DRY

A Journey From Source to Sea
Down the Colorado River

Jonathan Waterman

NATIONAL GEOGRAPHIC

WASHINGTON, D.C.

For my mother,

Katherine Adella Waterman (1931-2008)

Library of Congress Cataloging-in-Publication Data

Waterman, Jonathan.
  Running dry : a journey from source to sea down the Colorado River / Jonathan Waterman.
     p. cm.
  Includes index.
  ISBN 978-1-4262-0505-7 (alk. paper)
  1. Colorado River (Colo.-Mexico)--Description and travel. 2. Waterman, Jonathan--Travel--Colorado River (Colo.-Mexico) I. Title.
  F788.W28 2010
  979.1'3--dc22
                                    2010001704

The National Geographic Society is one of the world's largest nonprofit scientific and educational organizations. Founded in 1888 to "increase and diffuse geographic knowledge," the Society works to inspire people to care about the planet. It reaches more than 325 million people worldwide each month through its official journal, *National Geographic,* and other magazines; National Geographic Channel; television documentaries; music; radio; films; books; DVDs; maps; exhibitions; school publishing programs; interactive media; and merchandise. National Geographic has funded more than 9,000 scientific research, conservation and exploration projects and supports an education program combating geographic illiteracy.

For more information, please call 1-800-NGS LINE (647-5463) or write to the following address:

National Geographic Society
1145 17th Street N.W.
Washington, D.C. 20036-4688 U.S.A.

Visit us online at www.nationalgeographic.com

For information about special discounts for bulk purchases, please contact
National Geographic Books Special Sales: ngspecsales@ngs.org

For rights or permissions inquiries, please contact National Geographic Books Subsidiary Rights:
ngbookrights@ngs.org

Printed in the United States of America

Interior design: Cameron Zotter

10/WCPF/1

All the rivers run into the sea…

—Ecclesiastes 1:7

CONTENTS

INTRODUCTION

This book is about my five-month journey down the waters of the Colorado River. I had many escapades, made many more friends, and saw firsthand how these waters are parceled out to all of us living in the American Southwest.

The Colorado River is Calamity, arguing with its split personality, Beauty. From mountains to desert to delta, with breathtaking vistas and rapids, no other American river system has so many endemic fish species, lawyers, and silt. The river can be the color of dried blood or clear as hospital saline, squeezing and roaring through colorful canyons. More than a billion years of time can be read on the layered strata of surrounding walls. It has the most precipitous drop on the continent, two and a half vertical miles from the Rockies to the Gulf of California; and to the west, it is canalled another 200 feet below sea level, to the farms of Imperial Valley. In the unrestricted flows of a forgotten era that boatmen call the "Predambrian," the river carved out the Grand Canyon, carried 160 million tons of silt each year to the sea and routinely razed bridges, towns, and farmlands. In the Post-DamNation era, several hundred miles of legendary rapids—Byers, Gore, Glenwood, Westwater, Cataract, and the Grand—leave many white-water enthusiasts thinking that the Colorado River is intact. Sadly, it's not.

The delta is parched. Upstream, more than 300 miles of river are flooded by reservoirs and blocked by dams. Through a labyrinth of canals and aqueducts attached to these man-made lakes, the 1,450-mile river is diverted to several million acres of farms and 10 percent of the U.S. population. The reservoirs can store more than four times the river's annual flow. Several years before the national recession, the number-crunching water operators of the Colorado River Basin warned that the river's holdings were in danger of being overdrawn, with its customers living on false credit, its habitat on the verge of bankruptcy.

Like many Westerners, my well pumps water out of the ground before it can run into the Colorado River. After half a lifetime of far-off adventures on northern ice, I wanted to explore my arid backyard. I took my pack raft and kayak and then went to look for answers. I wanted to let the water carry me from source to sea so that I could understand the extent of the crisis, get to know the river, rethink my family's water use, and see what might be left for the future.

Mostly the business of running downstream kept me well occupied. I snowshoed, happily trespassed around dams and under barbed wire, paddled some rapids, and infected my feet in wastewater. In canyon depths, beneath snowy mountains, in solitude with multihued rock, or while bracing my kayak, the river moved me—sometimes right out of the boat. Because I didn't begin the trip as an expert white-water paddler, I found a new challenge around every corner. When in doubt, I portaged, accidentally swam, or brewed coffee on the shore and pondered my fate along with that of the river and its dependents.

The river touches countless lives. On my journey, I met many of these people—some at work, some at play. There were burly engineers devoted to reclaiming water and a belligerent rancher trying to kick me off the river as it flowed past his land. I spoke with a Las Vegas water manager who could spout out acre-feet figures as quickly as a blackjack dealer slings cards. I rode with boatmen who lectured adroitly on geology, bird identification, and photography—all in the midst of navigating rapids. I saw the devastating effects of the drying river on a Native American community. I met a water-conserving farmer installing underground drip irrigation. And I enjoyed food, shelter, and hospitality all along the way—from boaters on Lake Powell to Mexicans living along the dying delta.

Unlike other "us-versus-them" environmental issues, I found that the shrinking Colorado River is different. We're all in a similar boat trying to keep it flowing and understand what's at stake.

Of course, I survived, learned a lot about these waters, and had a ripping good ride. What remains is figuring out how to save the Colorado River for us and for our children.

—Carbondale, Colorado, January 2010

THE GRAND DITCH

On the last day of May, after the heaviest winter in 20 years, I shoulder a pack with a large satchel of my mother's ashes, a pair of snowshoes, and a deflated Alpacka raft with collapsible paddles. The Colorado River begins seven and a half miles and 1,500 feet above.

Early this morning, we drove for an hour from the arid eastern plains of Colorado toward Longs Peak, 14,259 feet. Plains farmers used to gauge their summer water supply by gazing up at the mountain's wineglass-shaped snow-field, visible from a hundred miles away. If the glass wasn't filled, it foretold a bad crop year. This year, the snow has spilt out over the entire mountainside.

Before the understaffed Rocky Mountain National Park rangers could begin charging at the park entrance, we drove above the tree line and past the oft-studied peak on Trail Ridge Road, confined by ten-foot snowbanks. A vertical mile below, we reached the Colorado River trailhead.

In contrast to the windblown eastern side, we're deep in snow. The Rockies rake incoming storms, pull the moisture onto the western slope, and funnel the empty winds out over the eastern plains.

The high altitude, opaque stream water beside us turns chocolate as the temperature rises, and water begins to pour out of untold ravines, unlocking mud banks, thawing snowfields, and bursting toward sea level more than a thousand miles away. The pace of my hiking companion, Brad Udall, quickens, even though his pack—freighted with heavy-metal backcountry skis and bindings—is a great deal heavier than mine. Brad is vexed that the Colorado

River no longer reaches the sea. The water beelining past our feet and wetting our socks should "slake the thirst of you, me and thirty million others who live in this gargantuan river basin, or evaporate from immense desert reservoirs downstream."

He talks with the slow cadence of a native Westerner. His mind holds a hard-earned map of the rivers and ranges of these parts. Nor does it hurt that five generations and two dozen of his kin have run municipal, state, or federal political offices. Since the mid-19th century, the Udall family dynasty, like all Western politicians, has trafficked in water. Or the lack thereof. So it's not a stretch to say that the river runs through Brad Udall's veins.

Brad, pushing 50 years old, churns out water facts as we follow the stream growing beside us. A former boatman in the Grand Canyon, he's fit from backcountry skiing those weekends he doesn't hit the lecture and sustainable water use circuit as the director of Western Water Assessment, based out of the National Oceanic and Atmospheric Administration (NOAA) offices in Boulder.

We ford a rivulet, climb another steep hill, and amid a thick pine forest, tiptoe across the crust of melting snowbanks, mined with three-foot sunken leg holes of hikers who passed earlier in the week without snowshoes. In a sun-drenched meadow, a kingfisher zippers through the air, rattling loudly against our intrusion. We stop and strip off our outer jackets as the now-meandering stream lowers its burbling a decibel.

In northern Arizona during the late 19th century, Brad's great-great-grandfather, John D. Lee, started Lees Ferry, pulling flat-bottomed boats across the river with a cable. A dozen miles upstream of this landmark, in 1961, Brad's uncle, Secretary of the Interior Stewart Udall—aka "Colorado River Master"—oversaw the building of the West's most disputed mass of concrete, the Glen Canyon Dam. His father, "Mo" Udall, was the one-time presidential candidate and Arizona representative who defended that state's Colorado River water rights, while Brad's brother Mark and their cousin Tom represent Colorado and New Mexico as congressmen now running shoo-in campaigns as senators. No one would dispute that Brad has found his calling as a spokesman for the river.

He says that today's growing problem with the shrinking river began with a climate miscalculation. Beginning in 1896, the U.S. government measured the Colorado River volume through acre-feet, the amount of water that would cover an acre of land one-foot deep. They guesstimated the river's average flow at 17.5 million acre-feet (maf), almost 6 trillion gallons per year. That's enough water to support 35 million modern households.

Yet scientists have recently figured out that the Colorado River's volume was calibrated following one of the wettest periods in its history. By measuring the distance between tree rings, hydrologists found growth rates that matched river volumes. Hydrologists determined that the region has experienced more severe droughts over the last several hundred years, Brad tells me, than yet experienced in the 21st century. This means that droughts are going to get worse before they get better. Over the centuries, the river has averaged little more than 15 maf per year—2.5 maf less than the seven member states and Mexico have divvied up. I'll learn more about the significance of these numbers as I head downstream.

I have come to the Colorado River to paddle all 1,450 miles and learn about what's at stake. Not only what's already been damaged, but also what we might lose in the future without proper solutions or conservation. Water, first of all. Then more cogently, the river itself, a living resource that includes wildlife and plant species, reservoirs, Native American culture, recreation, river-based economies, and the ever-shrinking wetlands of the delta. My family lives in Colorado and I want them to revel in the living resource of water—skiing the Rockies' snow, paddling its melt waters, and watering our garden—as I have for the last 20 years. But a half century from now, according to the forecasts of many climatologists, my sons are likely to see the ski resorts of Colorado go dry before their knees give out.

Climate models for the second half of this century show that up to 70 percent of the snowpack, which supplies the river 90 percent of its water, will disappear. Despite a whopping snowfall and long winter in the Upper Basin, the two biggest reservoirs created by Hoover and Glen Canyon Dams, "Lakes" Mead and Powell, are presently at half of their collective 50-maf capacities and are unlikely to recharge from the winter's big snowfall after meeting their downstream orders to create electricity and fill irrigation ditches.

If this nine-year drought continues on beyond a decade, as predicted, life throughout the river basin will be irrevocably changed. First, the sprawling economy created by recreational river and reservoir use throughout the river basin will go bust—crippling scores of towns and small cities along the river. Swimming pools will be drained and lawns browned in Salt Lake City, Utah, Cheyenne, Wyoming, and Albuquerque, New Mexico. Without Hoover Dam generating relatively clean and rapidly created hydroelectric power, Los Angeles will have blackouts. Without Glen Canyon Dam powering air conditioners, people will abandon sweltering Phoenix, necessitating the construction of more noxious, water consumptive coal plants on the far reaches of the energy grid. Several million acres of farms in the Southwest—including Imperial Valley, the fifth richest agricultural region in the country—will go fallow. Without radical change, citizens in Denver, Colorado, Las Vegas, Nevada, and San Diego, California, will have trouble flushing their toilets. Thirty million people will begin losing their drinking water. Finally, thanks to the antiquated Colorado River Compact, lawsuits will lock up what little water remains in what is already known as the most diverted river in the world.

Today, the driest states in the country are now among the most water-dependent and fastest-growing states. Eight decades ago, the Colorado River Compact split up the river between Mexico, Arizona, California, Nevada, New Mexico, Utah, Wyoming, and Colorado. In that time, the basin states' population of five million increased tenfold. Compounding this dilemma are droughts, an over-allocated river, and increasing global temperatures.

Brad's brow furrows as he discusses the shrinking river. He fires off facts and figures with the speed of a Wall Street ticker tape showing the futures market. Keeping to the Western Water Assessment's mission of science, he avoids the rhetoric of environmentalists, whom he refers to as "enviros."

Like the other jack Mormons in his family, he is lean and tall, with thick eyebrows, and a long jawline that contributes to a craggy handsomeness. As the snow deepens, Brad and I are happy to lighten our packs by caching our five-pound Alpacka rafts and paddles in a greening aspen forest. We strap on our skis and snowshoes. It would be vainglorious to try to boat down the snowed-over, steepening stream.

Brad points to La Poudre Pass, our destination, where the Continental Divide runs north to south, dividing Rocky Mountain National Park hydrologically. Waters on the west side form the Colorado River headwaters, running to the Pacific, while the east side drains to the Mississippi and the Atlantic. At least this is how nature intended it.

Above our heads, the Never Summer Mountains hold the snow that used to form the first drops of the river. Before this snowmelt can drain into the shrunken stream at our feet, a ditch intercepts the water, sluicing it over La Poudre Pass into Long Draw Reservoir, and off to the crops on the eastern plains.

The ditch appears like a surgical scar shaved across the heavily wooded face of the Never Summers. Farther west, a bulldozer rumbles along an adjacent dirt road, clearing out ice jams to keep the water from flooding over the ditch and into the valley below. Brad's congressman brother, Mark Udall, has championed a bill that will make this corner of Rocky Mountain National Park official wilderness. Five years ago, the ditch flooded the park's valley floor and caused $9 million in damage to dozens of historic cabins amid flower-strewn meadows. Now with protected wilderness status, the park can bill the ditch owners for the damage instead of suing.

Like other states in the river basin, Colorado developed around the ability to manipulate water. Financiers knew that "water runs uphill to money," and so does this ditch, pumped at a one percent grade over the Continental Divide.

As evidence of this water-as-gold maxim, in Colorado, we cannot legally catch rain in our gutters to water our gardens, because Brad and I live under the doctrine of prior appropriation—or first in time, first in right—meaning that someone below us already owns the water. These rights can be bought and sold separately from whatever rights we'd like to think we own on our roofs, high above and far away from any farmer. In times of drought, the owner of the oldest water right, regardless of distance from the river or its headwaters, reserves the right to use the water. This explains why ranchers and farmers 80 miles to the west in Grand Junction, Colorado, or 80 miles to the east in Fort Morgan, Colorado, own the water that falls on our Carbondale or Boulder roofs.

Yesterday, I'd met with Brad at the NOAA offices in Boulder, and his boss, the Director of the Earth System Research Lab. Sandy McDonald oversees 600 scientists studying weather and climate. In a small, empty auditorium, Sandy showed off a five-foot "Science On a Sphere" globe, lit from within by climate data. He pointed out Africa's Sahara Desert to remind me of the difference between a desert and a drought. We took several steps around the planet to North America and watched as a computer operator in an adjacent room programmed climate data onto the globe for 1970 and 2007, to show the effects of the drought. Over 37 years, the color change from blue to yellow over the Colorado River Basin showed a temperature increase of 3°F. Along with the globe's color-temperature changes, a numerical overlay displayed particulate matter in the atmosphere in 1970 and 2007, increasing from 327 parts per million (ppm) to 387 ppm, showing how greenhouse gases have caused the drought and changing climate by warming the atmosphere. In past millennia, similarly high levels have caused melting sea ice, a ten-foot rise in ocean levels, and a drier climate.

Amid these shocking statistics, I asked what NOAA, a government-funded agency, has forecast for future climate change in the Colorado River Basin. Sandy deferred to Brad, who replied that, by 2050, the snowpack will thin by a factor of 5 percent to 50 percent. In terms of the future of the river, even a 10 percent reduction in the river's snowpack water supply could trigger catastrophic reductions throughout the basin amid increasing population pressures for water.

"When you factor in the earlier runoffs caused by dust now overlaying the snow," Brad added, "raised by development across the West, and causing water to enter the river a month earlier than historic norms, there's another huge evaporative loss of up to five million acre feet when the water hits the reservoirs." He's referring to the heat gain caused by dark dust on the snow surface, absorbing the sun's energy and melting the snow in spring instead of reflecting the sun and preserving the snowpack until summer.

On this 68-degree day on the river's headwaters, because of the downed trees we're constantly forced to climb around, and my own breathlessness from chasing Udall uphill, I don't ask Brad to defend the science that explains changing climate. Those of us who live for their time spent out of doors in the West have already experienced obvious changes over the last two decades. Amid the rising temperatures, we've seen lengthening summers, haze caused by large Western forest fires, and watering restrictions brought on by drought. This is the first May in 20 years that we've needed snowshoes or skis at this elevation.

We're climbing over, walking around, and ducking under a direct effect of the drought caused by climate change. Here in the Colorado River drainages of Grand County and neighboring Summit County, beetles have infested a thousand square miles of lodgepole pine forests. As we climb to a deforested knob, downstream we can spy a sea of formerly green pine boughs turned dead as a red tide. Although I can't actually see the rice grain–sized *Dendroctonus ponderosae* beetles, we're surrounded by hundred-foot trees exhibiting sappy extrusions from beetles eating the inner bark and killing the tree. The lengthening summers have increased the beetles' reproductive cycle to twice a year. The lack of subzero, beetle-killing winters has created a tree-eating orgy. Brad explains that pine beetles have existed in the West since the Pleistocene, but this is the worst outbreak in state history. Foresters are predicting that beetles will destroy all of Colorado's lodgepole forest—an area the size of Rhode Island—in the next few years. Recently, the beetles have defied the former high-altitude cold barrier by jumping the Continental Divide and infesting eastern slope forests in the park and on toward the plains. At some point, fires will follow. In the past, without 50 million people living in the West, wildfires burned without suppression, regenerating the landscape with new growth.

With a sea of reddened trees standing like matchsticks waiting for a flame, the risks are obvious. Throughout public places along the Colorado River headwaters, "Survive Alive!" fliers are pinned up in eye-catching yellow and orange, instructing citizens to attend meetings and help create evacuation plans for when the "CATASTROPHIC WILDFIRE" arrives.

Weary from postholing the trail's softening snow with downed trees as high hurdles blocking our way, Brad takes off his skis, jabs his thumb north, and begins striding steeply uphill. I eye the gently contouring trail with a last bit of longing. As Brad bushwhacks at a right angle up away from the trail, breaking the snow up to his hips every few steps, I manage to keep him in sight.

After a half an hour of sweating and cursing labor, we reach a narrow dirt road alongside the several-foot-wide Grand Ditch. Out of the shaded forest, we apply more sun lotion as we walk. Ice bergie bits jam up, roll, and then sail no faster than our three-mile-an-hour pace.

In 1894, the Water Supply and Storage Company hired Chinese, Swedish, and Mexican laborers to dig the ditch, a thousand feet above what used to be called the Grand River. Until the early 20th century, the Colorado River didn't officially start until 451 miles downstream from here in Utah, at the confluence of the Green and Grand Rivers amid red rock canyons. The longest of the Colorado tributaries, the Green River originates from more than 700 miles north, in the Wind River Mountains of Wyoming. And because the Utah legislature knew that the Green River ran several hundred miles longer than the other Colorado River tributary then called the Grand River, they debated renaming the Green the Colorado River. At the same time, Colorado's representative Edward Taylor sought to bolster tourism in his hometown of Glenwood Springs, Colorado. In 1921, he proposed to Congress that the Grand River be renamed the Colorado. President Harding signed the bill, peeving both Utah and Wyoming lawmakers. Thanks to the allure of the well-known name, Glenwood Springs reaped a flood of tourists on the now-elongated Colorado River.

The state of Colorado is rife with dams, ditches, and tunnels that breach the Rockies, having diverted the river's headwaters long before concrete started pouring downstream. In 1936, backhoes lengthened the efforts of earlier shovelers on the 16-mile-long Grand Ditch. The Water Supply and Storage Company's "engineering marvel" intercepted over six million gallons of Never Summer Mountain streams and sent them plunging down the Cache La Poudre River to the distant eastern plains. The advantage of midsummer snowmelt is that farmers can open their ditches with all the convenience of filling a pitcher from the refrigerator. Also, the system has only one small dammed reservoir—Long Draw—minimizing loss from evaporation.

After the Grand Ditch was finished, the Colorado River below turned into a lazy creek, seen from a high switchback on the Trail Ridge Road as a looping brown intestine of water. During the last nine years of drought, the river has trickled out of the park and down to Grand Lake. Although flood cycles seldom recharge flora on the banks, valuable homes and ranches downstream remain intact. And so begins the long-justified saga of reclamation—protecting property from floods, growing crops, creating hydroelectricity, and providing recreation—from every ditch, diversion, and dam built between here and the sea.

As Brad and I round the final corner of the ditch road, breaking out toward the open meadows of 10,175-foot La Poudre Pass, we spy the Christmas-tree-shaped Long Draw Reservoir. Its descending waterlines have caused 50-foot-high bathtub rings, stained by minerals pulled out of the Never Summers. These bathtub rings are now emblematic of the drought lowering a hundred reservoirs throughout the Colorado River Basin, like a warning postscript to the reclamation saga.

"Nice view, huh?" Brad asks rhetorically. "It's for watering subsidized alfalfa to feed subsidized cows out on the plains." He continues with the suggestion that, if we raised the price of utilities instead of subsidizing the cost of water and electricity, we'd quickly find solutions for conserving water and electricity. "Just like what we're seeing with rising gas prices."

During the hike, I've learned that part of Brad's work, as both a Udall and the director of Western Water Assessment, is spreading the news that climate change is here to stay. "In terms of the Colorado River, the higher temperatures will increase the atmosphere's moisture-holding capacity and evaporation will increase, further draining the reservoir capacities," he ticks the points off on his fingers. "Then there's drought. The evaporation will increase water demand and summertime drying. And then there's the earlier spring runoff. . . ."

We cut across a meadow above a small lake shown on the map, but apparently long since dried up. It's late afternoon, and although Brad isn't showing any pain, I'm overheated and blistered from the hike. I pull off my pack. A Steller's jay wings a croaking, erratic path above us on the snow-covered meadow, but our day otherwise seems a subdued and unlikely beginning for such an iconic river.

Above, tall green trees—possibly still free of pine beetles—climb several thousand feet up the remnant volcanoes. In the distance, we can still hear a clanking, sputtering backhoe, scooping ice jams out of the Grand Ditch. I turn to the west, lift the bag high, and spill the ashes of my mother into the breeze above the remains of the Colorado River headwaters. It's a long story, but I'm hoping she'll join me during the long descent to the Pacific.

MOVING WATER THROUGH MOUNTAINS

In 1869, Major John Wesley Powell boated the Green River from Green River, Wyoming, to the Colorado River in Utah and through the Grand Canyon in Arizona. He also made nuanced scientific observations about the character of the river and its Native American people. Powell became the modern-day equivalent of an Argonaut by traversing unmapped terra incognito and working as the director of the U.S. Geological Survey (USGS) in Washington, D.C.—where he founded the Board of Ethnology and the National Geographic Society. He also advocated sensible growth and limited reclamation in the arid West, but his ideology put him at odds with politicians and developers who would exploit the Colorado River Basin's water. In 1893, Powell warned developers that bringing water to the desert for agriculture and unlimited development would be "piling up a heritage of conflict and litigation."

Although some have repeated his 1,000-mile journey down the Green River—in 1989, Colin Fletcher became the first to row all 1,700 miles to the sea—no one has run all 1,450 miles of the Colorado River. If I'm to get away with this plan, my objectives have to be clear. I was tempted to improve my kayak roll so that I might challenge the river on its own terms, but I don't want to be so gripped by paddling that it'll distract me from learning about the river. So I decided to surround myself with experts who can share their boats, experience, and a sense of place.

If survival is an issue on those rapids that are keeping me awake at night thinking about them, I'll portage or find a guide. With an experienced guide to help shepherd my wife and sons, we can spend several days together on the river. The plan feels liberating. I can honor both the river and my family. As I contacted various experts—rangers, lawyers, boatmen, outfitters, guides, scientists, engineers, Bureau of Reclamation workers, conservationists, Native Americans, water commissioners, and fishermen—I found that my schedule can be built around their availability so we could travel downstream together, allowing me to concentrate on the issues, rather than being simply focused on how to return home alive.

Nothing changes one's outlook faster than raising children. In retrospect, my former passion for exploring remote landscapes during challenging journeys seems a bit self-indulgent. What has become my priority now is the condition of the changing world that my boys will inherit.

As Brad Udall drives home, I scout the headwaters in my car. The park campground is closed due to unsafe conditions as chainsaw crews drop hundreds of standing dead trees. Nearing the park exit in approaching dusk, I continue looking for a place to camp. A dozen elk escort their calves through the river meadows, making me think yet again about my mother (now finding her microbial path down through the frozen headwaters).

She jump-started my adventure career when she dropped me off at high school one spring morning in 1974, and announced that she would be leaving my dad, me, and my brothers. I was initially relieved that I'd no longer bear witness to the fights and silent yet unconcealed anger that I would later come to learn is the hallmark of unhappy marriages. Within days of her leaving, though, my relief turned to a sense of unspeakable abandonment. Because my soft-spoken father had been rendered almost mute by the split and became powerless to direct my actions, I moved out of the house and into an apartment in neighboring Waltham, Massachusetts. I stopped attending school. What had only been an ill-defined germ grew into a dream of taking long adventures through little-known wilderness.

I didn't see my mother for two years. Still, we were close, if awkward, together. Although she potty-trained and raised three sibling rivals born in a span of six years, she could only hug with hand pats on our shoulders. We rarely kissed.

My mom and I respected one another if only because we were so alike. She had given me her willfulness, an inability to accept complacency, and a love of travel. So she singled me out among my brothers, whom she otherwise treated equally, by offering me her father's Hudson River pilot job—today it's still a career choice offered to direct blood lineage—but I refused. She had already initiated my fascination with water at her parents' lake house and during happy family seashore vacations from Massachusetts to Florida. Bodysurfing, water skiing, shell collecting, boating, and long runs on the beach became Waterman family pastimes.

Although I couldn't blame my parents for divorcing, Mom motivated me by breaking free of the parental yoke and starting a new life. Dad had already launched his career by inventing a theorem called the T-Matrix, expressed by the formula:

$$QT = -\text{Reg}(Q)$$

It took me a long time to figure out what it meant. And he was disappointed to see my failing grades.

Filled with the angst that defines most teenagers, even those not undergoing their parents' divorce, I followed my mom by using her departure to trigger my own. Far removed from those who could injure me, on unclimbed mountain routes or long river and ocean journeys on the opposite side of the continent, I found a new family in my expedition teammates. As my writing, photography, and lecturing career developed, I found a mission in sharing the history and beauty of endangered wild places, even if I failed at earning money to take care of the downtime between expeditions. Like my mother, I attempted marriage, but it ended in disaster if only because I didn't know the meaning of commitment to another person. Eventually, after being tested on dozens of expeditions, I found my own version of a graduate exam during a solo 2,200-mile kayak journey across the Northwest Passage.

Then I had the luck to meet June, remarry, and begin raising our children. Like neophyte parents everywhere, we gained new respect for our mothers' and fathers' child-raising efforts. Building our own house and being a committed parent made my expedition life and my wilderness spokesperson career look like child's play. But when Kay Waterman got sick with rectal melanoma, I realized that I knew less about my own mother than those remote landscapes I explored. Why is it that we don't know what we've got until it's gone?

During Mom's yearlong, painful reduction in her modest Durham, North Carolina, town house, she rarely accepted opiates. Nor would she concede to me, my brothers, or the hospice nurses that she was dying. She persevered in a steadfast state of denial. I showed her pictures and a map of the Colorado River, and told her what I planned to do. A month before her death, shortly before she lost the ability to speak, she licked her lips in an attempt to wet her parched mouth and cheerfully conceded that she too was going on a long journey. No deference to any god, an afterlife, or a world beyond, despite the visits of a chaplain, whom she suffered patiently. Kay Waterman—whom her tennis partners called the Steel Magnolia—wasn't going to drink anyone else's Kool-Aid.

I still cringe, on a daily basis, at the memory of my mom on her deathbed, shriveled and wordless. While trying to process those moments, I cling to thankfulness for all that she gave me. How she stood by me during divorce, teased me for taking "macho expeditions," and how, to steer her son toward a long and meaningful life, she accused me of having an adolescent death wish.

So, on the morning of June 1, I tell myself, I'm not starting down the river to claim any firsts, or to prove myself, or to don any more hair shirts than I've already been so foolish to wear. My survival *should never* be in question. With the blessings of June and my boys, Nicholas and Alistair, I'm merely taking the next year to continue my wilderness education and to pay homage to Mom while following her ashes down this dying river toward the sea.

Twelve o'clock is a languid time to start an ambitious descent down the remaining 1,443 miles, but it's better than procrastinating any longer. I'm stiff from yesterday's hike. There's no guidebook for the headwaters of this famous river and no telling what obstacles await us. Pete McBride and I are standing below the last snowbank on the Colorado River trailhead, red-facedly blowing up our Alpacka rafts. It takes a dizzying 15 minutes to inflate the raft by lung power, another 15 minutes to stretch, then another 10 minutes to try and remember what we've forgotten. Once we fold our legs inside the little yellow crafts, we cinch the waterproof spray skirts up to our chests.

From previous sorties, I have learned that the Alpacka is well suited to surf or turf, while running minor rapids, or for stuffing it in my pack for the long portage in Mexico. By the time we tie dry bags over our bows and start paddling—like Gullivers strapped into our Lilliputian crafts—the creek has gained a surging current, even though the Grand Ditch a thousand feet above has already stolen much of the volume. During this peak water weekend across the state's high country, three boaters will drown in the big water.

Each year, from late April through July, as a warm high-pressure system creates clouds that hold the heat below the mountaintops, high-altitude snowfields are primed to melt with the first rays of the morning sun. Here in the mountains or hundreds of miles below, the river is a dynamic resource, responding to the heat and movements of its headwaters. For several hundred miles downriver, onlookers will regularly pull over to the shoulder to get out of their cars and feel the wind preceding now dark brown snowmelt waters as the Colorado River scours its banks in what could resemble a biblical flood: uprooted trees waving past with green leaves and beavers ruddering their tails in glee while herons ply the banks snatching stunned fish.

Everything depends on the mountain snow melting here at the river's source and creating its volume, measured as cubic feet per second (cfs). This is the ruler of boatmen and dam workers. The river's health or flood potential can be checked at gauging stations all the way down to Mexico. Today, measured at the Baker Gulch station a few miles below Pete and me, surrounded by snowbanks purring with water, the river will double to 500 cfs—a rate that will fill an Olympic-size swimming pool in three minutes.

The biggest North American rivers, the Mississippi and the Mackenzie, have nearly 20 times the water of the Colorado River, which averages 3,937 cfs. Although one could argue that its 13,000-foot drop to the ocean used to be impressive, now the river rarely reaches the sea. Nor is it close to being the world's longest, an honor held by the 4,000-mile-long Nile, which drains 11 African countries and becomes the penultimate river—after the Colorado— for its number of bankside dependents. "The Colorado's modern notoriety, however," wrote Marc Reisner in *Cadillac Desert,* "stems not from its wild rapids and plunging canyons but from the fact that it is the most legislated, most debated, and most litigated river in the entire world. It also has more people, more industry, and a more significant economy dependent on it than any comparable river in the world." Reisner's précis, accurate two decades ago, is even more alarming today because ten million additional people have come to depend on the river.

As Pete disappears around a corner, whooping in a nondescript rapid caused by another fallen tree, I tighten the chin strap on my helmet. I plunge my hand in for a quick assessment: ice water! Worse than most white water, but not nearly as gripping as that of the lower river's rapids, the stream is ripping several miles an hour through a lot of dead and pine beetle–felled trees. Although benign in appearance, these tree "strainers" and other river obstacles such as fences cause more boating deaths than rapids. The rumor of many barbed-wire fences crisscrossing the river downstream has already deprived me of sleep.

At a beaver dam that sluices the water down a three-foot drop, Pete waits for me with his camera lens uncapped. I raise my paddle in the air, throw my body weight forward to prevent flipping backward, and "whoop."

I'm equally excited that the surrounding protected park habitat—the thick growth of native willows and gullies lush with aspen and cottonwood trees—shows how the river once existed along all of its length. The natural cycle starts with beaver dams that trap sediments and foster vegetation that prevents erosion in the river valley. Downstream, beyond the park, these dams are routinely destroyed by ranchers coveting the same water. Because the river lacks a healthy population of beavers, erosion has run rampant in the last century. Denuding of the river valley is also abetted by overgrazing. In tandem with changing climate that, in most years, has created early and rapid snowmelts, or felled pine beetle–rich trees that can no longer stabilize banks, the river corridor's capacity to withstand flooding has been crippled.

By the time we have portaged around a dozen strainers a few hours later, Pete has his Nikon closed up in its dry bag. We have plenty of time to get to know one another as the river breaks out of the forest and carves lazy oxbows. We pass meadows flowered with pink-laced spring beauties and populated by sagging old cabins. Recently introduced moose splash gangly legged across our path downriver.

Pete grew up tending a modest cattle ranch in Old Snowmass. His family embraces a conservation ethic that prevents development on their land, irrigated by Colorado tributaries. As a muscular skier and all-around athlete given to popping off handstands when we take rest breaks on the riverbanks, Pete found his calling behind the lens of a camera 15 years ago. At 37, he's been assigned to scores of adventures—boating, fishing, trekking, climbing, and skiing—around the world, and he brings awareness to unknown issues, from the dangerous work of Sherpas on Mount Everest to the Bolivian silver mines.

Pete's abiding interest above and beyond adventure junkets is conservation. He believes that keeping the old ranches in place, despite their water-intensive alfalfa crops, will preserve green spaces along the Colorado River corridor and prevent more housing developments that will deplete the river. While we discuss the merits of drip-irrigated ranching versus xeriscaped, low-density housing with recycled wastewater, we're both here to learn more about the river and what we might lose.

Over a long day that covers two dozen miles of oxbow river paddling, and no more than nine miles as the raven flies, we drift through a valley squashed flat 12,000 years ago by megatons of ice from the final Pinedale glaciation.

On each new turn east on a river that meanders toward all points of the compass, we catch sight of the first summer automobile tourists, accelerating toward Trail Ridge Road. As we float back west, we plunge into a world— except for the constant whining of chainsaws—that feels as primeval and wild as its beginnings.

To the west, the 20-mile-long Never Summer Mountains are a rare southern oxbow in the Continental Divide. These granitic-igneous mountains are smeared with olive and carroty colored lichens, and underlain by large fields of shed boulders. A century ago, visiting Arapaho, more accustomed to the canyon country heat a thousand miles away (along river tributaries that could be named Always Summer), the Native Americans first named these peaks *Ni-chebe-chii* (Never Any Summer).

We crane our necks in the opposite direction toward Longs Peak, first climbed by the wounded war veteran Major Powell in 1868. He learned that the peak's waters drain to the Atlantic rather than the Grand River 6,000 feet below. Although the climb had been organized by the self-promoting newspaperman William Byers, the 120-pound, five-foot-six-inch Major took charge. He had gained ten pounds since the war, and his stern gaze and the dark beard touching his collarbones made him appear larger in photographs than he stood in real life. As a geology professor from a small Midwestern college, he fell hard and fast for the rugged geography begging to be explored. On top, he made a speech about how they had accomplished a feat that others thought impossible, but they should pursue still greater achievements, like the river on the horizon. One of the party pulled out a flask of wine to make a toast, but two unnamed members—most likely including the autocratic Major—refused to partake. His teammates consisted of civilians and several students, and although all of their names would grace the peak as its first ascensionists, the climb was good sport rather than scientific accomplishment.

On the summit, they built a rock cairn and placed a can inside, listing their names, along with thermometer and barometer readings. One of the team jokingly inserted another can containing one of Powell's rock-hard biscuits—compact and as difficult on the teeth as the granite on that mountain's east face—as an "everlasting memento" of the Major. He removed it. As one of his biographers, Wallace Stegner, wrote in *Beyond the Hundredth Meridian*:

> There is no record which would indicate that he was being facetious or indulging in mock heroics [with his speech]. He took the climbing of Long's Peak seriously, far more seriously than Byers [or the others]. He

took seriously too the thought of other challenges to overcome, other unknowns to mark with writings in a cairn. A serious and intense young man, hardier in spite of his maiming than most of his companions . . . a young man serious and a touch pompous and perhaps even somewhat ridiculous.

Through his exploration of the unknown landscape on the horizon, and later running the USGS, Powell would help advance the principles of Western geology. As the rock layers that he and others would study showed, the river didn't exist 75 million years ago, because most of the Colorado Plateau lay submerged beneath the Cretaceous sea, which drained river systems from high ground in Arizona, Nevada, and western Utah. As the sea retreated, southerly river systems drained north across Wyoming. As the Rockies rose, western Colorado also began its drainages, making the headwaters of an ancient river form south of La Poudre Pass and north into Wyoming. The Major and other geologists of his day believed that the Colorado River started during this period, carving its way down to the Grand Canyon and notching it out over nearly 70 million years. This belief of the Grand Canyon's formation held sway until the 1964 theory of plate tectonics explained how colliding continents could reconfigure the American Southwest in a way that mere rivers could not.

Through these continent-building forces 65 million years ago, the Rockies continued to grow higher as basins in Utah sank, forming a large, shallow lake system called Grand Lake, spreading into today's Colorado River headwaters and southwestern Wyoming. Over the ensuing 25 million years, rivers that had been flowing north around Grand Lake into Wyoming began to run west to Utah as the region stopped sinking. As uplifts occurred in both Wyoming and Colorado, basin and range "stretching" dropped open new river channels in Utah—so a river like today's Colorado was rerouted yet again, west-southwest across the salt deserts of Utah and eventually, some believe, to the Pacific Ocean near Santa Barbara, California.

Farther south, the major tributary that resembles today's Gunnison River turned west and met the Colorado River two hundred miles from the headwaters, outside modern-day Grand Junction. Unlike most ancient rivers in North America, the Colorado is a geological infant, and humans could have witnessed some of its early cutting through the Grand Canyon. Still, the scientific establishment does not know to what extent and exactly when the river started carving the Canyon.

Farther north, roughly five million years ago, another uplift in Utah blocked the Colorado River's flow west. So the river turned south, spewing more silt across the vast deserts of southern Utah and raising the level of land across Arizona. There, the gigantic Hopi Lake surrounded Flagstaff and the northern rim of what was or what would become the Grand Canyon. Here is where another puzzle begins. Some believe that Hopi Lake was shallow and had nothing to do with the Grand Canyon's formation. Others, including scientific creationists, believe that the lake rose high above sea level, over-flowed, and punched out the Grand Canyon, just like Noah's flood.

As the river carved through the Grand Canyon and south to Mexico's Sea of Cortez, most geologists agree that the sediment, laid down in relatively modern times, came exclusively from the Colorado River. Upriver over the last five million years, the Gore Range and White River Plateau uplifts occurred in Colorado, forcing the river to turn and make its final carvings through Gore and Glenwood Canyons.

After climbing Longs Peak, Powell reconnoitered this route. He may have rejected running the Grand River because it lacked the aura of the unknown, having been traversed by countless miners and bordered by settlements. Also, a minimum of scouting would have revealed that several dozen miles of these rapids were unnavigable in a heavy wooden dory. The expedition might have ended badly if he had started here and attempted to row the most difficult stretch of white water on the entire watershed. Compared to the Grand or Cataract Canyons, Gore Canyon's rapids are rated a grade higher and are technically more difficult than anything found downstream. At the very least, the narrow Gore Canyon would have destroyed Powell's big boats, just like Capt. Samuel Adams's failed 1869 expedition. So Powell would follow the easier route down the Green River, which he repeatedly scouted over the winter, and could reach via the continental railroad.

Even with our high-tech little rafts and detailed maps, Pete and I narrowly avoid disaster on our second day of paddling. As we continue downriver, sitting with ramrod attentiveness in our boats, the Colorado Stream gains volume from untold washes, creeks, and gullies, bleeding white with snowmelt. Outside Rocky Mountain National Park, the current picks up. As suddenly as public land is replaced by barbed wire and No Trespassing signs, the moose and elk are replaced by fusty bales of hay, grazing horses, and million-dollar chalets showcasing yards of beetle-killed lodgepole stumps.

We pass denuded gullies and washes, carving 50 feet into the hillsides, allowing snow and rain and mud and all matter of detritus—sage bushes, plastic bottles, branches, and fence posts—to run unchecked into the headwaters. The resulting flood of waterborne sediment, unchecked by vegetation or beaver dams, can now only be slowed by farm ditches or stopped by giant concrete dams. No beaver worth its sharp teeth and mud-daubing tail would attempt to block this new, unruly river of rampant erosion. Two generations of Colorado River Basinites have come to regard these scoured banks as natural a part of the riparian landscape as mounted cowboys riding the range. This misconception in fact is owed to the cowboys and grazers.

Since the 1890s, a half century after trappers removed beavers from this river and its drainages, the introduction of cattle, horses, and sheep altered riverside ecology. Much of the thin layer of topsoil throughout the Southwest has been washed downstream as invading hordes of grazing animals have eaten and trampled the native vegetation, introducing invasive thorns and exotic weeds. The early days of unchecked grazing will take decades if not centuries to repair.

In the next dozen miles, we're aware of at least two sets of barbed-wire fences crossing the river. Two nights before, as a guest of the Winding River Campground and Resort, I had gotten to know the garrulous owner, Wes House. Wary of taking anything away from the resource, he had converted a sawmill into a dude ranch 40 years ago. Although ranching pays scant dividends to modern cowboys, tourism is alive and well, despite the pine beetle–maimed views of Arapahoe National Forest, resembling massive logging clear-cuts. Wes had to pay loggers $5,000 to clear-cut hundreds of his trees so that the standing dead timber wouldn't fall on his guests. The campground is now a sunny pasture of stumps, with little privacy between campsites.

When I asked Wes if it was okay to paddle past his horse ranch on the river, he warned me about the barbed-wire fences across the water.

"We've come prepared with wire cutters," I said, "so we shouldn't have any problem."

He was aghast until I explained I was joking. We planned to carry our little boats around his fences. "You bet," Wes smiled, "but you should be looking out for more fences downstream."

At noon on June 2, Pete and I duly pull out at each of Wes's fences and step over. We continue paddling downstream with our guards down, relieved that we'd gotten around the first two obstacles safely. Then, while paddling mid-river around a sharp corner in fast water, we spot another barbed-wire fence looming only yards ahead. I sprint for the left bank; Pete stays mid-stream to try and hop the lowest strand of wire, but it all happens so fast we can't communicate. Just as I reach the eroded bank, I grab the steel fence post to avoid the rusty barbed wire; I hit so hard with the momentum of the current behind me that the post bends backward, lifting the entire fence out of the water just as Pete begins his midstream hop to lift the raft's leading edge over the wire. The wire shoots up like a released bowstring and lifts his boat straight up, flipping him backward into the water.

As Pete is swept under, he dives deep and swims beneath the quivering fence wire. "You okay?" I yell as soon as he comes up for air in the snowmelt waters.

"Yeah!"

"Sorry," I cry, throwing my boat over the fence as I sprint after his paddle, spinning downstream as fast as the current. When we regroup downstream, river right, his sunglasses are the only gear lost. He's shivering but still smiling. His quick, cool-headed reaction, along with his lack of assigning any blame, makes me glad to have his company.

We've gained a new awareness of how easily we can get hurt, even in a nontechnical stream. We continue paddling down past more private land and barbed wire and a plethora of No Trespassing signs. We duck two bridges and wind our splashing way past cattle, a gravel plant, and subdivisions barely above the high waterline. In the distance, we hear the river tumbling over a Pinedale glaciation moraine. Suddenly, the fattening stream resembles the Colorado River of Powell lore: frothing, bouldered, foaming water that young creek boaters dream about. Standing next to our boats, Pete shivering anew, we take one look at one another and shake our heads. In the woods behind another No Trespassing sign, we deflate the boats for a mile-long bushwhack down the mountain, to my appointment with dam officials outside Grand Lake.

The first few balmy days of June are transformed by another two days of snow, dusting the mountain village of Grand Lake, population 500. Its boardwalks and bric-a-brac–filled main-street shops are spruced up in anticipation of summer tourists. Under the shadow of Longs Peak and the Rockies, the town is a Yankee version of Chamonix. Restaurants—advertising everything from cordon bleu to pizza—are affordable. Fishermen and cowboys and mountain bikers abound. And locals are gracious, at least to a lone tourist rather than the coming hordes.

The outskirts of Grand Lake, along with the larger, more blue-collar town of Granby, are havens for pricey second homes, owned by those who come to swim, water-ski, fish, horseback ride, hike, and play around Shadow Mountain, and Granby and Grand Lakes. The deep, 500-acre Grand Lake—larger than any other natural body of water in Colorado—is easily the smallest of the three connected lakes. Because lakes carved solely by glaciers are usually shallow, the deep bowl of the once grand lake is theorized to be an ancient, pre-Pleistocene crater. Although modern engineering would like to usurp the grandest acts of nature, a student of geology always has the opportunity to plumb greater earth works.

Standing above the Adams Tunnel, sucking Colorado River water toward the eastern plains, I can see how "ramp and pluck" mountainsides above the crater were later carved out by 1,500-foot-thick glaciers, flowing down from the Rockies: The lower "ramp" side of the glacier polished the rock shiny clean, whereas the deeper ice plucked off and carved the rock mountainside. As the ice retreated several thousand years ago, the glacial moraine further dammed the deep, clear blue waters of the lake. Before the Bureau of Reclamation arrived, you could have cupped your hands and drank freely from Grand Lake without fear of toxic indigestion.

In 1941, before Reclamation began pumping the Colorado River into Grand Lake and down through the tunnel beneath Longs Peak, Robert Pennak, a scientist from the University of Colorado, measured the clarity of water in Grand Lake at 30 feet. After Reclamation began pumping, the clarity dropped so low that Pennak called the lake "irreparably harmed." In the 1990s, locals resumed the clarity test and measured the average clarity depth to 12 feet before Reclamation began its summer pumping. After pumping the lake, clarity dropped to a half dozen feet.

Along with this mucking of the waters, and the pine beetle epidemic wreaking havoc upon the county forests, locals are also alarmed about the blue-green blooms of toxic algae spreading into their natural lake from the adjoining waters of Shadow Mountain Lake. These warm, shallow waters form ideal petri dish conditions for all manner of large and small plant life. Of course, local developers and realtors were oblivious to the biological foment in the waters below. The reservoir is rimmed with $10-million trophy homes and single-acre lots that cost over $3 million.

Reclamation is mandated by Congress to protect and preserve the water in Grand Lake. So two winters ago, Shadow Mountain Lake was drained for 56 days to freeze the toxic algae flowing into Grand Lake. By most accounts, this only intensified the algae. By the World Health Organization's (WHO) standards, the excessive amounts of toxic cyanobacteria in the algae pose a serious health threat. For two summers in a row, the levels rose high enough that WHO guidelines recommended swimmers and recreational water users be notified. Because the water is pumped from Lake Granby up to Shadow Mountain Lake and through Grand Lake to the tunnel, the cyanobacteria levels are higher in Grand Lake than in Shadow Mountain Lake. No one is saying if the water flowing east through the tunnel for farmers and metropolitan users is also contaminated.

In 2007, an independent consulting firm completed a study recommending that Grand Lake's waters could be protected through the construction of a pipeline bypassing the lake into Adams Tunnel, or a brand-new, expensive under-the-Rockies tunnel. Reclamation responded to these potential solutions with a civil letter, concerned, and cloaking the bombshell with bureaucratese, that only an act of Congress would allow them to take any action. Federal support* won't come any time soon, so the locals, represented by the Greater Grand Lake Shoreline Association, continue to try to clean the water by working through state government. Needless to say, the dead duck smell, pea green–colored clumps, and oily scum along the shorelines are making tourists and locals reconsider swimming, waterskiing, and fishing, not to mention selling real estate.

As I wait for my appointment outside an even higher barbed-wire fence surrounding the pumping plant on Lake Granby, I'm aware that those who profit spiritually or financially from the Three Lakes are not happy about Reclamation or the Northern Colorado Water Conservancy District (Northern). Initially, residents thought the Colorado Big Thompson Project (CBT) was putting them on the map with recreation dollars galore through the new reservoirs. Now their precious lakes are endangered by drought and toxic contamination.

The ten-foot galvanized fence rises like a drawbridge. I drive under the gate past a landscaper trimming errant tufts of grass from the curbs of a well-watered five-acre lawn. Dark clouds have lowered beneath the snowy peaks of the Rockies, and a cold rain turns the white sidewalks gray as the sky. Here on the northern shore of Lake Granby, 8,280 feet, the "Farr Pumping Plant"

---

*Reclamation charged the Northern Colorado Water Conservancy District (Northern) to operate and maintain the Colorado Big Thompson project (CBT). Northern, a public agency encompassing eight counties, offered to pay half the algae cleanup bill. The inference is that Reclamation should pay the other half.

is named after W. D. Farr's family, a clan of ranchers turned water operators and bankers in Greeley, 4,000 feet below and 70 miles across the Continental Divide. The concrete, windowless pumping plant was built in the aftermath of World War II, with two-by-sixes for forms rather than plywood, hoarded by the military. Clearly, the seven-foot-thick walls would have withstood a barrage from invading warplanes. The rectangular bunker stands only three stories above the lake, but its 130-foot plunge below the high watermark reveals a 12-story building—stained, like the reservoir shores, with the inevitable bathtub ring of crystallized minerals.

Noble Underbrink is the collection systems department manager for Northern. He meets me in sneakers and the dressed-up attire of the western slope: a collared, short-sleeve shirt tucked into a pair of blue jeans. As we walk to the door, he pats one of the retired six-foot-high pump turbines mounted into the concrete sidewalk. Noble buzzes us into the plant by sliding his barcoded badge through an encrypted card reader, making me feel we've just gained access to the Pentagon. In a narrow lobby, I sign into the visitors' book and wave to the sleepy-looking guard.

The cramped operation center is surrounded by tall computers and lit-up circuit boards reminiscent of the military command center from *Dr. Strangelove*. I raise my camera toward the five workers—who immediately avert their faces. When Noble requests that I not photograph the "high-security" floor on the lake bottom, I ask if they've had a problem with security.

"No," Noble replies, "we just don't want any pictures getting into the wrong hands."

"Yeah," I nod empathetically, "our world has really changed since 9/11."

At the elevator, he punches the button for Floor 6 and drops a line that takes me aback: "We're now going 101 feet below the water surface." But both Noble and I know that the drought has put Floor 6 no more than 60 feet underwater. I want to ask him what he thinks about the false promises that lured settlers west—to the dry plains that this plant irrigates—but bringing up Manifest Destiny to water operators would be akin to telling exploding shoe jokes in an airport security line.

"This is the Cinderella of water systems." Noble waves proudly with his arm as we enter the catwalk above three lifeless 6,000-horse turbines, gleaming with 18-inch stainless-steel shafts. He says that it takes only 20 million watts to start these babies up, but the Windy Gap Reservoir's pumping station downriver demands twice the wattage, creating a voltage dip and dimming lightbulbs in several surrounding towns.

I learn that the snowmelt waters of Windy Gap and that of another reservoir, Willow Creek, are pumped uphill into Lake Granby, on the opposite shore from the pumping station. On July 1, as the big winter snowmelt allows Lake Granby to fill and hide the unsightly bathtub rings surrounding its waters, the Farr pumping station will spin into work for ten months, *if* there's enough water, sending it north into a big pipe toward Shadow Mountain Lake, "with enough torque to push it 186 feet uphill," Noble says, continuing in his for-the-tourists monologue, "19 feet higher than Niagara Falls." Then the water flows toward Grand Lake and the tunnel beneath Longs Peak.

"Is it true that Grand Lake is now polluted?" I ask.

"We froze the algae out two winters ago by lowering the lake," he replies curtly. "There's no problem anymore."

Noble puts on his ear protectors and motions for me to do the same. With the screech of a locomotive's wheels, the steel shaft begins spinning, and it seems that the whole 12-story building must be vibrating. An electric pump gives off the distinct smell of burning ozone as we hear churning water. Noble's face lights up into a big smile that looks relieved. The job of pumping the river underneath Longs Peak toward an entirely different ocean has started anew.

In 1889, the Colorado legislature first proposed sending Grand Lake–Colorado River water east through the divide. Despite Colorado's $25,000 appropriation to study the project, the state of technology for transporting water across the Rockies, already shown by laborers hand shoveling the Grand River Ditch, did not surpass that of the Hohokam,* who dug 1,200 miles of canals with stones and baskets 1,500 years ago.

American farming changed in 1928, when the mother of all droughts hit. The Dust Bowl swept from southern Nebraska south through western Oklahoma to the Texas panhandle, from mid-Kansas west to eastern Colorado. To the biblically inclined, hard-working denizens of the plains, the widely

---

The Hohokam built the first dams in America, on Colorado River tributaries in modern-day Phoenix. Although other Native Americans survived in igloos or tepees, the Hohokam lived in grand adobe houses and grew tobacco, squash, beans, and agave. During silt-laden flood cycles, their dams washed out, allowing silt to wash downstream and recharge bankside growth. Unlike modern stone or cement dams that trap silt, the Hohokam engineers merely rebuilt their stick dams as the floods subsided. Still, the most industrious North American farmers were wiped out several hundred years later by overwatering their crops with saline runoff.

promoted concept of "water following the plow" was finally recognized as malarkey. It stopped raining for seven years. Crops were destroyed by huge black tornados of dust likened to the apocalypse. Livestock dropped in their tracks and covered the plains as desiccated bone bags. Then the Great Depression set in motion a "Grapes of Wrath" exodus toward the wetter promise of California. Those who stayed would never forget the storm of physical and economic drought.

East-slope Coloradoans who remembered "the Worst Hard Time" now had the technological know-how to move mountains or drill through them, and the nearest reliable water lay nearly a hundred miles west, across the crest of the Rockies. After the Dust Bowl, no one was going to let 14,259-foot Longs Peak stop them.

W. D. Farr, the former director of Northern who would oversee the proposed water diversion, experienced the Dust Bowl at 17. His family fought to shelter their cattle and sheep in the parched and wind-torn plains of Greeley, Colorado—east of the Rockies. "If we hadn't had the two things [drought, economic depression] at the same time," Farr said, "the Colorado Big Thompson Project would never have been built."

Counting wartime interruptions, the tunnel construction took 9 years: 6 years to bore the 13-mile, 9-foot-wide hole and another 3 years to line it with concrete. On June 23, 1947, W. D. Farr, the irrigation booster now known as "Mr. Water," witnessed the first western slope water flowing by gravity, 13 miles and 2,000 feet down from Grand Lake. Standing on the eastern slope, Farr first heard the roar of a train. Then "the biggest cloud of dust I ever saw came out of that tunnel ahead of the water," in what he described as the most exciting day of his life. "And it just covered us with dust. We were just filthy, our hats, our clothes." For several minutes, the workers surrounding him hugged, kissed, and threw their hats up toward Longs Peak. NBC broadcast the event nationally.

As the controversial tunnel faded from the front page, CBT stayed below the media radar, conveniently overshadowed by Hoover Dam. Although the world's biggest dam cost $58 million and took less than three years to pour, CBT cost $168 million and its ganglion of new dams and reservoirs took 19 years to complete.

Even at subsidized prices, water and electricity sales earned Reclamation millions. In 1987, Northern's 50-year-repayment date arrived. Rather than the $168-million overrun, Reclamation marked down the invoice to its original $25 million, and Northern repaid the Reclamation Fund less than one-sixth of the entire cost, interest free. Now a one-acre-foot share of water, formerly $5, fetches $15,000.

The six CBT power plants sell 759 million kilowatt hours of electricity a year, powering 58,000 homes. As hydroelectric power surged in the 1960s, dams created almost 40 percent of the nation's electricity. Today, an increasing number of polluting, coal-fired plants have greatly reduced hydroelectricity's share.

One of Reclamation's Public Affairs directors, Bob Walsh, believes that his agency's hydroelectric program can't compete with the low cost of easily transported coal. In an era where the immense popularity of white-water rafting and enviro warriors has helped to raise public consciousness, the downsized Reclamation advertises that only 3 percent of the nation's 80,000 dams generate hydroelectric power, which, they claim, is twice as efficient as its competitive energy resources. Wind and solar energy, of course, are not mentioned or found as supplemental energy sources on Reclamation power plant sites. One former chief engineer of CBT told me that Reclamation could create more than two coal-fired plants worth of energy per year—as long as the rivers don't run dry.

The Adams Tunnel has become one of 12 under-the-Continental Divide portals to draw from the Colorado River, catering to a flood of new settlers and swelling Colorado's eastern slope to 3.8 million people. The CBT water intended for farms now irrigates 620,000 acres but is also consumed by 800,000 people and various businesses—35 percent for irrigation, 65 percent for cities and industry. The Adams Tunnel allotment of Colorado River supplies 35 eastern slope towns and cities. In the next quarter century, that population will continue to grow. As underground aquifers beneath the eastern slope are being bought up and depleted, the municipalities continue to lay their money on the distant and thinning river, but no one can accurately say how long its water will last.

ONTO A NONNAVIGABLE RIVER

On the shores of Shadow Mountain Lake, a flock of white pelicans feed amid the algae next to the incoming rush of the Colorado River. Ancient moraines poke from the shallow lake like old vertebrae. Mist clings to the shore. A pair of mating osprey fish the waters, angling down, splashing, and angling back up, showing their empty talons. As I walk east across the reservoir and away from the river and boat moorages, the air becomes still and strangely quiet without moving water.

Reclamation has succeeded in creating a counterfeit water theme park. Their advertising bait—open to one and all to bring your speedboats and your fishing rods—has been taken. One can only wonder, as the drought continues, and eutrophication starves the lake of oxygen, if a sector of the motorboating, reservoir-loving public will realize how badly they've been bilked.

Amid ten-foot-high piles of clear-cut, beetle-infested lodgepole strewn throughout the campground, Arapaho National Forest still charges $20 per night per denuded tent site. At the bottom of Shadow Mountain Lake Dam, dozens of spin-cast fishermen await their rewards in the gushing reservoir outflow. Some poke their rods over the concrete abutment, while others stand along the muddy shore in hopes of hooking one of the sought-after exotics—the colorful rainbow or mackinaw trout—growing fat on the bacterial by-products drifting out of the petri dish above. If on the one-in-a-million chance that a bait fisherman were to hook into one of the surreal but unattractive natives—the humpback chub used to crowd these waters—the federally endangered fish would be thrown back in with disgust.

Rather than risking my life in the unnatural and wicked-looking rapid, I walk for another hour and watch the river froth over rounded boulders. The path is wet and wide from innumerable fly fishermen who work these waters.

After three miles of newly aerated existence, the river is quelled yet again at the gray waters of the next reservoir. In mind-numbing contrast, the elongated, drought-ridden banks of Lake Granby glow in a luminous green furze up to the edge of a lodgepole forest blackened by pine beetles. Standing in waders crotch deep, a dozen fishermen try to tease out a precious rainbow.

In the mud, I blow up my raft, dunk it in the water, then tiptoe in and begin paddling double-speed against the headwind. As the lake widens, the waves increase. Beneath the spray skirt, I'm getting soaked by whitecaps bound for eastern Colorado via the pumping plant.

I'm paddling a half mile an hour in the opposite direction, toward a dam hidden beyond the near hills, on a lake that drains 311 square miles. When I study my satellite photo through the clear, waterproof map case, the reservoir bears an uncanny resemblance to a seahorse. And I'm on the rear wingtip being blown backward. I have to get out and walk around the seven-mile tail of the seahorse, to walk another seven miles up toward its belly and illegally cross over a dam on its throat. Half full, the reservoir holds 96 billion gallons, enough water to fill the irrigation ditches and bathtubs of northeastern Colorado until this time next year. It might take me just as long to jump all the blowdowns while walking around this beast.

Under the cover of dusk, I jog past five No Access and No Trespassing signs on a dirt road and cut down a steep hill toward the bottom of Lake Granby Dam. Although Noble Underbrink said he could legally gain me access and a tour of the dam in several days, I want to see the dam on my own. In a low valley beneath more trophy homes, feeling shrunken and furtive beneath the 300-foot-tall, well-lit walls of the dam, I stuff my red shirt in the pack so that I'll be less visible.

High above, I hear heavy equipment, patching holes on the exposed walls of the dam. Even if the spillways were running with water, the earthen-filled Granby Dam has no hydroelectric generators. The 861-foot-long dam adds to a series of dikes that span five of the 40 miles of shoreline.

Because Reclamation needs to replenish the lake to begin pumping water to the Grand Lake tunnel, the river's outflow beneath the dam is a mere trickle. I resume my jog downstream, stopping only to climb a locked gate on the dam access road. The ankle-deep stream is busy with irrigation ditches, gates, small dams, and No Trespassing signs. Given the low water, I'm content to walk. Still, I arrive at Highway 34 feeling like a common criminal for sneaking around in the dark along roads, dams, and a closed-off public river. When I finish hitchhiking to my car, parked alongside the dam, I'm relieved that the local sheriff hasn't left a parking ticket on the windshield.

That night, back at my tree-barren campsite, a child wails and a dog barks—making me miss my family. To distract myself, I begin phoning ranchers downstream and asking permission to paddle through their land. Last year, a kayaking friend had been shot at here by a rancher, displeased by his portaging around barbed wire. In previous years, dozens of paddlers have been arrested for trespassing on Colorado rivers. Never knowing if I'm speaking to a hostile soul on the phone, I graciously explain that I won't be stepping off the river onto any private land—unless there's barbed wire in the river. One of the ranchers begrudgingly grants me permission, but warns that the Division of Wildlife cops will stop and arrest me if they see me on the river.

Unlike other Western states, Colorado has not resolved whether its waterways—even the famous Colorado River—are open to the public. In 1977, David Emmert was arrested here for trespassing after floating through the private premises of a rancher. The case went to the local court, which couldn't interpret the law. The rancher eventually appealed his case to the Colorado Supreme Court, hoping that the highest levels of state government would side with ranchers practicing one of the most revered professions in Colorado. The Colorado Supreme Court ignored the Colorado legislature's attempt to protect the public's right by excluding "flowing water" from its definition of premises. Because Emmert had briefly touched the banks along the rancher's land to get around the barbed-wire fence, he was found guilty of trespassing and was fined.

This state of affairs is a shame. The right to run rivers in small, human-powered craft existed long before the founding of the United States, under the common law of England, dating as far back as the civil law of Roman times. Water attorneys—who are in no shortage these days in the Colorado River Basin—call this the Law of Nature.

By obtaining permission from four different ranchers, I've gained some insurance against being handcuffed and taken off the river. Still, I'm nervous. More than 40 miles of ranchlands adjoining the river lie ahead of me, and it's impossible to call every landowner. In the morning, I obtain permission from the Ouray Ranch manager, out marking lodgepole pines with fluorescent green tape so that loggers can remove the infested trees. Like many of the subdivisions along the river, the several dozen homes are owned by fishermen, only four of whom are permanent residents. The manager happily grants me consent to use the river through his property, but like the other ranchers, warns me about more barbed-wire fences.

The good news about what remains of the Colorado River as it wends sluggishly between Granby Dam and Windy Gap Dam is that beaver dams often block the water. In turn, the creek bottom is lush with willows, the skittering shadows of trout, and, as I turn a corner, two close-mouthed fishermen, angrily glaring at how I have intruded upon their own Private Colorado. But because they don't try to stop me, maybe they're trespassing too.

For the first mile below Ouray Ranch, I'm forced to bushwhack around three barbed-wire fences. Under federal law, if a landowner obstructs a stream, they're obligated to provide a portage or a chute bypassing the fences. But complaining to a law enforcement official won't do me any good. Around here, the sheriffs all drink coffee with the ranchers.

Within two hours, I approach the muddy confluence of the Fraser River, listed as the third most endangered river in America. Last year, Meadow Creek Reservoir and Williams Fork Reservoirs trapped 85,444 acre-feet (27 billion gallons) of the Fraser's water and sent it east through the Moffat Tunnel to Denver Water. A strain this diversion imposes became evident two years ago, when a ranch foreman downstream opened up his floodgates for the Skylark Ranch. Before he'd collected his fall allotment, the river had vanished. "It was a holiday weekend and the fishing lodges were full," the foreman told the *Denver Post,* "and I dried up the Colorado." Because the ranch had water rights, the foreman felt obligated and entitled to take the water. When I asked a Reclamation representative about this shortage, she said the newspaper distorted the claims of the river drying up.

No matter who's telling the story, the water allocation is veering toward a tipping point. In eight years, Denver is projected to exceed its water demand. Without taking its full water rights of an additional 18,000 acre-feet (5 billion gallons), Denver won't have enough water for new suburban tract homes. No wonder the river is so thin.*

To avoid the headwind—and advertising my illegal presence on the reservoir to the traffic on Highway 40 above—I duck tight under the willows

---

*Northern has proposed that another $270-million dam be built to draw an additional 30,000 acre-feet (11 billion gallons) through the Adams Tunnel. Measured from the Windy Gap Reservoir that I'm paddling through, the 10 percent water decrease here will send a collective 70 percent of the headwaters through the two tunnels.

in view of even more No Trespassing signs. Next to a floodgate on the side of the dam, I slip under a hole in the fence just as a state trooper drives past on the highway, causing my heart rate to accelerate two dozen beats. I lower my raft back in, then jump into the fast-flowing water—spinning dizzily downstream until I can properly orient my paddle and straighten out, then furiously stroke away from yet another log strainer.

I paddle river left and into a slower slough to avoid the next riverwide cable, dangling a dangerously low No Trespassing sign midstream. I scouted it out a week ago, so it's no problem, but an inattentive boater could be guillotined in the six-mile-per-hour current.

I pass ranch fields for the next dozen miles toward Hot Sulphur Springs. Everywhere I look, bright green, three-foot-high alfalfa, *Medicago sativa,* sways in the wind. Although it has to be rotated with other crops, such as wheat or corn, alfalfa and its long-legged roots can withstand droughts, salinity, and even a frost or two.

Alfalfa gained notoriety in the cult-classic book *Catch 22,* in which a farmer accepts cash subsidies for not growing the crop, allowing him to buy more land and receive even more subsidies for not growing alfalfa. Once mowed and gathered as hay, it is fed to the same livestock that has trampled and fertilized the surrounding riverside into a moonscape of sage, cheatgrass, and thistles. Although the Grazing Act helped minimize transient herds of sheep and cattle, this stretch of river is still ruled by alfalfa, cattle, and dams. Alfalfa has the lowest economic value per acre-foot of water that it consumes. Colorado River farmers at sea level or here at high altitudes consider alfalfa the thirstiest flora of the edible plant kingdom, drinking down double the water of grapefruit, the second most water-intensive food crop in the basin. But growers know that, as long as they own cattle and as long as water is relatively cheap, they'll continue to grow alfalfa.

Of the three million acres of land irrigated in Colorado, only one-third of those crops are irrigated by the more efficient sprinklers or drip technology. In hopes of conserving water, Reclamation funded an alfalfa drip-irrigation study in 2002. The study showed that installing drip tape or tubing a foot below the soil will cut down water use by 25 percent without reducing the hay quality or production.*

---

*Reclamation has created its own catch-22: delivering subsidized, cheap water prevents more efficient use of water. Throughout the West, Reclamation's constituency is largely farmers, while the West's population has become largely urban. Most farmers along the Colorado River pay less than $5 per acre-foot for their water rights, whereas Denver residents who want to water their

At a mile and a half above sea level, with a short growing season, the ranchers' other crop choices are limited to wheat or irrigated pasture, both of which pay low and drink voraciously. As development continues flowing down the valley, raising land prices to that of Grand Lake and Granby, some of these ranchers will sell out to developers. Some of them have found alternatives: raising horses, opening dude ranches, or offering exclusive access to fishermen on a river that is supposedly closed to the public. Skylark Ranch recently built fisherman cabins along the river. I can tell from the glares and unreturned Hellos I get from several more fishermen that a paddler is considered persona non grata here. The county revenues from fishing come to $12 million annually, but only $6 million comes from rafting or kayaking—and paddlers mostly stick to the Fraser above, or Byers Canyon below.

Because the river campground at Hot Sulphur Springs is overflowing with trash and stinking of sewage, I happily pay for a hotel room, only to find a handwritten warning above the sink not to drink the water. The town water supply has been contaminated with E. coli.

I start paddling into the eight-mile-long Byers Canyon as mid-morning warms the day, just in case I'm forced to swim the cold rapids. The International Scale of River Difficulty rates rapids from an easy I to a deadly VI. During the spring high water that I'm riding today, kayakers have graded this narrow canyon a class IV+, meaning that it's "extremely difficult" and that "the risk of injury to swimmers is moderate to high . . . and a strong Eskimo roll is highly recommended." Although the latter skill is not my strong suit anyway, rolling a pack raft is impossible. I have oared many class IVs in bigger rafts, but paddling a Class IV alone in a pack raft is asking for trouble.

From my earlier walk and scout of the canyon from the highway, I saw that the railroad and road builders have bulldozed in hundreds of boulders, creating bottlenecks and unnatural rapids. So I've memorized the landmarks where I need to turn, stop, or lean forward and paddle like crazy. Although I could probably run the steepest drop through several standing waves without flipping, I'd become intimate with many sharp-edged boulders if I had to swim through a half mile of continuous rapids below. There's no

summer lawns pay $1,200 per acre-foot. Although the ranchers and farmers are conditioned to use more water than they need, Denverites complain that it's cheaper for the farmers to waste Reclamation water than save it.

guarantee I won't lose my raft, or take a bruising tour through a couple of nasty-looking whirlpools.

I won't be able to climb the steep embankment to the highway. But if necessary, I could clamber up to and portage along the railroad tracks, offering enough room for a train or a person.

I paddle through several minor riffles and drops, feeling a small degree of mastery, even though the water is fast and the stream is narrower than my family's kitchen at dinnertime. In the bouncy, water-absorbing Alpacka, my options feel limited. From previous experience, I've learned that the boat skates over some holes, but its front tube has a tendency to be sucked under by most eddies—which would throw me in.

I grip my paddle tighter as the current yanks me downstream. My rear end is soaked. My brain says *Focus* while my heart yells *Retreat!* That same organ also seems to be pumping louder than the river roaring below, loud as the passing of a freight train feet above, which I cannot afford to glance at. This must be how Burt Reynolds's character felt in the whitewater epic *Deliverance,* with the sodomites waiting on the banks above, probable death waiting in the rapids below. Just above the final drop, I avoid a nasty eddy by spinning left, then ferry river right to a safe eddy and grab a solid-looking branch on a precariously perched log above the lip of class IV+ water shotgunning 2,000 cfs down into the final half mile of frothing battlefield.

This kind of water probably wouldn't deter Burt or most hairy-chested boaters. But I'm scared witless. I'm more than relieved to portage-race another freight train down the last half mile.

Once I've bypassed the canyon, the class II–III rapids below are good fun. For the rest of the morning, I fall into a Zen-like trance of boulder and cable avoidance, while cumulus clouds race above me like tall ships through the blue ocean of Colorado sky. As I splash over a small dam, a flock of pelicans veers off into another field of alfalfa. Mallards honk. Scores of Canada geese escort their goslings downriver in a powerful current. On a stretch of river adjacent to the highway, another state trooper drives by, shaking his head at me but unwilling to stop and further burden the local courthouse's docket with a harmless paddler.

Two miles farther down, a rancher's billboard aimed toward the river and obviously designed for boaters reads:

DANGER: RIVER ELECTRIFIED. GET OUT NOW!!!

I reject the warning if only because electrifying the river sounds more fiction than fact. Given their difficult economic circumstances, I can understand why ranchers are angry, even if I can't yet understand why they're so territorial with paddlers in particular. How can a boater possibly hurt the ranching business?

Heightening the mystery, the river takes me through a ranch and past more scowling fisherman, into thick copses of shaded cottonwood. There's nothing I can do, except continue to be polite. A mile farther down, on a fast, narrow corner, I wave to four more fishermen sitting on a picnic bench. "How's it going?" I ask.

"Okay," says one of the three elderly men, all dressed in expensive-looking khaki vests with multiple pockets. But the fourth, a more agile 40-year-old dressed like a rancher in a worn Carhartt jacket, gets up and runs after me on the banks. "C'mere," he says out of earshot of his fishing clients, wagging his finger.

"Sorry, it's not safe to stop here," I say. "Besides, if I did touch the banks, I'd be trespassing."

"Hey!" he half screams so his clients won't hear him.

I wave again, "Have a nice day," keeping it civil, knowing that I'll be off what he thinks is his river property by the time he can take any action.

Out of the cover of cottonwoods, the wind is gusting over 40 miles an hour. Twice, I'm nearly bowled over as gusts catch the front tube. The cattle manure air is tanned with airborne dust. As the river meanders back north, a great blue heron repeatedly flies off and lands another hundred yards down, croaking raucously. In a fallow field, a much-maligned coyote glances at me, then bolts.

As I approach an old steel bridge, I hear a rancher's truck clattering over the rutted road in hot pursuit. He slams on the brakes at the bridge, jumps out, runs overhead, and yells down to me: "Get out, now!" It's the angry rancher from upstream.

"Well," I say as calmly as I can over the roaring wind, "I'm not getting out because you're hardly the law, but I will talk to you over there on the riverbank."

Out of the wind, he clambers ankle-deep through the mud, enraging him even further. His ball cap reads "Elk Trout Ranch," and I'm relieved to see that he's unarmed. "The sheriff's waiting for you down at Blue River!"

I call his bluff. "Why?"

"These are nonnavigable waters," he says, "closed to boating. Only fishermen can come in here, and they pay for exclusive rights to fish the river."

Now I understand. Fishing is the new cash cow. By boating down a narrow stream where fishermen are sold exclusive access, I'm seen to be jeopardizing the ranchers' survival. I can guess that further arguing my case will only turn up the heat. Instead, I take out my camera and point it toward him. "Can I take your photograph? I'm a journalist working on a story about the health of the river. "

"No," he takes a deep breath, "I'd rather you didn't take my picture. I'd rather be a nice guy and let you go."

I thank him, and he replies, "The river is going to hell in a handbasket."

Like enviros and water buffalos (coveting the resource for their own interests) working together throughout the basin, we have a lot to talk about. Until the Colorado legislature can act on its plethora of unresolved water issues, this rancher and I and the public at large are all in the same boat.

I hold out my hand and introduce myself. After several moments, he wishes me good luck and says that he'll call the sheriff and drop the trespassing charges. Whether it's true or not, I thank him. Now that the day's main difficulties have been resolved, I can turn my focus back to fighting the last six miles of headwinds down toward Gore Canyon.

Below the ranching town of Kremmling, the Colorado River is fed by an anorexic-looking tributary: banks shot by cattle hooves, sage receding into windblown earth. The Blue River was dammed 20 miles upstream by the Green Mountain Reservoir in 1941, compensating the western slope for water lost to the eastern plains through CBT. In 1963, Denver Water dammed the Blue River again at Dillon Reservoir.*

In the last half century, ranching towns like Kremmling have burgeoned as tourist destinations because of Blue Lake and other reservoirs known as the Great Lakes. During weekends or vacations throughout the year, fishermen and water skiers flee the plains heat and smog of Denver. Interstate 70 turns into a parking lot as urban dwellers follow water ditches and tunnels, crawling in their cars across the divide toward reservoirs, rivers, or ski slopes. On the wetter west side, turning lawn sprinklers off had been unheard of until 2005, when restrictions caused by Denver's increasing thirst hit subdivisions near the drying Dillon Reservoir. The last nine summers of drought have put a crimp in business on mountain reservoirs and their drought-wrinkled shorelines. Boat ramps come to ignominious ends in soft sand or axle-eating mud many yards above the waterline.

---

*At press time, 70,000 acre-feet (22 billion gallons) are pumped per year from the Dillon Reservoir through the Roberts Tunnel to Denver. The growing city wants to increase its annual harvest to 117,000 acre-feet (38 billion gallons).

From where I sit bobbing on the cool Colorado-Blue confluence, removed from asphalt or the interstate corridor, it looks like peak runoff as usual—as long as I don't look at the thin Blue River. A month from now, even the mighty Colorado River will run skinny as the snowpack dries up and ranchers open their floodgates against tunnels slurping back against the river.

Behind me, the river meanders east through the alfalfa and grazing highlands of Middle Park. Downstream, the river turns to the southwest and meanders toward the Gore Range and its 12,000-foot peaks rising with purplish and snowy distinction above the sluggish brown waters. The water has gone strangely still, each molecule backing up and waiting its turn to plunge into Gore Canyon as if the Colorado River has a mind of its own.

Spend enough time out here, I think, *and you can feel the river's pulse.*

Before the ancient river carved out the 2,500-foot deep Gore Canyon several millennia ago, the mountains had dammed an enormous lake back over Middle Park. Reclamation Service engineers and geologists wanted to repeat the same feat. In 1903, they jumped on the bandwagon with private dam builders who planned to flood Gore Canyon clear back to Granby and reap the fortunes of a hydroelectric plant. The proposal, pitched with characteristic arrogance, would have evicted scores of ranchers and flooded several towns.

Enter President Teddy Roosevelt, the consummate conservationist. He admired John Wesley Powell and possessed the consummate political skills that Powell lacked. In the spring of 1902, Roosevelt had shrewdly shown the idealistic Congressman Francis Griffith Newlands how to reinsert some of his and Powell's principles into the bill that would be passed as the Newlands Reclamation Act. Roosevelt threw all the power of the White House and his popular presidency toward encouraging Congress to pass the bill, which had stalled for 18 months because of Newlands's unwillingness to compromise. After the bill's passage, though, Roosevelt was irritated that the bill carried Newlands's name because reclamation had been a presidential agenda the first day Roosevelt took office.

Powell died that year, suffering from a stroke, and the act's lack of controlled development infuriated men of his ilk. As Stegner wrote in *Beyond the Hundredth Meridian,* "He would have said there is a difference between using a resource and mining it." Like Powell, however, Roosevelt saw the West pragmatically and wanted to encourage growth and conserve water in those places, like deserts, where water seemed essential.

Although complicated by imperialism, the budding land ethic of the early 20th century favored conserving water, forests, and grazing lands rather than preserving wilderness or wild rivers. With a huge expanse of uninhabited wilderness at America's disposal, natural resources weren't protected for their own sake—unless it involved creating parks for the people or reclaiming water for farmers. For Roosevelt and Powell, wilderness was experienced while hunting, mountain climbing, or river running. Both were nature buffs and animal lovers, but they could not foresee how many species and habitats would soon become endangered or destroyed. Even as the visionary environmentalist John Muir had begun to beat the drum of preserving wilderness after California's pristine Hetch Hetchy river valley was flooded for San Francisco water and power in 1910, few protested the proliferation of dams.

As for Gore Canyon, Roosevelt had hunted in the Colorado headwaters, and he wanted to leave the river alone for the same reason he espoused while setting aside Grand Canyon National Park—for the greater good of the people. Instead of damming Gore, Roosevelt authorized a $10-million earthen dam (eventually named after him) outside Phoenix, on the Salt River, another Colorado tributary. The project had no opposition because it would miraculously spread water across the desert. After squelching the Middle Park Reservoir, Roosevelt permitted the Denver and Rio Grande Western Railroad a right of way through Gore Canyon instead. The railroad provided a nondivisive and cheap way to expedite progress in the West.

Sixty years later, the German emigrant Walter Kirschbaum, who came to America as a kayak instructor and language teacher, first paddled Gore Canyon's class V rapids. Given the complexities of this river bursting through a shadowed crack in the high mountains, it boggles the mind to think of Kirschbaum in his old-fashioned fiberglass and canvas-topped kayak. Although he could Eskimo roll if a wave or an eddy knocked him over, unlike a modern short kayak, his big homemade boat leaked and moved slowly, whereas speed equals survival in the rock garden of whirlpools. Kirschbaum portaged the first two drops and confronted the final twisting waterfalls with a combination of technical expertise and seat-of-the-pants bravado.

The 296-mile Grand Canyon, which Kirschbaum ran in 1960, averages an eight-foot-per-mile drop; for five miles, Gore Canyon drops an average of 68 feet per mile. Kirschbaum loved the Colorado River for its muddy newness, compared to the gin-clear Old World rivers that carried little sediment. He continued nimbly bobbing and plunging through every Western white-water rodeo he could find—until he slipped and drowned in an indoor bathtub.

I had run Gore Canyon in a 13-foot paddle raft six weeks prior with Pete McBride and a phlegmatic guide, Chris "Mongo" Reeder. Mongo, a fan of Mel Brooks's movies, was named after a *Blazing Saddles* character on the trail who said little until nightfall in camp, when his loud flatulence spoke volumes. The contemporary Mongo is also a member of the U.S. rafting team and holder of a record, the 24-hour dash from Glenwood Springs to Moab down the Colorado. Taking a more leisurely pace on April 21, Pete, Mongo, and I started paddling from Blue River in mid-morning, trying to avoid splashing one another with the 44-degree water. A snowy headwind whistled in our ears, and we strained our tendons paddling for over an hour through the last meanders of Middle Park. As Gore Canyon began roaring in the background and Mongo knew he had our attention, he told us to avoid swimming in the icy waterfalls below.

My hands were shaking. I distracted myself by peering into the ten-foot tall, corrugated aluminum watchtower on the riverbank above the rapids. The "USGS Colorado River Near Kremmling" gauge has monitored the river volume for 104 years. Today, it's clocking 1,370 cfs, well within the limits for sane paddling.

Utilizing this gauge, Denver Water recently created a PowerPoint presentation to show how the city has tackled the thorny issue of quenching an enlarged thirst with a shrunken river. As the drought continues and anxiety mounts, the dilemma that Denver and other municipalities face is being addressed at crowded water conferences throughout the Southwest. The speakers and invitees include scientists, water buffalos, municipal water administrators, Reclamation bureaucrats, engineers, conservationists, and lawyers—all lugging laptop PowerPoint presentations. Using science to help simplify the complex water-rights issue, the Denver Water engineers displayed a line chart from the river's "Near Kremmling" gauge alongside reconstructed tree ring data measured by Connie Woodhouse, a respected NOAA scientist.

Woodhouse's work has shown that trees function as reliable river gauges. By boring harmless holes in dozens of headwater trees and withdrawing sample cores, she eventually dried and mounted three Douglas fir cores with timelines corresponding directly to the river volume. The thin rings show dry years; thicker rings denote wetter years. If Dr. Woodhouse didn't have supporting data, she wouldn't jump to conclusions about predicting droughts. In an ideal world, however, understanding the complex tide throughout history could allow users to draw from the Colorado River and its tributaries while still protecting the natural cycles of the river.

Standing next to the gauge near Kremmling, feeling the icy back breeze from the rapids below, I can imagine the river jumping its banks and plowing through the forest above. On May 26, 1984, the river crested high enough to flood the railroad tracks, scour roads in Utah, and eventually bypass ten more dams and reach the sea. According to the gauge's records, this last happened in what boatmen call the "Predambrian Era" (before the dams), on June 7, 1912, uprooting trees four feet higher. During the last five centuries, beginning in the latter Middle Ages, the vacillating tree ring graph shows four bigger deluges. The first and greatest flood receded as Columbus crossed the Atlantic. The last started as Powell finished his descent of the Grand.

Two years after Powell's death, the tree ring record chases the river gauge's zigzags closely in the Denver Water presentation. Imagine an electrocardiogram (EKG) readout hooked up to a human being, juxtaposed with a readout from a calmer twin. The calmer tree ring line does not jump above the river gauge line until 1940, and for three years, it exceeds the river gauge line by 250,000 acre-feet. So call it coincidence that, in 1941, Granby Dam construction had started upstream as Green Mountain Dam withheld large amounts of the Blue River from reaching Gore Canyon. Any attentive physician studying an EKG would be startled by similar declines, and even an untrained observer would be tempted to suspect that cardiac arrhythmia has been induced by placing so many dams in the river.

At the close of the 20th century, the drought graphs like a heart attack. Both lines waver, then plummet into a three-year million-acre-foot drop of volume. This drought, nine years and counting, has only been matched once in duration, but more than seven times in intensity according to Woodhouse's tree ring data, which shows droughts since 1437. In a 2004 paper about her work, standing out amid federally funded colleagues too timid to address global warming under the Bush administration, she wrote that "The climate of the future will not be analogous to that of the past because of the unprecedented effect of human activities."

Mongo finally opened his mouth and screamed, "PADDLE HARDER!!!" We strained to pull ourselves into the nine-foot waterfall called "Applesauce," versus being pulped in the rock-lined rapid several feet to the left. Gore, like Byers Canyon, is littered with boulders of granite and schist knocked from the walls 200 feet above when they built the railroad tracks.

The most difficult and constricted rapid, dubbed "Gore," is only partially named after the hunter Sir George Gore, who exterminated game in his namesake mountain range in the 19th century. Paddlers know its double entendre name from a raft-sized sharpened boulder, perfectly positioned to disembowel raft and passengers. So we lined the boat over a small waterfall on the far side of the river, then jumped back in and bounced like a pinball through "Double Pourover" and the eight-foot drop of "Pyrite Falls." Pete wisely debarked with his camera to get a good vantage point above the second most difficult class V rapid, "Tunnel Falls," below the railroad tunnel.

Now we were shivering, despite the warm sun. Even the reticent Mongo expressed hesitation about the volume of water pouring through this 12-foot waterfall and across a swirling black hole that looked like it could pin a swimmer until the river dropped again sometime in July. The whirlpool, referred to as a "keeper hydraulic" in boater lingo, had fully captured our attention.

"Let's do something I've never done before," Mongo said with a sly smile, narrowing his eyes and scratching his beard. "Let's approach Tunnel river left, along the bank, then just before the drop, paddle full speed so we can try and jump the keeper hydraulic below."

"What do you mean by *try* and jump?" I asked.

He didn't reply. While ferrying river left to line up for the coming drop, I asked Mongo, "You ever get scared?"

He growled.

I tried again: "Funny how being scared makes you respect the river in a way that wouldn't be possible if we avoided Gore Canyon."

Mongo replied: "PADDLE HARDER!" And shouted again: "NOW DUCK!"

We were lined up square, or so it seemed initially, as we flew alongside the hole in a blur of spray, Mongo on the right, me on the left, but tilting up like a blue pancake being flipped by the white spatula of river. I leaned hard left out toward the polished granite walls as Mongo got bumped half out toward the swirling, foaming hole. As the raft bounced against the water strangely upright, he nimbly pulled himself back in. The raft skated across the whirlpool, then stalled.

"PADDLE NOW!" Mongo needlessly screamed, this time an octave higher.

Six lung-bursting paddle strokes pulled us out of the hole and propelled us into an eddy beneath a boulder big as a soot-stained cottage. While waiting for Pete to jump back in, we high-fived.

"That was fun," I said, "huh, Mongo?"

He just smiled.

I slumped down in the raft, panting hard, trying to recover from flailing against the river. "Boy," I said, "I'm out of shape."

Mongo remained silent, but didn't seem to be lacking in breath as he pushed us off. While being flushed past another keeper in the swirling "Toilet Bowl" rapids, Pete lay on his back in the bow and photographed a wave of ice water cascading over his camera in a water housing and drenching Mongo—smiling in open-mouthed bliss—and me, ducking the deluge. Above "Kirschbaum" rapids, Pete jumped out onto the shore and photographed us paddling through a line of surf, hammering the raft—*"Cha-Chum, Cha-Chum, Cha-Chum"*—like a drum. We finished weaving through the slalom course of rocks, exhilarated.

"You ever wonder, Chris," I asked as we sped down the river toward our car at the Pumphouse takeout, "what would happen if the snow really does stop falling in the headwaters?"

"Yeah," Mongo said.

I gave him a moment to compose his thoughts. I could only guess that he had been thinking about his young children, his new line of "Mongo products" river gear, as well as his precipitation-dependent work on the river and as a ski patroller at Vail. This time he replied with full eye contact:

"We're screwed."

The evening of June 8, Bruce Kime and I can't get away from the Pumphouse boat put-in fast enough to escape the reek of fish guts discarded on the shore by a fisherman more interested in food than sport. It's astonishing how different bait and spin-cast anglers are from fly fisherman. Whereas the former takes from rivers, the latter—judging by the conservation efforts of fly fishing groups such as Trout Unlimited—gives back.

Bruce dips his oars, while swallows dip and hover alongside, among a hatch of nymph flies, and the sun dips below the rounded hills to the west. We thread "Eye of the Needle" rapids and the 18-foot raft judders past basalt cliffs and a beaver working a slough. Bruce looks visibly relieved as we emerge from the straightforward class III rapids, even though he's rowed this stretch before. Whatever the case, I'm happy to have a companion in awe. In less than two hours, we've covered a half dozen miles, so we pull over onto an island with a picnic bench.

For the next hundred miles, we're passing private ranches and the usual spate of No Trespassing signs alongside Bureau of Land Management (BLM) public lands created by the 1936 Grazing Act. Camping areas are groomed with designated tent sites and prebuilt fire rings. We gather driftwood for a fire, but because the Colorado evening has gone totally black, we opt for sleep instead. A half dozen times through the night, we're awakened by coal trains rumbling past and muting the roar of the rising Colorado.

In the morning, we leave early, jumping up and down to warm ourselves against the frost whitening the riverbanks. Every hour, we take turns at the oars as the day warms up an increasingly full and wave-strewn river. Snowmelt is rushing off the Gore Range behind us. As the heated ground air mixes in along the icy river corridor, light waves are bent, and the air wavers into a fuzzy mirage. Along the river, it's a lime green fairyland. Up above the mirage, the pyramidal, 13,560-foot Powell Peak stands out among the whitened chops of the Gore Range like an incisor biting into crisp blue sky. Longs Peak, although higher than Powell's namesake mountain, is a rounded lump in the sky by comparison.

The Major hardly qualified as an alpinist seeking out the great lines of unclimbed mountains in the mid-19th century. If he hadn't developed an eye for geometrically pleasing lines and ridges that led directly to summits, he had at least been smitten by virgin mountains. Two months after climbing Longs Peak in August 1868, Powell escorted one of his college students, Ned Farrell, and a *Rocky Mountain News* editor, Oramel Howland, toward the highest peak in the Gore Range. Upon seeing the steep snow and rock below the summit, Farrell tried to convince the Major to turn back. But they all reached the top on September 26.

Farrell recalled the Major's difficulties: ". . . he would not give up, and we cautiously moved on, passing many places where a single misstep . . . would be certain death."

Farrell did not exaggerate. Although they didn't need a rope on Longs, they certainly would have benefited from one on Powell Peak's steep, exfoliating shale. Powell got badly winded trying to keep up with his younger charge. So on this summit, exhausted and deferring to a younger civilian for once, he finally allowed one of his granite biscuits to be left in a tin can with a note, recording the date and their names. Sixty-seven years later, the Colorado Mountain Club carried the tin can and its note down, to be preserved for posterity. The "everlasting memento" to the Major had metamorphosed into a blackened pebble.

In 1979, I guided seven young Outward Bound students up Powell's route by fixing ropes up the mountainside to safeguard the passage. On top, with two students shaken to tears by the steepness of the peak, I sat impressed with the one-armed Major's audacity more than a century ago. The steep and crumbling shale on the ridge often required the use of two hands.

Bruce Kime is a neighbor and friend who runs the outdoor education program at Colorado Mountain College. Although he exhibits leadership, safety, and outdoor skills as tools for his students during frequent wilderness trips, back in the classroom he chooses environmental issues—climate change, resource extraction, and dam building—as the foundations of his outdoor education curriculum.

On our second day of rowing the river, we swap tales of our formative moments in the wilderness. He first started as a guide on the Colorado River in 1980, while working for the rafting company Timberline Tours (now owned by Mongo). As a greenhorn rowing his first trip down the relatively benign waters below Gore Canyon, Bruce flipped his raft and dumped a boatload of Girl Scouts into "Eye of the Needle" rapids. His barefooted, stoner partner rowing the other raft jumped onto a bank to help pluck out the girls, but stepped on a beaver-gnawed, sharpened willow stump and ran it through his foot. "Amazing," Bruce shakes his head while telling the story, "how much fat there is in a human foot."

Now I know why he looked so focused on the rapid last night.

As we spend a long half hour walking down to and scouting a rapid named "Rodeo," I realize that Bruce—unlike most river runners—has no interest in rivers as vehicles of adrenaline. He rows the raft perfectly into the "V," straightens it out, and lets the current do the work, pulling us through the class IV sleeper. We outrun ubiquitous mergansers and Canada geese, several weeks fatter than their newly arrived cousins appeared a hundred miles upstream.

As the river grows from dozens of incoming streams, we're coasting more than eight miles an hour. In a month, as these waters drop and warm fully into summer, this stretch will attract more rafters, fishermen, and inner tubers than any other section of the river for a couple hundred miles. Easy accessibility, canyon scenery, mild rapids, plentiful fish, inexpensive cabins, and cheap campgrounds draw the masses. By contrast, in the flood of peak runoff in uncrowded early season, the river feels wild, even intact. By late afternoon, Bruce and I are riding a surging brown deluge. But is it really a flood?

Normally, dry willows are waving with the river combing through their stems. Cottonwoods sweep past us in the current, waving their green leaves like warning flags. The river is so high that, in a nerve-wracking moment, we duck down flat beneath two bridges to squeeze through. To stop the raft along the bank-swept current of washed-over eddies, I have to spring out and quickly wrap the stern line around a tree.

There's no guarantee that headwater dams will prevent the river from taking out roads, houses, and even towns that have been built within the floodplain. Dams sometimes fail. Still, these dams allow profitable electric and water sales, irrigation, recreation for bait fisherman, and drinking water for distant cities. The amount of stilled Colorado River is impressive. One-fifth of its 1,450 miles are impounded by dams.

The impact of dams on rivers is not so obvious, because no order is so great as the chaos of nature. Controlled water releases from dams for electricity* have stopped the changing cycles of flow that used to occur daily, seasonally, and annually on the Colorado. These former sediment-carrying floods allowed myriad natural processes to flourish, beginning with beach building and island making. Consequently, habitat diversity and plant life are changed through loss of sediment.

The release of cold reservoir water from beneath the dams has significantly lowered and stabilized the river's temperatures. In addition, native cold-water fish—humpback chubs, bony chubs, pike minnows—can no longer reach spawning areas blocked by these dams. Native fish that used to be found from the sea to the headwaters are now only found in the lower basin or in small pockets of river or reservoir where fisheries managers struggle to reintroduce the natives amid aggressive, warm-water exotics, like trout, bass, and carp. The waving reeds or willows that we're seeing in these high waters, which used to rip from headwaters to sea, are now found in only isolated pockets—allowing invasive plants like tamarisk to take over.

A comprehensive report from the World Commission on Dams summarizes:

> The global debate about large dams is . . . complex because the issues are not confined to the design, construction and operation of dams themselves but embrace the range of social, environmental and political choices on which the human aspiration to development and improved well-being depend. Dams fundamentally alter rivers and the use of a natural resource, frequently entailing a reallocation of benefits from local riparian users to new groups of beneficiaries at a regional or national level. At the heart of the dams debate are issues of equity, governance, justice and power—issues that underlie the many intractable problems faced by humanity.

Bruce and I spend three days riding more than a hundred miles to Shoshone Lake, a small dammed reservoir upriver from Glenwood Springs. Over a thousand cfs

---

*Although hydroelectricity on these dams is advertised as a clean energy that doesn't use fossil fuels, it can't compare to that of solar or wind power. According to a recent, book-length report from the World Commission on Dams, the greenhouse gas emissions from the world's reservoirs contributes up to 28 percent of the planet's global warming because of vegetation rotting underwater behind dams.

is diverted through a tunnel to the Shoshone Hydro Plant, creating more "clean energy." Although most river runners hold dams in contempt as a simple matter of principle, because the Shoshone Dam was built one hundred years ago to create power, no one today can remember what the river was like without it.

Long before any other state in the West, in 1882, the Colorado Supreme Court overturned the Riparian Doctrine. This old English law, honored throughout much of the United States, entitled those living on a river's banks to use the water as they liked without diminishing it. The philosophy was that the river belonged to everyone to satisfy the needs of flock or fields, so long as they didn't exclude someone else's needs downriver. In an equalitarian society free of corporate landowners, the law worked.

In arid Colorado, however, farmers and miners and ranchers felt constrained by the Riparian Doctrine and wanted the opportunity to exploit the river. Operators took what they needed and then some. This prompted the 19th-century Colorado legislature to adopt the doctrine of prior appropriation. This revolutionary act of capitalism accelerated the clamor for water, put countless lawyers to work, and overloaded the court system. Within the vast water law, one rule abided for grabbing the water: *Qui prior est in tempore, potior est in jure*—he who is first in time is first in right.

As long as you came first, you could drain the river to its bones. If someone fought you for taking it, you hired a lawyer who would defend your rights under the Colorado constitution.

In 1902, before any other major dam or diversion, the Shoshone Hydro Plant obtained the right to take (or borrow in this case) 1,500 cfs, about 3,000 acre-feet a day, or over 1 maf per year, equaling 20 percent of the river's annual flow into Lake Powell. For up to three months, the 2.5 miles of riverbed between the dam and Shoshone Hydro is often drained to puddles. Underneath the plant, the water diverted from upstream returns in a munificent, 1,500-cfs water fountain. The turbines generate power for nearly 17,000 Colorado homes.

Because of the prior appropriation doctrine, Denver Water—a junior water rights holder, five places down the queue because its Colorado River rights weren't acquired until 1946—has to obey the "Shoshone call." If Shoshone Hydro was not calling the water downstream, then upstream water users could divert the water in priority long before it ever reached Glenwood Canyon; this would have given Bruce and me a much slower ride over the past three days.

Ever-expanding Denver may be separated from the river by the Rockies, but it is the fifth largest and fourth richest municipality—behind Los

Angeles, San Diego, Phoenix, and Las Vegas—clamoring for the Colorado River. Denver Water has an annual budget of a quarter billion dollars, over a thousand employees, and 1.2 million urban customers. Since the 1960s, Denver Water has been negotiating with Xcel Energy, which runs Shoshone Hydro, for a bigger share of water rights. In 2003, Xcel Energy reached an agreement that would partially shut down Shoshone during low river flows or droughts. As Denver Water appropriates Shoshone's water allotment, they compensate Xcel Energy for money lost due to inefficient power generation. To compensate for the 1,250 cfs not being blasted through the Shoshone fountain down to Glenwood Springs, the Colorado River District released an additional 1,000 cfs from Wolford Mountain Reservoir above Kremmling. As water disappears, these river horse trades are becoming more common.

As we walk past the tunnel diversion and around the water thrumming over the dam, the force of the class V rapids beneath our feet makes the prior appropriation doctrine seem irrelevant. A few hundred yards down the bike path, with the tires of passing semis vibrating against cast-iron joinery holding together sections of concrete Interstate 70 directly overhead and a drowned-out freight train passing silently on the opposite bank, we walk through the spray of cold water and hold tightly to the railing while staring into the most frightening section of river between the headwaters and Mexico. Before the 1990s "Bridge"—as locals call the $490 million interstate—construction blasted boulders and huge pieces of antique roadway into the river, this rapid was called "Cottonwood Falls." Now, with the new highway superstructure having splintered all cottonwoods from existence, the rapid has been renamed "Upper Death." No one wants to talk about exactly who died and when, including Bruce. We have to shout to hear one another over the thundering water.

"My God!" I say.

"Shall we do it?" he asks jokingly.

"Not even in my dreams," I yell back.

Below us, the central "haystack" explodes the river up and over an object the size of an abandoned locomotive. Provided you're not sucked into the ten-foot cavern below it, on either side downriver are sieves or giant keepers that whirlpool through concrete caves bristling with rusty rebar. No telling what else you might hit while being twirled around inside these keepers. Although it would help to be a skilled paddler, surviving the run would also require an equal amount of luck. To say nothing about brass balls.

HOME WATERS

Two weeks of sleeping on riverbanks and contemplating rapids paddled by hormonally imbalanced young men are enough to make anyone feel old. So on June 12, my 52nd birthday, I leave the river at Glenwood Springs, drive past the Roaring Fork confluence and two dozen miles up Highway 82 to my home above Carbondale. We live on an old potato farm mesa surrounded by juniper and pinyon pine, several miles and several hundred feet above the Roaring Fork River.

Four years ago on this site, we realized a dream: building an energy-efficient home so that we could teach ourselves and the boys how to live more sustainably. Because I'm not a tradesman, banging nails and playing general contractor makes my journey down the Colorado River seem like a vacation. For ten months after using a nail gun, I couldn't lift a paddle because of the tendonitis in my right arm. Unlike my job on the river, which I'll float and explore for another year, our house will always be a work-in-progress. Last year we installed solar panels that heat our water. In May, we built a greenhouse and a vegetable garden. Next year, we'll build a chicken coop and henhouse for laying hens who'll supply plenty of garden fertilizer. Sometime in the not-too-distant future, we hope to install a wind turbine and generate our own electricity.

Even away from the river—living in the semiarid ranch land rather than a subdivision—water plays a huge role in our lives. As seen from atop the roof where I'm repairing a vent knocked down by the heavy winter snows, our 360-degree panorama of high mountains and river valleys shows that it's the greenest summer in two decades. At the same time, our view of these verdant hills and bottomlands, not yet summer browned, is also alarming. Without continued rain or snow, we are surrounded by thousands of acres of forest, sage, scrub oak, and thriving grasslands. If the summer turns as dry and windy as it has in past years, they will dry out into a huge fuel supply for fast-moving wildfires. I'm standing on a metal roof looking down at recycled plastic decking and cement (rather than cedar) siding. And I'm hoping that these materials can prevent the house from burning down.

Two months ago, during a freak dry spell between snowmelt and spring, June was forced to drive the boys through a 70-foot-high, arcing wall of fire along Highway 82. With traffic behind her, and no option to stop with flames beside her, she floored it just moments before the dynamic flames jumped all four lanes up toward the hillside below our house. The cars behind her came to a screeching halt, and within minutes the fire department shut the highway down. Several hundred homes were evacuated. Luckily, the wind died down and the thousand-acre blaze ended as suddenly as it had started—by a rancher who incautiously let his irrigation-ditch burning turn into a wildfire.

Dry spells or droughts also affect the underground water supply. On the mesa near our home, ranches on the local reservoir ditch system recently switched entirely to sprinklers instead of flood irrigation. The change is a perplexing example of how a sensibly efficient act can upset the delicate balance of water conservation, potentially harming the underground aquifer by denying it recharge through flood irrigation.

Our 20 acres, adjoining my mother-in-law Carol's 20 acres, each came with 30-year-old wells that were drilled down into the aquifer. Twice over the last 20 years, Carol's well pump has sucked sand and mud as her aquifer water temporarily dropped. With our neighbors in the Missouri Heights Well Users Association, we've discussed mapping the unknown waters below, but a seismic survey of the aquifer would be incredibly expensive. We do know that the aquifer resides below basalt surface strata, held in semipermeable gravel and clay 200 feet below. The water, primed by an electric pump, flows directly into our house at 25 gallons per minute. I've wondered if the aquifer started in the last ice age because the water is so cold it makes your teeth ache. Like most of my neighbors in ranching country, we don't let the water run, indoors or out. Even while bathing the boys, June or I jump in to share the bathtub water.

Several years ago, we took advantage of the prior appropriation doctrine and adjudicated our well rights through the local water court. If a neighboring rancher sells off his land for a subdivision, and the new owners drain the aquifer, then that subdivision—under our water rights—will be obligated to supply us with water. This spring, after two years of writing letters and giving testimony to obnoxious development lawyers, our well users association convinced county officials to shut down construction of a subdivision that would have stacked a hundred homes sporting trophy lawns atop our aquifer. Because we live near the headwaters of three rivers seeded with abundant rain and snow, our small aquifer might be getting recharged at a similar rate to its discharge. Although a longer drought or subdivision rampant with Kentucky bluegrass could deplete the aquifer, our water supply near the source seems more secure than many large cities in the Southwest.

One hundred and sixty miles away live two million thirsty Denverites extending straws toward the distant Colorado River. On the surrounding plains, another 1.8 million Coloradoans poke shorter straws to reach one of four Denver Basin aquifers containing paleowater from the last ice age.

In our own small way, compared to the megalopolis, we are trying to retain a balance. After we finished building our house, rather than laying down water-consumptive sod on the surrounding acre of disturbed ground, we hydroseeded native grass and wildflowers so that we won't use up any water other than falling rain or snow. If we have a bad fire season, we'll mow the tall browned grass and then rake it away to protect our house with a fire perimeter. If we had planted Kentucky bluegrass—a plant as water-consumptive as alfalfa because the water evaporates off it rather than seeping back to the aquifer—an acre of this grass would drink 1,007,325 gallons per season.

Because our well water is free and sprinklers are cheap, we could easily turn our yard into a pampered country lawn. With a small loan, we could keep up with most of our neighbors' manicured properties surrounded by equally water-consumptive and diseased aspen trees, imported up to the evergreen zone. Thanks to the post-Victorian societal worship of the Green Lawn, my otherwise enviro mother-in-law lost her dogs to lymphatic cancer after landscapers applied deadly herbicides to her grass.

Our dog companions, Freddy and Teak, regularly use the grass as a toilet, which is as much fertilizer as our yard gets. To own a green lawn, we'd have to groom it with chemicals that would kill beneficial plants and insects, ultimately seeping down into the aquifer so that our neighbors will eventually fill their sinks with traces of this broad-leaf defoliant, renowned for thinning Vietnamese jungles. Manicured green grass is an ecological desert, killing diversity and native species. Our views are not widely shared: The lawn care industry in North America grosses $25 billion per year.*

While backfilling our house, we accepted a dozen free dump trucks loaded with dirt from an excavated Carbondale pasture. Initially it seemed like a great idea, enriching our acreage with remnant cattle and sheep manure mixed with tons of rich black soil straight off the Roaring Fork floodplain. As it turns out, the manure harbors exotic seeds that have become the bane of my existence. Although the sharp-spined thistle is revered in Scotland for repulsing barefoot Norwegian warriors, Scottish thistle is its own invasion in my yard. Several times a year, I tour the 20 acres and strain my back trying to uproot the plant, which starts ankle high, tentacling several feet of sinewy roots under boulders. When I pull them up, every millimeter of unobtainable root left in the belly of the ground, like the hydra of Greek mythology, pops ugly heads out within days. In the two weeks I've been out on the river, newly sprouted plants now rise over my knees. Even if I kill every living thistle on each square inch of our land, the seeds can lie dormant for 20 years, outwaiting even persistent droughts before they spring back to life. So the day after my birthday, I continue trying to stem the invasion with a sharpened dirt shovel. I spy, erupting amid the other native plants, another purple-headed thistle. I stomp the shovel in deep, pry out the root, then drop to my knees, and pull with both leather-gloved hands. I slay the many-headed monster and throw it onto our barren gravel driveway. The epic story of my backyard and its newly introduced species, I'm keenly aware, matches that of invasive species on the Colorado River.

Down in the corner of our property, underneath the shade of an ancient gnarled juniper, I cool off from the low nineties temperature while confronting a fresh cow pie fertilizing my favorite cacti. The fences built by ranchers to make us good neighbors are occasionally breached by stray "range locusts"— another burr beneath my saddle blanket. Most people call them cattle.

For as long as I can remember in public lands across the West, I have put up with the range locusts, spreading invasive species such as thistle and cheatgrass. Like many long-suffering wilderness users, I have learned how to stomach the cow pies and flies, the stench of urine and contaminated water, and the eroded landscapes.

---

*NASA has measured 32 million acres of U.S. lawns, much of it grown in arid regions—making homeowners' grass the largest irrigated crop in the nation. Many Southwest municipalities are now giving homeowners cash in return for tearing up their turf lawns.

In 2002, after reading Stephen Ambrose's *Undaunted Courage,* covering the journey of Lewis and Clark, I tried to follow their path down the Missouri River. Daunted after paddling a mere 200 miles down the headwaters, I quit. Rather than confronting grizzlies, like my pioneer predecessors, I had to share river campsites with bawling cattle.

During two decades of change I've witnessed in the Colorado River headwaters—watching rivers drop and fuel prices rise—and raising children who should be entitled to these resources, I've learned that diminishing water will impact the entire American West. My part in this water issue through the river, or my actions in trying to conserve water at home, can seem as indiscernible as wasted droplets evaporating off my neighbors' lawns. Yet, as our family lowers its consumption of water and fossil fuels and as thousands more take similar steps to conserve, we might make a difference. We have no choice but to try.

On June 14, I shuttle back to the Colorado River with Mike Freeman, a companion from Alaskan river trips and a sought-after school counselor who keeps threatening to retire and spend the rest of his life paddling and skiing. We put in our two kayaks where I left off below Glenwood Springs with Mongo in April. After removing my five-year-old child stowing away in the boat, I wave goodbye to him, Nicholas, Alistair, and June. I point the bow sideways to the current, and I'm swept off in a rush of water bound for Lake Powell. Despite elevated Interstate 70 nearby, the river is below the noise level of passing traffic and offers surprising isolation.

In the first hour, we see three bald eagles, white pelicans, and one osprey nest. Mostly we're riveted by angry, coffee-with-cream-tinted boils and steep wave trains. If the Colorado felt flooded above Glenwood Springs last week, the water below the confluence is running a mile per hour faster and 1,500 cfs higher. We're riding the wave of incoming Roaring Fork River, draining portions of four mountainous Colorado counties the size of Rhode Island. The water accelerating us west gains its initial momentum from snow melting two vertical miles above, from a half dozen 14,000-foot peaks, and hundreds more unnamed yet no less spectacular 12,000- and 13,000-foot peaks of the Elk and Collegiate Ranges. The Roaring Fork watershed supports more than 40,000 people, five ski areas, four Watermans on Missouri Heights, three under-the-divide tunnels, two large dams, and Aspen, the number one town of the rich and famous.

Freeman, from the former ranching-turned-tourism town of Glenwood Springs, lives within view of rapids he has paddled too many times to count.

Today, he's paddling a white flat-nosed Perception Pirouette. In this kayak, he can surf for hours or throw off showy enders—pirouetting the boat around on its bow. Still, his relic can no longer be sold or even given away. In the eyes of a new generation of afternoon kayakers shoehorned into ever-shorter play boats, happily surfing in the riverwide wave at the new Glenwood Springs water park, we're balding graybeard dinosaurs on a journey. No one takes kayak journeys on this section of river. I'm lolling in a 15-foot-long combination sea and river kayak, made in Germany by Prijon. This barge is loaded with wine, fresh groceries, and drinking water. If we tried to drink from the river, our water filter would be rendered useless by thick silt.

These particles softly ping and hiss against the hulls of our boats in midstream. Unlike a glacial river that carries rock carved out by prehistoric ice, the Colorado scours fresh earth during every flood cycle. In the spring and early summer runoff that we're paddling, the river is over 2 percent dirt—50 pounds per ton of water. The Colorado carries 35 times more silt than the huge Mississippi, making it one of the siltiest rivers in the world, behind China's Yellow River, which is twice as long. Like that river's surrounding earth colors, el Río Colorado—or *red* in Spanish, named by missionaries for its color during flood—will take on a red sandstone hue as we paddle past blushing sandstone in Grand Junction.

In the 90 miles between here and that town, the rapids are minor, but the powerful current could easily cause a quick drowning. Seen from a hillside above the river where we take our first break, the river, like fast-daubed oil from an omniscient brush, is painting mountain mud through sparkling green fields.

I watch Mike paddle up to a boulder surrounded by waves, where he catches an eddy, then angles out river right and surfs for a minute with a maniacal grin. I can't hear him from my position upstream, but I can guess what he's thinking. *I'll tell you what: We might be getting old, but this river knows how to show us a good time.* He finishes the session by pulling out into the current and deftly levering his paddle to take him on a riverwide arc.

I come in quick and hit the waves square but instead of continuing straight downstream, I get "typewritered" five feet sideways, rattling the fillings within my teeth; I throw out my paddle to one side and lean on it like an outrigger to keep the Yukon upright. Floating backward to watch the show, Freeman shakes his head. With all the snags and trees speeding along beside us, we know that swimming in this cold, fast water would test a beaver.

Freeman's dry suit is pinched shut by rubber gaskets at his neck, wrists, and ankles—restricting circulation to his brain, hands, and feet. Still, judging by his performance in eddies that I try to avoid, his brain is functioning just fine. I'm in dry pants, further gasketed at my hips, with a dry top counter-gasketing tightly over the spare tire around my midsection—which will deflate after another month of eating freeze-dried food. We've both heard the theory that most people who drown this time of year sink, in sudden horror, because the water's high silt content fills up their clothes as fast as a scrambling ferret. Although it seems unlikely that silt could pull a good swimmer under, neither of us is willing to prove the theory wrong.

Freeman is wearing his helmet. I forgot mine. We keep an eye on one another, whether laughing or poking into eddies for brief whirly tours. On slow sections, we receive the gift inherent to river trips by confiding in one another and catching up on one another's life stories since the last heart-to-heart, two years ago on the Kongakut River, atop the continent. We share the philosophy that our lives are better than good, but we need time gallivanting downstream to put our worlds in perspective and reassess our values.

On the river, we get what we need by riding in synch with those rhythms that we miss in our daily lives: Bird calls. The shape of wind as it crosses water. The tang of nature—greening willow limbs, a musty fox burrow, or spring beauties flowering along the banks—that can only be earned through the passage of miles and nights spent sleeping on the ground.

After every trip, we hope we are going home better human beings. Whether we succeed or not, having this opportunity provides yet another reason for sustaining the Colorado River: to provide spiritual renewal and necessary escape for thousands of tourists, boatmen, naturalists, and locals like us.

At midday, the thermometer on my kayak deck reads 86 degrees, but while sitting on a thick cushion of snowmelt and careening downstream fast as a river otter, it's cool enough to keep our gasketed dry gear fully zipped. At the second bridge in the town of Rifle, the entire river is swept left, exploding onto a concrete pillar that creates a reverse hydraulic big enough to hold a bus. Ride the current here into this aqueous roller coaster and you'd have all the free will of a twig. I read the trap with plenty of time, although I run the rapid backward, ferrying frantically toward the safe side of the river with no more than a kayak length to spare. This time, however, Freeman is not smiling. He'd witnessed another one of his friends drowning in a Colorado hydraulic more than a decade ago.

We shake our heads and keep moving, newly awed by the river's power. The river flattens out and loses speed while winding through a valley rife with alfalfa and poised to be subsumed by industry. I put my paddle down and watch a town repeatedly transformed by the pursuit of fossil fuel. Gravel pits surround the river. Oil and gas derricks clang to and fro like giant metronomes. Every other vehicle on the interstate is a pickup truck working the fields.

This is not the region's first oil and gas boom. On September 10, 1969, the Atomic Energy Commission set off a nuclear bomb belowground on a small mesa overlooking the Colorado River. It collapsed chimneys in the nearby town of Parachute, shook a passing helicopter, and vaporized the rock underground into a 350-foot-high, 76-foot-wide cavity. Protestors who entered the grounds above the experimental earthquake were knocked off their feet and then arrested for trespassing. The blast also achieved its desired effect: cracking underlying rock structures for hundreds of feet in all directions, freeing natural gas. And, just as predicted by opponents, millions of cubic feet of natural gas turned radioactive had to be burned off. CER Geonuclear and Austral Oil couldn't afford the public relations disaster of selling natural gas that would make customers' homes glow in the dark.

In comparison to the devastating 15-kiloton blast at Hiroshima, the explosion 11 miles southwest of Rifle achieved 44 kilotons. "Even small odds are unacceptable if the stakes are too high," Governor Lamm told a reporter, "and this was a case of blowing up a nuclear bomb in a way that could contaminate the entire Colorado River Basin with tritium. It was insanity."

In 1974, Lamm passed an initiative that would mandate a statewide vote before any atomic bombs could be set off again in Colorado. Congress quietly killed funding for the ill-conceived Project Plowshare, also known as PNE (peaceful nuclear explosions), which spent a decade blowing up 27 bombs and spending $800 million of taxpayer money. If successful in the gas fields of the Rockies, PNE had already sighted its crosshairs at water, planning to nuke together Arizona aquifers.

As we pass the sweet-smelling yet thorny bloom of invasive Russian olives west of Rifle, I wonder how the coming oil-shale development can be stopped if nuclear bombs were exploded here 40 years ago. We paddle underneath a huge cottonwood grove, shading us with a canopy that looks like cumulous shadows along the darkened surface of the river. Either side of the valley is guarded by gas rigs, laying claim to the Piceance Basin, a geological formation holding enough natural gas to heat 15 million homes for 100 years.

Driving I-70 at night, these lit-up drill rigs appear against the countryside like colossal stands of decorated Christmas trees. During spring high-water periods, drilling mud with diesel fuel and stray radionuclides occasionally leaks out into drainages, but the level of contamination is difficult to monitor. Ditto for the process of fracking, or injecting chemicals into the ground to extract small quantities of oil and gas, polluting the water table badly enough to sicken locals who drink it. Despite this, Rifle's population has swelled to over 8,000: roughnecks sucking up greenbacks and new businesses feeding on the busy oil economy.

To Big Oil, the natural gas is only chump change amid the wealth of fossil fuels buried below. Eight million years ago, Lake Uintah covered southwestern Wyoming, eastern Utah, and western Colorado. The freshwater lake and its shores teemed with life: matted with algae, fearsome megafish, giant horses, and fishing frigatebirds (now found at the river's mouth in Mexico).

Over the millennia, Lake Uintah eutrophied into a thick goop of carbon-rich life. Buried under accumulating sediments, mountains folded up and over the lake bed, and the earth's compression eventually created micrite, or oil shale. Each rock contains up to 40 percent kerogen, dripping with the lake's former life, morphed into hydrocarbons. Some of the kerogen was cooked by geothermal heat, steaming its hydrocarbons into the 100 trillion cubic feet of natural gas now being harvested. Most of the kerogen and organic matter was squeezed into blue-tinted oil shale, holding 63 trillion gallons of high-grade oil. The oleaginous rocks along the Colorado River contain nine times the oil found under Saudi Arabia, ten times the quantity ever drilled out of U.S. rocks.

Surrounded by the world's largest deposit of oil shale, Freeman and I can see earlier attempts to mine it on the opposite side of the river from Rifle, now a gated, several-hundred-home retirement community built like a castle overlooking its future kingdom. Battlement Mesa is the $5-billion ruin of the Colony Oil Shale Project, started in the late 1970s by Exxon. The operation went bust in 1982, on a weekend known as Black Sunday, as world oil prices plummeted and 2,200 employees lost their jobs overnight, creating scores of bankruptcies and home foreclosures.

Despite the king's ransom in the root cellar, the problem is that cooking oil shale, by turning an experimental oven up to 700 degrees, blows up the whole kitchen. The traditional mining methods aren't much better. As ably demonstrated in Estonia, oil shale causes 97 percent of that country's air pollution, 86 percent of total waste, and 23 percent of water pollution. China has similar mines; both countries' sites are as subtle as a Chernobyl meltdown.

Equally grave to the Colorado River is that mining oil shale consumes up to five barrels of water per barrel of oil produced. Then add the possibility of acid, heavy metals, and oil slicking the river. Mining oil shale consumes one-fifth the oil's ultimate energy to get it out of the ground, while emitting more greenhouse gas than any other fossil fuel extraction. This leads back to one of the causes of snow and water diminishment in the Colorado River Basin: climate change.

Before the atom bombs salted the subterranean with radionuclides, oil companies hounded every rancher and ditch owner for hundreds of miles, adding up to over 200 separate water rights that equal half a river. It's taken over a half century of boom and bust, but sniffing a new Saudi Arabia on the wind, the six oil companies (ExxonMobil, Shell Texaco, Chevron Texaco, The Oil Shale Corporation, OXY USA, and the Union Oil Company of California) have prevailed.*

Big Oil could grab enough water to challenge junior rights in Denver. This year's BLM environmental analysis is bleak: Oil shale development will transform western Colorado from an agricultural to an industrial landscape. Goodbye to the snow-making machines in most Colorado ski areas. So long to the Upper Colorado River Endangered Fish Recovery Program. And they can finish off half-empty Lake Powell, shrinking it to puddles by letting the oil companies inject billions of gallons of water into ground so hot it will transform western Colorado's sky into steam clouds.

Big Oil now owns what amounts to the entire four-state Upper Basin yearly allocation of Colorado River water. If these companies have their way with Rifle oil shale—performing a heat enema on underground kerogen, radionuclides, and explosive gas until the oil comes boiling out of the rock— it's hard to fathom what will happen to the landscape without a river. Never mind us folks who live here.

---

*Alaska's hard-to-access and incredibly fragile Arctic National Wildlife Refuge oil contains only 2 percent of the 800 billion barrels that the BLM estimates can be taken along the Colorado River. The six oil companies' 200-plus water rights per year add up to 7.2 maf (over 2 trillion gallons) of water needed to develop and process oil shale outside Rifle.

PANDORA'S BOX

North of the I-70 town De Beque, water cuts out of parachute-shaped sandstone canyons. Vultures draw lazy circles around the updrafts. Closer to our kayaks, perching in a giant cottonwood, as noble as the Swomee-Swans that used to eat the truffalo tree fruit in Dr. Seuss's *Lorax,* we pass a great blue heronry. Two dozen normally solitary big birds crowd onto one debarked tree, freighted with a bramble of huge stick nests that defy gravity. Anxious mothers croak up swamp noises from deep within their long throats, while their young test flap wings that look like broken tree branches.

At cocktail hour, we pitch camp on a floodplain caked with enough dried-out range locust droppings to fuel a campfire. Mosquitoes test their short proboscises against my thick socks as I take the map out of the case and measure the day by placing a string along the curls of Colorado River, and then match it to a legend in the bottom left corner: 60 miles. Although we paddled casually with a mid-morning start and several stretching breaks, I've never paddled the river this fast or full. Nor have I paddled class II waters with so many class IV consequences: barbed wire, keeper eddies, hundred-foot strainers, concrete abutments, and 49-degree ten-mile-per-hour current.

A downed cottonwood trunk serves as a backrest and gives us ample separation from a mound of red ants, commuting home from work. We drink merlot from our coffee cups.

"I tell you what," Freeman says as I torch the stove on with a lighter. "We were flying today. Flying!" We toast, inhale the chalky wine just slowly enough not to brand one another Visigoth guzzlers, and then agreeably refill our cups.

Being on the river—our tongues loosened by spirits—gives us a chance to reminisce about those moments we don't have time to indulge in during our busy careers. "I'm still not sure I can forgive you," Freeman begins, relishing his opportunity to cut a second hole in my kayak as he takes another sip, "for that day you undressed Margaret on the Tatshenshini River."

"Well," I reply, "you had your chance, Mike, but you were too busy swimming after the raft." We clink our coffee mugs. I can visualize the cottonwood strainer that flipped Margaret's and Mike's raft and threw them into the icy current. By the time I caught up to her several minutes later, she had turned stiff and blue with hypothermia. So I jumped out of my raft, peeled her off a rock, and swam her ashore to a sandy beach—where she collapsed. I stripped Margaret, dried her off, and we ducked into a sleeping bag together until I warmed her body back to shivering, 15 minutes later.

"Anyways," I say, "I had my eyes closed."

"Surrrrrrrh," Freeman says. "I tell you what," he concludes sincerely, "I still appreciate your quick moves on my ex-girlfriend."

"So long as you never return the favor," I add, "and warm me in a sleeping bag."

As dusk is thinly lit by a gibbous moon, the last nighthawks finish their long vocal dives, sounding like high-pitched model airplanes: *"BEErzh, BEErzh, BEErzhhhhhhhhhhhhhhhhhhh."* Coyotes then fill up the silence with a series of yips, followed by mournful howls.

Tonight, even in our dreams, we will never leave the river. Fish begin jumping in the moonlight. As the wind flips around and begins to pull in cool air, the cottonwood leaves rustle, and the smell of home cooking comes from a distant ranch house, while we crunch on al dente pasta. We polish off the wine and catch one another eyeing the bottle of scotch.

Mike talks about his complex relationship with his father, a basketball referee, who, like my dad, can't retire. I chime in with the Hemmingway model, which worked in fiction, but not in real life, because the author and his father both blew their brains out. However, in my favorite of his novels, the posthumous *Islands in the Stream,* Thomas Hudson takes his three sons fishing and, while helping young David land a marlin, he developed the ideal father-son relationship.

"Why is it so difficult," I ask, "for parents to dedicate time to their kids so that we can honor one another throughout our lives?"

"Right on," Mike adds with rhetorical flourish, "so that they don't become screw-ups like us!"

My mother is haunting me as always but I can't think of how to tell Mike without being maudlin. Like any good mother and son, our relationship is complicated. Even gone, she's in my thoughts more than ever.

Two hours and two cups of coffee past sunrise, the river's still running over 10,000 cfs. Warm nights on the river keep the flow running round the clock. It's not a rodeo, but while holding constant double-bladed paddle contact—dipping, sweeping, bracing—the current feels more invigorating than caffeine. As I-70 tunnels straight through sandstone, we ride the river on a long loop south, getting dumped back under a highway bridge and into the Grand Diversion Reservoir for the High Line Canal. Paddlers call the little lake's entrance Big Sur for its huge roller wave, created in 20,000-cfs-plus spring waters. Now with the advent of upstream river parks and a basin-wide drought, we have a becalmed Big Sur to ourselves. In previous years, the wave formed for weeks; now even in a big runoff, surfers are lucky to find the wave for more than a day or two.

On July 17, 1902, exactly one month after Roosevelt signed the Reclamation Act, the newly minted Reclamation Service announced it would be building a diversion dam and canals to carry water from the river 55 miles west to the fields of Fruita above the Colorado River. After ten years of court battles, the government acquired enough water rights and ditch right-of-ways to begin building the dam.

Yet, even before the dam's completion in 1916, farmers in Fruita, like their ancient Hohokam counterparts in Phoenix, realized that they were destroying their fields by overirrigating and poisoning both aquifers and soil through salinization. This "salt" buildup has been the curse of every civilization since humans started working the soil. To farmers, "salt" refers to the common sodium chloride and any number of naturally occurring alkaline chemical compounds, including chalk, barium chloride, phosphates, and nitrites.

No farmer would neglect to include selenium. Although the nonmetallic element has been found in humans and in the water before modern farmers used the river, by rinsing Colorado River over the ancient volcanic ash in the Mancos Shale formation underlying Grand Junction, selenium is leached to the surface. Too much selenium on the crops or in the local foraging cattle can then build up in humans and cause birth defects, sterility, or "dishrag heart." The selenium is so despised that, when I introduce myself and mention my hometown to downstream farmers, they raise their eyebrows and talk about how Colorado's Mancos Shale ruins their crops. When the river used to reach the sea, selenium levels were 14 times higher than the exposure levels recommended by the Environmental Protection Agency (EPA).

Upstream of Grand Junction, in the vegetation-abundant headwaters, salinization (and selenium) is minimal because constant rainfall and snows have long since washed the soils and carried salts to the ocean. The problem starts with the sulfurous Glenwood Springs hot springs upstream. Then, amid the scantly rinsed soils of western Colorado, dry for several millennia, the river becomes downright brackish as it rinses through the Grand Junction's infamous Mancos Shale.

Floods and irrigation leach the Mancos minerals to the top of the soil, or raise the aquifers until they too become poisoned. Unlike ancient peasants, modern farmers can flood their fields and continually rinse the soils with huge canals and electric pumps. Then, as the aquifers become oversalted, or raised high enough to poison the crops, the brackish groundwater is immediately pumped out into the river. As agriculture drains more salt into the river, the problem intensifies downstream. Flushing Grand Valley fields is a temporary solution for local farmers, but overirrigation of alkaline soils is akin to trucking contaminated nuclear waste from one state to the next. Eventually, even Grand Valley will go a whitened fallow trying to rinse away an ocean's worth of salt.*

Along the brine-caked banks, Freeman and I cautiously paddle to and fro above the roaring dam, avoiding the floodgate's powerful suction—like trying to run across a mag-chlorided highway during rush hour. Tamarisk trunks are encrusted with white scales. I jump out and salted weeds crunch underfoot.

In a 1971 study, the EPA estimated that 37 percent of the river's salinity comes directly from irrigation and 12 percent from reservoir evaporation. Human activities more than doubled the historic salt levels. In the surrounding Grand Valley, before improvements, irrigated agriculture added 580,000 tons (about eight tons of salt per farmed acre) to the river each year. After percolating through these farms and the ancient seabed, the borrowed river is returned 30 times more salty than it began.

In 1972, Congress passed the Clean Water Act to maintain water quality standards throughout the United States. Two years later, the Colorado River

---

*Before the dam could be built on the outskirts of Grand Junction, the government dug 400 miles of ditches to save thousands of acres and the aquifer from salt contamination. Shortly after the main canal was completed, the farm market collapsed. As the recession deepened in 1922, so did farmers' debts. Enter Congressman Edward Taylor, who worked out the farmers' 40-year repayment schedule to the federal government, writing off $1 million of debt.

Basin Salinity Control Act directed Reclamation to start reducing river salt. After three decades and two more Congressional amendments of the Salinity Act, Reclamation will line Grand Valley canals and build pipelines to prevent 116,000 tons of salt—precisely a fifth of the 580,000 tons created by local farms—from contaminating the Colorado River.

To make the costs of reducing Grand Junction agricultural salinity more palatable to the taxpayer, Reclamation reduces annual costs by diluting them in a half-century budget. Here's one of many pieces of math about the river: Add $168-million construction costs to $.6 million per year operating costs, divide by 50 years, and Reclamation has sweetened the cost to $93 per ton of salt removed.

Meanwhile, the U.S. Department of Agriculture (USDA) is installing more underground pipelines, gated pipe, concrete-lined ditches, land leveling, drip irrigation systems, and a variety of other practices that will help reduce the amount of farm water rinsing through the salty earth below.

Twenty-five years ago, Donald Worster shed a brilliant light on salinity in his book, *Rivers of Empire*:

> Could the lower specter of salinization ever really be exorcised from the western water empire? Some of its engineers and agriculturists had no doubt that it could be, that it was a temporary nuisance which a little time and expense could banish. Others were much less confident. Throughout history, wherever irrigation has been carried on intensively, they pointed out, salinization has come in its wake, like dust following the wind. It is the way of empires to believe they will be forever impregnable, that they will give the law to nature, not vice versa, that their power and expertise will conquer all.

The Colorado River faces more salt issues then any comparable or larger sized U.S. river. As an illustration, the most accurate calibration of water salinization is seen through parts per million (ppm) of dissolved salt, which is left behind after filtering out particulates and evaporating a liter of water. An evaporated liter from the largest natural lake in the United States, Lake Superior, contains 63 ppm, enough salt to sit on a dime. A liter from the largest reservoir, Lake Mead, yields enough salt to bury a quarter. Its 640 ppm water comes from the Colorado River.

The briny 70,000 acres of Grand Junction agriculture are merely the beginning of 3.4 million acres of brackish farmlands watered by the Colorado River. By the time this river is reused 18 times and returned to its shrunken bed in southern Arizona, the salinity levels will reach 2,600 ppm, more than enough to kill any crop the water touches.

As these larger concerns recede from my mind, we tiptoe out of the small reservoir's west shore through poison ivy and drag our kayaks up along the farm canal, running at about 500 cfs toward the Fruita farms through narrow tunnels that would grind us up like hamburger. Neither of us can shake the indignation that, although we felt like we belonged on the rampaging river above, we're interlopers here. This is how we've felt at other dam sites too. Although we haven't actually crossed the threshold of No Trespassing signs and set foot on the dam, kayaks simply don't mix with an impounded river. We wouldn't survive paddling over the main river's floodgates, waving our hats as we ride tens of thousands of pounds of water down into a concrete-lined, reverse hydraulic surlier than any natural rapid. So, in our Chaco sandals and wraparound sunglasses, clutching paddles in our callused palms, we must run the gauntlet of more dam officials.

While standing on the far side of the canal, we manage to scream a "HEYYY!" that strikes a decibel above the noise of water pounding below the dam. As if long accustomed to hand signals, a middle-aged woman signals with her index finger held up from the front screen door to wait a minute while she gets her husband. Their cottage is absurdly built near the wake of spray cascading from the dam's floodgate.

We introduce ourselves, and Leonard happily waves permission for us to cross the canal. As he pulls our kayaks in against the current, he asks, "You mean you're not going to run the canal?"

We shake our heads no, and he beams at us. We like him immediately.

He opens a three-foot gate and leads us across a bottle green lawn as sharply groomed as the 10,000 cfs pounding out of the roller dam's floodgate beyond, to the edge of five concrete steps, leading steeply down to a final six-foot vertical plunge into the terrible flood washing out from under the dam's European-style cupolas. "Leonard must think we're flying fish," I whisper.

We thank Leonard nonetheless and point farther downstream to a protected eddy. We hand our kayaks around an unmortared stone wall, its perfectly balanced rocks placed by diligent 1930s Civilian Conservation Corps workers. Down on the riverbank, we bushwhack through briny willows and over a rusting shopping cart, berried black bear droppings from last fall, a pile of antique fuses, and sticks gnawed to ankle height by hungry beavers. One can only wonder if they felt awed and impotent in the wake of the dam's six 14-foot-high roller gates, stretching five hundred feet across the river.

Within a half hour's sprint down the flood, we pass beneath the bridge of the Orchard Mesa power plant, setting off a laser beam–controlled robotic recording, but it's too garbled to understand whether we're trespassing. Like we don't have enough to worry about with the coming rapid.

The former dam site, combined with the Highlands diversion dam upstream and the Price Stubbs dam downstream, is the only section of main-stem Colorado River where a government agency has provided fish passage. Seen from the highway above, truckers can spy several dozen low three-foot-wide concrete piers making fish eddies along the eastern bank. We scout the water by walking a quarter mile west inside the guardrail of I-70, waving to cars honking their horns as if we're bare-ass naked. Exactly how I feel anyway, contemplating my potential fate.

The river roars into a solid, troublesome-looking class V wave crest. River left, beneath the whoosh of westbound semis, the riverbank of half-submerged concrete discs—part of the Upper Colorado River Endangered Fish Recovery Program—break the current for chubs, suckers, and pike min-nows. If these native fish—looking like mutants from the circus aquarium—haven't lost the genetic coding for swimming this far, they'll continue to the diversion dam weir, where Leonard and his colleagues will net them, transfer them up into the reservoir, and wish them Godspeed for repopulating the river up to Glenwood Springs, until they get stopped by the Shoshone Dam.

Alongside their concrete shelters, the water funnels down a rather straightforward-looking rapid. "You good?" Freeman asks.

I nod yes and grab my camera. As usual, he bobs through like a cork above the roiled waters, so there's no carnage worth photographing.

Because he has survived, and he now waves me onward, I have no choice but to enter the fray. I paddle swiftly into the smooth tongue, putting nary a drop on my face. Down past the waves, Freeman waits for me in a concrete eddy, and I nearly blow it by coming unbraced into the reverse current. Soon as my bow enters, the braking effect of the eddy rotates the cockpit sideways so I throw in a quick paddle brace to keep myself from going over and dent-ing concrete with my head. I know I did it right if only because Freeman is grinning widely. "I tell you what. You nailed that one, buddy!"

"If I was a real boater, I would've just rolled."

Freeman raps his knuckles audibly on his helmet, simulating a hollow head hitting concrete to show me why an Eskimo roll wouldn't work. We slap a quick high-five and then we're pulled under the I-70 bridge shade, sailing out of the last canyon in a wind that warms the orchards and vineyards of

Palisade. For a dozen miles, irrigation pipes repeatedly return warmed and increasingly more alkaline Colorado River water back to the source, dripping green mossy beards down sandstone walls as cliff swallows hover and glide through hatches of bugs.

We pass another recently completed fish ladder at the Price Stubb Diversion Dam by paddling river left over shallow boulders. A mile above the Gunnison River confluence, we can no longer see snowy mountains. To my surprise, the water feels pleasantly cool rather than cold. The air temperature has hit the triple digits. I drift with my hands in the water and doff my cap to a gaggle of mergansers in punk red hairdos.

Rounding a corner, beneath a bridge, we greet the first boaters we've seen since Glenwood Springs. Three bearded and shirtless pirates are riding inner tubes like cushioned commodes. One inner tube holds a large red cooler. Although it's not noon, on each belly balances an open can of beer. We also notice that they need no paddles. Both of us feel suddenly silly in dry tops.

"Wanna beer?" one of them shouts.

"No, thanks," Freeman replies.

"Howzat yakking?" they ask.

"Good fun," I reply. "Where you headed?"

"Mexico!" the leader giggles, to which the three musketeers all raise their Budweisers in a solemn toast.

Out of sight around the next corner, on an eddy above the Gunnison, we sheepishly pull off our dry gear, changing into T-shirts and shorts, while Freeman stows the helmet. "Jeez," he says, "they give real boaters a bad name."

"Maybe an honest portrayal, though," I say, "Mr. Boater," shoving him over toward the water and jumping back into my kayak, steering around five more half-naked kids in Kmart pack rafts before Freeman can catch me.

As we plunge through the gray cloud of incoming Gunnison River water, I check my altimeter: 4,550 feet. I've now dropped 5,000 feet and 250 miles from the headwaters three weeks ago—even though with my lollygagging pace and research along the river, I have been paddling for only 12 days.

The Gunnison River is the fifth biggest tributary on the Colorado, running 180 miles back through three dams and reservoirs to the cow town of Gunnison. Although many Coloradoans are familiar with the Black Canyon of the Gunnison—one of the deepest, longest gorges in the world, with an incredible whitewater run truncated by a huge dam—few have heard of the Colorado pike minnow (formerly squawfish), one of the largest and most endangered minnows in the world.

Shaped like a torpedo, with the migratory drive of a salmon, *Ptychocheilus lucius* (folded-lip pike) evolved three million years ago, with the wooly mammoth and mastodons. Pike minnow bones have been found on Colorado tributaries in Hohokam archaeological sites dating back to 500 B.C.

Although it once grew as large as I am tall, now a three-foot pike minnow is a record. While the state of Colorado down-listed the fish from an endangered to a threatened species ten years ago, it will never be federally delisted because of the dams. Fish numbers are believed to be stable here along the Gunnison confluence, even though the U.S. Fish and Wildlife Service (USFWS) call these remnant populations "fragmented."

In the Predambrian Era, pike minnow evolved to survive the droughts of the Colorado River partially through their 50-year longevity. As droughts wiped out one region of fish—such as those on the Gunnison River—genetic testing has shown that a population from the San Juan River would eventually swim upstream and repopulate the Gunnison. The voracious fish survived because of an innate homing ability to swim 600-mile laps. Below Grand Canyon, few pike minnow are left; in the former Hohokam farming grounds along the Salt and Verde Rivers, modern dams have wiped out the fish. Among 100-plus Colorado River Basin dams, there are only three fish ladders for species like the pike minnow. Although hatchery programs do a booming business with exotic trout and bass, the program to reintroduce native fish has shown scant success. True, extinction has locally been reduced by the three diversions above us, but eliminating the sediment-trapping dams and their cold-water flow is the only act that would save the pike minnow and other indigenous Colorado River species. Natives need warm, sediment-rich water and the opportunity to migrate the length of the river.

Playing God by building fish-stopping dams alters the river's food chain. Colorado pike minnows were the supreme predator. Rodents, swallows, frogs, chubs, bugs—anything that fit in their mouth became fair game. On the Green River, one fisherman used to bait a setline with mice, tie it to the bumper of his truck, wait a half hour, and then drive out with pike minnow.

The absence of pike minnow along much of the Colorado shows the ecosystem's failing health. In its place, thriving in the frigid water released from reservoir bottoms, we now have newly introduced cold-water exotics: scaly carp begging for handouts at the marinas, trout trolling for flies, and bass, teasing the myriad bait fishermen Freeman and I wave to along the banks.

That afternoon at the takeout, I trade kayak for pack raft. I bear-hug Freeman, and he loads the kayak into his truck and heads upriver to his home.

Now I feel oddly trapped in sprawling Grand Junction. After last night's pleasant sleep on the ground, 40 yards apace from Freeman's snoring, I'm dreading a sterile hotel—there are no campsites along the river. Nonetheless, I get a smile from the Holiday Inn clerk, who is politely amused by the dark smudges of ground-up mountains on my face, happy to check in a customer with sandals and shorts in lieu of a jacket and tie.

My digs are quite different two mornings later, 17 miles downstream. After I've had my fill of instant oatmeal, I emerge from an illegal campsite amid a thick stand of tamarisk and make my prearranged meeting with entomologist Dan Bean at the Loma Boat Launch, next to a sign advising motor boaters of a dream destination:

LAKE POWELL 190 MILES

It's a slim chance that anyone interested in boating that far would have the expertise to navigate two different waterfalls along the way, the Westwater and Cataract rapids. To BLM's credit, they have laminated a photograph of a green aluminum canoe wrapped around the final rock below an insignificant rapid 16 miles downriver.

I throw my dry pack and raft into Dr. Bean's pickup. As we drive a few miles west on a side road, he nestles a jar of tamarisk beetles in his lap. He has brought me two gallons of water, and the first quarter of these jugs goes down in one rapid swig. I'm in my usual T-shirt, baggy shorts, and ball cap— smeared with the day's Elemental Herbs sun lotion. Dr. Bean, like Darwin en route to his equatorial species, is more wisely clad for severe sun in a long-sleeved white shirt and a shade cap that resembles a safari helmet. He wears long, loose-fitting pants to protect his legs from snakebites.

In the 1970s, the USDA realized that a scourge had swept western rivers in the form of a pink-flowering shrub. Tamarisk (from the Latin *tamarix:* tree) has a dozen different Eurasian subspecies from the family *Tamaricaceae,* imported to the American Southwest in the 1800s, to form windbreaks or ornamental shrubs. As home owners admired its delicate-laced, oriental green fronds, the gregarious plants began flourishing faster than water engineers could plant them along canals for erosion control, where the long, iron-legged tamarisk stabilized shifting sand banks. Although the process took decades, the emigrants slowly spread their roots toward an unforeseen plant succession. American bugs can't stomach the salty plant, while birds and bees spread its pollen. In Asia, 200 different bugs feed on tamarisk, and because the prized ornamental never goes haywire on the opposite side of the world, Dr. Bean's Chinese contemporaries are called in only to eliminate marauding bugs rather than the tamarisk itself.

In America, the tamarisk invasion could have been nipped in the bud except for another piece of exquisite timing in the modern opus of controlling nature: the dams arrived in the 1930s. These concrete walls halted the floods that rinsed out alkaline soils. Denied water, the native cottonwoods, willows, and mesquite trees along the high waterline perished in a vegetative era as deadly as the bubonic plague. In their place flourished the drought-resistant tamarisk.

Lacking any native predator within the American ecosystem, millions of tamarisk shrubs sociably crowded upriver, became trees, and conquered the riparian habitat from El Pókar, Mexico, to Eagle, Colorado. By 1990, tamarisk crowded most U.S. stream banks west of the 100th meridian and south of the 38th parallel. Bushwhack-challenged river runners began carrying saws for what they called "the cockroach tree," but the inexhaustible plant disagreeably smoked out campfires. The USDA classified it as a "noxious weed," an exemplary bureaucratic understatement, because the tree can grow up to a foot a month, to a height of 30 feet.

Mature species can guzzle 200 gallons of water a day, which isn't unheard of for its native equals, until you consider that no native plant grows in such dense thickets. According to a 1989 report from the American Society of Civil Engineers, tamarisk uses more water than all stream bank species. In a 2000 book, *Invasive Species in a Changing World,* one of several authors concludes that the plant can lower water tables, reduce stream flow, dry up desert springs, and reduce availability of water for agriculture, municipalities, native plants, and wildlife. Astonishingly, the cost of water lost to tamarisk in the Southwest is estimated at $285 million annually. The 10 subspecies of tamarisk are now found in 14 western states and as far east as Florida. Although the plant has several common names and a multitude of slurs, most people call it salt cedar.

Dr. Bean works closely with the USDA, which reported in its 17-page, 2003 "Proposed Program for Control of Saltcedar," that it's "capable of utilizing saline groundwater by excreting excess salts through glands in the leaves causing an increase in surface soil salinity. This increase, combined with dense canopy of saltcedar plants and higher likelihood of fires within stands of saltcedar, results in the elimination of native riparian plants."

"Tamarisk is the star of all noxious weeds," Dr. Bean says, "because it's found in recreational areas, it sucks up a lot of water, and it drops salty leaves that make undesirable wildlife habitat." With one hand on the wheel, the other safely clutching his beetle jar, he steers us down through private land back toward the Colorado River.

Dr. Bean also believes that warming temperatures will encourage tamarisk to migrate north. "I'll bet with climate change, it'll be more invasive in Canada, where it's presently not found."

The other domino effect of this noxious invader emerged as native riparian habitat died out: The southwestern willow flycatcher began to vanish. As the thorny mesquite, shade-giving cottonwood and prime nesting willows fell, this unprepossessing, six-inch songbird—given to concealment along the river's edge, and unknown to all but the most attuned of birders listening for its harsh, burry song—lost its vital habitat. By 1995, the USFWS put the western species of *Empidonax trailii* on the federal endangered list. Its departure all too neatly coincided with the departure of its former habitat. In 2005, as tamarisk prospered in the river corridor, a strange reversal occurred. Biologists excitedly found new flycatchers migrating back from Latin America into the new tamarisk thickets, sheltering billions of thriving insect prey. Thirteen hundred of the endangered birds remain in the western United States, mostly in New Mexico and Arizona. Along the lower Colorado River, 61 percent of their nests lie in tamarisk trees.

Last fall, word of the tamarisk invasion finally reached the Oval Office. Over the last couple of decades, land managers have bulldozed riverbanks, loosed hungry goats, and—at $3,000 per acre—chainsawed the trees down and painted their stumps with herbicide. Tamarisk still seemed to be winning the battle. An offensive had to be mounted. A tamarisk-control law authorized $15 million each year to eradicate the plant.

Dr. Bean explains how his USDA colleagues searched foreign shores to study hundreds of insects that would eat tamarisk. Eventually, they found a tamarisk-feeding specialist, *Diorhabda elongata*. No one knew if the beetles would harm native plants or crops. So, ten years ago, these beetles were imported to USDA quarantine laboratories in Texas and California. Again and again, the Kazakhstan and Chinese beetles would starve to death if offered native plants over tamarisk.

Outside Lovelock, Nevada, in 2001, the USDA arrived with carefully sealed vials of precious beetles, mindful that they had to stay several hundred miles north of the endangered songbird habitat in southern Nevada. The team carefully released 1,500 beetles onto two acres of tamarisk. By fall of 2002, the trees were defoliated. By 2003, the flourishing emigrants had chewed up hundreds of tamarisk acres in western Nevada. After *Diorhabda elongate* ate the leaves, the trees grew more leaves, but the beetles returned to feed until each plant's trunk and shadeless branches, unable to photosynthesize light, withered and died. By 2006, tens of thousands of acres had been denuded throughout western Nevada. Then another release took place in Delta, Utah. In only a couple of years, the beetles spread like a healthy pandemic.

We pull to a bumping stop and let the dirt road's dust cloud settle before jumping out. Dr. Bean lifts up his jar to make sure that his centimeter-long, yellow-and-black-striped beetles enjoyed the ride. Watching them wave their antennae with the fascination of a mammalogist observing an orca, he mumbles that *Diorhabda elongata* are not spectacular as individuals and that they do their best work en masse. We step out alongside a wall of green yet suspiciously yellowing tamarisk, dwarfed only by the red Wingate sandstone walls across the whooshing river. Dr. Bean opens the jar and gently shakes pet beetles onto his hand. Without wind to help them fly, they excitedly crawl back and forth on our fingers, as if animated by the smell of nearby tamarisk. After several minutes of playing with these pet beetles on the hood of his truck, he loads them into a tiny plastic vial and slides in a sprig of tamarisk to bring them to ecstasy.

Three years ago here, Dr. Bean began the first Colorado state release of 5,000 Chinese beetles, authorized by the USDA. He refers to some grownup Mormon "boy scouts" who scooped up thick masses of Kazakhstan beetles from Delta, Utah, into empty ice cream cartons and then began releasing over a hundred thousand beetles on several Colorado River sites near Moab, Utah. Because they hadn't been authorized to release the beetles on federal land, the boy scouts let the beetles feast on privately owned land, all but sinking from the impenetrable stands of tamarisk. One can only imagine how quickly these landowners had given permission to let the beetles tackle the salt cedar.

Dr. Bean taps his passengers out of the vial, using his index finger as a bridge for the Chinese beetles to climb out onto the feathery fronds of a tamarisk. Judging by pods of tiny off-white eggs glued onto the black branches, and yellowing fronds above us, beetles have been feeding, although not so voraciously as in Nevada and Utah. Dr. Bean is puzzled by the complexities of *Diorhabda elongata,* perplexed about why his Chinese beetles work so slowly, whereas across the border in Utah, their Kazakhstan brothers have "trashed wholesale acreage along the river. I think it has everything to do with latitude," he concludes.

The Asian beetles had been shrewdly selected by the USDA. South of latitude 37°, along the northern border of Arizona, where the willow flycatcher nests most thickly along the Colorado River, the summer days are shorter than 14.5 hours, which makes the beetle enter a state of dormancy called diapause, and stops all its reproduction.

As the last bug crawls from his finger, Dr. Bean smiles with great poignancy. Reading his mood, I ask, "How long will it live?"

"Two months, and she can lay nearly 700 eggs," he says with a soft-spoken smile. "But life out here is dangerous and she'll probably be eaten by lady bugs or ants long before then." At chest level on a ten-foot tree, he finds a native inhabitant. "It's a female and she's coming out of her nine-month winter diapause!"

In five sites along the river in Utah, scientists have used infrared satellite sensing to document extensive defoliation. Half the Upper Colorado River Basin's 2,000 miles of tamarisk-laced streams are now populated by the Kazakhstan, rather than Dr. Bean's Chinese, invaders. Only time will tell if the USDA has opened, as enviros warn, a Pandora's box.

As I paddle 15 miles downriver, the BLM sign advertising four species of endangered fish has been rendered unreadable by overgrown fronds of tamarisk. I've passed nesting bald eagles, copious tamarisk, and ancient sand dunes preserved in Wingate sandstone. Now I'm in the throat of Ruby Canyon, surrounded by soaring black-varnished Entrada sandstone walls, minarets, and towers. An overactive set of railroad tracks frequently rumbles alongside the north side of the river. Directly south is the newly created Black Ridge Canyons Wilderness. These 75,000 acres contain the second largest set of sandstone arches in North America, after the more famous Arches National Park in Utah.

Last night, I walked to the exact position where famed Colorado photographer William Henry Jackson stood to take an 1891 photograph. On the far shore of the Predambrian image stood a towering cottonwood tree, shading a wide sandy beach above the Colorado River. In the foreground, an engineer posed next to a steam engine. One hundred and seventeen years later, as a coal train thundered past, I repeated the black-and-white photograph. Across the river, the cottonwood had long since vanished, and the sandy beach had been taken over by a 30-foot-wide bank of tamarisk. As I retreated to my campsite, in the cool, shaded air after sunset, I had to douse a fire started by the train throwing sparks onto creosoted railroad ties.

Now I refocus on my day job: getting through "Black Rock Rapids" without hitting any boils. Dr. Bean had assured me that it would take a herculean effort to drown in the class II water, even though a few bumblers had managed to wrap their canoes around the final boulder, as depicted by the BLM photo at the put-in. Still, the river in flood makes minor rapids into hydraulics beyond a mere canoeist's ken. The angry red water is at its peak surging through an ominous keyhole of polished black crystalline rock, 1.7 billion years old. The water surges through in a smooth yet powerful tongue, licking under the widened river below and bubbling back up in an unpredictable witch's cauldron. I coast over the tongue with a breeze on my face, thinking that this must be how mastery feels as I pull hard, hunting for calmer water around the big eddy. Skirting the biggest boils, I get hit by a secondary boil: sucking my front tube in and flipping me upside down into the Colorado River at its biggest flow in a decade.

While cinched in by the pack raft spray skirt, I crane my neck up out of the water, fill my lungs with air, then resubmerge and pop open the Velcro. I come sputtering free on the surface, relieved that the water isn't cold at least, until I see a keeper eddy 40 yards down that will hold me under the final, giant boulder of the wrapped canoes. So I let go of the paddle and raft and begin stroking like Johnny Weissmuller for the north shore. But in three strokes, my pack raft stern line wraps around my foot, pulling me downstream toward the eddy.

I'm going to die, I think, *and become famous in a rapid famous for never killing anyone.*

I take another deep breath and go under, untangling the line from my foot by removing my tightly strapped sandal. It'll be a long walk without a boat, so I grab the pack raft line with one hand and frog-kick madly, breathlessly, toward the tamarisk bank. I crawl to shore on my hands and knees, feeling more fish than Tarzan.

Beneath the hum of cicadas in the tamarisk shade, I'm happy to be alive, but stung that I didn't have the common sense to portage the rapid. I take five to catch my breath. My hands are shaking from the adrenaline flooding my body; I have to stretch to uncramp my calves. The camera is secure in its dry bag, the raft is unscathed, and the waterproof pack has kept my spare clothing and food dry.

Yet, I'm up a river without a paddle. It's not visible whirling round the eddy, so the paddle can only be headed downstream.

A group of guided rafters on the far shore have been amused by my swim. I shout across: "SEE MY PADDLE?!"

They wave downstream with a motion that simulates waving goodbye.

I resist screaming the obvious answer and instead shout: "Do you have a spare paddle I can borrow?"

They consult one another. Then their guide comes to the riverbank with great authority, holds up a blue blade canoe paddle, and shouts across: "You'll have to swim over to get it!"

I'm stunned. Although I know I'm a bonehead for running this big water in such a small craft, the guide has to be out of his mind to suggest that anyone swim the river in the backwash of a rapid running over 30,000 cfs. And it would evidently be too much to ask him to row his oar frame across to deliver the paddle to me. This time, straining for a polite goodbye, I yell, "No, thank you! Have a nice day!"

Eight long miles away lies the Westwater Ranger Station, where June and the boys will pick me up later this afternoon. I will not make a cramping defeat march in the desert heat, where I would risk being poached like an egg on the sizzling railroad tracks. So I begin searching the railroad grade for detritus that can be made into a paddle. Within a half hour of scavenging, dodging two freight trains, I find a one-foot-square piece of rubber and a three-foot steel bar. I punch four holes through the hard rubber with my knife, lash it to the bar with parachute cord, and I begin paddle-ruddering my pack raft downriver within an hour of being capsized.

The fear-driven tremble leaves my fingers so now I can constructively engage the water. I will not allow myself to entertain the notion of river mastery again for a long time.

Corrective J-strokes aren't a strength of this thrown-together paddle. So, as the raft performs a half spin in one direction, I paddle on the opposite side. My forward progress is nine-tenths clout, one-tenth elegance, with a lot of splashing thrown in between. Still, I've always perceived resourcefulness as the mother of all invention.

In two miles, the river slows a beat and swirls out of Ruby Canyon at the Utah-Colorado border along a lush plain of irrigated alfalfa farms. A headwind noisily sways seed-filled reeds like rattling venetian blinds.

My near-miss swim turns my thoughts toward my mother. Ever since the headwaters—alone or with friends, sighting ducklings with their female guardians, drinking her favorite red wine, or scenting tomato sauce on a stove (she cooked a mean lasagna)—my mom has joined me along the way. But I have no intention of joining her any time soon. I feel foolish for letting down my guard and risking my life in such a minor rapid. Judging by how distraught and confused I have been by my 77-year-old mother's death, the very idea of my children trying to cope with the premature death of one of their parents makes me nauseous. To say nothing of the burden that would be placed on June's shoulders.

Bundled together with *The Sibley Guide to Birds* and Reisner's *Cadillac Desert* at the bottom of my pack, I have been consulting my dog-eared copy of *The Tibetan Book of the Dead* (BOD) that I found on Mom's bookshelves. Although it's hardly a panacea to cover my sense of loss, I have nothing else to turn to.

I struggled to express myself in my journal during the days surrounding my mother's death. I had to force myself to write, and then to begin even identifying my confusion. Just looking at the journal still returns me to a disconnected hodgepodge of conflicting emotions.

Losing a parent is a consuming and guilt-laden challenge. All the normal miscommunications and all-too-human resentment for the lack of time I'd spent with my mom in later years has now come bubbling to the surface like the strange boil upriver that flipped me topsy-turvy. I could never convince Katherine Adella Waterman to come see the new house we had built. Plus, two years before her death, she showed a maddening lack of patience toward my sons during one of the few occasions we visited. After one night in her home, she had become so tart and short—yelling mercilessly at the boys for chasing Cocoa, the epileptic cat—that we packed up, found a hotel, and I made a lame excuse about a migraine headache. Fortunately, this incident and other past behaviors can now be explained by the melanoma she'd been hiding from us. Only after her death did we learn that she'd quietly sought treatment from an out-of-state doctor for a small tumor on her leg. Still, it's only natural to wish that our final memories of a parent would contain the same blissful circuitry of our youth: the playful beach vacations, tennis matches, jumping off the dock at Grandmother and Grandfather's lake house in northern New Jersey, and even as far back as being bathed in the sink as a toddler.

It's unrealistic to think that my mother could have been my good friend. But I do wish that we could have known one another better.

In my journal, the description of her last hours and what she looked like and how she struggled to speak are all accurate, if horrifying. Her cheekbones were distended and her shoulder bones rose eerily from her collapsed chest and bird-like arms, a cruel caricature of my once attractive mother, the same loving soul who changed my cloth diapers and set me free as a Gore-Tex-clad adult. As a former rescue worker, I had tended to more than a few dead bodies, bloated in rivers and frozen on mountainsides. Although each experience took days to reconcile and process, touching my own mother dead and still warm on her makeshift bed five months ago will not leave me alone. This and her last reductive days remain my waking nightmare. So I try to spurn the journal and corporeal images in general. Maybe after the passage of more time, I can eventually confront what happened and discover some small sense of peace with her absence.

Instead I turn to the comforting *Book of the Dead,* known more accurately in the East as *Liberation Through Understanding in the Between.* This belief of rebirth after death resonates within me. As if perchance, there are small consolations to be found.

Part One, as translated by Robert A. F. Thurman and introduced by His Honorable the Dalai Lama, is entitled "Preparations for the Journey."

My mother loved to travel. Although she lived on the East Coast, she often came to Colorado and volunteered on trail crews or borrowed my car to see the Southwest. Perhaps these journeys helped remove her from preconceptions and the all-too-familiar trap of cynicism by experiencing the same sense of wonder in the natural world that she encouraged in me throughout my adult life. Through growing up as a single child after the Great Depression and through World War II, she'd become a lifelong skeptic, foiled in conventional romantic love and scornful of Christian dogma. She had expressed interest in Buddhism, but like me, she hadn't studied it. In Christmas 1996, knowing her curiosity, I'd given her a photo book about the Dalai Lama and Tibet.

The last words she spoke, nearly a month before dying, were, "I've given up with the struggle and I'm now getting ready to take a journey." Clearly, she rejected the Judaic version of heaven and hell, politely tolerating the chaplain but refusing confession. We don't know if she read the book, underscored by my older brother Rick's pen. Nor can Rick remember how *his* book ended up at her house; by all rights, it should have been kept in his library. So I consult it with the hope that she deliberately left it in her town house for all of her sons to profit from.

After she died, Rick and I sat with her on the bed for a couple of hours after midnight waiting for the ambulance. Dying struck me as an industry of waiting. Waiting for her to wake up from the operations. Waiting for her to be admitted to an experimental drug therapy. Waiting for her to get better (until the last month or two she wouldn't admit she was dying). Waiting for her to take the last breath. Waiting for her to tell us that it was all a bad dream and we could go home. I also really wanted to believe that she was waiting for it all to be over with. It scared me how much she seemed to relish and privately own her pain. She resolutely refused painkillers, as though she wanted to feel every last moment on the planet Earth.

Still, Rick and I wanted to feel relieved that she no longer had to suffer, and we did feel relieved that we no longer had to wait for her to die. I kissed her—this woman who had spurned hugging her grown children—goodbye. As she grew cold, we waited some more, both holding her hands. Neither of us felt like crying, so we just sat on her bed. Numb and too tired to sleep. I tried to be businesslike about it all, to move on, as she would've wanted me to, but I was psychologically hobbled. Even this brief contemplation of her on her death-bed, while bobbing along with my lame excuse for a paddle, is depressing.

So I turn to more positive thoughts. Rick and I had become more communicative brothers during my mother's illness. Also, before my mom's death, I had become estranged from my younger brother, Jerry. But long before the final day, honoring Mom's wishes along with our being brothers, Jerry and I showed up together and spontaneously clowned at my mother's bedside: drawing the kind of smile from Mom that would disappear during her final months.

After Mom died, the supervising hospice nurse finally showed up driving a shiny silver Mercedes with a satellite navigational system glowing on the instrument panel. I walked her back across the dark driveway to guide her into the town house. I already knew that I needed time, privacy, and plenty of distance to deal with my own sorrow. But for the sake of my sons, I asked the supervisor—who had seen many dead mothers—what I should tell Mom's grandchildren. This kindly yet sleep-deprived Nigerian put her hand to her mouth and said she forgot the manual. I almost laughed, but she had to be serious—no one jokes in the home of a dead person. She gave me her business card and suggested that I call her later. Then she touched my shoulder with a sudden thought, "For your children," she said, "why don't you put your mother's death in the context of a journey?"

I paddle toward a dirt boat ramp carved out of a riverbank at the Westwa-ter Ranger Station. I've studied the banks for signs of my lost carbon-fiber kayak paddle, but I'm still performing the splash-spin downriver dance with a Neanderthal oar.

Despite the upstream cock-up, I'm three hours early. I'm anxious to see my family and leave the raging river alone for a night.

At the ramp, I hit the back-whirling eddy, tip up as the water throws me into a sudden wheelie, and correct a capsize by frantically thumping back at the water, while a boater standing in the shallows politely looks the other way. Eddies, after all, showcase the stuff of which paddlers are made. The boater has just come down from Ruby Canyon, and on the right side of his raft's oar frame is my lashed-down paddle.

"Missing something?" he asks.

"Yes, where'd you find it?"

"A few miles upriver. It looked like an otter swimming past us. We had to row hard to catch it."

"Thank you!" I say. "I went swimming and lost it."

He looks like he wants to hear more, but I'm too embarrassed to share the story.

"You should put your name on it; it's a nice paddle." He hands the paddle over and asks, "No spare?"

I show my steel bar lashed to a rubber square, lifting it up like the outgoing letter flag on my mailbox.

He looks disdainfully at my state-of-the-art Alpacka as if it's a mere Kmart rubber ducky and sarcastically says, "Nice boat."

"Thanks. They cost a thousand dollars." I see him pause with confusion, so I change the subject: "Where you headed?"

"Westwater Canyon," he groans. "Been a few years since I've kayaked it, but I think I'm still up to the task." He's shirtless, tanned as an islander, and lashing down his wife's small raft, both of which are serving as support for him and his kayak. "Where you going?" he asks.

"Mexico," I say.

He shakes his head and turns back to lashing the raft with a wry smile.* I've seen this reaction before, even said it to myself while encountering less experienced yet more ambitious outdoorsman who might be biting off more than they can chew in an unforgiving wilderness.

It takes an hour to re-sort, hang up my swimming gear, and splash the river sediment off. As my yard sale dries in the afternoon heat, I retire to the cottonwood shade, write a few journal pages, and ponder *Liberation Through Understanding in the Between*.

I shut the book as June arrives, and hug her and the boys tightly, and throw the boys both into the air. The boys' maternal grandmother, Carol, follows in her car as we caravan toward Moab, Utah. I neglect to mention my morning swim lesson, knowing it would upset June. Eventually, when I'm through with the river and she won't have the option of lying awake and worrying about me, I'll tell the tale.

In a word: Turkey.

CANYONLANDS

Early in the morning, Carol, various cousins, friends, and two dozen strangers ride a Navtec outfitters bus loaded down with rafts back upriver to the Westwater put-in. Nicholas begged me to bring him with us, so I had earlier approached the lead guide, Brian, and asked if my son would be okay if I watched him through the big rapids.

"I'll take care of your child," Brian said, his eyes hidden by oversize sunglasses, "but if she falls out of the boat, you'll have to say goodbye to her." Fair enough, I thought, no questions about that decision. And Mom's etiquette teachings prevent me from correcting the guide about his mangled pronoun use. So June and the boys will join our extended rafting family below the class IV rapids, outside the abandoned hamlet of Cisco, Utah.

In the front of the bus, as we pass the abandoned cars and graffiti-laden shacks of this once-prospering railroad town, Brian tells about how a drug deal gone bad and a murder boosted the local population (formerly two) to the highest crime rate of any small town in the country. Other stories follow about equally twisted desert rats and now I'm glad that my oldest son is safe with his mom in Moab rather than listening to this boatman. I'd need all afternoon to explain what marijuana is, why you can get rich from something that's against the law, and why our guide says "shit" instead of "poop" even though he's not talking about going to the bathroom.

The bus pulls to a halt in the middle of the desert, along the mostly abandoned and spider-webbed cracks on Route 128's worn tarmac, 45 minutes out from Moab. Brian announces: "We're going to stop here and check the rafts for *leaks*," he winks broadly, "in case anyone else feels the urge."

So it continues to the put-in. Brian gathers all the clients in the shade and performs a group safety talk, passes out personal flotation devices (PFDs), and puts the fear of God into everyone. "We haven't had any drownings yet," he says with a throaty bark that would do justice to a drill sergeant, "and if you listen to us, we'll keep it that way." This kind of pep talk can be heard up and down the river this time of year, from Colorado to Arizona, in hopes of boosting tips from clients overjoyed at their deliverance. Some guides will even concede that they want a modicum of control for a river that, even dammed, remains uncontrollable. Through repetition, Brian has become intimate with the river and climbed to the top rung of a career commonly known for its high burnout, lack of pay, and employment that dries up each year as snowmelt stops engorging the Colorado River.

Downstream, like most geologically astute boatmen, he holds forth on canyon rocks and history. Now that we're below the Jurassic period's sun-tanned Entrada sandstone in Ruby and Horsethief Canyons, Brian rows us further back in time below a nonconformity rock layer, created when erosion replaced the old rocks. Around the next bend, the 208-million-year-old Chinle conglomerate juts out on south-facing cliffs, topped by the younger and reddened Wingate sandstone, sandwiched by the purplish Kayenta sandstone. As Brian drones on like a college professor, we reemerge into the 1.7-billion-year-old ebony granite and gneiss that dominates for a dozen miles—it won't reappear until 421 miles downstream, in the Grand Canyon's Vishnu schist band. Even at six miles an hour, we've passed enough millennia to make a geologist squirm.

Brian warms up his oars on "Upper" and "Lower Dolores Rapids," then splashes us through Marble Canyon and "Staircase Rapids." It's restful to leave the driving to someone else. While Brian tells unctuous jokes, I take pictures of Carol hanging on for dear life and bail water onto June's fun-loving cousins with a five-gallon bucket. Although it was not regularly paddled until 40 years ago, I learn that, in 1916, Colorado boatmen Bert Loper and Ellsworth Kolb paddled covered canoes to become the first to run Westwater.

Like the legends of a century past, along with all those who have slipped through Westwater since then, we come to the bend we've all been anxiously awaiting, "Skull Rapid." Even though the class IV rapid is subdued by high water, Brian works the oars hard to stay river left and avoid being pulled into a black-cliffed corner called the "Room of Doom," infamous for trapping rafts in a giant whirlpool. The tension in Brian's strokes is plain through oars rasping arhythmically against the oarlocks, muscles cording his neck, and our raft jerking in a radical ferry angle away from potential disaster.

In no time, we're flushed out of the canyon and the river flattens out. Powerful hydraulics and periodic splashing created by water colliding against the riverbed swirl up to the surface. At Brian's prompting, I tighten my PFD and jump out to float downriver, periodically being spun through small whirlpools, my arms flung out to either side, eyes closed in delight. The river's power is palpable. I rinse reddish brown water through my mouth, and although it is cool and thick rather than salty, my teeth are quickly flossed with grit—I spit it out. If this water were bottled, it would conduct electricity and occasionally set off Geiger counters.

Sand cut out of antique dunes and dissolved uranium ions and old marine salts mixed with selenium and calcium fish microns cooled by snowmelt toss me like another particle in a nuclear accelerator, as relentless sun burns my head, and the river's forceful weight saps my will. I clamber back into the raft by torquing a foot over the roped D rings and flop aboard like a fish.

Two weeks ago, as the Utah border gauging station measured the river at its decadal zenith of 40,000 cfs, a recording instrument shot voltage through the water and measured conductivity through inorganic, dissolved solids or salts called microsiemens. At peak flow, the river carried only 300 microsiemens per centimeter, better than the level of most drinking water, good for fish. By the New Year, this section of river will lose 93 percent of its diluting flow. Then the gauging station will record the river at its yearly high of 1,200 microsiemens per centimeter, well beyond the range of safe drinking water.

Today's low microsiemen count combined with the three-digit air temperature equals great timing for a swim. Cousins Cynthia and Lisa jump in, 30,000 cfs swirling them beside the raft like rag dolls. The water is a relatively warm 59 degrees, so Brian rows on past, as Carol and I anxiously watch Cynthia and Lisa get pulled back and forth through a series of eddies a quarter mile back. Our guide is surprisingly unfazed. Finally, when we can no longer see them, I cajole Brian into rowing back upstream. They climb back aboard shivering and shaken—but like me, oddly humbled—by their blender journey into understanding the river.

As the flotilla of a half dozen rafts pulls out at the Cisco landing, June jumps aboard with the boys and Lisa's ten-year-old daughter, Uni. After Brian tells the kids that the river will carry them away if they should be "so stupid as to fall in," we continue downstream in two rafts. The other guide is a 19-year-old from Grand Junction. Carmen is petite and stands at the oars in a technique she has successfully employed from here to the Grand Canyon's last rapid. She's as mellifluous as a canyon wren, breaking out into the sad ballad "Bert Loper," about the legendary 79-year-old miner turned boatman, who lost his rowing job, then disappeared (or committed suicide) during a solo journey through the Grand Canyon.

Boatmen have come to define the spirit of fun found throughout the Canyonlands. In the 1970s, Brian's and Carmen's employer, Navtec, became the first company to guide Cataract Canyon, 112 miles downstream. Owner John Williams is the grandson of "Doc" Williams, who promoted both physical and mental well-being of Moabians, and before dying as a centenarian, helped found Arches National Park on the town limits.

Navtec had to compete with many outfitters, all vying to make Cataract or Westwater Canyons as well known to would-be clientele as every single rapid is to experienced boatmen. At first, the glut of leftover World War II pontoon bridges—lashed together with aluminum crossbars to become whitewater boats—meant that anyone could afford rafts and become a river guide. Outfitters soon switched to sturdier Hypalon rubber. In the 1980s, Williams shrewdly retrofitted his pontoons with motors and advertised Cataract Canyon day trips instead of three-day overnights. Business flourished for Navtec, until other companies starting putting more and more horsepower on their boats. As corporate rafting began buying out the smaller companies and throwing out expensive marketing outreach, Navtec is challenged to stay afloat.

Although John Williams was surprised by my request to lose the noisy outboard motors on the relatively flat water two dozen miles from Cisco to the rapids above Moab, he graciously acquiesced. Now we're hearing complaints from the tightly wound Brian, who grumbles to Carmen about having to row rather than motor through the gentle section of river he calls "the Nothings." No rapids, no sandstone cracks for the rock climber Brian to stick his fists into, and while my sons play on the raft, there's nothing for Brian to do but pull hard against swirling brown eddies infringing upon his downstream progress through Paradox Basin.

Yet, to a geologist, the passing countryside is the antithesis of nothing. To the east, the snowcapped La Sal Mountains, over 12,000 feet high, were named in 1776, by Spanish explorers for the salt beds that the Utes "hereabouts provide themselves." We're passing a bleached salt valley, surrounded by high, rocky fault lines. Five hundred and seventy million years ago, the region we're rafting through had been repeatedly covered by oceans, lakes, and rivers. As the waters subsided and evaporated, more than a mile's thickness of salts was deposited, along with gypsum, potash, and carbonates. Salt proved omnipresent in the canyonlands formation, evaporating through no less than 29 cycles, then pushing up against the earth.

Soluble salt at ground level has been carried down into the aquifer, waiting to be flushed out by agriculture or floods. Whatever salt hasn't dissolved lies in rock-hard subterranean formations.

Two hundred and ninety million years ago, after the reptiles, the rising Uncompahgre Highlands to the east dropped the first red rocks of Utah and began forming the Paradox Basin by pressuring the salt layers below. Dinosaurs came 50 million years later, roaming huge lakes and the lazy Mississippi-sized rivers of the Triassic period. At pontoon level, we're now passing low-angled Chinle slopes of the same era, formed by lake bottoms or streams and filled with a potpourri of limestone, shale, clay, and sandstone. The Chinle often holds uranium that formed during the Triassic, from an overlying thick layer of windblown volcanic ash. Like the salt, the water-soluble uranium leached out of the ash and down into the Chinle where it hardened into a uranium-vanadium-radium stew of pitchblende.

As leathery-winged birds evolved, lakes and rivers receded to carbon-filled swamps along the edge of Utah's last sea. The dinosaurs disappeared 66 million years ago, and a vast sand desert covered all.

Throughout the Tertiary period, volcanoes exploded and filled the basins of Utah with igneous sediment that cooled into rocks resembling Swiss cheese. Forty million years ago, as Lake Uintah receded to the north, a river not unlike the Colorado swept west, along with others, carrying rock and sand and carving out canyons and paper-punching the solidified dunes into sandstone arches.

As volcanism ended 1.6 million years ago, glaciers surrounded eastern Utah, and the Colorado River carved deeper into its canyon pathways. Ice melted to gravel atop the cooled remains of La Sal volcanoes.

For 150 million years, from the Permian reptiles to the dinosaur heyday of the Jurassic, the salt did not initially dissolve so much as the earth smothered it with layers of sediment. The soft masses of evaporated salt sank thousands of feet beneath the weight of these depositions, then flowed up and across the millennia in great viscous globules of putty, pushing apart layers of rock until it breached the earth's surface—forming grabens, domes, walls, and enormous basins. Elsewhere, these gigantic humps and dips, or anticlines and synclines, would be formed by regional earth movement. Here in the canyonlands, however, we're looking at the blobbing, unstoppable movement of salt. From here to 40-mile-distant Moab, the river will cut through more uranium-rich Chinle, along with three more salt-formed landscapes—Castle Valley, Salt Valley, and the Moab salt walls—spiking the river with conductivity and radioactivity.

Nicholas and Uni refill their bottles with this water and squirt one another as their mothers plead with them not to drink it. As our guides continue to denigrate the passing landscape to "the Nothings," the views of snowcapped mountains and blushing sandstone walls are made even livelier by great blue herons rattling up into the air and Alistair employing his kaleidoscopic binoculars.

In early evening, we stop at the deserted cheatgrass rug that floors an obscure campsite known as Hotel Bottom. The roof for our rooms is formed by towering cottonwoods with outrageously long and muscular limbs, shading the soil against marauding tamarisk.

Nicholas can't get enough of the spray bottle. In the desert heat, no one seems to mind being squirted. In the shade, Brian pulls off his sunglasses and hat to reveal severe brown eyes and hair standing-up straight. Nicholas, fascinated by poking beehives, is similarly drawn to our guide's intensity. He can't resist giving Brian a quick spray. And because Brian is uneasy with children, he chides Nicholas with his gravelly tenor: "You'll be sorry if you keep squirting me."

Two squirts later, I should've seen it coming. Before I can move to stop either my squirt or his squirtee, Brian abruptly picks Nicholas up and carries him to the river alongside the raft, then drops him in with a splash that seems unusually loud and ruder than a spanking to such an innocent child. Nicholas—remembering Brian's caveat about how the river will sweep him away—wades ashore in utter panic, consumed by tears. I rush to my five-year-old, lift him into my arms, and walk far away from his boogeyman. If not for two boys who model themselves after their dad's behavior, our guide would also have been thrown into the river.

In the way of all children, the water war is quickly forgotten. Nicholas is fascinated by the legions of mosquitoes, glommed onto the outer surface of our bug tent and poking thin brown straws in toward his hand. Fortunately, these buzzing moments will outlast all memories he brings home from the river.

Every Westerner knows that Moab bustles with river runners, mountain bikers, rock climbers, and jeepers. The pathways for these desert rats were created by an earlier generation of workers who cut thousands of miles of roads throughout the canyonlands. Their mission first lit the sleepy farming town aglow, back in the sleepy farming days near the end of Doc Williams's era. You can read about it on strange bumper stickers:

COLD WAR PATRIOT
Uranium Mines
We Did Our Part to Keep America Free

You can also see it on the dirt-creased faces of stooped-over, white-bearded men with hacking coughs who shuffle into City Market and Wal-Mart—avoiding the pricey tourist shops.

When a short-lived yet intensive radium boom dwindled in the first decade of the 20th century, the discarded pitchblende tailing piles of uranium and vanadium revealed that the latter ore would increase the tensile strength and elasticity of steel. Utah's vanadium industry briefly flourished.

During the Cold War, the radium tailings were revisited yet again for uranium. The Atomic Energy Commission sank millions of dollars into building roads, paying prospectors, and artificially inflating the price of uranium. This clamor for bombs would create a modern-day gold rush.

The big strike came in 1950. Down-on-his-heels geologist Charles Steen had been fired from an oil company for insubordination. Too broke to afford a Geiger counter, he lived in a Cisco tar-paper shack for several years, feeding his three young children and wife with poached venison and beans. Steen defied local wisdom by borrowing a diamond drill bit and boring into the 70-foot Chinle formation as if probing for oil. Working geologists of Colorado and Utah—poking through rocks with Geiger counters or overflying in airplanes outfitted with scintillometers—called this "Steen's Folly," at least until he hit the uranium mother lode. Overnight, he put Moab on the map.

The town became known as the uranium capital of the world and tripled to 6,000 people. The surrounding district eventually produced 25 tons of uranium oxide for bombs and, later, nuclear reactor fuel. Meanwhile, Steen invited all the local residents to annual airplane hangar parties and donated money to a local hospital and schools and many other causes, including top-heavy investments in uranium mines. In 1960, as the Atomic Energy Commission accumulated enough nuclear weaponry to repeatedly blow up the planet, the price of uranium plummeted and Steen ditched his riverside uranium mill.

The Atlas Minerals Corporation took over and expanded the mill, trucking in radioactive ore from 300 mines surrounding Moab. Uranium mine workers jokingly blew on and set off Geiger counters like breathalyzers. As the public learned the horrors of uranium-caused cancer, two decades of court battles ensued, as radiation victims sought compensation.

In the 1970s, yet another uranium boom supplied nuclear reactors for power plants. For every ounce of uranium produced, the Atlas mill created six pounds of radioactive and oily, toxic waste. All was dumped into a pond of radium, arsenic, lead, mercury, uranium, thorium, polonium, ammonia, molybdenum, selenium, and nitrates. Mill workers bulldozed more "hot" dirt into tailings surrounding the unlined pond. By the end of the decade, the oily waste pond, wetting the top of a terraced pyramid alongside the Colorado River, easily dwarfed Steen's Olympic swimming pool. By 1984, the 16-million-ton pile of toxic nightmares had risen 110 feet high, covering 130 acres. Never thinking about the consequences, the ascendant Kings of Uranium had brazenly built their pyramid to the Cold War and nuclear power in the floodplain of their River Nile.

As Congress finally ruled to compensate radiation victims in 1989, Moabians complained about the wind blowing radioactive dust into town. Atlas, no longer producing uranium here, was required to spray a synthetic binder over its mill pyramid. Until this day, longtime locals continue to joke about how they glow in the dark.

When Atlas learned that it would have to pay for the expensive reclamation, the company plowed its buildings into the pile along with the rest of the contamination, declared bankruptcy, and skipped town for the Bolivian gold mines—leaving its $4-million bond for a cleanup that would run over $1 billion. Its legacy was passed like a hot baton from the Nuclear Regulatory Commission to the Department of Energy (DOE).

Naturally, downriver users began to question the safety of their drinking water. The Metropolitan Water District of Southern California (MWD) complained of increased radioactivity in the river that supplies water to 16 million of its customers. Uranium is found throughout the Chinle riverbanks, so no one has yet proved that the Atlas tailings have contaminated the water with uranium. Also, scores of other abandoned uranium mills in the Colorado River Basin are washing their soluble contents downstream or into river-leaching aquifers.

The USGS calculates that Atlas leaks 57,000 gallons of contaminated water per day into the aquifer that discharges into the river. They measured leaking ammonia concentrations as high as 1,500 ppm (2 ppm of ammonia is considered lethal), killing any fish exposed to it.

The hazard that keeps water operators alarmed is the prospect of the Colorado River jumping its banks and washing the red pyramid and its enshrined contents downstream and into the intake pipes for Las Vegas, Phoenix, Los Angeles, and San Diego. According to the Moab-based Grand Canyon Conservation Trust, Atlas will "shrug" when the river hits 45,000 cfs—a mere 5,000 cfs higher than this year's peak flow.

"No," said the DOE director of the Atlas cleanup, Don Metzler, "it would take *65,000 cfs,*" when I met with him at the site.

At noon on a day that has even locals seeking shelter from the heat, Metzler hands me a hard hat inside the guard station at the former mill site. He's wearing jeans with a stylish Western belt buckle and tasseled work boots with steel toes. As he looks me in the eye and shakes my hand firmly, I'm thinking rancher rather than bureaucrat.

The river runs a couple hundred yards to the south, dark as the rubbled Chinle formation, mixed with plenty of sandstone. A couple hundred yards north are the massive tailings, shining an embarrassed red. I won't ask to go look at it and Don would never think of offering because we don't need any radiation therapy. Seven 20-foot-high steps lead to the top of the pile, and several of the terraces bristle with impervious salt cedar, hinting that this species will dominate after apocalypse.

Earlier, I'd circled No Trespassing signs and climbed the adjoining cliff beyond the mill site. A tanker truck drove along and sprayed the pile to prevent a growing breeze from blowing off contaminants. I studied the rectangular, blackened evaporating lake, wide as the river and several hundred yards long, that could accommodate (and then dissolve) the nearby Colorado River highway bridge along with every nuclear-free building, truck, and person on the surrounding mill site. The pile is conveniently centered over the Moab fault line.

The summit is encircled with a couple of miles of white retaining boom, as if this would prevent an earthquake from boiling the toxic waters. Men wearing masks and bright haz-mat suits inspected the dirt with Geiger counters.

At what I hope is a safe distance below, Don escorts me to a pump that pulls a hundred gallons per minute out of the river and sends it up through the pile in a series of wicks. As the water rises to the top of the pyramid, it's channeled into the black lake, where Colorado River water evaporates out a crystalline concentrate of lethal toxins.

Don shrugs about my river sandals, even though his two DOE colleagues are shod in steel-toed boots. Next to the pump, a sign with the yellow-glowing radioactive symbol reads

CAUTION
CONTAMINATION AREA

Still, Don poses with two hands full of dirt scooped from beneath the sign. "Clean enough to eat off," he says, almost like he's prodding me not to believe him.

"We want to protect the river," he says, pointing to the distant pile. "Our contaminants stay on top." He volunteers that the ammonia is toxic to fish and that only a flood could leach radioactivity from the site. To prove his point, he walks me down to the riverbank and shows the stick and mud detritus, ten feet below the pumping station, deposited a couple of weeks ago during the 40,000-cfs event.

Along the riverside road, a stone's throw from the river, he takes me to 41 wells, all 30 feet deep, all monitoring for ammonia and other toxins passing through the groundwater. No botanist would fail to notice that the red dirt between here and the artificial mountain has been replanted with native cottonwoods, whereas along the river, tamarisk yellows under the weight of invading beetles. Between here and the river, a line of sandbags had been spread as part of DOE protocol, anticipating the 40,000-cfs flood two weeks before it came.

Don suggests that, until the pile is moved, his agency's biggest task is simply watching the water. Moab Creek runs through the site in two different places. "These wells make a tenfold capture of water moving under or around the pile," he says. We both know that this is a 16-million-ton mess, and he isn't going to soft-sell it, even though the DOE has been hampered for years by politics and a lack of funding.

Once the old railroad tracks are rebuilt, Don says, the trains will carry the tailings 30 miles to Crescent Junction, miles from human habitation. Over 18 years, in trains departing once a day, the contaminated dirt will be lowered into impenetrable Mancos shale bedrock, isolated from any aquifer. "Same rock underlying my home in Grand Junction," he says. "Once the hole is capped, the tailings will be safe for a thousand years."

This isn't Metzler's first contaminated mess. Under his supervision, the DOE has cleaned up several smaller uranium mill sites in the Colorado River

Basin, among 17 inactive mill sites now under its charge in the West. Just before departing, he drops a warning for the future: "Uranium had dropped to $9 a pound on the open market and now it's back up to $90 a pound." He shakes my hand again, wishing me luck on my journey downriver, expressing envy that he can't join me.

On June 22, I'm paddling toward Cataract Canyon and some of the river's biggest rapids. Over the last two days of raft travel from Castle Valley, the riverbanks have passed in a thick parade of browning tamarisk slumped with fattening beetles. In light of the illness that took away my mom, I'm seeing tamarisk as the cancer and beetles as the chemotherapy. It's hard to know which is the disease and which is the cure.

Alive or dead, the tamarisk thickets are humming with legions of mosquitoes. And because the sky is at least temporarily hung with shading cumulus, I try to avoid the buzzing banks of the river. It is a well-kept secret that mosquitoes plague Moab, the word a phonetic match to the word Ute Indians used to describe the valley's mosquito water. Nineteenth-century Mormon settlers who kicked out the Utes named their town after the biblical Moab, outside the Israelites' promised land.

In front of the tamarisk, on drought sandbars and newly exposed sand islands, lines of native willows are vying for a comeback, waving their tops out above this year's flood. I follow the strongest current by paddling outside the scum of pink tamarisk buds inside the eddy lines.

For the next couple of weeks, I'll be passing under the Jurassic Wingate formation. These red, iron-oxidized cliffs stretch hundreds of feet vertically overhead, lighting the river horizons afire with every sunset and sunrise. As Manhattan skyscrapers define the steely Hudson, and the Alaska Range the milky Susitna—Wingate, Navajo, and Redwall limestone redden the Colorado River. The walls are varnished tan, brown, orange, and black from microscopic plant particles interacting with dust and daubing hundred-foot-high abstract murals on thousand-foot canvases.

Business on the river is brisk today with jet boats and rafting clients. While paddling past motorless rafts drifting with the current and fizzing with freshly opened beers, I pass Brian. He and another small Navtec raft are outfitted with Scottish clients and headed toward the big rapids. Brian's fellow guide Colin asks about my time upriver, then politely cuts to the chase: "Do you know what you're in for downstream?" I do.

Two days from now, I'll be camping near the Green River—doubling the flow. After this, the rust-colored Colorado will be carrying freight trains of mostly dissolved Rocky Mountains. Three miles below the confluence, the river will explode down the first set of rapids, vibrating the riverbanks.

Cataract Canyon, unchecked by any local dam, is the river's corset-busting maelstrom. In normal snow years, flows exceed that of the Grand Canyon. Rafts routinely flip, and swimmers sometimes drown. Even experienced boatmen say their prayers to the ongoing aqueous thunderstorm. After all, most of these transient youths have been trained in the more casual drought waters of the Cataract.

Becalmed above this pandemonium, I am repeatedly asked by the guides if I'll be taking my little boat through "the Grand Ditch" (Grand Canyon in local boatmen parlance)—*if* I survive Cataract. So I explain that I'm here to learn about the river, not drown in it, while I continue to Mexico. When they ask how I'm getting through Cataract, I say that I'm hitching a ride with the Canyonlands Ranger Steve Young. Each time I mention his name, the reaction is like saying that I'm riding with Barack Obama through Chicago. Then I'm feted with cold drinks. Once the guides approve of the company I'll be keeping, only the clients continue interrogating me.

Many people don't know about the river's origin and its end: "Where's Rocky Mountain National Park? How many miles? The river doesn't reach the sea?"

Large motorized boats cut their speed and wave as soon as they spy my tiny raft. It's still 40 miles to the confluence and Cataract Canyon, so I paddle hard as silt patters like rain against my boat. "Too thick to drink, too thin to plow," as early ranchers said.

In sweltering mid-afternoon heat, I paddle four miles around a jutting gooseneck of dense rock that the river can't cut, forcing me and its waters around in a great circle tour. Above the cliffs off my bow, paddling north, I spy people a thousand feet above in Dead Horse Point State Park. A few miles later, I'm paddling south, and four people up on the White Rim Trail to the west are rolling rocks down to river level. They shout down to me, clearly audible, although mere specks against the sky. Through my silence, I take small satisfaction in letting these boulder trundlers think they're too far away and insignificant amid this landscape to be seen or heard.

I pass out of BLM lands and into Canyonlands National Park. Planners were thwarted in creating a park here for a dozen years, trying to work around uranium interests seeking hot sandstone. During a lull in uranium prices in 1964, President Johnson signed a bill to create what would eventually become a 528-square-mile park.

Seen from outer space, the Green and Colorado confluence forms a northwest-tilting anchor, hooking the park into three unique landforms. To the north looms the Island in the Sky, a broad mesa 1,200 feet above the White Rim bench. To the south, the Needles district bristles with red-and-white-banded pinnacles, grabens, and arches. And west of the confluence are the inaccessible hinterlands of the maze, an easy place to get lost and study ancient art panels.

This is still uranium country. Prices are climbing, and several uranium mining claims within the boundaries legally predate the national park's creation. On other federal, state, and private lands adjoining the river from the state of Colorado to Mexico, Triassic rock and old uranium mining claims abound.*

I stop at Lathrop Canyon to explore the ruins. The main campsite has been taken by a guided group, Tag-A-Long Expeditions. While introducing myself, I say that Ranger Steve Young will be picking me up at the confluence to take me through Cataract.

"You mean T-berry?" the lead guide Dave asks.

"You know him?"

"*Everyone* knows him," Dave replies. "Wanna beer?"

Then I'm invited to dinner and escorted to a prime tent site along the river. Rather than using my own waste bags, Dave graciously allows me to use their toilet—perhaps the ultimate compliment a boatman can pay to a stranger.

Toilets, or "groovers," are typically green army surplus waterproof ammo boxes. The name emanated from a 1970s river guide, who noticed one of his clients returning from the ammo box bathroom with her bikinied bottom imprinted with a conspicuous set of parallel grooves, 18 inches long and 8 inches wide, from sitting on the narrow-lipped ammo can. The name stuck even though modern groovers are usually capped with comfortable toilet seats.

Emptying one's bladder in the toilet will piss off any guide because overflowing toilets are as deadly as the 20-mm shells that used to fill the ammo boxes. Even the Park Service recommends peeing in the river rather than killing local vegetation.

Three hundred and ninety-five uranium claims exist along the river corridor. Recently, 800 new uranium claims have been filed within five miles of the river. Even if only a few of the 1,195 mines are opened, it would only take one more muscular Atlas to contaminate the Colorado River. Because stricter federal regulations are no guarantee of stopping uranium wastes from leaching into groundwater, Southwest water operators are on high alert.

As a nonguided boater in Canyonlands, I'm required to get a free permit, carry out my wastes, and take care of the riverscape. Because outbreaks of dysentery among the 14 outfitter groups here could cause a slough of evacuations, guides are required to offer two hand-washing stations during every meal and three basins for dishwashing (including a bleach basin), and store their perishables and meats atop the ice on the bottom of the coolers. Guides must have first aid certification, carry a medical kit, and if their raft is motorized, a spare outboard.

Dave's clients include a ramrod-straight German couple, a Seattle man, and a family from Massachusetts who are having the time of their life jumping from a small cliff and cooling off in the strong current. I don't want to ruin their fun by telling them about the contaminated Atlas mill site 40 miles upriver.

At sunset, I paddle across the 50-yard-wide river to visit a ruin site. The mosquitoes hustle me through a dark cave hacked out of tamarisk and onto a path that meanders uphill around fragile cryptogrammic soils. For 30 years, I've returned to the canyonlands to photograph and examine ruin sites. Like other aficionados, I've learned that each new dilapidated ruin offers a fascinating glimpse into a gentle people who drew impressionist art on the walls, threw pots, wove baskets, and grew corn, while Europe raged with the Crusades.

Sunset transforms the river into a bronze mirror of reflected heat, so I stand in the cool shadows next to a chest-high stone granary, flat stones mortared together with clay. The granary had been built a thousand years ago to protect corn from the same genus of ravens now cawing overhead.

The ancient Puebloans (formerly Anasazi, "ancient enemies" in Navajo) migrated into these canyons centuries before Christ. Until 800 years ago, tree rings show that these people lived in a desert habitat with enough rain to prevent drought. They wore fur or feather robes, plant-fiber sandals, and shell, bone, or stone jewelry. Women gathered pinyon nuts, wild rice, and sunflower and mustard seeds that they ground into flour. Their elegantly striped pots are now scattered in shards buried along riverbanks from western Colorado to northern Arizona.

The Great Drought came in the 12th century. Throughout North America, the long summers and lack of rain resembled the first decade of the 21st century. For 300 years, this climate change reduced the river and seared the land. Combined with the arrival of warlike Utes, according to some archaeologists, the drought forced the ancient Puebloans to abandon the canyonlands.

Upon a north-facing wall around the corner from the crumbling granary, I find a remnant of these people. A man held his hands against the wall and spat out a mixture of gypsum, urine, and yarrow, creating negative prints of hands the exact size of mine. A foot below, he spat again over the smaller hands of his child. Both prints reach toward the heavens, acting like signatures for adjacent drawings of bighorn sheep and a crescent moon. Of all the chilling anthropomorphic beings and bizarre fertility symbols depicted alongside hundreds of other ruins throughout the Southwest, these common handprints hint of flesh and blood: showing off a child just as I would photograph my sons. I palm the thermal mass of Wingate beside their antiquated prints, careful not to smudge any oils from my hands near their signatures. The layers of rock above and below unveil history, uniting me with the ancients. I can imagine this father and son feeling the heat of the wall, looking up in awe and squawking back in mimicry of the raven. They could've been here yesterday.

Two dozen miles downriver, I awaken to baking midsummer canyonlands from an early afternoon nap, dreaming of my cool mountain home. Grass imprints my back and bare legs. My sweaty head rests on my PFD. Ten feet below, water gurgles against my life raft tied in the eddy. I swig down 90-degree water from a jug. When I stand over the river to pee, it's barely yellow—a good sign: I'm not yet dehydrated.

As dark clouds build overhead, I rush out from the sheltering trees and stand naked with arms outstretched and mouth tilted underneath delicious cool rain and wind. Within two minutes, the sky's water evaporates and the rain disappears. The wind stops. I'm back in the oven again.

Climbing high above the tight bank of tamarisk and cottonwoods for a view, I can see the Green River tinting the muddy Colorado. This week's upriver gauges—the Green at 15,000 cfs, the Colorado 20,000 cfs—show how the latter carries more volume.

John Wesley Powell first reached the confluence in mid-July 139 years ago. After climbing up the walls above me, he wrote about the view in *The Exploration of the Colorado River and Its Canyons*:

From the northwest comes the Green in a narrow winding gorge. From the northeast comes the Grand, through a canyon that seems bottomless from where we stand. Away to the west are lines of cliffs and ledges of rock—not such ledges as the reader may have seen where the quarryman splits his blocks, but ledges from which the gods might quarry mountains . . . .

I stroll closer to the confluence. West of the Green River end, running from Wyoming's Wind River Mountains, lies a ten-foot-high Wingate erratic, frost broken and tumbled down from the cliffs high above. It had been shakily carved by one of Frank Brown's two surveying expeditions:

STA 8489 + 50

DGC 988 P. PA

MAY 4th 1889

The barely legible "STA"tion marker would have benefited from studying ancient Puebloan art.

Nineteen years after Powell, the ambitious Brown expedition came to survey what Powell denigrated as a foolish railroad grade from Grand Junction, Colorado, to Yuma, Arizona. Powell refused to give their expedition precise navigational information about the river, so the second-in-command Robert Brewster Stanton would devote himself to correcting the romantic Powell and his popular book.

Stanton, nephew of the famous abolitionist Henry Brewster Stanton, had grown up with a silver spoon in his mouth. Through his well-connected Presbyterian clergyman father, Robert Livingston Stanton, young Robert repeatedly met President Lincoln in the White House.

Stanton and his nemesis, Powell, could not have been more unalike. Powell cut a bulbous-beaked profile and was called by his sister "the homeliest man God ever made." He also proved to be an autodidact with a ravenous curiosity for natural history. Lacking an arm below his elbow, Powell could still swim like a fish. Stanton, a foppish dresser from a pedigreed family, parted his hair stylishly down the middle, and studied at Miami University in Ohio while his father served as its president. Stanton had lost use of one of his arms and never learned how to swim.

Powell spent seven, then eleven days portaging around the rapids he named Cataract Canyon in the relatively tame runoffs of 1869 and 1871. When Stanton arrived in the spring of 1889, the rapids below the confluence were running at a furious 45,000 cfs. He would spend more than a month mapping and surveying Cataract Canyon. Each night, he tended to his meticulous diary and filled a surveying book with topographical information and detailed drawings. The leader, Frank Brown, a realtor and recent founder of Cañon and Pacific Railroad in Denver, Colorado, had tightfistedly denied his men life jackets even though Stanton had put them on the necessary list of provisions. Even worse, Brown brought flimsy low-freeboard boats that were constantly being swamped and breaking up against rocks.

As a visionary, Brown saw an opportunity to pad his legacy as a railroad man by delivering the wealth of gold and coal mines directly to California. By sticking to the river, his railroad wouldn't have to cross any mountain ranges. And Stanton, his chief engineer, had never met a landscape he couldn't conquer with a railroad.

Several miles below the confluence, Brown's inexperienced crew lost or destroyed valuable survey equipment and a camera while trying to portage or line their boats through chaotic water. On June 4, they destroyed one of their boats and Stanton wrote in his diary:

Talked to several of the men and find a good deal of dissatisfaction among them as to the way Mr. Brown is managing the expedition and the way Hughes and Reynolds (guests of Brown) try to boss the handling of boats. I will have a talk with all the men at breakfast tomorrow.

Brown was driven to tears when the boat *Mary*—named after his wife— disappeared in the rapids, and his stupor demoralized the men. Instead, they began to look to Stanton for leadership. Through his methodical, bulldog manner, their high jinks through terrifying rapids merely allowed him to focus more diligently on the task at hand. Along perpendicular cliffs above the narrowest section of river, he confidently wrote of building a 1,500-foot tunnel. Above booming rapids, he described how he would use cliff material removed from the grade to create coves in the river.

The team spent whole days submerged in the water, and an equal number of nights shivering under wet blankets. Without life jackets, repeatedly forced to swim for their lives in whirlpools and through the huge rapids that define Cataract Canyon, each man began wondering when their number would come up. The repeated boat stave-ins and capsizes cut their 75 days of food to less than three weeks. Through all the hardships, Stanton kept his eyes glued to the survey sights, obsessively studying Powell's book.

On June 13, he wrote that his survey

line of today was run too high. This on account of my supposing that these rapids were where Powell's "75 ft. fall in 3/4 mile" came. But on getting the levels this evening I find that the fall is only about 55 ft. in two miles, so that I can easily maintain my 16 ft. per mile as a maximum grade.

On June 16, Brown confided to Stanton that he had been rushing the team through the canyon so that he could meet with a "syndicate" in New York by mid-August that "represented $50 million who had agreed to take hold of the building of this road if the Engineer's report was favorable." Stanton made his finest act of judgment by dismissing the leader and letting him descend to Hite Ferry below the canyon to resupply. Stanton nearly starved, but without Brown and his cumbersome guests, he completed the Cataract Canyon survey.

As evening shadows round out the jagged corners of canyon heat, Ranger T-berry motors into the eddy below the confluence and I jump aboard. He's six-foot-four, broad shouldered, and slim hipped. T-berry is dressed in sun-bleached Park Service regulation green shorts, a requisite badge on his gray uniform short sleeves, a green cap with the arrowhead, and nonregulation flip-flops. Neat and functional, but hardly ironed. If he has a gun somewhere, I can't see it, even though most rangers pack guns on their Sam Browne belts. If you spend enough time in national park backcountries, the rangers and their uniforms will tell you whether they're cops (crisp and pressed) or mountain men (sweat-stained and wrinkled) long before they speak.

The boat is carrying my buddy David Schipper (Skip), the wildlife biologist Bill Sloan, and ranger apprentice Jeremy Snyder. Among these garrulous passengers, T-berry is reticent and businesslike. If his leadership defies words, his physical presence and captaincy is indelible: He's the guy whom we'll be looking to if the raft flips "black side up."

He stands wide-legged over his twin 60-horse Mercury outboards, twists one of the throttles like he's driving a Harley, and puts the raft up into something resembling trim. His four-stroke engines reduce noise and carbon emissions, and will soon be required equipment for all motor outfitters in the park.

The river has become a fat water snake, lazily coiling three miles down to Spanish Bottom. T-berry yells over the purring engine, "You can feel it right here"—he releases the throttle and mimics the flat, slow-moving water with his slow horizontal karate chop—"the way the river backs up like a lake, getting ready to drop down into 'Brown Betty' rapid," named for Stanton's cook boat that capsized all of their food and pots here. T-Berry, a closet historian, then recommends that I bring Stanton's diaries with me through the Grand Canyon later this fall.

The 22-foot J-rig he's driving costs taxpayers $28,000, plus $15,000 for the outboard setup. Measuring dollars spent against lives saved, this boat might be one of the most cost-effective tools in the National Park Service arsenal. Although people routinely perish elsewhere in the park's dry canyons, because of the park "catch and release" program—fishing out human beings from the rapids, then releasing them on the shores—the Park Service has efficiently pared body evacuations from their river budget. Catch and release begins whenever the rapids crest over 50,000 cfs. Then T-berry and the rangers set up camp at the bottom of the "Big Drop Rapids" for a month, where most of the oar boats flipped in this year's high water end up. In state-of-the-art jet boats, rangers can motor up hair-raising rapids, grab the hypothermic and dazed "bobbers" (few can swim in this turbulent cold water), and haul them onto the rescue boats. All day long. Each year, over 6,000 people run these rapids. In high-water years, it's better than life insurance to have T-berry and his ranger cohorts watching you smash into 30-foot waves in Cataract, then weave past jagged rocks with all of the control of a pinball dinging through the bumpers. And if you have to run "Big Drop" in what he calls the "Terrible Thirties" (water levels over 30,000 cfs), you'd be best off hitching a ride in his boat.

T-berry angles river right toward an empty beach, gooses the Merc, and levers the outboard up out of the water as we slide up onto the sand. Ranger Snyder takes the bowline and loops it around a stout tamarisk. Then, with his boss's reminder, the youthful assistant-awaiting-a-uniform hefts the pungent 20-mm ammo box and walks away in search of the ideal groover placement. T-berry backs up Snyder's flimsy tie-off.

The neophytes pitch tents, while T-berry and Bill throw their sleeping bags on sand. We're surrounded by shriveling stands of tamarisk gone brown as dandelions beneath herbicides. Every tree in sight wriggles with Kazakhstan caterpillars, ready to molt into centimeter-long tamarisk-munching machines. Along the sandy beach, thousands of larvae writhe like caraway seeds. Even though we're 52 miles below the last release, the beetles are ubiquitous. For the last couple of years, T-berry has been fielding complaints from irate visitors about these beetles ruining their wilderness experience. The insects get in their eyes, buzz in their faces, fall into the food, and are squashed on tent floors, forming deplorable brown stains that look like skid marks.

"They must be exaggerating by saying *skid marks*," I say, "right?"

"Okay," T-berry throws up his hands, "don't believe me."

As we gather around the aluminum cooking table—command central for all river trips—Snyder says he's relieved that the leaf-eating beetles have replaced the mosquitoes at Spanish Bottom.

Our camp is pitched below high escarpments of sandstone, on a flat river bottom a third of a mile wide, created before the river more than 300 million years ago. The Spanish Bottom sinkhole formed over the Paradox Formation of ancient sea salt. Throughout the narrow, steep-walled Cataract Canyon, the Paleolithic Paradox Formation reemerges along the river bottom, like a glimpse of buried treasure below earlier and denser layers of geologic time.

In the 1700s, Spanish missionaries may have crossed the river here, while in the mid-1900s, Butch Cassidy and the Sundance Kid passed through on their way to a desert hideout. Stanton's photographer recorded the view in 1889, showing undisturbed soil crusts and an unimpeded view of the river. I first visited Spanish Bottom 30 years ago, hiking with nine Outward Bound students. They each took three-day solos—not talking to or seeing anyone—along the riverbank, hidden in willow and sparse tamarisk, promising not to step on the delicate and crusty soils. Now the soil is covered in invasive cheatgrass. Tamarisk has supplanted the native willows.

As for the supposed solution to the tamarisk, I've seen the exotic beetles for 200 miles, from Horsethief to Cataract Canyons. Along with jeopardizing the willow flycatcher, the largest biologic control experiment in history is making Canyonlands National Park an unwilling guinea pig—as T-berry puts it.

Skip boils water for pasta, Bill studies his Bible, and Ranger Snyder consults T-berry about one of the many complexities of their difficult job. "It has to be flat, with a good view and privacy," T-berry says about proper groover placement. T-berry has taken off his badge and no bobbers are evident in the river, so it's time to relax. I offer to fill everyone's cups with red wine, and all but Skip passes, if only because wizened boatmen in hot canyons drink cold beer.

T-berry wears many hats on the river. His biggest responsibility, taking care of the park and its visitors, intersects with his least favorite duty of playing cop. He's written two tickets already this summer for boatmen doing their duty without ammo boxes. He also serves as a medic, rescuer, search party organizer, engine mechanic, walking information booth, janitor, health inspector, historian, and fireman. Last summer, a boatman burned down Spanish Bottom while torching his toilet paper—sending the rangers into action with shovels, water buckets, and a well-deserved toilet citation.

Over the last seven weeks, T-berry has been called out on four fires, an airplane crash, a hiker falling off a cliff, and a fruitless search for a well-hidden suicide victim. In less than two months, he's logged more overtime than in the past five years. "The kids don't even call me Dad anymore," he moans, running fingers through his Fu Manchu. "I'm just some dirty guy sleeping on the couch. Most nights I don't even get home until 11."

He met his wife, Eve, more than a decade ago while working as a freelance boatman on the river. They were filming a television commercial, and although another hotshot male kayaker had been slated to steal the show, the filmmaker loved Eve's unfeigned look of surprise every time she face-planted Cataract Canyon waves. So she repeatedly capsized her canoe, take after take. Off camera, T-berry repeatedly rescued her. He would snag her PFD shoulder strap and levitate her straight out of the water, away from scary hydraulics and beater swims through the rocks. It's implicit in his story that "picking up" an attractive woman and drying her off yield a lifetime of rewards. Even the irreverent boatmen know that, if he hasn't rescued them or their clients yet, there's always their next trip downriver. So most boatmen show him unconditional respect.

More than any boatman I've met, T-berry has an encyclopedic grasp of river history. Like most well-read boatmen, he tolerates and even quotes from the hyperbolic Powell, but shows more interest in other Cataract pioneers such as the little-known Stanton and Loper (1907) and the Kolb Brothers (1911). As the resident expert, he frequently accompanies scientists to hunt down sites and repeat photographs taken during early expeditions.

He spent most of May stationed below the "Big Drops." This year's record high, 63,000 cfs, has only been matched once in the last decade. Unlike the years preceding 1998, T-berry believes that the drought has accustomed a whole generation of guides to easy or moderate flows. This is a civil way of saying that he has to spend a lot more time holding the guides' hands than they have a right to expect.

He also believes that the park is going to be in "*rapid* trouble" if the drought continues. "We're going to see Cataract Canyon going downhill fast," he says. "I might be trolling this river in a canoe because that's the only thing that will make it through."

Six years ago, during peak run-off season, the river dropped to a mere fraction of its present size. No motorboats could fit down the shallow canyon.

Boats repeatedly flipped against exposed boulders; T-berry repeatedly rescued swimmers and rigged pulley systems to remove trapped boats. "Cataract is different from the Grand Canyon because Glen Canyon Dam gives a steady flow for its boaters," he says. "Here, we take whatever nature gives us, and it's been slim pickings the last decade."*

T-berry shares the hope of boatmen and naturalists the length of the river: "I think Glen Canyon Dam is going to go bye-bye," he says, referring to the concrete wall 213 miles downstream, stilling river into lake a dozen miles below Spanish Bottom. In Powell's day, there were 52 rapids to be run. Today, thanks to the dam, Cataract Canyon has only half that number, depending upon the dropping levels of the reservoir. "We're going to drink the damn thing," T-berry says about the need for the dam to come down, spurring everyone to raise their cups for a toast.

This is hardly insurrection. T-berry is one of countless park rangers who now see the handwriting on the concrete wall. Rather than a flight of imagination as proposed by former ranger Ed Abbey's terrorist *Monkey Wrench Gang* characters, "dismantling" Glen Canyon Dam has been frequently discussed in cities—Phoenix, Albuquerque, San Diego, and Denver—that depend upon Colorado River. In the eighties, 20 million people depended upon the river for drinking water; now it's 30 million people. Add another 10 million people, plus a couple degrees of heat to these warming cities, and the reservoirs will drop so low that dam turbines will no longer be able to create electricity. Unlike Lake Mead, Powell provides no municipal drinking water. And each reservoir loses over 260 billion gallons of water per year through evaporation—more than twice what Las Vegas takes each year from the river. So dismantling the dam, sans explosives, has become an ideal as pervasive as putting an African American or a woman in charge of the Oval Office. If it came to a vote tomorrow, the only defenders of the dam would be the tourist agencies and thousands of water skiers, exotic fish fanatics, and motorheads of the reservoir.

"Wait until you paddle across Lake Powell," T-berry says, "and you'll see what I mean. The lake is a showpiece of the Darwin theory and mankind's de-evolution."

Now that we've dispensed with the essentials discussed around most river campfires, Ranger Young explains that his two-decade-old nickname comes

---

Since 1923, Cataract Canyon has recorded four different decades with each year's peak flow totaling over 600,000 cfs. Over the last decade, these high river flows have ebbed to 353,000 cfs.

from an episode of *The Simpsons* about "Tonzo Berry." His fellow Outward Bound instructors needed a catchy and original moniker, so they shortened it to T-berry. Despite its cryptic and mostly inexplicable origins, the handle stuck and it's now practically synonymous with Cataract Canyon. He's run it several hundred times more than John Wesley Powell.

As the night cools to a bearable 85 degrees, the storytelling loses its ardor. The black sky is lit only with stars, framed by canyon walls. Bats flit and dive, then hover amid the alien bug invasion.

I have crawled back into my tent through its unzipped door when I suddenly sense company. So I turn on my headlamp and shine its beam on several hundred Kazakhstan larvae squirming across the floor and walls. It's bizarre that they somehow homed in on my tent, as if following a scent. I escort them out, but each gentle swipe squashes two for every one of the soft, precious infants that I manage to sweep out the door. By the time I'm through, the blue floor is streaked with brown skid marks.

In the morning, we motor back above the confluence and along the Green River to count desert bighorn sheep. T-berry stops to chat with passing canoeists, politely inquiring about their groovers, and answering questions with a patient, no-nonsense charm that belies how many times he's answered the exact same questions.

I jump out on the riverbank and join white-bearded Bill. Sitting masochistically in the direct sunlight, he takes off his long-sleeve light blue cotton dress shirt, dunks it in the river, and pulls the dripping garment back on over his dark blue T-shirt. We have a choice of being temporarily cooled by 60-degree water of indeterminate contaminants, sitting in the sun, or hiding in the tamarisk. I sit in the shade. Bill sits in the sun and repeatedly dips in his shirt. He's waving his telemetry antennae back and forth, trying to pick up a signal from a score of sheep wearing radio collars, among more than 350 sheep in the park.

Bill has the patience of Job tending to an unseen flock. His skin is impressively pale for someone so disinterested in sun lotion. As he scans the vast canyon walls above, he chats about his life's work. As I ask questions, the antennae waves, and he answers questions without taking his eyes off distant cliffs.

Bill's mission is to count the sheep, transport healthy specimens to other protected Southwestern parks, and patrol the river to observe any changes in their habitat. Ill clad in hot blue jeans, wearing a pinched look of pain and a Y2K ball cap "01-01-00," Bill could be mistaken for a miner survivalist.

Among the ancient ruins of the Southwest, bighorn are routinely featured in rock art. One can only imagine how prolific the sheep must have been a thousand years ago. To invoke the skill of these 200-pound beasts nimbly climbing steep sandstone, the canyon people wove sheep dewclaws onto their fiber sandals, and fantasized of their bighorn powers while scrambling dizzying heights above the river, up to their cliff dwellings, vegetable granaries, and otherworldly panels of art.

Several hundred years later, early explorers found the same large flocks throughout Southwestern canyons. As the Ute and other tribes were pushed into reservations in the mid-19th century, a flood of emigrants introduced their European livestock. The bighorn were decimated through exposure to domestic sheep pathogens and hungry explorers like Powell.

After his river experiences, he wrote in his journal-styled *Exploration of the Colorado River and Its Canyons* about sighting bighorn sheep a hundred feet above Cataract Canyon. While Powell waited regally in the boats—he couldn't safely climb up the cliffs with one arm—he heard his companions' gunshots go off above. Like most passages in his book, Major Powell is often removed from but oddly part of the action: He couldn't row, so he directed the men pulling at the oars, commanding them what to cook or how to hunt his dinner. Compared to the usual ornate mid-19th-century prose, Powell augmented his narrative through an athletic combination of lordly omniscience, frequent adjectives, and active verbs. Whether spot-on or just keenly embellished, the book continues to be widely read by an armchair readership who can revel in a frontier experience on an uncharted river, hunting and eating wild mutton to survive in a wilderness that filled the author with awe.

After a pause in the action, Powell heard more gunshots. No 19th-century college could have taught Powell, a self-educated writer, how to color his scenes as well. His oft-exclamation-marked narration reveals both an untrammeled river and a bombastic vision that drove him toward mastering Western water:

> We lash our prizes to the deck and go on for a short distance; but fresh meat is too tempting, and we stop early to have a feast. And what a feast it is! Two fine young sheep! We care not for bread or beans or dried apples tonight; coffee and mutton are all we ask.

Powell mentions sheep seven times. In those days, although desert bighorn were almost extirpated, some remnant populations managed to outrange the domestic sheep diseases and outwit the prospectors. Working their cloven hooves like suction cups against the secure grip of sandstone, the sheep climbed onto inaccessible ledges and hid from guns, germs, and steel. Still, by 1964, wildlife technicians found less than 100 sheep remaining. Canyonlands National Park was established in the nick of time.

The park closed down grazing and hunting. Over two decades, wildlife technicians transported the hardy survivors from already populated zones into no-sheep zones. Eventually, the sheep population tripled.

Good park management gives researchers like Bill plenty of leeway. His research has shown that *Ovis canadensis nelsoni* has been impacted by the park's 325 percent increase in human visitation from 1979 to 1994. During human hiking encounters, bighorn fled 61 percent of the time, versus encounters with vehicles (17 percent fled) and mountain bikers (6 percent fled). Desert bighorn also appear to be suffering from the drought, even though the subspecies has adapted to long periods without water, which would kill its more common, larger cousins, the Rocky Mountain bighorn.

Through his telemetry headset, Bill can hear repeated high-frequency pings, indicating life somewhere high above. Still, his high-power binoculars have not revealed a trace of megafauna. We're here to find sheep, so Bill sends three of us up onto the cliff sides in hopes of herding his charges out onto more visible ledges. Then eagle-eyed Bill can count the flock and make a cursory inspection of their health.

An hour later, as I stand 1,500 feet above the river, the 22-foot boat has shrunken to a white speck amid the backed-up waters of Stillwater Canyon. More discernible is a colossal battleship of sandstone cliffs, afloat on a dark brown pontoon of tamarisk, surrounded by the river's most-storied confluence. Although distant sheep usually stand out against dark rock, it occurs to me that the wise old bighorn—genetically refined into the ultimate survivors—could be sleeping in tamarisk shade a few dozen yards from Bill, waving his small-horned antennae, Pentax glass glued to his eye sockets. Through my binoculars, I can see T-berry, shaded beneath the canopy of his überboat. Bill continues to sit in the sun, looking for sheep, or so it appears. The two are sitting up as though they might be busy, but they could just as easily be courting their well-deserved midday siesta as weathered desert rats.

Skip, Ranger Snyder, and I have each consumed a couple of quarts of water. Still, it's so oppressively hot and dry that the sweat immediately evaporates off our skin. As our kidneys shrivel, Skip keeps smearing on lip balm. If we were so clueless to prostrate ourselves on the sandstone ledge, vultures would circle in. So we continue to stand, staring dumbly through the earth's geology, feeling reduced to microsiemens amid the timeworn scenery enveloping us.

Distant cumulus clouds to the east loft a white line of rain through the thick and superheated sky. To the south, a shimmering blue mirage of water floats above Lake Powell. As the air stills and heat covers the Southwest like a thick blanket, air conditioners are being cranked up in Phoenix, L.A., and San Diego. Responding in kind, like the shore clamoring for sea, penstock gates crank open at Hoover and Glen Canyon Dams and the river runs once again—if only until the cool of evening—for a few megawatts more.

As we J-boat downstream, several canoeists at Spanish Bottom tell us about a collared sheep emerging from the tamarisk along with a small flock and coming down to water's edge to drink out of the confluence. Like a camel, the species can sup one-fifth of its weight in water. "Those buggers," Bill says angrily. He figures they're the same sheep he's been listening to all day, hiding behind him in the tamarisk.

Before heading into the rapids, T-berry tightens his PFD and gives us a lecture about holding tightly onto the boat if it flips. Swim hard for the shore, look out for the holes, and keep our feet downstream so we don't split our heads like watermelons against rocks. It's intriguing that he's suddenly talking with great modesty, as if he'll have no control over our passage down the river.

In contrast to most modern rangers, he's working from his gut rather than Park Service protocol. He also understands that he's long overdue to be tossed into the cauldron. He might have come to Cataract many years ago with a swagger, but the Colorado River defines and even rules his life.

Despite the sincerity of his warning speech, I'm all the more confident that he won't flip. Only the humble boatmen, so they say, keep their gunpowder dry. As we head into "Brown Betty," I sit with Bill up in front, his legs straddling the right pontoon, mine the left, so that we can cool off and receive the full brunt of the waves.

If we experience any disappointment as we hit the first five rapids, holding on for our lives and getting soaked, it's because T-berry has the river so wired. He shoots the rapid, and because of the outboard, he's able to spin the boat, ferry slightly upstream, and hook into an eddy that would be unreachable by oar power. Brown Betty turns out to be a minor rapid, even though Stanton's cooks capsized here.

As we continue down, elegantly feinting toward each catastrophic drop, then quickly gliding around it, T-berry scouts every rapid ahead, even benign-looking class III chutes. If there's no eddy to park in, he finds a slow spot in the river and holds the boat stationary by running upstream so that he can assess weird holes, dangerous rocks, or anything that looks new amid the ever-shifting riverscape. Although almost any other boatman would confidently use this überboat to quickly dispatch all of the rapids, T-berry takes nothing for granted, like this is his first time down the river.

I share his sense of caution, even though I'm only a passenger, because the river hasn't shown waterfalls one-third this big or technical since the "Upper Death Rapid" at Glenwood Springs several weeks ago. For 16 miles in Cataract Canyon, the river drops 30 feet per mile. Although it's only one-quarter as steep as Gore Canyon, the difference is obvious. Cataract Canyon has more water thundering through it than any modern rapids on the Colorado River. Even at a moderate 35,000 cfs, the water is vibrating the banks, pushing boulders downstream, and showing hydraulics big enough to hold airplanes.

Three miles downstream, in 1985, a Cessna Turbo 210 making an illegal ice-cream drop crashed into the river. The pilot and passenger sat dazed out on the 36-foot-long wingspan as a giant eddy spun them in circles until a guided group pulled them aboard their raft. The victims had minor injuries, the sort of outcome that warms T-berry's heart: Nobody died, but the brash pilot received a huge lesson about hubris. The six-seat, 28-foot-long plane remains at the bottom of one of many deep Cataract Canyon eddies, home to only the pike minnows.

We pass Rapid 6 by avoiding the rocks on river right. For a better perspective of the river, I jump out to photograph T-berry running Rapid 7, better known locally as "the North Sea." Today it gives the ranger boat a bucking wet ride, completely submersing the pontoons until only their heads appear—wide-eyed and open-mouthed—above the water. A month earlier, the waves here reached 30 feet high and flipped any rower brazen enough to test them.

We stop and visit every outfitter's camp. T-berry is not in a hurry to get through the final Big Drops. Clean-shaven and understated, he makes the dutiful inspections, refusing proffered drinks. When it's time to leave, he drags the voluble Bill from ample beer coolers; no one would think of refusing a thirsty man a drink, particularly if he's working for the Park Service.

Preparing for a flip, T-berry lowers the canopy and tightens every lash strap on the boat. Provincial Cataract guides, looking to boost their tip money, will hitch up their pants, pull their lash strap belts tight, and dramatically analogize these Big Drops to the Grand Canyon's hardest rapids, like squeezing "Crystal Rapid" up against "Lava Rapid." Even Powell couldn't help exaggerating this section of Cataract.

As we tilt into the Big Drops, T-berry has the water's action as wired as a sport climber who has memorized and choreographed a cliff. He points out how the rapids are created by the river colliding with boulders rinsed out of Teapot Canyon. Through the uneventful first drop, T-berry pauses for a quick look at Niagara. The infamous drop has recently developed a powerful current that only a quick oarsman or a powerful motorboat can avoid. T-berry knows better than anyone that 11 of the 14 river deaths in the park occurred here—mostly drownings during flips. Niagara, normally a pourover rock, has become a thirsty hole with a huge wave on its end. Although rafts have survived a passage into the awful-looking drop, welded boat frames have been bent in two, oars snapped like matchsticks, and bobbers beaten senseless by the broken-off, sharpened pieces. The trick is not only to run Niagara or Big Drop 2 properly, but also to be aligned at its end so that the boat isn't completely debilitated by the house-sized Teapot Canyon boulders and holes lining the riverbanks along Big Drop 3.

T-berry again wraps the nylon webbing around his right hand to hold himself down and then twists his outboard throttle to outflank the wicked-looking "Satan's Gut" on river left. Propeller boats sometimes hit the wrong section of backwash in Big Drop 2, causing their props to churn powerlessly in aerated water, condemning their boat into the Gut.

Like all good boatmen, T-berry doesn't stare into the demonic, legendary abyss, but looks downstream at several towering waves, then swings into a quick ferry. He pours on the power, straightens the neoprene autoclaved pontoons in the direction and speed of the current, and crashes us through a high spray of river water. We shoot our fists skyward in approval.

We beach at the campsite called Lower Ten Cent. Before the boat can be tied up, Bill leaps off and slips away through the tamarisk and trots upstream for cocktail hour at Brian's and Colin's Navtec camp below the Big Drops.

We've come an hour late to perform catch and release, so Brian has picked up the clients and pieces on his own, after Colin flipped his raft at Little Niagara. Normally jocular, both guides are uncharacteristically quiet, kicking the sand and trying to assemble a kitchen after losing their gear in the rapids.

Like the cooks of a century ago in the Brown Betty, the guides still have to get their Scottish clients Tim Hurton and Glenn Barnes to Lake Powell, and they have only a battered pot and a spare stove to feed them.

Glenn is still shell shocked as he tells us the story. When they flipped in Big Drop 2, they were aligned for disaster. While clinging to their black-side-up raft, Colin quipped to Tim that maybe Satan's Gut would flip them right side up; Tim blanched in horror, wondering if he would survive a second flip. Glenn ill-advisedly let go of the raft and tried to swim for shore. Within seconds, the current swept him far from the boat. Just as he signaled to Colin that he was okay by putting his hands atop his head, the corkscrewing Satan's Gut sucked him in. Instead of being whirlpooled down the evil drain, according to onlookers, the force of circulating water lifted and threw him 30 feet through the air into a midstream boulder. He could only remember fighting for every breath and being dragged across rocks. He hit sidelong and absorbed the impact with his body instead of his head, so he remained conscious and continued stroking hard for the bank.

The story comes out in reluctant stops and starts, like he's gasping for air all over again. Somehow, he reached shore fighting to breathe and "coughing my guts up." As he finishes the story, he looks again up into the sky, almost like he's asking forgiveness for sharing the tale of his survival so publicly. Glenn knows he's lucky to be alive.

Watching T-berry perform an inspection with Glenn's guides, Colin and Brian, it's hard to tell whether they're verbally subdued from this recent river spanking or naturally cowed in the presence of T-berry. Brian opens a small ammo box with a clank and a rattle, passes over his first aid certification to T-berry, and with a sweeping flourish, pulls out a large dildo from the same waterproof box. Brian, dressed in a black short-sleeve print shirt adorned with red chili peppers, waggles his latex toy up at the sky as if to taunt Park Service authority and Satan's Gut upstream. Because T-berry has observed plenty of machismo in Cataract Canyon, he pays no attention to the boatman's antics. If Brian continues guiding, his karma will eventually bring him full circle.

As we walk back to camp, T-berry explains that if guides don't see the significance of their near misses, clients do. These are life-changing events. If nothing else, flipping a raft and surviving the wicked hydraulic called Satan's Gut gives clients either a lifetime of bragging rights or a sense of redemption. They will reward their guides more handsomely in tip money for this than any other act on the river. (After giving generous gratuities,

Glenn and Tim would underwrite a night of celebration in a Moab saloon with their guides.)

Outside camp, T-berry nimbly jumps over crusted sections of biologic soil, also called cryptogam. Although he professes a lack of knowledge about the many plants surrounding us, he skips over a few more rocks in a continued show of deference to the black rumpled rug of microorganisms thrown over the sand. This live dirt used to cover most of the desert.

Dozens of frozen-looking footprints left by the less wary dent the two-inch-thick desert epidermis. Oblivious boaters have crunched through a minute yet thriving community of lichens, mosses, and cyanobacteria that fix nitrogen for surrounding plants. Long before the rocks around us were formed, as oceans covered the world to the depth that we're tiptoeing across on the Paradox Formation, cyanobacteria, or blue-green algae, lay above us as a great surface scum. Cyanobacteria absorbed carbon dioxide and created oxygen that made life flourish on planet Earth. For T-berry and me, the equation is simple: "Bust the crust" and we're literally squashing our own beginnings.

In the early 20th century, as domestic sheep and cattle overgrazed the bottom of Cataract Canyon, they trampled these live soils. In their droppings, they left spores for the invasive, long-rooted cheatgrass and Russian knapweed, which robs water from the living soil. Yet the most devastating change to these little-known yet abundant crusts comes from the unprecedented modern development in the Colorado River Basin.

Besides the disturbances in water flow, the soils are also vulnerable to climate change and off-road vehicles. Although the cyanobacteria can take decades to recover, lichens and mosses within the crusted soil need centuries. Botanists and snow scientists have recently determined that the destruction of these cryptogrammic soils creates another problem in the river basin. Without the protective rug of microorganisms holding onto rainwater, desert soils lose their wind resistance, turn into sand dunes, or blow away.

The dust is carried into the atmosphere and blown around the world. For the last two decades in my valley and along the mountains above Denver, prevailing westerly storms carry this red dust onto high-altitude snowfields and plaster the mountains. Isotope tracings and satellite pictures have proven that the dust storms come from disturbed desert soils.

Driving through the springtime Rockies, the visual effect is stunning. Most springs, the snow-covered mountains are glued over with a thin veneer of reddish brown dust as if they've been daubed with war paint. Instead of reflecting most of the sun's heat back into the air, the ground-up desert crust forces the snowpack to absorb the heat and melt several weeks early.* The premature runoff sends most of the snowmelt down into Lake Powell in May, and by July, the quickly evaporating reservoir's water supply is cut off until the next spring.

With Lake Powell still refilling, T-berry can run three more rapids that are normally covered by the reservoir. Seen through my 400-mm lens from the shore at Rapid 28, T-berry looks remarkably cool as the J-rig stern plops into a big hole. For a half minute, the boat disappears from view, but when T-berry pops back into sight, he's still standing rock solid at the tiller, coolly facing downstream.

Back on board I tell him, "You looked like you were out for a Sunday drive on that rapid."

Out of earshot from his apprentice, Ranger Snyder, T-berry confides: "Well, my outboard cut out, and I spent a frantic 30 seconds trying to restart it."

A couple miles later, the water slows and lightens from iced mocha to latte. As I point this out to T-berry, he yells back, "The cube root of the velocity equals carrying capacity." In other words, the reservoir has slowed the current so that it can no longer carry the dark-colored river silt, falling to the river bottom.

We pass Dark Canyon and its ancient cliff dwelling, now inundated by Lake Powell. Two hundred feet under silt and water are the remains of a rapid that Predambrian Era river runners thought the equal of any in the Grand Canyon. "Dark Canyon Rapid" dropped 25 feet in a mile, but may have had the quickest, sharpest drop of any rapid downstream from Gore Canyon. Sadly, Dark Canyon Rapid and 20 more have been stilled.

The rising reservoir is now submerging tamarisk and willow that haven't felt water this high for seven years. T-berry stands with a hand on each throttle as we speed across the lake. The twin Mercs are throwing up a rooster tail of water behind us. He's watching warily ahead for shifting islands of silt hidden just under the water. On my request, he pulls over to a high sandbank that lines the riverwide reservoir like dirty interstate snowplow berms. He cuts the engines. After two days of roaring rapids, the quiet of the lake is jarring. No birds sing. Even the wind is hushed.

---

*Over the last nine years, peak river flow into Lake Powell has occurred in May, except for one year when the peak flow came in early June. Over previous decades, June peak flows were common. Scientists believe this is caused more by Southwestern development—disturbing the biological soil crust—than climate change.

"One of the bad things about this place is that the lowering lake exposes human feces from recreational motorboaters without toilets," T-berry says. "Then the rising lake covers it all up again and raises the water's fecal count."

He scoops a handful of fine silt from a 20-foot-high bank plowed to a sudden stop by the reservoir. "But this is the final indignity," he says, letting the fine particulate sift through his fingers like a dropping hourglass. "One of the siltiest rivers in the world can no longer carry its mountains to the sea."

LAKE FOUL OR JEWEL OF THE COLORADO?

T-berry warned me not to paddle across Lake Powell amid the heat and crowds of summer. Still, with 900 miles remaining to the sea, I can't wait any longer. Plus, it will be interesting to experience the reservoir in its full glory during peak motorboating season. Each year, the reservoir draws over a million tourists who spend $500 million riding speedboats, recreational watercrafts, houseboats, skiffs, or any matter of floating craft powered by fossil fuels. Human- or wind-powered craft have no business being here.

Seen from a zoomed-out perspective on Google Earth, the lake resembles a lightning bolt zigzagging 180 miles across the desert, from the Cataract Canyon in Utah to the Grand Canyon in Arizona. Tourism bureaus boast that its canyon-cut shorelines are longer than the U.S. Pacific coast. Traveling in my freighted kayak, I can average only several miles an hour. So I'll need more than a week to reach Glen Canyon Dam.

I'm soon standing ankle-deep below the Hite Marina, cramming water jugs into my kayak. Like most boat launches, the shore reeks of fish guts. The marina is surrounded by the flooded mines of Hite City and White Canyon, which shut down its uranium mill in 1959. As the reservoir filled several years later, it inundated 20,000 pounds of radioactive tailings. The U.S. Department of Health, Education, and Welfare concluded that the lake would dilute any leaking radiation, the isolated site posed no risk, and that the river sediment would bury the tailings pile.

With my toes buried in the squishy substance, I can see that silt is a force to be reckoned with. Over 40 years, the 27-maf reservoir has lost 4 percent of its capacity as the river has deposited, according to Reisner's 1986 computation, an ocean liner's worth of silt each afternoon.

As the drought struck, the Park Service poured another concrete boat ramp. After the second ramp began drying in the desert sun like the first ramp, though, they gave up. Six years ago, the dry-docked marina closed. I'm standing far below the ramp on a slanting bed of silt recently covered with water—thanks to last winter's heavy snowfall—that temporarily resurrects Hite Marina.

Up above the concrete ramp are nine trucks parked with empty boat trailers. "This is the most business I've seen at Hite in six years," says Brett, the resident ranger for Glen Canyon National Recreation Area. He's been kind enough to let me park my car at his house. Apparently drug runners from south of the border are fond of utilizing the nearby dirt airstrip, then stealing cars parked at the secluded Hite Marina—although Brett denies this rumor. Because the recreation area's visitation numbers are parched by the drought, Park Service staff does not want to discourage more business.

Brett is watching me carefully, making note of how much water and survival gear I'm carrying. I have ballasted my kayak with the usual assortment of books and maps, ten days of food, two cameras, a shade umbrella, a tent, a sheet to sleep under, a foam sleeping pad, sun lotion, a flask of Glenfiddich scotch (red wine would only spoil in this heat), and ten gallons of water. Because I've given up on producing any more children, I might consider drinking from the lake if I'm dying of thirst. I've learned that desert travel is remarkably similar to subzero expeditions. Both require constant temperature regulation (here I can jump into the lake to stay cool) and plenty of water for hydration, to prevent frostbite or heat debility. Ranger Brett mentions heat stroke as a possibility—the 110-degree temperatures would fry an egg on an asphalt driveway—and I nod my head in agreement.

Rangers who dream of living in the great out-of-doors but who end up regularly handcuffing vacationing miscreants can't help being standoffish and authoritarian. By contrast, Brett is in a celebratory mood. He's just gotten word of his transfer to a park in Montana. Although the Department of the Interior is skimping on his moving costs, he's overjoyed—like most rangers seeking transfers from Glen Canyon National Recreation Area—that his exile on a polluted reservoir frequented by drunken boat drivers and sandstone graffiti vandals has come to an end.

At the crack of noon, inauspicious timing for desert travel, I push off with my feet in the air and paddle out where I can dip my toes overboard and rinse off the sticky silt. Large masses of driftwood clutter the low-angled lee shores. On steeper lees, the driftwood hangs more than 50 feet above like spiky hairdos styled by the receding reservoir.

It takes 20 minutes to paddle to each red buoy that marks a mile's progress toward the 140-mile-distant Glen Canyon Dam. Although I can often see the next buoy rising above the surface of the lake in a mirage, paddling each new mile is fatiguing. Sweat blocks my sunglasses. The air feels as thick as water every time I pull and push my double-bladed paddle. Although the water is a warm 80 degrees, compared to the three-digit air temperature, it feels remarkably cool. So at each new buoy, I cup my hands and allow myself a splashing reward in the face.

Wingate formations stretch hundreds of feet above me with sweeping hand cracks. If I still actively climbed rock, it would take me a long time to get to the dam. Amber-colored lizards perform push-ups on ledges. Walls with spalls cut by the wind aspire to archdom. Sandstone formations that Powell once stared at are still birthmarked with blackened cyanobacteria that breathe in carbon dioxide and pump out oxygen. Still, the air smells fecund, like something bad baking in the oven.

I've passed four carp floating belly up. Surely this is from fouled water rather than an old-age die-off. The fish are so renowned for sucking up decay that no sensible North American cooks dare to bring the species into their kitchens.

Five more buoys and I can't take it any more. Under the shade of an overhanging Chinle formation that looks like freeze-dried mud, I lay down on a thick white bed of invasive Asian shells. Before I close my eyes for a siesta, the profile of my mom's nose and undercut chin juts out above me.

More than a million years ago, volcanic activity built the Colorado River's first great dam. Unlike the puny Glen Canyon Dam, the lava flow of Prospect Dam rose a half mile above the river and backed up the ensuing lake all the way to Moab. The Colorado River took 20,000 years to dismantle Prospect Dam.

Over the millennia, a dozen lava dams followed, along with a dozen catastrophic floods. While the rising Colorado Plateau poured out billions of tons of superheated basalt, the heated anger of the underlying earth couldn't match the relentless flow of the Colorado River.

Ancient Puebloans engineered the first human-made dam in Glen Canyon a thousand years ago. For several hundred years above the main river, they held back a spring with a double-walled masonry dam, used to feed ditches. Six hundred years later, backed up by Glen Canyon Dam, the waters buried the dam and over two thousand ruin sites.

The flooding of this reservoir in 1963 galvanized the modern environmental movement. As a trade-off to save Dinosaur National Monument on the Green River from being flooded by Echo Park Dam, the Sierra Club and other environmental groups conceded to flooding the waters of Glen Canyon. Called *The Place No One Knew* in a coffee-table book eulogy, Lake Powell has become the symbol of environmental tragedy caused by reservoirs. In place of a hushed, exploratory wonderland, the flooded canyons now host the masses for motorboat recreation. According to Wallace Stegner, "In creating the lovely and the usable, we have given up the incomparable."

On July 4, my first full day on the lake, I leave at sunrise and paddle almost 20 miles before the heat and headwind force me to slump lower in the plastic butt bucket. As I draw within a dozen miles of the popular Halls Crossing and Bullfrog Marina extended boat launches, the lake is congested with motorboats. I pass under a brilliant burgundy Wingate wall holding a majestic football-field-width black varnish of microscopic creatures inside iron oxides, like a living blanket sent from the carbon-rich heavens to smother global warming. Its billions of cyanobacteria spores ventilate double-time to boat traffic spewing carbon dioxide.

In the growing wake, I repeatedly paddle-brace to avoid capsizing. High vertical walls on either side of the lake amplify the man-made waves, whipped higher by the west wind. Many of the boat drivers are lofting cans of liquid refreshment as their water-skiers race past, repeatedly splashing me. Yet the unpredictable traffic keeps me more alert than a game of dodgeball. I'm sipping from a long-strawed backpack of drinking water, occasionally swallowing anti-inflammatory tablets to preserve clicking wrists and shoulders while paddling at a speed that seems like slow motion. Although I have a Day-Glo orange bicycle flag waving from a wand several feet above my head, and I know that the traffic might see me clearly enough not to run me over, not a soul from more than a hundred passing boats has waved back or acknowledged me. A kayaker is persona non grata.

Whether they're bikini-clad women, corpulent fishermen, laughing teenagers, or muscular skiers—they're having fun, and I'm not. So maybe they're just leaving me alone to my misery as I continue slogging away, like a windup toy battling across a bubbling hot tub of noisy motor jets.

In the sandy cove of Sundog Bar, occupied by two houseboats, I pull my kayak up onto a protected shore. The calcium carbonate brine caking my legs matches the high-water stains up on the sandstone walls. The temperature has cooled to 102 degrees, and I pitch a shade tarp along a sparse grove of tamarisk, oddly free of beetles.

Although I've sipped three gallons from my imported water supply, I'm dehydrated and wracked by diarrhea—probably caused by accidentally swallowing a few microbes of E. coli–tainted reservoir water. So I break out some electrolyte drink mix and wash down another two tablets of Pepto-Bismol. I'm sharing the shade with a similarly lethargic-looking canyon wren. Its long down-curved bill, white throat, and red tail form a stark contrast to the green-feathered fronds of tamarisk. We watch one another, *Catherpes mexicanus* and *Homo erectus,* eye to eye. Then he sings out the descending notes that could easily be mistaken as a memorial dirge to a river-gone-reservoir. It begins as a cascading whistle, "*Twi twi twi!*" falling into a pool, "*Towi towi towi*" broken by the final and slow "*toowi toowi toowi.*"

The song cheers me up, as if I'm not alone in lamenting the river. I spring to action by cleaning up the beer cans, cigarette butts, and used toilet paper on my sandy campsite surrounded by old fire pits. Because my stern compartment will fit a five-pound trash bag, I stuff it all up out of reach with a paddle.

To cool off, I dive six feet under into the lake's surface, down to a cold-water layer not yet warmed by the relentless sun. Curious carp circle my legs, gasping around me with overblown white tuba lips. Introduced to the river in the 1880s, these scaly Asian weed feeders grow over two feet long and dominate the reservoir bottom. If not for a lack of sharp teeth, my toes and other appendage would be fish food. I burst back onto the surface just as my neighbors pull up in a small boat pushing a lot of horsepower.

"See any boils?" asks a jovial giant, wearing a Broncos T-shirt and holding a beer.

"Not since the rapids of Cataract Canyon," I say, "it's been flat since then." We introduce ourselves, and he explains that boils are caused by bass coming to the surface to feed. Harvey invites me to their 40-foot houseboat for drinks and dinner. I pull on my T- shirt, grab my camera, and he drives us across the small cove.

Inside their houseboat, a double-wide trailer on two floats, the air conditioner is turned on high. Gooseflesh breaks over my arms. Harvey's smiling wife, Elvira, presses a margarita into my hand to remove me one step farther from the desert.

Harvey introduces me to his buddy, Homer, in his early forties: "Meet Jon, he's an *environmentalist* kayaker." No one misses the emphasis in my introduction. Then he adds, with a wide, lopsided smile, "Guess who we're eating for dinner!"

"Since we only met a minute ago," I ask Harvey in a friendly tone, "what makes you think I'm an environmentalist?"

"I smelled it soon as you stepped on my boat. You need a bath, you don't have water skis or a fishing rod, and you take a lot of pictures." Harvey good-naturedly presses a Miller Lite into my free hand and continues chatting.

He's now celebrating the best part of his high school gym teaching career: June, July, and half of August. Harvey says he's a progressive Utah resident, and this—sweeping his arm toward Homer and his wife, Lulu, and Elvira—is not an LDS crowd, even though he adds: "The *Deseret News* obituary section is famous for the line: *He loved his lake.*"

Homer works for a power company, and the two women are in real estate. Everything about these good-looking, amusing couples—upwardly mobile Utah Con-Libs—shows that they have found their peace here on their lake, away from ringing telephones.

A platter of pork chops is handed to me and I politely pass it on, taking an extra large helping of potato salad instead. Harvey looks at me in wide-eyed astonishment: "Don't tell me you're a vegetarian?"

I smile back, "I won't."

"Then I'll have yours," he says, reaching over my shoulder and helping himself to the last pork chop.

"I've been reading Powell's *Exploration of the Colorado River,*" I remark.

"Yeah," Homer bites, "an amazing explorer."

"Also a visionary for his reclamation plans for the West," I add. "I'd bet he's spinning in his grave with this lake named after him. Because he didn't believe in irrigating the desert."

Silence . . . *oops.* Homer stops chewing, Lulu looks away from the table, Elvira looks amused, and Harvey's eyes go to a squint.

I quickly change the subject: "Anyone read any interesting books this summer?" More silence. Then I hit bingo by asking Homer how he catches striped bass. Although not much is involved aside from a good lure and casting into the boils, finding the boils is a trick. He gets out his tackle box to show me his best lures—which mimic shrimp and small fish.

They turn off the generator-powered air conditioner because the gas will cost them over a grand for the weeklong vacation,. We throw our paper plates into the trash and move out to the stern deck. "Back to the contemplation of the great out-of-doors," Harvey says, "for our good ol' nature boy!" He slaps my shoulder. He then gestures to the water-cupped-out holes of sandstone—huecos—on the low-angled Wingate above their boat.

"You like natural history, right?"

"Yes," I reply, perking up at the potential of finding common ground. Harvey has taken off his shirt, and he has a way of pressing his six feet four inches close enough and flexing his biceps repeatedly enough so that any sensible soul can see that it's best to agree with the big man. "Those big huecos are caused by pissing Miller," he points. "The small ones are caused by pissing Bud. That's why you will be seeing so many big huecos on this lake."

I smile gamely.

Homer asks, "You know where all those so-called pictographs came from up in Moab?"

"Yes," I reply, taking the bait again, "I'm a fan. I've spent a lot of time coming to the desert to look at them."

"Well then," Homer goes on, "then you know as well as I that the mayor of Moab drew them to stimulate the tourism business." Harvey is laughing, so I join in briefly too, just to let them see that I'm a good sport.

Harvey tells me that the rock climbing is no good here because "the sandstone is too brittle to accept the hammered-in wedges." I don't mention that pitons were banned decades ago because they destroy the sought-after hand cracks throughout the desert. Elvira and Lulu are nodding their heads intently. It seems best to remain silent, nod, and not rock the boat.

Homer suddenly turns deadpan and asks what I'm doing here.

I reply, "To learn why everyone loves this lake so much."

I tell them about my journey to Mexico, estimating it'll take another couple months of paddling. "Why," asks Harvey, "would anyone want to do something like that?"

"To see what's left of the river and learn what's at stake for my sons," I reply.

Homer, a crew-cut veteran of Lake Powell, says with an uncharacteristic furrow across his graying brow, "There's people who want to drain this lake." He looks me right in the eye because I'm the only one accused of being an enviro. "Heaven help us if we come to that because it'll be war."

"I've never been here before, so I haven't decided what I believe yet," I reply. "Maybe you can share with me what's at stake?"

"You bet!" Harvey roars. "We'll hit the fireworks tonight at Bullfrog and you'll see what you've been missing!" He lifts open the cooler and passes around another round of Miller Lites, even though I'm still wondering how

I can graciously get away with pouring out the warm, barely sipped can in my other hand. Although I don't mind Harvey downgrading me to a "pussy environmentalist" for drinking so slowly, refusing a beer among a tribe like this might be perceived as an insult to all that they hold holy.

That's not all I have on my mind. I made a promise to my family that I would survive the Colorado River. Yet Bullfrog Basin is more than a dozen miles away, it's getting dark, and thousands of drunken boaters are reputed to crowd into the bay to witness the Fourth of July fireworks. According to Ranger Brett, the spectacle so stirs onlookers with patriotism that fights break out, boats crash, and the victims get airlifted to distant hospitals.

Homer has only had ten beers. Although Harvey claims that he's a more advanced drinker, having raised the level of the lake this evening with his Miller Lite output, even he seems to know that his dedicated effort toward "solving the supposed drought problem" will disqualify him from driving us to the event. Only Homer will be allowed to touch the powerful controls of his finely tuned speedboat. As Harvey steps aside to continue filling the lake, Homer whispers that he has a hundred more horses on his runabout boat tied to the houseboat's starboard than Harvey's runabout tied to port.

Before I know it, holding a beer in each hand, I'm being whisked off to Bullfrog Basin at 40 miles an hour, faster than I've ever traveled in a small boat. We're surrounded by ominously shadowed sandstone walls. The lake is black, sloshing, and unfamiliar to me. And Harvey nixed my request to grab a PFD from the kayak.

Homer discusses the number of hours he's worked on the engine, how the runabout ($20,000) costs more than his houseboat ($10,000), and how he lives for his time on the lake. "It used to be a mess, toilet paper and beer cans everywhere, but now it's been cleaned up," he says as he tosses the beer can overboard.

I try to concentrate on his words and trust that he won't hit anything—a swimmer, driftwood, or a rock—in the dark, even though Harvey is shining a powerful floodlight off the bow. "I come here to water ski, go tubing [being dragged behind a boat in an inflated truck-sized tube], play [water] basketball, go Jet Skiing," Homer yells with one finger loosely hooked over the wheel, the other hand fully encircling the koozie-insulated beer just handed to him by Harvey. "If I can't do those things, I *fish*."

I feel oddly privileged that these jack Mormons have taken me in. They've invited me to drinks and dinner in their floating home. Now they're taking me out to share in a holiday ritual so coveted as a summer highlight that thousands of people haul in boats from hundreds of miles away. We come from different walks of life, so I'm struggling to find our common denominator, and I haven't a clue what it might be.

As we turn out of the darkened and cliffed passageway five hundred feet above the Colorado riverbed, we arc northwest into the eight-mile-wide Bullfrog Basin. We're confronted by a sea of red and green lights, bobbing from the port and starboard sides of hundreds, no, *thousands* of boats. I try to take it all in. The lights of the distant marina and hundreds of cars alternately hit their red glowing brake lights and flash their high beams along the shore, illuminating long, sandy beaches. The stars are dim by comparison. Boat air horns blare. Stereos broadcast the bass beat of rock and country music. Above the din, we can make out the clipped voice of bullhorned authority bellowing from a National Park Service boat, trying to restore order within the chaotic, jostling parking lot that has no speed limits or yellow lines, and even less sobriety. Although the wind has stilled, the churning of thousands of propellers and cheering revelers jumping up and down on their boats has created an artificial wave action. More times than I can count, we're fended off from crashing into other crafts with boat poles and Harvey's strong arms. I've never seen such a spectacle. It'll be tough for the fireworks to top this scene.

Each time we free ourselves from another hull, Harvey goes back to working the floodlight, shining it, I assume, toward the waterline of other boats so that Homer can see where he's driving. Still, curses are directed toward our boat as we avoid each new near collision. Lulu remains below. Homer shouts directions. Elvira and I watch silently, and I sense a passing kinship if only because we're both trying to keep our sense of humor without showing how aghast we feel about the surrounding mayhem.

As the first Fourth of July blast concusses our eardrums and lights up the sky with a purple mushroom of sparks that sends an audible "Ohhhhhhh" throughout the bay, I catch a glimmer of Homer's and Harvey's excitement. This is not awe though—this is the primal anticipation before seeing a quarterback sacked. I can't imagine how we'll extricate ourselves when the show stops and everyone races through the dark chaos back to their private floating double-wides, replete with televisions, microwaves, and swamp coolers. I briefly consider swimming ashore, but given the odds of getting diced up by propellers, it seems smarter to remain aboard.

Under the cover of darkness, I've poured out the two beers and put the crushed cans in my pocket. I've even managed to fend off Harvey's end-the-drought campaign of beer refills by clutching my camera with the hand that's not clenching the boat rail.

The explosions in the sky above have at least quelled the shouting. Lulu has emerged from below decks, shyly trying to master her motion sickness. Harvey hits the jackpot by shining the floodlight directly into the cockpit of a Park Service patrol boat. As soon as the ranger recovers his sight, he steers over, and with a clunking shift into neutral, he angrily rushes out of his pilothouse like he's about to clear leather with his sidearm.

"Put that floodlight down and stop shining it in people's eyes!" he screams. "What the fuck are you thinking?" Harvey deserves to be dressed down, in light of what I now recognize as reckless behavior behind the floodlight, but a short fuse is not the best tool for park visitors in need of an education.

As soon as the ranger drives out of earshot, Homer complains: "Every experience I've had with the Nazi rangers is like that. They stop us and tell us not to stand up in our boats, but then they do nothing about moving hazardous logs from mid-channel. They try to tell us how to be safe in our lake, but what do they know about driving a boat like mine?" He gives his instrument panel an adoring pat and takes a long calming swig of beer.

The grand finale explosion signals everyone that it's time to race back to their camps. The basin suddenly roars to life, filled with the fumes of ancient hydrocarbons. Homer pulls down the throttle, swings the boat back toward canyon darkness and, as Lulu retreats back below, we thud through a reservoir gone bipolar with cross-directional waves. In a perfect storm of alcohol-enhanced skippers, we skid away from one near collision after another, as Harvey resumes his position on the bowsprit, hollering and gesturing and blinding those boat drivers whom Captain Miller Lite can't outpower.

"Homer," I shout, "do you have any PFDs?"

He shouts to his mate below decks. Down in the tight berth, as we thud and bang through the chop—where Lulu's motion sickness has forced her to worship the porcelain god—she should be wearing a helmet. She appears seconds later, white as a ghost, and hands me up a life jacket. Up on the bow, standing like the Statue of Liberty clutching a cowboy hat crown on his head while his other hand shines the beacon, Harvey lip-synchs another "pussy" in my direction as Elvira and I tighten down our PFDs.

"Scared?" she says, not entirely sympathetic.

"You bet," I nod.

Homer has slid his beer into the gyroscopically mounted cup holder so that he can clutch the wheel like a fighter pilot. I crouch down low, death-gripping my seat so that a sudden crash won't propel me overboard.

After half an hour's carnival ride through darkness, with my kidneys badly shaken, we succeed in beating or intimidating those nocturnal motorheads who unwisely chose to jockey with us back up the lake. Now Homer's only challenge is navigation. He can't find Sundog Cove. The air is thick with gray smoke that stings our eyes. "Fires in California are screwing me up," Homer says. "Normally I can find my way home in the dark easy."

Harvey points excitedly toward every other cove. Lulu emerges, looking spent, and offers a comment about slowing down, but Homer curtly sends her back below decks: "I know what I'm doing, *honey*." While he and Harvey bicker about where to turn, Elvira smiles coyly at me, as though to acknowledge that the evening's farce has not gone unappreciated.

For five hours after dawn, I paddle across glassine waters. Alone on the reservoir, I relax and try to absorb what the infamous Reclamation commissioner Floyd Dominy wrote in his 1965 booklet "Lake Powell: Jewel of the Colorado":

> Sired by the muddy Colorado in magnificent canyon country, a great blue lake has been born in the West. . . . Lake Powell holds working water—water for many purposes. And one of those purposes is to provide the people of this country with the finest scenic and recreational area in the Nation.

In his office, Floyd Dominy hung a photograph of himself arm in arm with his engineer son who built dams with the Corps of Engineers, speeding across this lake in a motorboat. In these activities, Dominy described finding "peace. And a oneness with the world and God." The fearless commissioner, described by former Secretary of the Interior Stewart Udall as a marauding elephant, happened to be a bully, an alcoholic, and an unrepentant borrower of wives who played every political trick in the book to plug up more rivers and build his own power base. He demanded passage on Air Force One and convinced Congress to give him his own airplane. After the zenith of his political career, Glen Canyon Dam, he built a monument to himself with the first skyscraper that went up in Denver, falsely cloaking the building expenses under budget line items as another dam. Today bureau workers in Denver call it the Federal Center.

Fired for his excesses by the Nixon administration, Dominy truly believed that the only good river was a dammed river. He even held until late in his life that the Grand Canyon, like Glen Canyon, would have been better off as a reservoir because recreational lake tourism outstripped the usefulness of mere national parks. To his credit, the former commissioner never tried to dodge an interview. He loved the limelight along with a good debate. In a 1994 interview, Dominy identified himself as "Satan personified" to the nascent environmental community. During a 2000 interview, when he was in his early nineties, he said that his name should have been "Dominate."

The dominant dam building years have long since waned. In the new millennium, Reclamation mostly provides janitorial services and obeys water calls delivered to concrete creations like Dominy's. In 2006, Reclamation published its version of the story in a book called *The Bureau of Reclamation: Origins and Growth to 1945*. After several pages devoted to "Dominy's Drive and Energy," the author William Rowley tells of a divide in the agency: "Some use the word 'decline' and others describe a 'beleaguered Bureau of Reclamation.'" In the seventies, the agency schizophrenically changed its name to Water and Power Resources Service, then back again. In the 1990s, a progressive new commissioner, Daniel Beard, identified revised priorities: water conservation, mitigation of environmental problems, power and water for urban communities, support for Native American water rights, and so on. As political regimes shift, so flows reclamation. In 2002, although the White House denied climate change, yet another Reclamation began talking about working "with all water users to leverage resources and make use of developed water supplies."

Today the agency remains surprisingly top-heavy with engineers. Reclamation still labors under the outsize stigma of Floyd Dominy, trapped in a back eddy as the societal mainstream pushes government to sustain dwindling natural resources. Dominy thought of conservationists as "posy sniffers," and although this manly point of view still finds voice in the backwoods of America, contemporary naturalists in the desert Southwest harken to the call of author Ed Abbey.

Abbey denied being a naturalist, even though his first nonfiction natural history book, *Desert Solitaire*, received wide critical acclaim.* His most

---

Abbey promoted civil disobedience by recommending that readers throw their beer cans along highways, while his fictional characters poured sugar in bulldozer gas tanks and chainsawed down billboards. His own calling, he insisted, was that of a novelist. Eight of Abbey's novels remain in print as cult hits, many of them loosely based on his own life of defending wilderness and free rivers. In his nonfiction stories and lectures, he decried overpopulation and consumption of natural resources while fathering many children with several wives and proudly driving a gas-guzzling, pink Cadillac.

popular book, *The Monkey Wrench Gang,* details a half-fictional gang of idealists who dream of blowing up Glen Canyon Dam, while being chased by its Mormon defenders.

Abbey's explorations of the desert Southwest gave him a knowledge base and a platform that allowed him to plunge a knife into the underbelly of what he called "industrial tourism." He also held forth on the evils of the "techno industrial military complex." Before development changed the Southwest, he floated Glen Canyon for ten days in 1959. In 1967, he worked as a ranger for five months in Bullfrog Basin. In his 1981 essay, "The Damnation of a Canyon," Abbey accurately foresaw that Hite Marina would have to be abandoned in 20 or 30 years.

He complained about "Jewel of the Colorado" being published under taxpayer expense through the Government Printing Office, and scoffed that Dominy's idea of getting closer to God meant "about five hundred feet closer. Eh, Floyd?"

Abbey closed the essay by setting Dominy straight on the ultimate Creator:

Within a generation—thirty years—I predict the river and canyons will bear a decent resemblance to their former selves. Within the life-time of our children Glen Canyon and the living river, heart of the canyonlands, will be restored to us. The wilderness will again belong to God, the people, and the wild things that call it home.

Because those who don't know history are doomed to repeat it, I try to imagine what these canyons looked like from Abbey's and Powell's perspectives, five hundred feet below, riding a winding canyon river unslicked by motor oil. I stop to stretch my cramping legs below a series of Moqui steps, carved out of the rock by ancient peoples, leading down to the river—if not for the drought, the steps would be underwater. I curl my fingers into inch-deep holds and find that the impossibly steep rock has been made into a ladder, even though the discreetly scraped-out steps would have been invisible to passing river enemies.

Like all boatmen since Stanton, I pull out my copy of Powell. One hundred and thirty-nine years ago, he wrote about climbing up above this section of the river: "I search about for a few minutes for an easier way, when I am surprised at finding a stairway, evidently cut in the rock by hands. . . . Here I stand, where these now lost people stood centuries ago, and look over this strange country, gazing off to great mountains in the northwest. . . ."

In the immaculate waters of Glen Canyon, he found a poetic voice to replace his upstream exaggerations about Cataract Canyon's waterfalls. He described immense sandstone walls that looked as if they'd been carved with an architectural purpose.

As motorboaters sleep off the previous day's excesses, I can almost imagine the place that Powell first wrote about. Still, as I put in the requisite miles before another day begins, I'm wishing for a scuba tank to see what's hidden below.

Nearing the gas station and overpriced grocery store at Halls Crossing, in the building wake of waterskiers and motorboaters, I paddle through the lee shelter of hundreds of vacant houseboats floating amid the beer cans. In the shade of a picnic area on a massive floating dock, I wash down more Pepto-Bismol with a gallon of cold electrolyte drink. At midday, the marina comes alive with boatmen sport drinkers, filling coolers with ice, as their children feed Wonder bread to a school of over a hundred carp next to sign that reads "DON'T FEED THE FISH," until a Park Service woman chases the kids away. The woman disappears; the carp wait five minutes, the kids return, and the feeding cycle resumes.

At the floating National Park Service office, the on-duty ranger is still bleary-eyed from Bullfrog Basin's Fourth of July madness. "Seven thousand people crowded into that bay to watch the fireworks," he says. "No one died. A miracle."

I recognize his modulated voice. Even in his air-conditioned office, he's tightly wound, ready for gun-slinging action.

He tells me that the crowds are flagging compared to other summers. Gas prices have made everyone wary about traveling the lake, and those who still come to pay homage to the two-stroke engine are sticking much closer to the marinas. I ask about the highlight of the holiday, and he tells me about a big, obnoxious drunk on a boat, blinding other boat drivers with a floodlight. "I should've thrown the whole boatload in jail to dry out for the night."

"Sounds familiar," I say, subtly sliding my camera back around my back so that he won't recognize the Canon I wore while photographing Harvey and company.

"We get all types," he says, running his hand over his shining hair and a neatly trimmed Fu Manchu. "Every year about six deaths, a murder, a rape, and lots of would-be cliff divers."

I point to the stunning Park Service poster, plastered throughout every marina on the lake, featuring six sequential photos of a man in 75-foot freefall off a Wingate precipice toward an unforgivably hard landing on the reservoir. Given the end result, it seems an ill-considered campaign—a Siren's song to the hormonally challenged—for the Park Service to promote such an activity by blowing up the photos and labeling it dangerous. "Seems like a very nonsubtle advertisement to invite more cliff divers?" I ask.

"An interesting frontal cave-in of a skull," he replies, dodging my question, to talk about the jumper's death, "because he looked down at the last instant and that made his day."

The ranger is cool amid the day's strange humidity, squinting with steely, brown-eyed curiosity at the sweat running down the side of my face as if he's seen me before. He has. No sense getting him pissed off again. So I pull my ball cap visor down lower, continue to distract him with questions, and eventually find common ground if only because of my former employment as a ranger—performing rescues rather than law enforcement. Like Brett, today is this ranger's last day of eight years of service on the reservoir before transferring to a southern Arizona park, where he's looking forward to more straightforward visitor contacts: arresting drug runners crossing the border. I thank him for his time.

On the desk is a pile of brochures, and because I'm hooked by the opening line advertising Glen Canyon National Recreation Area—"Throughout history man has altered . . ."—I take a brochure back to my reading area in the shade. Then I wait like a lizard for nightfall to begin.

Out of nowhere, rain then hail comes down in angry torrents, threatening to punch holes in the floating marina and blow it away, but within minutes, it's hot and sunny again and people emerge from the boats complaining about the weather.

This is the Southwest summer monsoon cycle. Although "monsoon" is commonly defined by the tropical Asian phenomenon, this regular North American summer event has provided scant relief from the long drought. Unlike the winter winds that bring rain and snow from the west, the summer monsoonal shift to southern winds, combined with low pressure over the Sonoran and Mojave Deserts, pushes up moisture from Mexico. Thunderstorms are often the result.

When darkness falls, I creep off behind a thick stand of tamarisk and clandestinely camp within a stone's throw of the ranger station. As I do every night, I write in my journal, trying to make sense of this artificial lake that I've deliberately avoided throughout three decades of living in the West. The people that I've been observing for the last few days would not come to Glen Canyon if it still contained a wild river. By virtue of taming its waters behind a massive concrete wall, the government has delivered some implicit guarantee of security, as though we have achieved the goals of Manifest Destiny: vanquishing the wilderness that our forebearers feared in the American West. Without engines to help our species master the waters safely, the lake would be empty. Except for a few paddlers.

The whole chaotic scene is beginning to make sense to me. I write:

Lake = accessible recreation area

River = wilderness + danger

I circle it, close the journal, and twist off my headlamp. Now it's time to try and enjoy what's left.

When Powell and his men rowed through the last miles of Glen Canyon in early August 1869, they shot another desert bighorn, which helped curb their growing hunger. This time they dried the meat, so it wouldn't spoil like the sheep they'd shot up in Cataract Canyon. The men frequently grumbled about Powell's leadership, along with disparaging his wild-eyed brother, Captain Walter Powell, performing sorrowful songs in a deep baritone and nursing his post-traumatic stress syndrome from the war. If not for Jack Sumner's intervention up in the rapids of Cataract, pulling the oxlike Walter out of the river by his hair, he would have drowned a crewmate who showed disrespect to the Major. Sumner, the wanna-be mountain man, believed the captain suffered from a bad case of "petticoat dementia," or syphilis.

In the pacifying waters of Glen Canyon, the Major was so moved by his brother's singing of the angry ballad "Old Shady," he named the reverberating cavern Music Temple. The ballad of an escaped slave showed the brothers' devotion to the Civil War cause and their upbringing by a staunch abolitionist father.

In the meantime, Sumner and the other men rowed their boats tight to the walls, following the current's gentle riffles, while the captain and the major shouted out obvious directions downstream—further irking each boat's pair of rowers. The muddy waters rippled with native chubs, suckers, and pike minnows. The worrywart George Bradley wrote in his journal, "Fish were very plenty as we passed along today, but they will not bite as they get plenty to eat all along; where the water is still we could see them catching small flies that that river seems covered with."

Near a castellated butte shaped like a gun sight, they found recently bleached cattle bones from Ute and Navajo rustlers, who forded the muddy Colorado with animals rustled from Mormon settlements to the west. Here at the Crossing of the Fathers, for the second time since Green River, Wyoming, they intersected the trail of earlier explorers.

In July 1776, in Santa Fe, a Spanish city for 171 years, businessmen dreamed up a journey that would later inspire Jefferson to launch the Lewis and Clark expedition. The Spanish wanted to establish a trade route to their mission in Monterey, California, and bring Christianity to the heathens throughout the territory with an eye toward eventual colonization.

Ever since 1540, when Hernando de Alarcón rowed from the sea to present-day Yuma, Arizona, followed by one of Coronado's men discovering the Grand Canyon, the river had fired the popular imagination of Spaniards. Alarcón first named it El Río del Buena Guia (River of Good Guidance). Later Spaniards named it the River of Burnt Wood, and finally, the Colorado (or Red) River.

Among a dozen horseback riders, in 1776, were the Spanish priests Franco Dominguez and Silvestre Velez, often called Escalante after his hometown. They traced the eastern edge of the Colorado River Basin, following the North Star toward Wyoming. After shooting and jerking the meat from a lone bison, they forded the Green River, which they named Río San Buenaventura long before the mountain men arrived. They got lost, nearly died of thirst, and evaded Shoshone raiding parties as their supplies dwindled and they cut new holes in their belts. The devoted diarist Escalante wrote, "The horses began to be deprived of their lives so we would not have to forfeit ours."

Although the leader Bernardo de Miera argued with the priests to continue to Monterey, Dominguez and Escalante outvoted him. So they turned back east, praying to find a direct route back to Santa Fe.

They searched for ten days, passing up the Pariah River leading to Lees Ferry and found the only route—later named the Crossing of the Fathers—penetrating more than a hundred miles of steep canyons. They cut footsteps with their axes down a short section of steep slickrock for their horses to reach the Colorado River. Down on the canyon bottom, desert bighorn tracks potholed the sand so densely it looked as if a domestic sheep herd had passed through.

"We were stopped for a long time by a strong blizzard and tempest consisting of rain and thick hailstones amid horrendous thunder claps and lightning flashes," Escalante wrote in his elegant script on November 6, during a period that tree rings show as a prolonged drought. "We recited the Virgin's litany, for her to implore some relief for us, and God willed for the tempest to end." The next day, with the river at low ebb, they walked across. Escalante laconically described firing guns in celebration.

Nine days later, they reached the Hopi village of Orabai. After a rest, they passed north of Humphreys Summit and onto Santa Fe on January 2, 1777. Their exploration had taken them 2,000 miles across unmapped country. In the boldly inked map that Bernardo de Miera produced a year later, he shows their route taking them by the "Río San Juan," then around Moab through the Spanish Fork and the Dolores River. The map repeatedly and mistakenly labeled other rivers the Río Colorado.

Forty years later, their route opened up the Spanish Trail to California. After this climax of expansionism, Spain gave up New Mexico, New Spain, and the river—its southern portion marked "Tierra in Cognita" on the Spanish map. After California was mapped by the gold rush, the map of the Southwest still contained a blank section below the Crossing of the Fathers. Although the Army Corps of Topographical Engineers produced another map in 1855, it revealed nothing new, except for the bold and single word superimposed over southern Utah and Arizona: "unexplored." Powell couldn't resist.

To beat the heat on this scorching day, I boat several miles north up into the shade of a snaking labyrinth through a flooded canyon. The Escalante River had been named after the Spanish father by a member of Powell's 1872 expedition. Above the reservoir most of the year, the Colorado tributary is a 20-cfs creek, but to the delight of kayakers checking USGS online river gauges, it swells tenfold during floods.

Several miles up the drowned Escalante, I turn due west into a narrower canyon, past the sky blue eye of La Gorce Arch, lapped by the reservoir's high watermark. If not for the motorboats, time would stand still in these canyons. Although half-flooded, the wind and water-hewn rock still fires the imagination.

Lizards flicker into fissures just beyond the grasp of a canyon wren bobbing in and out of the shadows. The air alternately cools in the shade and glows on walls stretching hundreds of feet toward the thin sliver of sky. Two-stroke engines echo up and down the canyon.

I wave to families, old folks, and even the waterskiers. And why not? Whether they've been inspired by Dominy or Abbey, we're all here to explore, and the wonder of what remains will inevitably imprint us all, like the varnish staining the walls above.

I stop and camp at the final waterfall splashing out of Davis Gulch. The pictographs on an adjoining cave wall were made famous by a 1955 *National Geographic* magazine story. Holding a copy of the photograph in front of my face, I pinpoint the exact location, several feet above my head. The remnant white gypsum dots of anthropomorphic beings clad in strange armor were drawn by ancient Puebloans a thousand years ago. I set up a tripod and rephotograph the remains. The once extensive mural has been whited out by the mineral-rich, receding reservoir and the recently scratched-in, four-foot-high graffiti reading, "USA."

Twenty miles down the Colorado River, I paddle into the red-walled Music Temple. Young men on recreational watercrafts circle like overgrown hornets. The amphitheatre of high sandstone is shrunken by the reservoir, although the acoustics still work, judging by the whine of two-stroke engines deafeningly echoing against rock.

Powell described the 200-foot-high walls where his brother regaled them in his baritone at their campsite. They were shaded by box elder and cottonwood trees, with a deep pool of green-rimmed water, all lit by a narrow fissure of sky. Here, at the height of his descriptive powers about the river, Powell built wonder through context and his delight at finding an oasis amid the arid canyons.

Nowadays, the grove of trees are deeply submerged, the pool inundated, and instead of moss, the rock is caked with bathtub rings. Although the curving natural band shell formation is unusual, in a drowned state, it's hard to see it as a place that inspired Powell to write that it had been "made for an academy of music by its storm-bound architect."

Asking if Powell would approve of this reservoir being named after him frames the controversy that pits tourism bureaus against those who believe in free rivers. The answer can be found, in part, by traveling the reservoir as the Major did—rowing or paddling—with his book close at hand.

Floyd Dominy, who named the reservoir after Powell, said in a recent interview:

Powell probably had more to do with the enactment of the federal reclamation project act than any one individual. He'd been making speeches and writing about the development of the west being dependent strictly on the management of water, that you couldn't have a large population in a semi-arid and arid area, unless you had a water supply that was dependable and the erratic western streams were not dependable without storage.

Yet in Powell's 1878 call to reform, *Report on the Arid Lands,* he advocated a stripped-down irrigation of efficient farms built close to water. During his later congressional-supported "Irrigation Survey," he espoused community-controlled, small dams rather than government projects. Powell grew up working his family's small wheat farm in Wisconsin—so in later life, he was naturally drawn to support small, sustainable irrigation rather than the agribusiness and desert cities that mega reservoirs would supply. He warned against developing the American desert.

So the swamped Music Temple has lost the source of Powell's poetry. He would not have traded massive irrigation and flood prevention, new jobs, and the reservoir's tourism for the loss of Glen Canyon's natural treasures. The reservoir has desecrated both his memory and his longstanding patriotic service.

On my fifth night out, camped on a kayak-sized beach, I watch the stars wink between steady yellow tracers of circling satellites and blinking airliners bound for the West Coast. I've escaped the houseboats under these walls of towering sandstone, glowing red under the new moon. I dive into the cooling lake and then stand naked on a high dome of slickrock. Bass dimple the water. Tamarisks sigh in a cooling breeze. The San Juan River confluence is marked below with a flashing yellow beacon, but the tributary that once contributed two maf per year is now no more than another amputated arm of the reservoir.

On the evening of November 12, 1922, politicos at a posh lodge in New Mexico divided the San Juan and other Colorado tributaries down to the last acre-foot. The seven-member state representatives for the Colorado River Compact came to a handshake agreement about divvying up the water. According to the minutes, Stephen Davis, vying for New Mexico's Colorado River appropriations through the San Juan water, said only "aye" after an hour and a half, as the party agreed to split the Colorado River in two at Lees Ferry. New Mexico, unlike the six other states, did not adjoin the river, and its main source of water, the Río Grande, had been taken by farmers.

The representatives also knew that most of the Colorado River water comes from the state of Colorado. Even the San Juan (formerly one-eighth the volume of the main-stem Colorado) drains an area the size of West Virginia from four corners of the mountainous states surrounding it. Although New Mexico has more land along the river than Arizona, Utah, or Colorado, the San Juan Mountains of Colorado provide 90 percent of the namesake river's snowmelt. Among the four major tributaries of the Colorado River, the 400-mile San Juan is the shortest and the saltiest. Like the bigger river, the San Juan flows from snowy mountains to parched desert.

Compared to Nevada's 4 percent share of river, New Mexico made out like a bandit in the 1922 compact. New Mexico took 11 percent or 840,000 acre-feet from the San Juan River. Forty years later, New Mexico tunneled 110,000 acre-feet of this water beneath the Rockies into the Río Chama and Río Grande for Albuquerque.*

I wake before my alarm at 4:30 a.m. Unlike most mornings at home, I jump to action, excited about the dawn, curling my toes into cool sand. I boil lake water for oatmeal and coffee on my hissing stove, stuff my sleeping gear into a waterproof bag, and stow it in the kayak. It takes me several minutes to eat, stretch, and pour my coffee into a splash-proof cup. Then I'm paddling.

I'm alone except for a croaking raven, swooping behind me to inspect my campsite for scraps. He'll find nothing. I erased my footprints from the sand, bagged up my waste, and have taken only photographs. If not for the still hours following the dawn—along with its promise of new discoveries in a quiet wonderland of sculpted rock above clear water—I would hitch a ride off the crowded reservoir.

The water is a crimson mirror gathering up the day. As the sun climbs higher in the sky, I can see sandstone stretching down into a looking-glass world of drowned ruins. Even paddling as fast as I can, it seems like I'm going nowhere. Above the surface, morning glories brighten ledges beneath vertical Wingate towers and spires and the tips of buried mountains.

By mid-morning, I'm once again aware that the beaches and red ledges I'm paddling past are rife with litter. Recently the marina concessionaire Aramark, dismayed by the Park Service's lack of action and concerned about declining tourist visitation, implemented a volunteer "Trash Tracker" program. Because the Park Service's bags were too flimsy to hold more than napkins, Aramark donated a skipper, a houseboat, food, a barge, and sturdy trash bags. Last year, a hundred volunteers plucked up thousands of cigarette butts, 1,500 golf balls, hundreds of feet of rope, over a hundred chairs, various boat parts, scores of tires, plastic bags, aluminum cans, bottles, toilet paper, condoms, food wrappers, and broken glass onto a barge. Each year, they retrieve and recycle over 25 tons of jettisoned trash.

The San Juan River is half depleted, its silt deposits and former sand waves quelled by the Navajo Dam that Dominy built in the headwaters. Now the Navajo, along with two Ute tribes and Apache, are pursuing their water rights from the New Mexico allocation. Eventually, the state will take its full San Juan allocation, and Lake Powell will shrink farther down its silted banks.

At the witching noon hour, I steer west as if I were paddling down a river. The rapids come from large speedboats, repeatedly swamping my cockpit with their wakes. Again and again, I pull out the hand pump from the under-deck netting above my knees. Several minutes of pumping allow me to suck all the water out and resume paddling. To ease my creeping tendonitis, I change my stroke and raise the blades higher in the air, envisioning the paddle as a metronome, setting a four-mile-per-hour pace.

In the oppressive heat at the remote Dangling Rope Marina, I tell the district ranger that the recreation area has developed policies that exclude kayak travel. Then I ask if action can be taken against the number of wake-producing boats that are breaking Utah law by cutting close and swamping me.

"If we pulled over everyone traveling less than a hundred feet from stopped boats," she replies, "we'd never get anything done."

She's overworked, so I commiserate. In the 50-mile Dangling Rope district on Lake Powell, eight rangers deal with an average of 35 search and rescues and 60 medical problems a summer. Contrary to lower figures cited by the Halls Crossing district ranger, the Dangling Rope district ranger says the lake's death rate has climbed to a dozen per year. Many deaths occur from carbon monoxide poisoning, brought on by leaky generators, or swimming under and being towed behind boats. Last week, a man sleeping in his houseboat died from the "mystery illness."

When I detail the charcoal-smeared damage to an ancient art mural at Reflection Canyon, she replies, "We want to deal with graffiti, but we're too busy being reactive rather than proactive." She says, "We're running ragged." (Six months later, she won't reply to my repeated e-mails about whether her colleagues checked up on the vandalism.)

By stocking up on a gallon of cold fruit juice, I defy my ban on paddling through the afternoon heat in the interest of leaving the reservoir more quickly. Confused by large canyon intersections and balancing through boat wakes, I lose my sense of direction even while looking at the map. The most reliable direction beacon proves to be the large white plumes of smoke rising from the coal plant at the 30-mile-distant Navajo Generating Station.

By the time I reach Gunsight Butte near the end of Glen Canyon, after seven days of paddling from Hite Marina, I'm hopeful that I can find the 232-year-old inscription from Escalante. But I already know what to expect.

Although Glen Canyon National Recreation Area does not have an archaeologist, rangers have mapped more than 80 sandstone walls that have been defaced by graffiti. So the National Park Service has coordinated the

Graffiti Removal and Intervention Team (GRIT). Volunteers board a house-boat, *True Grit*, donated by diehard John Wayne fan Bill Williams, and then travel to sites etched with hundreds of initials and dates. These modern art-ists possess the same sense of entitlement to Utah sandstone walls that street gangs take to underpasses and subway tunnels. In all my experience through-out the modern West, graffiti in the backcountry seemed as rare as gunplay. Until I came to Lake Powell.

Above a popular anchorage, I follow an ill-defined path up through the tam-arisk and into a narrow passageway that bisects Gunsight Butte. Because GRIT has recently scrubbed the formerly graffitied walls with water and wire brushes, this is not the place the padres passed through—the Park Service prohibits vol-unteers from erasing graffiti alongside fragile historic artifacts or murals.

After an hour's search, I find a shaded alcove deep within a sandstone cleft. In November 1776, this refrigerated fissure would have shown the Spaniards' breaths. Hundreds of names and slurs and hearts pierced with arrows decorate 50 yards of varnished walls between Park Service signs that warn offenders against defacement. I try to imagine Escalante's hunger, the growing terror that he would never reach Santa Fe, and despite his elaborately kept journal, how their travels would be lost to history.

In the midst of a dark stone patina that he thought would preserve his passing for posterity, he employed the same calligraphy found in his journals:

paso por Aqui
año 1776

His words, "I passed here in the year of 1776," are encircled and nearly obscured by a large heart shape and crude graffiti:

Rob
+
KATHI-1994

When I reach the dam on July 11, paddling atop more than 500 feet of water, I feel an overwhelming sense of relief that I am through with the reservoir. Even the mighty Glen Canyon Dam is an anticlimactic, curved wedge of gray concrete, aligned with the paler bathtub rings rimming Glen Canyon's last stretch of bright Wingate. A cable of floats with "Keep Out" signs prevents me from paddling the last hundred yards to touch the dam. And bam!—like a million others who have read *The Monkey Wrench Gang*, I wonder what a well-placed parcel of dynamite would do to the ominous-looking structure.

On a suspension bridge above and behind the dam, traffic crawls across Highway 89. Towers of hydroelectric lines lead south, feeding the grid that keeps Phoenix cool and well lit.

At water's edge below the footpath, a man repeatedly casts a lure into the water. I hold out my hand and introduce myself. I try to contain my surprise as he replies, "Mario Escalante."

"Any relation to the famous Spanish priest?"

"Not to my knowledge," he says politely.

Each day, in his private contractor truck, he leaves Flagstaff at dawn carrying the U.S. mail to Page. Then he fishes for six hours alongside the dam for bass, picks up the outgoing mail, and brings his daily catch back to his wife and high school daughter for dinner. From years of fishing at this spot, he believes that the water is contaminated with oil and fecal chloroform, so he only drinks from a plastic gallon water jug. He offers me a swig as a respite from the day's heat. I pull out my own bottle to show him that I'm in good shape.

"Last night there was nowhere to camp," I say, "So I paid $150 to sleep in a bed at the Wahweap Marina Resort, but it's the worst night of sleep I got in over a week of lying on sand." We laugh together.

For the first time in 140 miles, someone is asking me detailed questions about my trip, excited about the adventure rather than his own preoccupation, and curious about what I will find when the river runs out in Mexico. As we exchange e-mail addresses, it strikes me as odd that someone from a different culture would take more interest in my trip than all of the Anglos I met on the lake behind me.

In contrast to the plug of concrete seen from reservoir level, from below Glen Canyon Dam is an apparition of imposed order and curving symmetry, 1,500 feet wide and 700 feet high. Refrigerated lake water flushes out from its bottom. Although the dam embodies a function that has outlived its builders, the narrow-waisted and broad-shouldered architecture lures the eye away from the surrounding canyon walls. It's the most muscular piece of concrete imaginable: humankind flexing its power against nature.

Three hundred feet thick at the bottom, the superstructure hums with surging electricity, while the river is hushed into a translucent, subdued velvet. The reverberating cries of unseen birds swoop at the cold miasma slipping from underneath the dam. Passing semi trucks on the suspension bridge are reduced to insects.

The symmetrical pattern of grids across the dam shows hundreds of forms for the cement placements made a half century ago, while reservoir seepage has drizzled the gray concrete white with minerals. A train-tunnel-sized portal at river level regularly disgorges tourists (200,000 come each year to tour the dam) who board iceberg-colored mega rafts and motor downstream with their heads turned to admire the horizon-dominating structure upstream. The visitor center where they started their tour appears as an elliptical spaceship landed beside the dam's crest.

I'm standing on the same boulder that Stanton's photographer clambered onto 119 years ago, carrying a tripod and a revolutionary lightweight film camera. Frank Nims had already seen plenty of epics and deaths on their expedition, and this boulder gave him a relatively safe stance compared to a cliff ledge a week later, when he fell 22 feet and broke his leg. It took days to carry him out on a litter.

Compared to Nims's December 1889 photograph of unimpeded river, the sandbars are gone and the banks bristle with tamarisk. The river is also worked by anglers gracefully penduluming lines back and forth from boats to the river for rainbow trout. One-third of the way up the Wingate cliffs are reservoir seepage lines, rimmed with vegetative slime for a half mile below the dam. The cliffs' greenery is watered by leaks around the dam and through sandstone fault lines. Engineers call this escaped reservoir water "bank storage," supposedly predicted before the dam had been built. The 6-cfs leakage around the dam dumps over three million gallons per day back into the river.

OF DADS, LAWNS, AND DAMS

After kayaking 15 miles of a somewhat intact Glen Canyon on the Colorado River below the dam to Lees Ferry, it's time to find a way home. I miss my family. Plus, I need to put the river in context with our daily lives to better understand water conservation and preservation of this living resource.

I leave my kayak with a friend in Page, Arizona. Created while Glen Canyon Dam cement was *placed* ("poured" is a malapropism to the exacting dam engineers) in the early 1960s, the company town took its name from the sixth Reclamation commissioner, John Page.

The town of Page is suffering an economic dry spell from a tourism downturn. So it is burgeoning with discount motels. Oblivious to its location in the desert, Page is equipped with big box stores, a flourishing library, and a John Wesley Powell Museum. His *Emma Dean* dory replica resides under a cupola. The shifting crowd of homeless people and foreign tourists rival the unusual number of boats parked along sidewalks and in dry docks stretching across town.

No road leads directly from Page to Hite Marina on the far side of the reservoir, so I charter a small plane. For an hour, I'm glued to the window as we fly east over the lake. From the bird's-eye perspective, one can see how once-narrow canyons were flooded into Warm Creek Bay, Padre Bay, Last Chance Bay, and Rock Creek Bay.

From several thousand feet above, the reservoir is spumed by white wakes of boats circling and weaving. We fly over the dead-end canyon of Dangling

Rope Marina, rife with more boats. Then over the straight-as-an-arrow, isolated brown hogback of the Kaiparowits Plateau, shooting northwest. As the San Juan River continues east in its flooded lake incarnation, we turn north and follow dizzying canyon walls over the elaborate curves of the Escalante River banks, coiling in blank, stunningly curved and bulging sandstone.

The pilot won't risk landing at the potholed Hite Marina airstrip, so we descend toward the Bullfrog Marina. Below, hundreds of boats and strange green lawns appear as cancers against the beautifully blistered slickrock and living red soils. We land at a deserted airstrip.

I spend the rest of Sunday holding out my thumb to hundreds more boat-trailered SUVs headed home for the weekend. These are the same race drivers who nearly capsized me in my kayak, so I give their swaying speedboats plenty of room by standing off the pavement. After five hours of no progress, giddy from the heat, I hide the paddle to prevent any prejudicial drivers from identifying me as a kayaker and hold out a $50 bill. The second car stops.

He's a boat mechanic from the uranium mill town of Ticaboo, Utah. Jeff Welker is happy to drive another hour to Hite Marina, because he's never seen so little boat repair work as this summer. Everyone is broke. "They're still launching at the reservoir," he says, "but since gas is so expensive, they anchor a mile or two outside the marinas and turn off their engines."

During one more day of driving east to Colorado, I delete my mother's number from my cell phone, hoping this will speed me toward closure.

For the next month, it will be my good fortune to keep June and the boys within constant sight. My sons are initially confused to have me home, and although it takes no time to be a fulfilled dad again, we spend several days falling back into our old routines.

I read to them from our favorite conservation classics: *The Lorax, The Little Prince,* and *The Wind in the Willows*. Nicholas is a rapt listener, a sponge soaking in the world. Whether it be the Lorax trying to save natural habitat from destruction; the Little Prince who learns that "You become responsible, forever, for what you have tamed"; or animals who treasure "messing about with boats" on their river. The power of language and well-crafted narratives has made him more interested in the stories than the pictures. Although he's too young to grasp the full import of metaphors, he knows why turning the lights off and using compact fluorescent bulbs will keep coal plants from emitting more carbon dioxide emissions. Or why we keep the faucets turned off: to conserve water from our mysterious aquifer.

Two-year-old Alistair is curious about water and the Colorado River: *Where did you sleep? Did you drink the water? Can I go with you when you return?*

At night, to cool off from the 90-degree days of our semiarid mesa, we leave the windows open. The buzzing nighthawks have stopped their ritual dives, while the magpie family too is quelled after ravens raided their nest. We can no longer hear the mountain snow coursing through the Roaring Fork River, settled down into a summer lull in the valley below. To fill the void, coyotes are tuning up for their fall symphonies.

We take long walks on the game trails through sage and juniper clinging to stony ground amid thumb-sized cactuses and alien-headed thistles. Coyote and fox sign are abundant, but we can't find any of the local mountain lion scat. The wild alfalfa and grasses surrounding our house have browned and ceased pollen production. We're thankful that our well still gushes. Through judicious watering and pruning, June has transformed our greenhouse into a jungle of tomatoes, broccoli, squash, potatoes, and lettuce. Once a day, we dump our garbage into a compost barrel and give it a quick spin to hasten the process of enriching the soil in our greenhouse. We eat dinners on our deck overlooking the Roaring Fork River Valley and take turns sitting in the south-facing chairs to inspect the view up above the greenery to the snowcapped 14,000-foot peaks: Capitol, Snowmass, and the Maroon Bells. Passing thunderstorms frequently generate double rainbows arching over Grandmother's house to the east. Because we know that most people in the world lack this connectivity to the earth and the resources that sustain us, we take turns saying thanks for our food and family.

Our lives are tied to the cold, clean subterranean water that lets us flourish on our high mesa. It's hard to conceive of living here without water, so we respond by honoring this living resource. We buy organic groceries, those we can't grow in our greenhouse, from local farms, instead of supporting agribusiness supermarkets. We set up a barrel to collect rain from the south-facing roof, and we dispense with a gutter on the north-facing roof to help keep the wild grass green. If everyone could revere water, even in small ways, we might change the world through our wallets and our actions.

I can think of no better place to live than Carbondale, Colorado. Bicyclists, mountaineers, and conservationists abound. Mostly, if locals' necks are red, it's because they spend a lot of time outdoors. Thanks to a progressive town council, big box stores are banned. Farmers' markets abound in the surrounding valley. The Community Office for Resource Efficiency and our local energy company gave us cash rebates for our expensive solar panels, and new businesses in town are required to utilize solar power. The subject of water conservation is often broached in one of several newspapers, on public radio stations, and in local conferences.

On my mom's birthday in late July, I prepare the ground for three cinquefoil shrubs, one for each of her sons. This native plant, with yellow flowers and soft leaves, is as abstemious with water as my mother was with all of her pleasures: a single glass of red wine several nights a week, her simple yet comfortable possessions, and a natural garden along her side yard. I shovel out the rocks, add a bucket of our neighbor's horse manure, and set in the plants along the path leading to our front door. Now every time I leave and return home, I'll think of her. Also, I don't mind showing visitors that the Watermans are unburdened by a fertilized lawn or pruned rows of showy exotics.

We don't pretend to have all the answers on sustainable living. The solutions to reducing our water or carbon footprint are complex, and often confusing. Should we thoroughly rinse used glass jars before driving them 20 miles to a recycling center? Can we justify a relaxed use of nonconsumptive household water because the water is returned through our septic field into the ground? Is it better to buy organic foods shipped from far away? Or non-organics with a smaller carbon footprint? We do keep asking the questions, remain receptive to change, and rethink the model of our natural resources as a horn of plenty.

While at home, I stay close to the river—taking walks and bike rides alongside it, reading about it—so that I can begin to understand how we might sustain this living resource. As the presidential campaign heats up, Senator John McCain visits Colorado Springs and tells the media that the Colorado River Compact has to be changed. As an Arizonan, everyone knows what he's thinking: Colorado has to give up some of its water for his parched Arizona. In the swing state of Colorado, where whiskey is for drinking and water is for fighting, this gaffe will cost him dearly.

In mid-August, we fly east to celebrate my dad's 80th in Cape Cod, Massachusetts. While my sons and I take turns in the window seat, we study the landscape as it unveils the secrets of Western expansion and irrigation practices. The Platte River, replenished by recycled Colorado River, curls east toward the Atlantic instead of the Pacific. From high altitude, we watch the desiccated high plains—hoarding less than 20 inches per year—polka-dotted by green irrigation sprinklers. As we cross over the 100th meridian and approach Missouri, these circular irrigators disappear, and, because plentiful water no longer has to be diverted long distances,* the land is continuously lush, taking in more than 30 inches of rainfall per year.

As we walk through Boston's Logan International Airport, the elder of our observant sons struggles to understand the people around us, speaking about "cahhh"s and "pahhhkin" with the accents I grew up around. The abundance of pale faces shows a difference between a land of sun versus a land of rain, while jogging suits have become haute couture for the leisure class. Driving out of Boston in rush hour to Cape Cod is an experience more stressful—with sudden accelerations, blaring horns, and rising blood pressure—than any traffic in Colorado.

I greet my dad at his door in West Yarmouth. As with my mom, the hug is quick and unnatural, but I'll take it any day over a handshake. "Ahh," he says, running his hand over my shaved head in lieu of a hello, "you've discovered the cure for baldness!" Along with his wit, I've always been amazed that my father, a lifelong New Englander, doesn't have a Boston accent.

Nicholas and Alistair get to play with their uncles and cousins, while their grandfather—dressed in shorts, a button-down shirt, and his traditional comb-over—fields precocious questions, then retreats to his study and closes the door as young people's voices climb. He's relieved to be free of child care duty after raising his own three boisterous hellions. Father child care in the sixties equaled rushing off to work and changing the occasional weekend diaper.

Looking in vain for body surfing, my brothers and I are deterred by the surfeit of trash and people clogging the seashores—unlike our boyhoods back in the day. Although climate change has plenty of traction on the East Coast, partly through the prediction that the oceans will rise, trying to promote water conservation here would be like introducing the electric car to Saudi Arabia. Where I live in Colorado, 15 inches of rain falls each year; New England receives three times as much.

Crossing the divide of culture that separates the West from the East is equally difficult. Visitors who come from the East Coast to our home in

---

*The U.S. Census Bureau's Mean Center of Population map shows a historical Western expansion directly tied to irrigation. In 2008, the national population's balance point lay in Missouri. As my sons reach their thirties, the balance point is predicted to move several hundred miles west—making more people dependent upon the diversions and dams that supply water to the arid region west of the 100th meridian. As we fly east toward Indiana, the population map shows how Western expansion stalled until the mid-20th century, moving west rapidly after Hoover, Grand Coulee, and Glen Canyon Dams were built.

Colorado take protracted showers as if our aquifer tapped into an infinite ocean. Also, New Englanders speak "wicked" quick before you can drop a punch line, and Westerners slowly say "you bet" like they don't get it. I moved west 30 years ago in search of prevalent sunshine and a low-density population amid an expanse of undeveloped wild lands. In New England, unless you're in a park during midweek after Labor Day, you're in a traffic jam or waiting in line.

On our third muggy day in West Yarmouth, we forgo the beach and substitute skinny-dipping in ponds behind my dad's home. This comes as a shock to my stepmother Karen and all those modest souls spying on us from nearby windows.

I came east partly to spend some time alone with my father, to bridge what I perceive as our vast differences. One afternoon he introduces me to a twist on a father-son ritual we took more than 40 years ago. Dad has always buried himself in books, but he rarely buys them. So instead of taking me back to the library, we drive to the neighboring town's "Swap and Shop"— locally pronounced "Swapppp and Chop"—thrift store in his unending quest for more free mystery books.

In the car, we stop talking to listen to President Bush on the radio, denying climate change. Dad used to have security clearance for Pentagon briefings that showed, among other things, how the brass could make battleships "disappear" from radar screens by cloaking them with a cloud of microscopic particles. The sane position for a scientist like my father was to remain apolitical, because the work he accepted from the military could also be used in peacetime. After the commander in chief sound bite finishes, Dad abruptly clicks off the radio and says, "Ahh," then delivers a riposte that needs no reply: "Hardly the intelligentsia, eh?"

Retirement would put him in the grave, so each morning he limps up the stairs to his home study, sits down in front of his legal yellow paper pads and computer, and enters the universe of theoretical physics that sustains him. Four decades ago, he invented the broad-reaching "T-Matrix" theorem. Within several years of this breakthrough, he retired from the world of corporate think tanks surrounding Boston and devoted himself as a full-time freelancer to the work that renewed him. After my mom left, he became a suburban recluse except for playing tennis. His natural introversion allowed him to focus exclusively on his work. Now, because his knees have betrayed him on the tennis court, he clutches the T-Matrix like a double-bladed paddle taking him down the river of his passion, studying the scattering of light particles.

Every week from China to the United States, another scientist continues to expand the known universe by releasing another paper showing the application of the "Transition"-Matrix. On this visit, Dad wrote it down for me:

$$QT = -Reg(Q)$$

where the matrix elements of Q are integrals of products of wave functions over the object surface, and Reg means "the regular part of," i.e., singular outgoing wave functions are replaced by regular wave functions.

The formula enables one to compute how light reflects from nonspherical objects to reveal their shape. The matrix can accurately unveil the volume of a drop of blood or the unknown parameters of an interstellar dust particle.

Dad is often invited as a guest of honor and speaker at the Electromagnetic and Light Scattering by Nonspherical Particles Conference. Because this annual get-together of the cerebrally endowed yet socially challenged is rarely held in the United States, and because Dr. Peter C. Waterman is not a traveler, he declines. Although he is perfectly cognizant of how airplane wings achieve lift, he would prefer not experiencing it.

"Would I need a translator," I ask Dad, "if I went to that conference to try and understand what they're saying?"

"No," he replies with classic deadpan, "just a calculator."

For all of my adult life, I have struggled to understand my father's work, but I see only hieroglyphics in his published papers. Anything beyond his most basic explanations leaves me dumbfounded. To my dad's way of thinking, mathematics is a universal discipline, and if applied correctly, we can discover new boundaries and solve the problems of the world. So I never give up trying to get on his wavelength.

We are alike in at least one way: My father has never chased the almighty dollar. He underbids the competition to win his contracts, he says, which will allow him to finish his final T-Matrix paper. Knowing Dad's humility, he'd probably get the contracts even if he came in as the highest bidder. How could they reject Dr. T-Matrix?

I don't bring up Mom, if only because their marriage fell apart long ago and flogging old times isn't Dad's strong suit. Once, in free fall after my failed first marriage 15 years ago, I asked him for advice. "I kind of liked her, Jon," proved to be all he could muster on the subject. So some memories are better left unvisited. Still, as tennis fanatics and eternal penny-pinchers, my mother and father were not unalike. Dad has recently taken to reminding me that, because he served abroad as an Army private in World War II, he gets a free plot in the local veterans cemetery.

I know that discussing the grief I'm shouldering about Mom's death might be cruel, opening my dad up to a melancholic chapter of his life that might lay beyond reconciliation. Also, to be honest, I don't want to induce another long silence punctuated by "Don't know." The price of respecting my father came through accepting his reticence, just as he has acknowledged my willfulness.

My brothers and I scheme of lists of questions or other techniques that will allow us to extend our short, long-distance phone calls with our father. Undoubtedly, he picks up on our tactics when one son repeats a question another son has already unsuccessfully asked. When Dad doesn't answer e-mails, I resend the query until he has no choice but to reply. But real conversation is not about obstinately hitting "send." To find a connection, I have recently taken to reading all of the books he recommends. Michael Connelly and John Sanford are among the authors I can discuss garrulously in our impromptu long-distance book club. I seldom find a mystery that transcends its genre and takes me beyond climactic narrative, but I've been seeking the common denominator to my father all my life.

My older brother, Rick, a doctor, has tried discussing the likes of Stephen Hawking and Freeman Dyson with Dad, who listens respectfully yet offers little in return, if only because the mathematical probabilities of the mystery genre are better suited to the wiring of his brain than quantum physics. My younger brother, Jerry, a computer technician, has found success in discussing the Three Stooges or ancient Mickey Mouse cartoons that my dad has memorized and rerecorded on DVDs and sent to his grandchildren.

Bring up the T-Matrix, of course, and none of us can get him off the phone.

Throughout my visit, I repeatedly ask Dad about his well-being. Unlike Mom, he is happy to own up to his health issues: a shortness of breath, high blood pressure, and heart arrhythmia. If I were in his shoes, I'd be scared about my failing health. He's more fragile than I've ever seen him, and he concedes that his mind isn't as quick as it used to be. As for matters of the flesh, it's the same aging that my sons will observe in me: the receding hairline, increasing knee problems, and hearing that fades proportionately to the amount of hair that begins growing out of the ears. He offers me a goodbye handshake but I bypass it to a hug, wondering if I'll see him again.

We return home in late August and drive east along the Colorado River toward its headwaters. At Devils Thumb Ranch Resort, above the Fraser River tributary, we'll meet up with June's family and friends to celebrate her 40th birthday. On an oiled dirt road, we stop above Gore Canyon and look down a thousand feet at five kayakers bouncing through the last rapid surrounded by banks of lichen-covered talus and tall lodgepole.

Through Middle Park, the river sluices clean as air over and around barbed-wire fences, while in Byers Canyon, the once-dangerous rapids of spring are now shrunken to summer riffles from lack of rainfall or snowmelt. I could pass through unharmed in a blindfold.

At each new vista, I describe and point to landmarks for June and our boys: the white pelicans, surly ranchers, and the hotel that I stayed at in Hot Sulfur Springs with the sign that warned me not to drink the water out of the tap. Through including them in the conversation, we try to raise our children differently from the ways that we were brought up. Although we keep the radio and TV off and avoid exposing them to the media that would clutter the wonder within their still-forming brains, I never hold back on describing my own rambunctiousness. Better to celebrate than subdue what's inside of us, because our sons share parts of their parents, as we share parts of them.

I talk about how easy it was to hitchhike back and forth to my car along the headwaters, despite my dirty and unshaven countenance. As long as I held a paddle in one hand, cars would pick me up. I tell how psyched I was to find a hole in the fence atop Windy Gap Reservoir Dam that allowed me to sneak through down to the river below, just as a cop drove past on the highway, making me feel like a fugitive on a river that should be wide open to the public.

The moments come flowing back to me and then out of me as stories. From remote canyons to railroads and even along the highway, as we drive alongside the river, compressing two weeks worth of memories into a two-hour drive, I realize that the river doesn't necessarily lose all of its wildness through this highway accessibility. Birds and mammals become habituated to the noise. Barbed-wire fences keep out range locusts. And once you're encapsulated in a boat that is surrounded by the blissful "whoosh" of current, you stop hearing cars on the highway.

"Seek and ye shall find," I tell the boys.

"What's that mean?" asks Nicholas.

"Adventures are hidden down there on the water, out of sight from the highway behind the willows, and you've got to go look for them."

"Pooh-pooh," Alistair adds.

"That too, right, Dad?" Nicholas responds, because boys are fascinated by the processes of the lower intestine.

Nicholas and Alistair are animated in the backseat, listening to their old man describing boyish escapades and wilderness ideals. But as we turn south and continue up Highway 40 along the Fraser River and in the shadow of Granby Dam, we've plunged into the land of pine beetle kill. As far as we can see, the forest is brown and dead. We all grow silent driving through booming Granby, stopping at one traffic light after another toward a horizon of thinning rivers and dilapidated forests. Instead of asking me about the river, Nicholas wonders aloud how long the insects take to kill each tree.

"Don't know," I finally say, surprised by what sounds like Dad's laconic voice coming out of my larynx.

"What do you mean, *don't know?*" he asks.

June looks at me knowingly. "Your son's asking you a question."

"Ahh," I say, trying to transcend my father's genes, "let's look it up and find out, then discuss it, okay?"

In early September, I set up a drip irrigation timer for Mom's cinquefoil: 15 minutes every other day, knowing that by late fall, the plants will be hardy enough to live on their own without watering. Then I kiss June and the boys goodbye and make the lonely two-day drive back to Page, stopping frequently to study the river—as if learning more about Nicholas's and Alistair's future world can justify my leaving them behind.

On September 7, I meet with the director of Glen Canyon Dam. Lonnie Gourley is an affable, administrator in his mid-fifties, immeasurably proud of the structure, "How d'ya like the view?" he asks.

Lonnie waves his arm expansively toward the office picture window framing towers of concrete above a square mile of cabled-off reservoir and garishly stained sandstone walls. This is the pilot stern house for driving Glen Canyon Dam.

The wall behind Lonnie's desk contains a large framed photograph of the dam's crest as parking lot with a hundred vehicles. Another half dozen photographs feature an aerial of the dam, marinas, boats, and Rainbow Bridge reflected in a reservoir perilously close to the natural treasure. For understanding how an engineer sees the world, these sterile photographs speak volumes on how machines and man-made structures can so easily dominate nature.

Lonnie's outbox is empty, his in-box, half full. His desk contains neat stacks of paperwork, waiting to be read, responded to, or filed. A safety video, presumably about catastrophic events here, is marked "unclassified."

"What would happen if the dam was breached?" I ask.

"There have been a number of dam failures in history," Lonnie adds slowly. "If that dam just vaporized . . ." he pauses, "it would be like letting Niagara Falls go for a few hours. It would wash through the Grand Canyon at an extreme rate for about a week."

"What's the flow of Niagara?" I ask, remembering how water engineers often cite America's largest waterfall.

"One million acre-feet per second." Now he's excited, smiling. "Boy, if I had a million acre-feet per second, I could fill Lake Powell in two weeks!" (Later I learn that the St. Lawrence River runs five times smaller over the famous falls at peak flow.)

"If the Glen Canyon Dam breached," I ask, "would Hoover Dam stop the flow?"

"If both Mead and Powell were full, Hoover couldn't bypass all that water." Lonnie pushes the glasses up on his nose and patiently explains that, since the drought, they've been on an equalization program, keeping both reservoirs at the same levels. According to the Colorado River Compact, he has to deliver 8.2 million acre-feet from the upper basin view outside his window to the lower basin downstream of the dam. Then he has to satisfy the enviros, whom he says, will require 12,000 cfs later this fall "to study beach building in the Grand Canyon." He says this innocuously, like a lieutenant taking orders, even though it's inaccurate: The high flows are for electricity demands, and agricultural water calls for more than any scientific or environmental studies.

Amid the math to satisfy the Colorado River Compact and environmental needs, Lonnie's supervision of water releases has to factor in what he refers to as complex electricity calls. Unlike the nearby Navajo coal plant, Glen Canyon Dam's hydroelectric power generation can respond to peak demands immediately, in the case of an unpredicted heat wave, when 1.5 million people in Phoenix all turn on their air conditioners simultaneously. Lonnie knows the system well, and beams about what most engineers refer to as "green electricity." Still, I'm uneasy with his agency's claim that hydropower has nothing to do with atmospheric emissions.

Reclamation is in need of an agency-wide retrofit so that it can join a modern world seeking solutions to climate change. Dams, contrary to popular opinion, are a huge source of greenhouse gasses. Initially, these emissions are released from billions of tons of concrete and other off-gassing construction materials. After reservoirs flood, inordinate quantities of methane, carbon dioxide and nitrous oxide are released in turbines, spillways, and downriver. The gasses come from rotting organic matter that existed before the reservoir's creation—such as dirt, trees, and other vegetation—and an ongoing mega production of plankton and algae on the stilled, warmed-up waters. Then considerable methane releases are created by clearing land and increased agricultural irrigation served by the dam's water.

Although no one has yet calculated the total climate impact of dams through carbon dioxide releases, each year, according to the International Rivers Network, an estimated 104 million metric tons of methane is released from dammed-up reservoirs. This makes dams the largest human-generated source of methane, causing one-quarter of the world's methane emissions.

Seen through Lonnie's office window, the Navajo Generating Station coal plant, with its smoking stacks, produces more electricity each year (17 million megawatts) than all the hydropower facilities on the Colorado River combined (9 million megawatts). Now with the drought and less water passing under the dams, Glen Canyon and Hoover hydropower turbines are only waiting to be compromised.

For the time being, Glen Canyon Dam will keep drawing visitors, pulling power, and releasing water to serve the Lower Basin. Until the dam is decommissioned—within the decade or two that it takes for climate change to force our hands—no one is arguing that we shouldn't use the electricity. But *dams do not create "green electricity."*

As my mind wanders, Lonnie is talking about how cubic feet per second translates into megawatts called for by downstream power users. Right now, for 12 hours each day, he says they're releasing 8,000 cfs to spin the turbines and transfer 300 megawatts of power into the yellow generators atop the huge turbines spinning in the basement of the dam. Meanwhile, the three smokestacks of the Navajo Generating Station, puffing out white hydrocarbon steam clouds like giant cigars taunting the dam, show that hydroelectricity is scant justification to build dams—particularly if new technology will reduce coal plant emissions, along with the development of wind and solar electricity.

Lonnie has guided many tours over the years and knows what to expect from his visitors. "You can't float through this point here," he says, "you've gotta portage around." In reference to canoeists who would appreciate the loss of white water caused by a dam, or the fact that the reservoir hasn't recharged in years, he adds: "It's definitely a little calmer than it used to be here."

As expected, I learn more about the dam's construction and history. The hundreds of grids on the downstream face of the dam show the forms, poured by a 24-ton capacity cement bucket from an aerial tramway strung across the canyon. It took a half million of these buckets—five million cubic yards of concrete; 25 feet wide at the crest, 300 feet wide at the base—pouring every day for three years, to finish the dam. Lake Powell was born when they plugged the diversion tunnels (connected to the bypass tunnels) with 300 feet of concrete in March 1963. Seventeen years later, snowmelt finally filled the reservoir.

Lonnie explains that the only "hiccup" in the dam's half century of operation came in 1983, as the reservoir hit "full pool" and management approved a "bypass event" to stop the rising water from slipping over the top of the dam and "vaporizing the structure." Because big dams like Glen Canyon contain generators at their bases, river bypass tunnels were drilled through the sandstone walls on either side, so the release of floodwaters wouldn't damage the power plant.

In late May 1983, they got a chance to test the tunnels out. The water raced up to 120 miles an hour, then hit a deflection ramp at the end of the two tunnels, shooting harmlessly into the river. Freak rainstorms then turned to unheard-of snow. They opened the spillway higher, until 20,000 cfs ran through the tunnels. The power plant and normal river outlet were already maxed out by an additional release of 40,000 cfs. Lonnie says his colleagues on their normal rounds working inside the dam were "disconcerted" by the concrete walls vibrating and rumbling. Onlookers saw chunks of rebar, concrete, and sandstone shooting out into the river below.

Reclamation officials had no choice but to shut down the bypass tunnels and inspect the damage. The pressure-building mixture of air and water, or cavitation, caused the rerouted river to bore through sections of three-foot reinforced concrete down to Navajo sandstone. Still, with the reservoir rising, Reclamation had no choice but to re-raise the arms of the spillways. The dam's vibrations increased to a constant shaking, punctuated by even more disconcerting jolts and rumbling.

Then another event occurred: "Hydraulic jumps" or waterfalls occurred in both tunnels. They were forced to open the gates farther and increase the flow to reduce the jump of waterfalls, intensifying the cavitation against newly exposed sandstone inside the tunnels. On the high country surrounding the reservoir, snow melted and added to the reservoir volume. Rainstorms continued until they could no longer close the spillway gates. Fortunately, during an earlier shut down, Reclamation had quickly assembled and inserted eight-foot "flashboards" on the spillway gates to prevent the structures from washing into the tunnels.

As the release peaked at 92,000 cfs, the river below went the color of sandstone. The National Park Service airdropped flood warning notes to Grand Canyon river runners: "Camp High, Be Safe." Steven Hannon, one of several authors who have published novels about Glen Canyon Dam being destroyed, researched the 1983 "hiccup":

> Navajo sandstone was being excavated from within the dam abutment like soil before a placer miner's hydraulic nozzle. Down in the employee dining room, located at the base of the dam adjacent to the left abutment, a worker later said that it sounded like the artillery barrages he had experienced in Vietnam. Everyone was "pretty nervous and on edge," he said.

A month and a half after it started, the flood stopped, six feet below the crest of the dam, a foot below the steel flashboards. Lonnie says that crews of concrete "dentists" came to the dam and spent months performing oral surgery to repair the cavities created by lake water rushing through the bypass tunnels. The deepest hole carved 50 feet into the sandstone. Two thousand three hundred yards of concrete were required to fill the holes.

Since the bypass event in 1983, the reservoir has reached full pool another three times, with only one other major release. For several days, they released 50,000 cfs, but the repaired tunnels held thanks to a deep slot that workers had chiseled into the tunnels that reduced cavitation by allowing air to vent along the top of the tunnel.

As Lonnie walks me out onto the crest of the dam, he gestures down to its toe. We stretch carefully over the lip at sternum height and look down at the curving arch of concrete, 710 feet down toward the subdued river. I can't help smiling because the view reminds me of the well-publicized event, orchestrated by Ed Abbey and his friends from the newly formed civil disobedience group EarthFirst! Three men, undeterred by park rangers, hustled along the crest of the dam carrying what appeared to be a rolled-up rug. At midpoint, they stopped, leaned over, and unfurled several hundred feet of tapered black plastic down this wall, simulating a crack in the dam. If I were to try such a stunt today, the largest bureaucracy in the world, Homeland Security, which has replaced the park rangers around the dam, would haul me away in handcuffs.

If human or natural catastrophe caused this dam to fail, even in drought conditions, hundreds of lives would be lost in the ensuing flood. If the ensuing wave breached Hoover Dam, 363 miles downstream, thousands of lives would be lost in a disaster worse than Hurricane Katrina. Downstream, a half dozen small cities and dozens of small towns would be inundated, 30 more water-dependent cities—especially Los Angeles, Phoenix, and Las Vegas—would be crippled, and many agricultural areas devastated. Nearly half of the 30 million people who depend upon the river would suddenly be faced with water shortages. If the flood occurred in midsummer, blackouts would cripple numerous cities until power outages could be resolved.

Recently the Living Rivers organization argued that a catastrophic failure of Glen Canyon Dam would cause such an impact to the region that Lake Powell should be drained naturally. In the ensuing court battle, the organization failed to force Reclamation to show the "inundation maps" that would detail the impact of Glen Canyon's fall.

I'm thinking about these issues as we take an elevator down into the catacombs of the dam. Along darkened concrete sidewalks, periodically lit by dim lightbulbs, a gutter directs an additional 1.5 cfs of seepage—about the size of a small brook—out of the leaky dam. The dam's bowels are supercooled by the deep reservoir waters pushing against concrete. Although my host is relaxed, proudly displaying his copious engineering know-how, I'm anxious. I can sense the pressure of water—"200 pounds per square inch," says Lonnie—pushing against the wall 20 feet from where we stand. Underneath my hand, the concrete wall is clammy-cold and alive with vibrational adjustments to water levels, temperature changes, and the movement of distant turbines. In a darkened end of the hallway, the concrete suddenly gives way to tunneled sandstone walls. A downspout from the ceiling bank storage burbles more cold reservoir water into the floor gutter. I feel like Jonah swallowed by the whale.

Finally, at river level, we emerge into blinding sunshine and walk toward the turbine room, vibrating like a battalion of tanks. The dam was dedicated on September 22, 1966, by a cast of political luminaries, including President Johnson's wife, Lady Bird. Up on the crest, she spoke into the microphone to a crowd of thousands: "As I look around at this incredibly beautiful and creative work, it occurs to me that this is a new kind of writing on the walls, a kind that says proudly and beautifully, 'Man was here.' I am proud that man is here."

Two governors and one Navajo representative also came to the podium. All three speakers took the opportunity to deride the Sierra Club's opposition to the dam because they assumed that its activist director David Brower would not be present. Brower had been taking out expensive and damaging ads in newspapers across the country, trying to prevent more dams from being built on the Colorado River.

Then Commissioner Floyd Dominy came to the microphone. Characteristically, he blew everyone away:

> Dave Brower is here today. Brower is not here in an official capacity but as my guest. We're going to spend several days on Lake Powell, so I can convert him a little. Then we're going down the river, so he can convert me.

Lonnie points to an unlikely green lawn of bluebells, wedged into a void between the bottom of the dam and the river. He gets the same schoolboy look on his face that he had while imagining Niagara's flow, and he shares a final tidbit of oral history that has been passed down to each new keeper of Glen Canyon Dam: As Dominy escorted Lady Bird toward the turbine rooms, she pointed matter-of-factly at the brown wedge of dirt and told him, "Y'all know, that there would look beautiful planted in Texas bluebells."

The next day, bobbing in a boat next to the "Keep Out" signs 200 yards upstream of the dam, I'm talking with the director of the Glen Canyon Institute (GCI), Dr. Richard Ingebretsen. Reclamationists perceive his organization as the radical fringe.

"Rich," 50, is a devout Mormon and soft-spoken boatman. In between practicing emergency room medicine and running a staff of four at the GCI, with 1,500 active members, he teaches physics and medicine at the University of Utah. Unlike civil disobedience protestors or nonprofits filing lawsuits to save the river below the dam, GCI focuses on restoring Glen Canyon and draining Lake Powell.

The year after Lady Bird's dedication, Rich came to Glen Canyon as a ten-year-old Boy Scout. The infant reservoir had begun flooding the Colorado River banks. They rode a boat from a put-in at the unfinished Wahweap Marina to the entrance of Forbidding Canyon, and began hiking several miles to Rainbow Bridge. The scoutmaster said that the pools they were drinking from and splashing through would be flooded the following year, but Rich couldn't process that information. Finally, in what seemed an eternity to a young boy hiking through rugged canyons, they caught their first sight of the enormous natural sandstone bridge, framing Navajo Mountain in the background.

The experience stirred Ingebretsen's soul. They had been worried about getting lost in the little-traveled canyon country. They were thirsty. But the impossibly high bridge—built by God, they were told—made their difficult journey worth all the hard work.

He came back a half dozen years later on a high school field trip, and because Forbidding Canyon had been flooded, he didn't recognize the stilled, shrunken canyons from his speeding motorboat. The pools and walls that had enchanted him in 1967 were gone. They, along with hordes of other tourists, quickly visited Rainbow Bridge and left. The students were unimpressed. Their destination had become merely another goal to be checked off a list. "It was painfully hard to see," Rich says. "The smell of gas, the crowds." When Rich tried to describe the pools he'd played in as a boy, his classmates seemed apathetic. They all wanted to go waterskiing. "It hurt my heart that it was all underwater," he says.

In 1989, his fiancée died, and Ingebretsen, heartbroken again, plunged himself into work. But saving patients from septic shock and teaching physics wasn't enough. In 1995, he formed the GCI. That fall, he staged a debate at the university in Salt Lake City between former Reclamation Commissioner Floyd Dominy and David Brower. Seven hundred people attended, mostly cheering for Brower.

The following year, Reclamation announced that Lake Powell annually evaporated one maf of water. This news came as the final straw of resource depletion, spurring Western conservation groups to action. GCI sponsored another rally that drew 1,500 people to see Brower's photographs of an undammed Glen Canyon. The science was reviewed for several years, while the Sierra Club and conservation groups protested. All to no avail. The dam's tangible benefits outweighed the hard-to-gauge detriments of losing canyons that no one really knew or appreciated. An environmental impact statement concluded that artificial floods could restore the river below the dam, and for the time being, the public accepted that the government could look after the river. Even the big guns of the environmental lobby felt like Davids against the Reclamation Goliath. Sierra Club and the others threw in the towel.

Ingebretsen never lost hope. For a decade, GCI stayed on track, trying to work with municipal water managers throughout the West. They laughed him out of their offices. They told Dr. Ingebretsen he'd never drain Lake Powell. He was a dreamer.

Part of his mission to restore Glen Canyon includes reaching out to schools and the Latter-day Saints community. "Mormons are extremely water conscious, and many church properties practice water conservation or speak of curbing growth [in arid regions]," Rich says. "Historically Brigham Young and Joseph Smith often wrote of preserving the land too." (In terms of water, Ingebretsen is right: Even Powell admired Mormon irrigation.)

"The problem," he explains, "is that Mormons love the lake. The Glen Canyon Institute has been instrumental in showing them that God did not create it."

He debated with groups such as the motorboating Friends of Lake Powell. The passionate 8,000-member organization's representatives said they'd never drain their lake. He told them they'd have to. "When it comes to supplying water to Los Angeles or Las Vegas," he said, "the economics of Page and reservoir boating aren't going to matter."

"What about power?" I ask.

"Buddy," Rich says in his Western patois, "nothing matters but water. Electricity, environmental politics, or recreation doesn't matter when it comes to slaking the thirst of 30 million people." He dips a hand into the warm reservoir: "This water needs to be charging Lake Mead and going to people's faucets. We're going to run dry."

Although modern water managers might not be passionate about restoring Glen Canyon, in light of the ongoing drought, they're paying a lot more attention to Rich's campaign to drain Lake Powell. Even Reclamation thinks the drought might reach crisis levels by 2025. "They don't laugh at me anymore," he says.

Rich doesn't care how Reclamation might affect the dam's decommissioning. "That word," he says, "does not exist on the federal register. Now nothing matters but water."

When I ask him again to explain how he felt about seeing the canyons and pools flooded by the reservoir, he repeats emphatically but without elaborating: "It just hurt my heart." Like his close friend Brower, who openly wept about the flooding of Glen Canyon, Richard Ingebretsen, PhD, MD, understands the issue on another level. He believes, "GCI has a really good shot at restoring Glen Canyon if I do it right." The ultimate success of his mission will not be accomplished solely through educational outreach about sedimentation and the West running out of water. Restoring Glen Canyon will ring the church bells when the public develops a compassion for the river and its canyons.

Because I've only experienced Lake Powell in a kayak, I'm guessing the reservoir will appear different while standing over an engine throttle. So I borrow a friend's motorboat and spend ten days on the reservoir to visit those places I lacked the time and energy to paddle to.

Nothing changes. If I don't slow down as the big tour boats pass, the 12-foot *Osprey*—imported from New Zealand and used by researchers in Grand Canyon rapids—will flip in the enormous wakes. Although the graffiti is ubiquitous, if I hike more than a mile away from the reservoir to see ancient art panels, they're undamaged by modern vandals. Park Service employees are still burned out from their summer with merrymaking visitors.

At Rainbow Bridge National Monument, within Glen Canyon National Recreation Area, I meet an anonymous ranger who is embarrassed and apologetic that he's sneaking a cigarette. I assure him, as long as he doesn't blow smoke in my face, that it's none of my business. He's kind enough to respond to my unusual entreaty and show me a hundred-year-old crude Navajo carving of a horse, hidden on the arch. As I mention my work and pull the camera from its pack, he asks if I've obtained a photography permit. I reply truthfully that the park public information officer said that I didn't need one. The ranger, now looking stumped, tells me that he can't radio in to verify my claim because headquarters is closed.

"Well, it's quitting time," I say, looking at my watch, "I imagine you're ready to go home. Thanks for your help." He takes the hint and leaves me alone.

After sunset, the air cools with inimitable desert speed. I lie on my back contemplating the eerie form rising above me. Technically speaking, because of the stone's 42-foot thickness and 33-foot width, it's a "bridge" rather than an arch. With water below, the *Queen Mary 2* could easily pass under it. Fortunately, the reservoir is at low pool and the nearest water is a mile downstream. If the reservoir ever reaches full pool again, it will flood underneath the world's largest natural bridge and—Rich Ingebretsen says—jeopardize the bedrock foundations. This seems unlikely, if only because the sandstone bridge originally was carved out by water rushing down from Navajo Mountain above.

While lying down on my back, I look at lengthening shadows curving almost 300 feet above. Rainbow Bridge bears a startling resemblance to the snout of a gargantuan elephant, trumpeting its consternation about being betrayed by the Colorado River Storage Project's "adequate protective measures to preclude impairment of the Rainbow Bridge National Monument."*

The bridge is a popular tourist destination, so I feel privileged to spend time lounging alone underneath it. Before the reservoir was built, it could only be seen by those who walked or rode a horse for two days. Now it's accessible by a two-hour, high-speedboat ride. Floyd Dominy, of course, considered this a great success. "Rainbow Bridge gets 300,000 or more a year now," he told Ed Marston at *High Country News* in 2000, "when it had only 15,000 in 50 years. The Colorado River [Grand Canyon] float trip was limited to about a six-week period, haphazardly, when it was available in the flood season. Now you've got 20,000 people a year going down it every year."

Dominy also made the case that, when the river went through its Predambrian fluctuations, dropping below several thousand cfs, no one could boat the Colorado River trickling through the Grand Canyon. As nobody's fool, Dominy had figured that, amid that constituency of 20,000 Grand Canyon raft riders per year who didn't like dams or a white-water season extended by several months, they still couldn't hold a political candle next to the annual floodlights of two million who came to his beloved lake on motorboats.

David Brower sued. But in 1974, the Tenth Circuit Court of Appeals ruled that Congress's lack of funding to protect the bridge took precedence over the explicit language of the act. The Navajo also sued to have access closed. In 1980, the Tenth District Court of Appeals ruled against the claimants, in favor of water storage over Navajo religious ceremonies, which would violate the religious freedoms of all citizens.

*Scattering ashes at the Colorado River source with Brad Udall (right),
at La Poudre Pass, Colorado.*

Grand Lake (left), dwarfed by the reservoirs Shadow Mountain and Lake Granby.

Blue River confluence (left) in Middle Park, showing the Colorado River above Gore Canyon, near Kremmling, Colorado.

Carter Reservoir with Colorado River water near Fort Collins, Colorado. CBT spillway pipe (right center) leading from the tunnel under Longs Peak (top).

The author and Bruce Kime below Burns, Colorado. Note the passing train.

Nicholas, Alistair, and June Waterman sheltering from mosquitoes at Hotel Bottom, Utah.

Handprints of ancient Puebloans in Lathrop Canyon, Utah.

Lake Powell, with former Colorado River through Glen Canyon (right) and Wahweap Marina (top center).

Ranger Steve Young (T-berry) on a rock, avoiding the carpet of biologic (cryptogam) soils in Canyonlands National Park, Utah.

The author hitchhiking back to his car amid weekend Lake Powell motorboat traffic.

Glen Canyon Institute Director Rich Ingebretsen and the dam that he would like to take down.

Brian Dierker finessing Mile 231 Rapid, Grand Canyon.

Fritz preparing to release humpback chubs found in Grand Canyon.

Intact ancient Puebloan pot, Grand Canyon.

Desert bighorn sheep on the river's edge in Grand Canyon, Arizona.

*After Lava Falls' V-wave, a Grand Canyon rafter bucks through the
tail waves and scrapes around Cheese Grater rock.*

Southern Nevada Water Authority's General Manager Pat Mulroy in her office, considering the crucial living resource of Las Vegas.

How much longer can arid Las Vegas flaunt water?

The author paddleboarding behind Izzy Collett in Black Canyon below the Hoover Dam.

The author and London Bridge, Lake Havasu City, Arizona.

Alfalfa and cotton fields in Blythe, California. Note the levees that prevent the river from spreading out over its former floodplain.

Colorado River canal loaded with DDT, fecal chloroform, and E. coli in Palo Verde, California.

*Riverman Smokey Knowlton with invasive giant salvinia, surrounded
by giant cane at Walters Camp, California.*

*Yuma Desalination Plant Operations Manager Len Martin showing
Reclamation's warehouse of reverse-osmosis piping.*

*Mexican border fence and the All-American Canal diverting the
lion's share of Colorado River west to Imperial Valley.*

One of many salt-laden Imperial Valley drains into the Salton Sea.

*Cocopah elder Colin Soto and the emblem of his people
on a tribal building in Somerton, Arizona.*

*Pete McBride on the Mexican delta at river's end,
with Sierra Mayor in the background.*

THE GRAND CANYON CHUB

Lawsuits against the dam and its reservoir continue. A Flagstaff-based non-profit, Grand Canyon Trust, is suing Reclamation for policies that are harming fish—specifically the humpback chub—and habitat downstream. The chub, as scientists call it, is one of the few native fish survivors in the Grand Canyon. Less than five years after the dam was completed, in 1967, the chub joined the endangered species list.

In 1973, the Endangered Species Act potentially gave the chub some protection against the cold water and erratic surges needed to create hydropower. Still, their population dropped to 5,000, or a quarter of their original number in the Grand Canyon. The USFWS petitioned for a change in flows to save the fish. Reclamation responded with more scientific studies. As the government dithered, the pike minnow below the dam vanished. In 1992, Senator John McCain's Grand Canyon Protection Act—limiting the severity of fluctuating flows—gave the chub limited protection from the dam's erratic flows. But this new law cannot change the Colorado River Compact and its water deliveries.

Five million years before all the legalese, the chub evolved as a member of the minnow family. Along with its other eliminated and endangered cousins—the pike minnow, bonytail, razorback sucker, and roundtail chub—the fish developed unique survival strategies. They can't swim to save their lives, but their fin adaptations make them flutter or drop like submarines. Their bodies are barracuda-shaped for speed, but rather than speeding *through* the water, the chub employs its shape to cope with the speed *of the* water. On the end of a fishing rod, they're like pulling in a stone.

The old, native minnows have thick skin, embedded scales, and small eyes to cope with turbulence and silt. Unlike the keen eyes of sport fish, chub eyes are underdeveloped because of neuromast chemoreceptors on their heads, allowing them to smell faraway food. They sense sound through a lateral line of tuning-fork sensors along their sides, sending vibrations to their air bladders and inner ears, allowing them to home in on a struggling insect invisibly passing by in the turbid floodwaters.

The chub's humped back hydrodynamically allows it to hold flat on the bottom and remain upright in raging floods—so beauty can be found in form, even though it's a strange, ancient-looking creature. For spawning, the chub needs warm back eddies and thick sand beaches. Hatcheries, or well-designed aquariums,* can simulate these conditions, but tank fish prove inferior slugs next to those hardy survivors reared in the flash-flooding currents of the Colorado and its tributaries. The problem is, ever since the dam closed its gates, the first 60 miles of the Grand Canyon river bottom has been denied those floods, carrying six million metric tons of sand a year. As the reservoir climbed toward full, the cooled, bottom-level water released into the Grand Canyon proved perfect for Texas bluebells and newly introduced trout. But the dwarf-headed, cartilaginous-backed, ugly-duckling chub could no longer migrate past the dam, let alone succeed below it in the Big Chill.

Scientists found that the 46-degree water cooling the habitat below the dam limited chub growth to one millimeter per month: ideal snacking size for hungry trout. In warmer waters common to the Grand Predambrian—when chub, suckers, pike minnow, muskrat, otters, and mesquite once thrived—the chub grew up to seven millimeters per month. These scientists and researchers, funded by USGS through the Grand Canyon Monitoring and Research Center (GCMRC), have been studying the dam's effect upon the river for a couple of decades. Based in Flagstaff, GCMRC is the yin to the Reclamation yang under the Department of the Interior, fueled by boatmen and PhDs to balance the administrators and engineers working the dam.

---

*The best place to observe Colorado River native fishes is the huge aquarium at the Cabela's hunting and fishing store in Phoenix. Opposite the tank of natives are three showstopper tanks featuring a giant catfish, trout, and bass. The scores of human visitors spend no more than a minute glimpsing at the natives. Compared to the familiar-looking catfish and thin-skinned trout, the chub and its cousins are reclusive creatures of the deep: scared off by humans standing close to the glass.

The recent lawsuit is partially directed at the cold water–enhancing non-native species that prey upon the shrinking chub. In addition, Grand Canyon Trust claims that the dam is denying the chub habitat without the backwaters created by natural floods.

Saving the ancient fish is going to be as challenging and expensive as building another dam. GCMRC and other scientists have proposed solutions:

The dam could re-create more regular floods (Reclamation allowed a three-day bypass in March, but most researchers think of it as an artificial media ploy) and send less-erratic flows into the Grand Canyon. Silt trapped in Lake Powell could be injected into the river through a slurry pipeline. Or a temperature-control device could withdraw warmer reservoir water from the surface water above Glen Canyon Dam.

In hopes of understanding these options, while getting to know the Grand Canyon and its fish, I sign up as a GCMRC river volunteer. On September 20, a taciturn yet revered woman nicknamed Fritz calls the team of 18 researchers to order at Lees Ferry. She divides us into ten rowing rafts to perform beach surveys (the *sed-heads*), fish seining (the *in-saniacs*), and vegetation studies (the *veg heads*). The boatmen are a fit collection of amiable, well-educated, and outspoken transients. Judging from their brown and prematurely leathery hides, all are candidates for melanoma screening. Collectively, they've spent decades serving as guides for commercial river outfitters, but because the seasonal employment and limited wages aren't enough to keep them busy, they've developed other skills—as filmmakers, surveyors, waitresses, writers, teachers, or equipment designers—that allow them to continue enjoying the Grand Canyon.

Fishing and mountain guides routinely make two to three times as much per day for an equal amount of work. The apprenticeship here—rowing baggage, swamping (bailing boats), and performing groover duty—is done pro bono for several trips, until the rowers show such cheerfulness, exceptional dishwashing skills, and willingness for hard labor that the boss has no choice but to pay them subminimum wages.

Because GCMRC science trips don't pay tips, but the salary jumps $65 per day above commercial guide wages, boatmen are only obligated to bring their tie-down straps, row, and pitch in with each day's research. In reality, they all hustle either in hopes of getting more rowing assignments and/or because they love the work. From day one, these river devotees are also quick to share their considerable knowledge of geology, human history, hydrology, and natural history. Any one of them could teach advanced-level geology courses.

Mixed in with every raft are the no less erudite scientists and technicians from Arizona Game and Fish, the USGS, the USFWS, and Reclamation. A scientist, two teachers, and a biologist intern round out the crew as volunteers.

The trip is run as an egalitarian group because they all know their jobs, but like any well-oiled village, they have an unofficial mayor. When I shake Fritz's hand, I can feel the callused yet oddly soft grip of a 51-year-old mother and veteran of more than 200 trips through the canyon. She believes that the Grand Canyon won't be restored to the ecosystem that once existed in the Predambrian. She knows that the system of politics trumping science needs fixing, even if the dam isn't likely to be decommissioned anytime soon.

Although not a scientist, Fritz is intimately acquainted with the river and the mission at hand, so even the oldest, most grizzled boatmen—many of whom tower over this diminutive, solemn woman—defer to her, and are even intimidated by her. *If you can make Fritz smile*, the boatmen say, *walk away because it's not going to get any better.*

Like many of the men who compete for a plum job like Fritz's, she often pees standing up, her rear jean pocket carries the round wear marks of a Copenhagen can, and her storytelling prowess is burred with the slow cadences of a Southwestern native, even though she grew up in the Lehigh Valley of Pennsylvania.

Put her back East, and men would be flummoxed by what they perceive as a switch in genre roles, the girl next door on steroids. Here in northern Arizona, her take-charge manner, boating résumé, and intelligent brown eyes instill respect, even adoration. She is a tribal elder amid the take-no-prisoners, wisecracking coterie of boatmen.

As the youngest of four siblings—all but Fritz would stay in Pennsylvania with the family landscaping business—she grew up as a tomboy interested in science and nature. She found her calling at Arizona's outdoor-liberated Prescott College and created her own curriculum for a degree in natural history, but more important, she learned how to paddle a kayak, tie knots, and rig rescues.

The normally nonchalant Fritz became excited while she worked as a Park Service ranger in Dinosaur National Monument in the 1980s, counting hundreds of native pike minnows, still undiminished in the river. She refused to get a law enforcement degree, which put the kibosh on her Park Service future, but it thrilled her to see the pike minnow flourishing on a protected river—despite Flaming Gorge Dam upstream. After another decade of rowing clients through the Grand Canyon in rafts and dories, the river had marked her.

While serving as a guide on the river, Fritz describes finding a stray dollar bill that she had neglected to take out of her pocket before entering the canyon. In an epiphany, she realized that while rowing the river, money meant absolutely nothing. The material constraints of life were subsumed by the pleasures of living in the Grand Canyon.

If you wanted a drink at noon, you cracked open a cold one. You slept on your boat, alert to the movements of the river, and you opened your eyes when the sun crested the rim, never missing a sunrise or sunset. You read a lot of books, but more important, you developed a sense for the mood of the river until its ever-changing rapids and water levels were transmitted through the oars to your fingertips like braille. The phone didn't ring, and there were no cops or bills to pay once you made it past the check-in rangers at Lees Ferry. Once finished with the baggage-rowing, swamping apprenticeship, you joined a close-knit tribe who understood your needs and a potential future.

For a self-described rebel and nature girl, river guiding spun Fritz's clock, until midlife and marriage loomed. Then, ten years ago, GCMRC offered her the job. Because she felt the river embodied all the best parts of her life, and she could help coordinate the science that might save the place, she couldn't say no. With GCMRC, she had climbed up an unconventional career ladder to her dream job.

With the pick of many boatmen, she settled on one. As Dirk and Fritz raised a daughter, she felt even more strongly about why and for whom she wanted to preserve the river. As if she doesn't have enough oars in the water, she also oversees a program called Grand Canyon Youth, introducing city kids to the splendors of river life.

Once our Team GCMRC has cleared Lee's Ferry, Fritz points to a backwater and frantically rows river right. The other in-saniacs race into action, tracking the Pied Piper. They jump out, tie off rafts, and grab surveyor's rods, thermometers, fish rulers that Fritz built by gluing a clear metric ruler into a sushi-sized tray, seine nets, plastic buckets, dip nets, and bubblers. After measuring the length, depth, and temperatures of the backwater—fragrant with the methane and microbial matter that passes through the dam's turbines—the in-saniacs repeatedly swim through with ten-meter by one-meter nets to catch and identify every fish.

Given the thrilling vascular constriction experienced while wading chest deep with a net, it's easy to empathize with the native fishes' spawning challenges. Even in a still, sun-drenched backwater, the river feels so refrigerator-dispensed and designed to inhibit life that the prolific trout are a sporting miracle.

We reach the shallows in a collective shiver, clutching ice cream headaches and pulling out several wriggling pounds of skinnier-than-sardine-sized fish. We gently pick out our catch and place them in five-gallon buckets to be identified. Fritz wades back in to grab the can of chew that floated out of her pocket.

The waters are rich with trout, bass, and other exotics. In a time-honored tradition, the first carp is passed around for the in-saniacs to kiss. Although the four-millimeter trout and bloated carp number in the thousands, the day's natives—blue-headed and flannel-mouthed suckers under three millimeters—number less than two dozen. Every species and its size are accounted for on the data-intensive clipboards. Suckers, with their rounded pouty lips blowing Fritz more kisses, are taken out of the bubbling and well-oxygenated bucket and poured lovingly into the backwater. If Fritz isn't looking, trout and carp are deliberately left flopping on the beach by researchers long ago grown weary of the prolific species.

This night, alert to "dammed fluctuations" of the river, the boatmen sleep on their rafts, bobbing up and down and bumping against one another in the eddy lines below "Badger Creek Rapid." Outside the light of the campfire, bats are clicking in rhythm to the night, chasing errant mosquitoes, caddis, and mayflies. The Milky Way sparkles in a heavenly glow, silhouetting the canyon rims a thousand feet above like penlights illuminating a deep cave.

In the morning, Fritz's spare monologue, delivered from behind her creaking oars to her devoted in-saniacs, unveils the map inside her mind of every twist, rapid, and new beach to be found on the river: "This one's bullshit too," she says, "lack of a backwater!" She wants to find a chub, and in a place where passengers, even boatmen, are worrying about the next rapid, Fritz will swim through a hydraulic rather than miss a backwater.

At mile 11 below Lees Ferry, we drop 16 feet through "Soap Creek Rapid" and take on several cups of river. As the river curls back west, we pass a short stretch of boulders named Brown's Riffle, where Stanton's boss fell off and drowned more than a hundred years ago. Although most rivers are assigned the international scale of I to VI ratings, Grand Canyon rapids are rated from 1 to 10, often with a hyphenated range of numbers to show that everything changes according to the fluctuating dam releases. As for difficulty, the boat-men in rare agreement believe that rapids here are all about choosing the best line. If you want to bolster your reputation, hit the holes. To boost the tips, aim for the biggest waves. If you have working researchers on board, follow the leader and keep everyone dry. Soap Creek rates a 5 to 6, accord-ing to my pocket-sized Belknap's *Grand Canyon River Guide;* most boatmen favor an ammo can–sized *Stevens Guide,* detailed with natural history. Below Soap Creek, the unrated "Brown's Riffle" has a name only because the would-be railroad builder died here. Today, on the more widely used international scale, Soap Creek felt like a II—which is to say, you'd have to dive headfirst onto a rock to drown. But on the day that Brown drowned in Brown's Riffle, high water built up the already strong eddy.

Harry McDonald, the head boatman, worked the rudder as Brown sat at the oars. They were making repeated stops for Stanton and Nims to take photographs, so McDonald steered abruptly into the bigger than usual eddy near a beach, hit a wave, and both of them were thrown into the water. Their boats had been designed for lake travel, and the keels made them unstable in rough water. According to McDonald's testimony in Stanton's diary:

> We both went under, when I came up Mr. Brown was already up, I being in stern of boat was thrown into current & Brown being in bow was thrown in whirl[pool] between current and eddy—I was car-ried down & turning my head "Halloed" to Brown "Come on" he answered "All right" in a cheerful voice. . . . As soon as I got out of water I climbed up on rocks & turned immediately & saw Brown still in whirl[pool] swimming round . . . .

By the time they rowed Stanton's boat upstream to help, Brown had disappeared. They sat watching the "whirl" for hours, paralyzed in hopes that their leader would resurface from the eddy. Then they walked the river for a mile and a half looking for his body, until giving up. Stanton ended his diary that day by quoting an anonymous expert: "This river seldom gives up its dead."

Utterly disheartened, they tried to continue. Temperatures climbed to 130 degrees as they performed their surveys, looking to blast out a railroad through a sheer canyon already filled by a river. Five days later and a dozen miles downstream at the moderate "25 Mile Rapid," Henry Richards sug-gested portaging; Peter Hansbrough replied that they should row through it.

"Well if you say so, we'll go that way," Richards said while unlacing his boots, getting ready to take on water. As an African American servant for the Stanton family, Richards had to defer to Hansbrough. Even though Stanton had given him the choice of going around the rapid, now his pride was at stake. Richards continued: "That's a bad place to smash a boat, but of course there's no danger to us."

Stanton pushed the two off the beach and recommended, "Your safest course is to keep well out in the current way outside of the rocks."

"Yes," Hansbrough answered, "we will." But their boat inexplicably turned into the cliff, pinning them beneath a three-foot overhang. Modern-day boaters in a flat-bottomed rubber raft would have bounced off the wall and back out into the current, but their keeled boat hung fast. As they shipped the oars and began shoving with their hands against the cliff, Stanton thought they'd get back out into the current. While pushing against the cliff with an oar—a tricky maneuver at best—the tippy-keeled boat capsized. McDonald sprang to action in a boat below, rowing flat out to rescue the swimming Richards—who sank before McDonald could reach him. Hansbrough too disappeared. In the days before dams, trying to swim without life jackets proved doubly dangerous, as sediment filled up the men's clothes and pulled them under. They recovered Hansbrough's body 19 miles downriver, and buried him downstream of the rapid at Hansbrough Point.

Now three men were dead, but the railroad survey somehow had to go on. After taking the temperature of his demoralized men, Stanton reluctantly called it quits until he could come back with life jackets and better boats later that year. The men hiked out over the canyon rim back to Lees Ferry.

Soap Creek and 25 Mile Rapids are the second- and eleventh-rated drops of the 161 Grand Canyon rapids. Although Brown's railroad would be thwarted, the three deaths put his team first on a list of 60 Grand Canyon river fatalities over the next century.

From 1869 to 1937, one in 20 explorers died (seven on the river, three off the river). After commercial outfitters arrived and 25,000 people—mostly paying clientele—began riding the river each year, the survival odds improved vastly.

Seen from the context of 277 miles, 161 brief rapids show that the Grand Canyon is actually a long, scenic run. Stanton hubristically wrote that, with the exception of tunnel and bridge building, the relatively continuous grade would make railroad building a piece of cake compared to the ups and downs of mountain topography. When Stanton returned with life jackets in December, his eye pressed to the theodolite, he couldn't help but enjoy the continuously changing geology, wildlife, and alluring side canyons that created the white water.*

Colorado River rapids upstream—Byers, Gore, Glenwood Springs, Westwater, and Cataract—are caused by a multitude of boulders, slumping, landslides, debris flows, and rotational geology. In the Grand Canyon, however, virtually all of the rapids are created by side-canyon debris flows. As recently as 1995, these flood-raised tributary concoctions of clay, silt, and boulders wash into the Colorado River and congeal into unmovable, bulging river bottoms.

The irony of Grand Canyon rapids is that dams have increased the duration of the white-water season along with the severity of the rapids. Without large-scale natural floods that once groomed the boulders from these debris flows, Grand Canyon rapids are growing narrower and steeper.

Since the motor moratorium began a week ago, we have plenty of time rowing placid water between rapids to get to know the place and the people shaping its history. Although Fritz is reluctant to talk about herself, as she stands up and works the oars forward with short piston-stroke pushes, we learn with a bit of prying that she first came here as a 22-year-old in 1979, paddling a covered canoe. She swam four times in the biggest rapids. Paddling a tippy canoe would have been an audacious move for an experienced Grand Canyon hand, let alone someone who'd never run the river before.

"Were you scared?" a passenger asks.

"Naww, it was fun!" She explains that people rarely drown in the Grand Canyon. The reputation of the rapids here has elevated the perceived danger. Because most of the rapids drop into placid pools below the debris flows, swimmers either stroke to the nearest beach, jump back into and bale their boat, or get plucked out of the water by boatmen.

On average, the river is 300 feet wide and runs several miles an hour. In the rapids that many clients promote as their Battles of Stalingrad, the water

---

*President Theodore Roosevelt first protected the canyon as a game preserve in 1906, expanding it to a national monument in 1908, and after scores of mining claims were sorted out, Grand Canyon National Park was signed into law in 1919 by President Woodrow Wilson. Since then, visitors have found many ways to meet their maker: 240 have died in airplane crashes, over 50 have committed suicide (occasionally driving their cars off the cliffs à la Thelma and Louise), 50 have accidentally fallen to their deaths, 23 have been murdered, 70 have died of natural causes (with heat stroke leading the list), 30 have died from acts of God (lightning or falling rocks), 7 have died in flash floods, and an additional 20 have died by drowning while not running the river. With proper boats, life jackets, river experience, a standby Park Service rescue helicopter, and river maps, Stanton's team too would have found the Grand Canyon a relative cruise.

can accelerate up to 15 miles an hour. Less than 100 yards later, long enough to hold your breath or emit several screams, the adrenaline is quickly replaced with awe for the scenery. Even your clothes will dry before hitting the next rapid miles later. I don't mean to imply, however, that there's no skill involved, particularly to a kayaker or a boatman laboring with a ton of ice chests and clients bouncing out of the boats. Moving an 18-foot raft in a moderate current is like pushing an overloaded wheelbarrow up a hill with a half-flattened tire. In the rapids, you need the deftness of a race car driver to hold the angle steady or to react 50 yards before hitting the big hole hidden behind the sleeper boulder.

Collective boatmen wisdom holds that the rule of thumb in the Grand Canyon is that there's no rule of thumb. The rapids demand unerring technique, but even the best rowers can go black side up (under the intensive peer review of their tribe, most boatmen would sooner have a car accident than flip). A rapid that looks moderate when the dam release slows before bedtime can become a man-eater when the tap slowly turns on again by midday; a rainstorm can make conditions even worse. The river can be ankle deep or 80 feet deep. Although beer is cooled in the water here at mile 12, the 14-degree-temperature increase barely refrigerates trailing drink nets by mile 250. Boatmen are predisposed to storytelling—such as the time Fritz rescued dozens of clients from a flood by stringing a rope across the Havasu Gorge—but it's hard to seine truth out of fiction.

While rowing, Fritz multitasks with a notebook of aerial photographs, numbering backwaters and beaches. At the next potential spot, Fritz announces that the backwater has been destroyed: "It's a stinking flow-through," she yells. "Fuck!"

She is not angry about being denied the opportunity to painstakingly sift out every bit of wriggling fish life or detritus—dead or alive—from yet another backwater in hopes of finding the chub. She's pissed because the daily 12,000- to 4,000-cfs dam fluctuations have destroyed many of the beaches and backwaters built by the winter dam release or tributary floods.*

Fritz often mentions Major Powell. Along with collecting scientific data, he first discovered that the Grand Canyon is North America's most awe-inspiring autopsy of geologic time. Between hoped-for backwaters, Fritz gives us a quick lesson.

The Grand Canyon Protection Act prohibits fluctuations greater than 8,000 feet per day, which can only be drawn down at 1,000 cfs per hour, or raised up at 1,500 feet per hour. Scientists believe that even this slow-changing artificial tide sucks the water-soaked beaches downstream as the river recedes.

At Lees Ferry, the geologic clock began ticking backward at the Moen-kopi formation of light-colored sandstone and shale, formed 250 million years ago, in the Paleozoic era of the dinosaurs, by a sediment deposit. This was preceded by the darker Kaibab formation, deposited by shallow seas and loaded with marine fossils. Unlike similar rock formations that I've seen upriver, the Grand Canyon carves continuously back into the geologic past for more than 200 miles, revealing one layer after another, as if you're plung-ing back through the years on a time machine.

"Best way to remember it," Fritz says, sticking another wad of tobacco in her lower lip, "is the mnemonic *Know The Canyon's History, Study Rocks Made By Time.* She waits for me to pull out my journal and says it again: "*Know*—Kaibab; *The*—Toroweap; *Canyon's*—Coconino; *History*—Hermit; *Study*—Supai group; *Rocks*—Redwall limestone; *Made*—Muav; *By*—Bright Angel shale; *Time*—Tapeats."

Bronzed as the Kaibab, Fritz periodically pulls up her reading glasses, reaches into a stainless steel locker and pulls out her sun-bleached copy of Powell's *Exploration* to entertain anyone who'll listen about how the red mud of the Colorado never ran clear, the bacon went rancid, and how the glorious chasm was formed long before man had arrived, through thousands of years of a stream trickling through rock layers.

Although Fritz worships the chub, Powell found his god in the Grand Canyon through geology. As the other men chafed about surviving the next rapid, the Major repeatedly stopped to climb up for a better view of cliff layers, where he could potter through the rubble and identify more rocks. If nothing else, Powell became famous among the academy of modern geology for naming those layers that are still a mystery: the unconformities. For all the millions of years so clearly represented here through *Knowing The Canyon's History, Studying Rocks Made By Time,* millions more years of time are missing in the nondescript broken debris of the Great Unconformity—sandwiched between the Tapeats and the Sixtymile formation—and the Greatest Angular Unconformity, topping the ancient Vishnu schist.

The impatient boatman Bradley wrote in his journal about Powell's obses-sion: "If he can only study geology he will be happy without food or shelter but the rest of us are not afflicted with it to an alarming extent."

Powell advanced many well-educated guesses to the origin of these geo-logic layers. After he emerged from his first descent of the canyon, through public talks and writings, he helped elevate geology as a science apart from the Great Flood that 19th-century Americans believed had created the

Arizona chasm. Although Charles Darwin's *The Origin of Species* showed the world how science could explain the miracles of nature, Powell—a fan of the book—also read the writing on the walls. His father grew up with Darwin in Shrewsbury, England, and raised his son to be a strict Methodist, but the Major learned an entirely different lesson from the depths of the Grand Canyon. John Wesley Powell couldn't be content with being simply the first to explore terra incognita. He needed to tell the world how it had been created.

Each day's travel and work seining, surveying, or identifying plants all ends at an evening campfire in a comfortable lawn chair outfitted with a recessed cup holder. Sparks fly from Pariah River driftwood. Lies are swapped. Voices rise as the lone Republican among the researchers is disparaged, then praised for his boldness in identifying himself. Eventually, one by one, all retire to their outrageously thick Paco Pad mattresses as friends—with the exception of two newfound lovers, who row a hundred yards upstream to ride their waterbed in privacy.

The carp can also be heard in flagrante delicto, vibrating the reeds while sucking up gunk in a nearby backwater. Elephant grass sighs in the wind. When the campfire smokes, then burns dead, sparks drop from the sky as falling stars.

The sunrises are a melodrama of light that wink down into the canyon and then flood the river with light, like a cactus flowering under rain. If one could sleep through this display, the smell of five gallons of cowboy coffee and the chanting of peeved lesser yellowlegs—"*tew, tew, tew!*"—prove too much for most dawdlers. Sleep through the dishes, and you might get handed a cold cup of coffee, as well as an order to clean and dissemble the inordinately redolent groover.

As we row farther downstream, the egrets flying overhead are so dazzlingly white that I pull my sunglasses on. A great blue heron stands in a backwater, holding out its wings to draw overheated trout into the shadows. Even the ordinary mule deer—with huge racks lofting like mesquite trunks above a copse of willows—seems transformed into a higher genus, which one of the state game wardens identifies as a Kaibab buck. I watch it for several minutes through a long lens until the porcelain figure finally comes to life: batting an eyelash and flickering a nostril.

At another study plot, helping the Arizona Department of Game and Fish's Dr. Jeff Sorenson search for the endangered Kanab ambersnail, I unknowingly crouch one foot away from a pink rattlesnake, coiled and ready to strike under a red glowing monkey flower. The tall, thick grass saves me from being bitten. In an entire morning of crawling through plots of ambersnail terrain beneath the spray of an incoming waterfall, our crew of a dozen white Anglo-Saxon volunteers finds 11 of the endangered brown invertebrates.

Placed upon a fellow volunteer's pinky fingernail, the stalk-waving slug in a shell takes two minutes to crawl onto skin. The perennially upbeat Sorenson takes it as good news that the snail is not on the verge of extinction. The species had been mistakenly listed in 1992. After a 2007 continent-wide search for this biological equivalent of a lost contact lens, impartial scientists located robust snail populations in Alberta, Washington, and Nebraska. DNA testing has shown that these populations are more alike than different from the ambersnail. Still, Sorenson means to restore Grand Canyon habitat disrupted by unnatural dam flows.

As we float on in search of other endangered species, backwaters, and beaches, we are sucked through more debris flows and splashed by cooling rapids. The silt from incoming streams softens the river's emerald glow.

Although the tamarisk is occasionally thick, the Park Service has removed almost a half million trees across five thousand acres in side canyons over the last five years. On the main river, given the concern for the willow flycatcher and ongoing GCMRC studies, tamarisk is left alone.

Other nonnatives are abundant along the river: camelthorn, ravenna grass, Saharan mustard, and Mormon tea. The GCMRC botanists, equipped with presses, plant books, and maps (rather than herbicide and shovels that the Park Service employees carry), stop at every new beach, get out, and identify each species. If any plant is taken, the lead scientist gingerly picks only a stem, pressing it inside her plant book.

Among several government agencies represented in our flotilla of rafts, the National Park Service is conspicuously absent, even though they are officially in charge of this stretch of river. Although the Park Service—notably lacking in scientists to perform the studies—keeps Fritz dancing with red tape and river permits, GCMRC nabs most of the federal funding for scientific studies.

"The Park Service is the fox guarding the henhouse," one of several scientists explains to me in a raft, "and that's why we do all the work." The comment may be one part natural rivalry between federal agencies and one part real gripe.

Between backwaters, a scientist elaborates on his frustrations during a recent lunch date with a senior park administrator. He patiently explained to the park representative how the ongoing political wrangling could lead to a sedimentation pipeline or temperature-control device on the dam, pending more study. Putting down her hamburger, the park representative complained, "Why don't people just let us administer the park as we're supposed to?"

"Because the Colorado River runs through it," the scientist explained, "and 30 million people depend upon it."

As we approach the warmer waters of the Little Colorado River, Fritz leads other in-saniacs in another round of chub dances, arms extended in queer pantomime of otherworldly petroglyph beings, as a prayer to the ancients to catch one of these disappearing fish in the seine nets. The veteran in-saniacs and scientists don't believe, despite Reclamation's token March flood, that the chub will spawn in Colorado River backwaters again. Even if restorative dam floods were to become a regular event, the cold backwaters will continue to serve as dining rooms for hungry trout.

In 1912, Ellsworth Kolb had no trouble finding chub and other native fishes in the river when he traveled from Wyoming to Mexico. He wrote about the Grand Canyon:

> On the opposite side of the pool the fins and tails of numerous fish could be seen above the water. The striking of their tails had caused the noise we had heard. The 'bony tail' [humpback chub] were spawning. . . . The Colorado is full of them.

Matthew Andersen, supervisory biologist with GCMRC, says the chub population has recently risen to 6,000. Like all of the scientists floating downriver, he's broad-minded, easygoing, and here to learn as much as to share knowledge.

As we bounce through yet another rapid, he talks about the high hopes he and his colleagues held for native fish in the undammed Yampa River, a tributary upstream on the Green River. In the last few years, profligate bass have voraciously devoured the last vestiges of a healthy chub population. Although the Endangered Species Act would seem to favor the restoration of Grand Canyon waters for the humpback chub, biologists like Matthew see the species' life insurance as the spring-fed turquoise waters of the Little Colorado River—a 315-mile-long tributary not controlled by Reclamation. Because of incoming Little Colorado River warm water, the Grand Canyon has the healthiest count of humpback chub among five other struggling populations above Lake Powell.

Several miles upstream of this tributary, Fritz is fretting about the tens of thousands of nonnatives she's been catching in the seine nets for the last week. Her distraction has already shown in a minor rapid, where she misread her rowing route and got "surfed"—held along the edge of wave and reverse hydrau-lic. Although less experienced boatmen in the entourage have already taken worse runs, Fritz's minor rowing error puts the boatmen in a state of tongue-wagging wonder. No one misses a trick. All day long they say, "Hey, Fritz got surfed!"

At a shaded backwater under the Bright Angel shale, in the heart of chub land, Fritz and Matthew are still hopeful. Handful by handful, the in-saniac crew deposits another squirming mass of fingerlings in a bubbling bucket. Fritz puts on her reading glasses and joins Matthew. As the other in-saniacs go silent, she begins the nuts and bolts of her nine-to-nine post: pulling up a seat in the soft beach, knocking the sand from her lap to make a desk, pick-ing out fish from the in-bucket and measuring them, releasing them to the out-bucket, and calling out fish names. After finding more than a hundred of each species, as per protocol, she stops measuring and only calls out their names: "Another flannie [flannel-mouth sucker], eight carp, three carp, two flannies, six RBT [rainbow trout], one fathead."

"Fathead minnow," Matthew says, "probably released from a wastewater treatment plant."

Although he's technically Fritz's boss, an important level of respect is at play as Matthew defers to her on handling techniques and she asks him about science. His conclusions are drawn from a rigorous analysis of endless field observations and data collection—the data collected, of course, by Fritz.

Matthew waves a hooped radio receiver over the larger fish, listening for the crackling beep that identifies previously tagged fish. On untagged fish, he injects a harmless dot of a radio transmitter into their bellies so that the fish can be tracked. "Once had a flannie swim from here to Glen Canyon Dam, then all the way downriver to Lake Mead and into Havasu Reservoir," he says, lifting his eyes with delight. "No one knows how it got around Hoover and Davis Dams without fish ladders."

A lithe boatwoman from Montana, covered in mud up to her ankles, stands above, making hash marks in the appropriate columns as Fritz deject-edly calls out names of everything except chub: "nine dace [speckled dace], seven carp, two blue [blue headed sucker], five flannies, one flannie, six RBT, one plains killifish."

Matthew interrupts the count: "The killi is a bait fish," he says. "Don't know how it got here. Probably someone dumped out their aquarium up in the headwaters of the Little Colorado."

Fritz continues, "Four carp . . ." then hesitates, elbowing Matthew, injecting another sucker with a radio tag at her side, as she screams: "TWO

CHUB!" Researchers drop their nets, boats are abandoned, a thermometer is dropped as everyone comes running toward the fish buckets. Fritz is shaking.

She holds them out in proud display, silvery clean and glinting in the morning sun, forked clear tails protruding from the main body. Held in just the right light, the gossamer-thin tail on this thick-skinned fish can be seen to spread like the wings of a butterfly, allowing it to soar and glide in turbid floods. Unlike the wriggling, squirming, and flopping nonnatives, these two are calm and perhaps too cool: The water is only 50 degrees. As fry, their signature humpbacks have not yet developed, hence their need for protective backwaters. The stalk behind its body elongates like the tail of a military helicopter, suspending the rotors to improve acceleration.

Chubs do not exist in any other river basin. The fish, Fritz knows, is the last great piscine hope for the Colorado River. If it survives, the effort will provide new hope for endangered riparian species everywhere by showing how science on a river *can* trump the politics of dams.

Fritz coos: "Aren't they cute?"

This kind of talk from the tribal elder elicits a giggle from the other boatwomen basking in her presence, because it's so *not* Fritz. She delicately releases them to the bucket and then to the river with a high step. Fritz heads straight to a cooler and throws out a celebratory beer for all present. "To the chub!" she declares and, as the toast is returned and beers swilled, it's clear that we're drinking for the salvation of both the fish and the river that runs through the Grand Canyon.

But something's amiss: Fritz is smiling. Boatmen begin backing away.

One early morning on a narrow stretch of river, Fritz swears everyone in her boat to secrecy about our location. She waits like a flight attendant at the exit row getting her yeses from passengers, then pulls over and ties off with an instinctually thrown bowline, threaded through a hole worn in the sandstone by a once-surging river. She steps nimbly up ledges and barefooted past cactuses to a small fissure in the rock, at a point above 200,000 cfs, beyond reach of the river for the last millennium.

Because Fritz is quiet, our quarry is either going to be a well-established boatman prank or an object that transcends words. On the other side of her outstretched finger, sitting on a ledge inside the fissure, half in shadow, half in God's light, is a soccer-ball-sized, clay-colored pot of the ancient Puebloans. Completely intact, marred only by tiny oxidization bubbles, and still carrying the scratches of its maker, the pot sits where its user placed it full of grain 800 years ago. Fritz still hasn't spoken as she descends to the river. When I look at Matthew, he's speechless too.

For miles downstream, Little Colorado River alkalinity crusts the Colorado River water-level Tapeats like Paleolithic bird droppings. Amid the dizzying voids and multicolored rocks that define the Grand Canyon, as one descends through time, the passage has a way of shaking out elemental truths. For the last couple of days, I've been obsessing about my mother: how I hugged her too hard and saw bits of dried-out scalp and brittle hair fall out onto her bed. Toward the end the suffering had transformed my mother. Her friends had to stop visiting because it was too painful to see her. Seven months later and I'm still feeling guilty about the broken shower, the funky drier, and the ceiling hole I wanted to repair—since I couldn't fix her—before she died.

I'm dreaming about my mother because we're looking for a fish that has been chilled to the brink of extinction, on a river that appears similarly doomed. Government agencies have applied many potential cures over the years. The trout have been electroshocked out of the river, the dam has applied bandage floods, the tamarisk and other nonnatives have been surgically removed, and yet the studies continue as if no one really knows how to affect recovery.

The similarities between this river and my mother are disconcerting. At mile 84, above the popular hiking destination of Phantom Ranch, I'm talking obliquely with Matthew about taking care of my mother. Sharing a thwart on a raft for days on end builds friendships and encourages confessions. At first, I say, the chemotherapy offered some hope, and as my mother grew sicker and lost weight that she couldn't afford to lose, the proscribed radiation treatment caused her hair to fall out. A long remission followed, and just before breathing a sigh of relief, the CAT scan showed a walnut-sized tumor in her brain. I took her to surgery thinking that I'd never talk to her again, but the next day, she outran the physical therapist up the stairs to show that she should be released immediately.

Several months followed, with another course of chemotherapy that only made her desperately sick and dingy. As a final indignity, Kay Waterman was invited to participate in an experimental drug study, but the participating doctor wouldn't return her calls. When she fell and hurt her hip in the bathroom, we took her to a nursing home. Again she demanded to be set free, and within several weeks, we brought her home. At this point, it seemed the end had come.

Still, my mother kept trying to bargain. For all I knew, she was trying to make deals with the doctors; if she believed in God or some higher power, even the devil, she would have been ready to talk. She said she would get over her "illness." Until this point, we found new ways to be hopeful at every step of her battle with cancer. "When she told me that she would beat it," I say to Matthew, "I wanted to believe her."

By the time we row under the suspension bridge to Phantom Ranch, I'm trying to hide my eyes. I've embarrassed myself. Still, Matthew understands the metaphor I'm working like a dog with a bone: We poke and prod with our science in hopes of fixing mother earth. I debark with everyone else and then go for a walk alone to clear my head.

None of us wants to lose those whom we love. And the river, I keep telling myself, is a living resource that should outlast us all.

I'm tempted to revisit *The Book of the Dead,* but from a non-Buddhist perspective, the book can be an abstraction. So I need to talk with *my* tribe. Immediately. At the ranch restaurant, bustling with hikers, I stand in line and wait for my turn to call home on the outdoor pay phone. None of the GCMRC crew is here, but maybe this trip has become such a ritualistic journey for the boatmen that no one wants to call family until we emerge from Diamond Creek next week.

A half hour of talking to June and Nicholas and Alistair, letting them know that I'm okay, releases a weight from my shoulders. I tell them that we'll go for a hike when I get home, jump on the trampoline, read stories, and wrestle. Nicholas tells me about a ton of tomatoes he hauled from the hoop house. Because I won't be able to taste any fresh tomatoes from the garden, he says that they've started canning enough *fruits*—

"*Vegetables,*" I interrupt, testing him.

"No, Dad, it's a *fruit* and we'll have enough stockpiled in jars until you get home and all the way up to next tomato season."

I describe yesterday morning's scorpion: clambering up a sand bank that appeared through my macro lens as a castle along the Colorado River. I remind June that she's my source of gravity and then thank her again for letting me be here while taking such good care of the boys.

What's a river worth if we don't have anyone to share it with? I return to the raft with a bounce in my stride—like sharing Fritz's joy at finding a chub.

Below Phantom Ranch, scores of spiny lizards perform push-ups on shiny black Vishnu schist. The air is sweet with Baccharis plants, as if we're floating past an Italian eatery cooking with rosemary. Desert bighorn half hidden in the willows watch us float by as though we're the captives in *their* zoo.

We break through drifting skeins of webs from a spider hatch, flying in the cool upriver breeze as light-test fishing line, tickling our faces and carrying spiderlings upstream on their magic carpets. A bobcat's tracks line the beach, and bank beaver are busy between rapids. At night, we find black widows guarding their eggs inside elaborate cone-shaped webs under sheltering cliffs. I even meet a sociable, palm-sized tarantula, hairy as a dog.

For several hours every morning, it's jacket weather, then the clouds lift and we're suddenly back to T-shirts. While the sed-heads repeatedly stop to level their tripods and measure beaches vanishing from the March 45,000-cfs flood line, I get out and walk among knee-high barrel cactuses lining the banks above high water like the muscular calves of Lippizaners.

Sheep beds are kicked down to soft sand between the cactuses, pebbled with neat piles of steel shot–sized scat. I clear one out and perch as a sheep would, camera on my hooves, contemplating the smell of air through the canyon, pushing butterflies and tickling webs of more migrating spiders. The river runs green, laden with thin fingers of gauzy silt released from a distant rainstorm. A lone cottonwood rises above the willows and reappears on a large pool of river as mirror, transposing the rock layers from above.

For the last couple of days, the distant hum of airplanes flying as wary specks above the canyon rims leaves us in relative peace on the river. But today white ash drifts down to the river from a forest fire on the North Rim. Helicopters buzz back and forth with fire suppressants, but as we tighten the boat straps and point into Hermit Rapids, the roar of white water removes us from those unknown catastrophes scorching the real world above.

The Redwall limestone glows beneath the Supai layers of sandstone toward the North Rim. Above and beyond these layers, as we sink deeper in time through a chasm carved west, the winds cool with autumn as the sun arcs further south. We feel the rhythm that comes with a sense of place, alert to the changing of the seasons.

Backwaters are increasingly hard to find. In today's carp-filled hole, a scientist launched a "trash fish" 50 yards through the air and back into the river with a resounding splash—emphasizing his anger about the Canyon's dwindling native piscifauna. Undaunted, Fritz is now traveling with a pet carp swimming in a plastic jar, rescued from the same backwater and named like a stray cat. Carpe Diem will go into an aquarium for her five-year-old daughter.

"National Geographic," she calls me because I'm photographing Carpe Diem, "don't tell the Park Service."

From the time the campfire is started until it dies down after 9 p.m., she listens to the chief sed-head pontificate about beaches. "Amazing! Could you believe the size of it?" he asks rhetorically before continuing, "It went two-thirds of the way across the river." No one doubts the veracity of what he's saying, although he's said it so many times on top of so many gin and seltzers, he could be talking to the theodolite that he's spent ten hours squinting through every day for ten days. In the depths of the canyon, obsession is a respected part of a boatman's repair kit for the river.

Fritz adds that, in normal flows, she'll come upon 120 backwaters. But this trip we've scarcely seen 70. In the presence of scientists, no one wants to say what this might mean to the chub, but judging by Fritz's frown, worn like a barometer before the storm, even the healthiest population of chub is going to need more than the Little Colorado River.

The research work prohibits us from taking leisurely hikes up side canyons, so we can't explore Havasu Creek. The place is famous for periodic and destructive flash floods. Last month, the Park Service mobilized rescue helicopters to save several hundred people trapped here by a rising wall of water.

I convince a boatman to row up the creek for a quick photograph. The milky calcium carbonate waters fume clouds of turquoise up to the surface before being swept off and absorbed into the green Colorado. As the other in-saniacs flit past us in the river, led by Fritz, I tease out the story of the dramatic rescue she performed here three decades ago.

A woman amid macho boatmen (she's never referred to as a boat*woman*) in the seventies had a lot to prove to the doubting Thomases who ruled the Grand Canyon—particularly while rowing wooden dories, a more precise and sporty vehicle than the slow-moving, flat-bottomed rafts. The hazing routinely practiced upon new boat boys didn't bypass young Fritz—a suspiciously masculine nickname. Although she minimizes the role that gender played in her Colorado River beginnings, to meet the mark set by other boatmen, she became a hard ass, showed no fear other than in the requisite respect of scouting rapids, and found a knack for cursing that would give pause to sailors.

In her third trip as a baggage-rowing vassal amid a male-dominated crew, she pulled into Havasu Creek gone angry brown with a flash flood during a heavy rainstorm. Fresh from her park ranger job on the Green River, she happened to be wearing the distinctive Ranger Rick broad-brimmed hat to keep the rain out of her eyes. She rowed her submarine-prone dory right up to a dozen clients from another guided trip that were stuck on the wrong side of a creek, with rising waters trapping them in place. Even worse, their guide had just dislocated his shoulder and had his arm in a sling.

They looked at Fritz and said, "Thank God! The Park Service is here. We're saved!"

If she had been the Park Service, she would've radioed out for a helicopter. But, unlike most rangers, Fritz knew how to rig a Tyrolean traverse. As the rookie of her crew, she immediately set it up, giving directions to the men, anchoring the rope up high on both sides of the canyon. Fritz tested the rope: It held. Within no time, they started slinging clients to safety on the far side of the flooding creek. No one drowned. And so began another Grand Canyon prodigy.

We catch up to Fritz at the next backwater, looking for fish. We find eight more backwaters this afternoon, but just as many more potential fish spawning holes are high and drying in the sun. The Reclamation biologist on Fritz's raft jokingly suggests calling the dam on his satellite phone and asking for a large water release. Fritz does not miss his reference to a famous Floyd Dominy line from floating through the Grand Canyon with David Brower in 1967.

As told by the author John McPhee in his book about Brower, *Encounters with the Archdruid,* Upset Rapid looked perilously low to their river guide, needing more water to make the run safe. "If you want to sit here 24 hours," Dominy replied, "I'll get you whatever you need."

Times have changed since then. The Reclamation biologist accompanying this GCMRC trip, Dave Speas, is a garrulous, Jack Daniels–packing outdoorsman from Salt Lake City—Dominy packed Jim Beam mixed with river water. Today, river runners still drink their source of locomotion, but not until pumping the river through filters. Unlike Brower and Dominy trading barbs all day long, Speas jumps in with Fritz and gets dirty at every backwater, identifying fish. Like most scientists here, he's looking for solutions. Rather than extolling the virtues of man-made lakes as Dominy did, Speas is quick to point out the foibles of the agency he works for. In rapids that fill up the boat, he bails with a bilge pump rather than a bucket—Dominy merely sat back and smoked his cigars. When asked about the role of litigation in prompting the March dam release, Speas prefers to take the Fifth Amendment, other than saying, "That was and remains a low point for me and my colleagues in our work."

This evening in front of the fire, he chats knowledgably about modern authors such as Jim Harrison, Ed Abbey, and Peter Matthiessen. Dominy, it turns out, had read these environmentalist authors only to get a leg up on his enemies who supported free-flowing rivers. After Dominy retired to his Virginia property, containing a large number of stud bulls, small dams, and trout ponds, Reclamation mostly stopped building dams. Since then, supporting water conservation in the West has become a political agenda for conservatives and liberals alike.

Dominy oversaw the construction of three major dams in the Colorado River Basin—Flaming Gorge, Navajo, and Glen Canyon. As a hardworking adolescent survivor of the Nebraskan Dust Bowl, Dominy believed that bringing water to the parched Southwest showed patriotism, community service, and a way to rise above the hardships presented by the cruel forces of nature. He repeatedly spoke about dams as leading the way for a more "prosperous America."

Ten years ago, Rich Ingebretsen visited him in Virginia and asked if he took delight in flooding Glen Canyon. "No," Floyd Dominy replied, "I took *absolute* delight in flooding Glen Canyon."

In Marston's 2000 *High Country News* interview, Dominy spoke of the chub:

Sure, we've changed the environment of the river, but that doesn't mean we've made it worse. I happen to think that Homo sapiens is what the Endangered Species Act ought to be addressed to. I'm no fan of the Endangered Species Act. The thing that they're talking about now is that we've destroyed the humpback chub, because he can't live in clean water. Well, hell, all the archaeological digs around the world prove every day that various species have been evolving—flora and fauna—and expiring over the years.

Dominy's vision for reclamation, like any fundamentalist point of view, might not be in touch with the times. The Colorado River Basin population has doubled since his heyday, thanks to Reclamation supporting both agriculture and flourishing cities. Consequently, the region has attracted new ideas and progressive thinking that make resource protection and restoring the Colorado River a higher priority. McPhee's and Reisner's books about the river, featuring Dominy as an archetypal head case who can't keep his cigar burning through Lava Falls, have become required college classroom reading. Dominy's taxpayer-financed propaganda booklet, *Jewel of the Colorado: Lake*

Powell, is long out of print. He did more as an arrogant antagonist to jump-start the fledgling environmental community into a lobbying power than David Brower could have done without him.

Widely heralded as the champion of the modern environmental movement, Brower died in 2000 at 89. On December 3, 2009, Dominy turned 100 years old, still the outspoken and natural-born raconteur. He celebrated his birthday in Washington, D.C., a week later, telling stories of his glory days to a respectful gathering of enviros and conservatives. If Brower were alive, he would have attended.

A half century after Dominy's reign, our team of researchers camped at Grand Canyon river mile 176 is still trying to gauge all the damage he wrought. In the eerie three-mile calm upriver from the sawmill of Lava Falls, Fritz gives the morning speech with the usual work assignments, concluding: "Don't forget we have a rapid today too," as if any boatman needs a reminder.

At mile 178, we slink around a 60-foot black basalt tower spy-hopping out of mid-river like the vulcanized head of a whale. In dramatic contrast to the colorful sandstone upriver, we've now entered the volcano.

In the time-honored tradition of every Grand Canyon passenger, we climb up the well-worn trail to the overlook and stare down at Lava Falls. If a tape recorder had been hidden on this bluff for the past year, the tape would play back "Awesome!" hundreds of times.

Powell wrote, "What a conflict of water and fire there must have been here!" Although most boaters are too preoccupied to study geology here, the northern bank features a 350,000-year-old black lava flow. The lava flows repeatedly formed half-mile-high dams and backed up a lake that would have been the wet dream of Commissioner Dominy. Just like in Glen Canyon, these ancient volcanic plugs were structurally unsound because of their vertical, columnar formation. In the context of geologic time, the river quickly undercut the dams.

Powell spent three hours hauling boats around the rapid, wisely leaving the first descent of Lava Falls for Stanton 21 years later. Stanton took one look, and after losing Brown and others upstream, he spent two hours portaging. Six years later, the trapper George Flavell became the first to run Lava Falls.

Flavell epitomizes the modern boatman more than any early explorer who passed through the canyon. Unlike the hardworking Powell and Stanton, Flavell had no professional interests in publishing or building anything about the river. Like Stanton reading Powell, Flavell had been inspired by looking at the pictures in Stanton's article about the river journey in *Scribner's.*

Flavell's motivations were: "First, for the adventure; second to see what so few people have seen; third, to hunt and trap; fourth to examine the perpendicular walls of rock for gold." He showed up in Green River, Wyoming, in late summer 1896, built a flat-bottomed boat, and rowed it 800 miles to Lees Ferry in early October. He named his boat *The Phantom,* mistakenly misspelling it in his breezy journal, posthumously published as the *Log of the Panthon.* Famous for his bluster, he ran many huge rapids without scouting. Halfway through the Grand Canyon, he told his scared-green passenger Ramon Montéz: "There is only one stone we must not hit, that we must miss at all hazard—our tombstone!"

He also cracked open modern white-water technique by building a rowboat that allowed him to face forward rather than sitting backward and blindly stroking downstream while taking orders from a superior in the stern. He hadn't spent a lot of time on the river, so he mistakenly ran *The Phantom* with its bow downstream, and pushed on the oars instead of placing the bow upstream and pulling away from obstacles. Unlike Powell and Stanton, blindly rowing straight into each new disaster, Flavell navigated through Lava Falls by watching and then athletically reacting to every wave and current. Although the early upsets and deaths could be attributed to still-developing technique, many Grand Canyon rapids prior to the dams grew into sediment-filled, eddy-fenced, whirlpooled showstoppers.

This morning, at its usual 12,000 cfs, perhaps even lower because of the surging, washing-machine dam releases, "Lava Falls" is at its "follow the burble" stage. No question about the line. You have to miss the initial hole in the center, which Fritz says would result in raft *carnage,* and stay right of center down the gentle trough or burble directly into the infamous V wave. Here you ship the oars and hang on tight. You try to stay trued up through several tail waves and miss the thick slab of abrasive-looking volcanic rock—"the Cheese Grater"—on river right.

River left of the V wave is a submerged rock that rakes the rapids like a fin. It's no coincidence that boaters, attuned to the iconic fish of Grand Canyon, have adopted their own name for the central feature in the river's most iconic rapid "Chub Rock."

Up above, the "chub queen" is holding court on the overlook, still gesturing to disciples about how it's done, while waiting for the sed-heads to finish working upstream. It's nerve-wracking for Grand Canyon boatmen to linger more than an hour, contemplating the mother rapid of them all. They have plenty of time to eyeball the line wisely, and establish landmarks that line up with memory as they ride through in mounting terror. Those who take the trouble to walk down and look upriver at the rapid see the face of a 13-foot Waikiki wave sweeping the river's width. By virtue of busting through a couple of hundred times, Fritz knows that after the initial setup, squaring off her boat correctly for the biggest wave, the outcome is really not up to her. This is one rapid where smart boatmen show humility and contrition for any past transgressions committed against the river.

Depending upon flows, Grand Canyon has more challenging rapids. Like Lava, they're scouted before being run. In big water, "Crystal" (rated 7 to 10) has been deadly for six boaters. Then there are the confused waters of "Granite" (7 to 8) and "Hermit" (6 to 8) with its 30-foot drop. If a debris flow runs out of a side canyon during a rainstorm, even the tamest rapid can suddenly turn wild.*

Up at the overlook, I witness a sudden, collective about-face. "Let's do it!" is shouted with slightly less enthusiasm than Fritz showed during the chub dance. But I've never seen boatmen run to their boats and untie from the shore so quickly.

The only GCMRC boat that comes close to disaster is piloted by the accident-prone chief sed-head—helicoptered out after breaking his leg in Lava several years ago. As soon as he hits the legendary V wave, he's knocked out of the boat and disappears into a river shaken to the consistency of an exploding seltzer bottle.

Directly behind, on the verge of dropping onto the smooth tongue that leads to the same wave, I point out the chief sed-head's disappearing act to my young boatman. Because he's struggling to find his own calm before the storm, and get correctly lined up into the burble, he shouts back, "Shut up!"

Amazingly, before the sed-head's boat can get swatted by the tail wave, he leaps back from underwater into the raft like a salmon, and throws all his body weight onto the right pontoon to prevent the raft from high-siding all the way up and flipping over. He crests the final wave in acceptable style, in need of a good baling, but avoiding the Cheese Grater.

Next up in the batter's box, I'm balancing behind my gripped boatman with a camera in a waterproof housing. Part of the joy in being a passenger

---

Until December 3, 1966, Crystal was a riffle that not even Major Powell saw fit to comment on. Then, after a rainstorm that dropped more water than the dam releases, along with boulders, debris, and cottonwood trees, a new rapid was born. The hole in its middle gave many river runners sleepless nights. In 1983, when Lake Powell began spilling 92,000 cfs to prevent the dam from being breached, the debris flow boulders were pushed out of Crystal.

over the last two weeks has been to experience and capture the river in a way that would otherwise be impossible while rowing similarly gripped.

I clip the camera housing carabineer to my PFD and then pull it tight. At the crux V wave, upright like the Major behind the boatman—so I can photograph him being inundated with water before I'm inundated with water—I feel like we're driving over a widened rubber speed bump at high speed in a rainstorm. Then I quickly learn that standing up is the wrong choice. I'm thrown down clicking the shutter release while the boatman screams, "HIGH-SIDE RIGHT!!!" signaling that we should jump onto the right pontoon because the wave will flip us left. But we have so much momentum along with several hundred pounds of newly imported river that we too crest the final tail wave effortlessly, if slightly askew, before we decelerate into the calm pool below: like skidding away from a semi truck head-on into the breakdown lane.

My photos all turn out to be underwater abstracts.

Fritz's boat—identified by its trademark seine nets lashed neatly on the starboard tube—is piloted by a volunteer who's never paddled Lava before. He's all alone in the boat, and he makes a perfect run. The advice he'd taken, about holding his line and letting the river do the rest, came from Carol Fritzinger. No one uses her family or given names because boatmen here leave their pasts behind to reinvent themselves on the river.

Fritz is one of only a few pros who will trust her boat to a neophyte. In the rapid under the volcano, no less. She's sitting as a passenger in a nearby raft, smiling with her bottom lip characteristically bulging, enjoying the ride and one of many Grand Canyon moments of unadulterated animal joy: letting your body plunge through a white wall of water so you can come out laughing on the other side and see a world looking a bit brighter. She likes the idea of surrounding herself with volunteers who will work their way down the river, the same people who can't afford to pay three grand for a commercial outfitter who won't let them pull the oars.

She waits until the black-bearded Reclamation biologist Speas comes through in the last boat, standing in the bow, pumping in fury to lighten the boat's newly acquired ballast, and then raising his fist up in the air with pure delight on his face. I see a lot of people thankful that they've made the passage black side down through the most famous rapid rendered small by the grandest national park of them all. Although no one is talking about decommissioning the dam, the crew has worked obsessively to study the problems created by the structure. This will continue, I imagine, for many years to come.

THE LIGHTS OF LAS VEGAS

At Diamond Creek, on a guano-adorned snag above a river eddy, a cormorant is hanging out its wings to dry. The dirt road access through wild burro habitat is the only place to haul a boat into the Grand Canyon below Lees Ferry, 226 miles upstream. The river continues carving 55 miles north to Pearce Ferry on Lake Mead, then plods another 410 miles in fits and starts through Mohave, Havasu, and Imperial Reservoirs to the Mexican border.

My companion for the next week of paddling to Hoover Dam is larger-than-life Brian Dierker. For the first two days, a half dozen friends accompany us. Among our crew is a bird biologist and advocate for tamarisk as the salvation of willow flycatchers. The shrinking reservoir has created a fearsome rapid at Pearce Ferry, trapping the biologist's small motorboat. Brian, it turns out, is the jack-of-all-trades riverman who will rescue this unsuited-for-white-water boat by finessing it directly through the strange new reservoir rapids.

On our way there, we take turns paddling a surfboard and three kayaks. At the biggest river rapids, at mile 231, I jump into our support raft and take pictures of Brian, plowing through waves in his kayak, giggling as he's done for the past 40 years, ever since he was a 15-year-old on his first Grand Canyon youth trip. He had already grown six feet tall, and while college football scouts had their eye on the outsized young lineman from Flagstaff, Brian couldn't stop thinking about the river.

At 16, he went on a $10-a-day payroll to row other kids down the river in ungainly four-oared "snout" boats. They ate freeze-dried food, and when hunger knocked in their stomachs, they bonked carp and ate them out of the river like cave kids. Brian hastens to add, that in the seventies, you could walk across the river on the backs of these trash fish. More than 450 Grand Canyon trips later, he has come to know the place with unmatched intimacy.

In stark contrast to the indulgent modern river trip, the survivalist mentality of his early Grand Canyon youth trips cast Brian in a different mold. He ate with his fingers sans tables, and if his fellow guides snuck in a can or two of beer, he learned to pull the tops underwater so his innocent passengers wouldn't hear the fizz of his overindulgence. Brian remains a minimalist amid new millennial boatmen taking the kitchen sinks.

He cups his hands and drinks from the river. If the water goes unappealingly brown, all the more reason to break out the amber-colored bottle of Jameson.

He's a font of river lore, and straddled against the raft, his voice a bullhorn echo against the passing canyon walls: "I gotta tell you guys about ole sausage fingers, a 300-pound hydrographer I hauled around the Grand Canyon in my boat who got attacked by a condor." Although the obese scientist ate only vegan food in front of the boatmen, he broke out a stash of sausages and junk food each day in the privacy of his tent. A recently released radio-collared condor, accustomed to dining on animals killed by biologists to simulate its new wilderness diet, ripped open the napping hydrologist's tent to share the oily meat. Brian heard the man's screams and arrived just as the bird flew away.

A new story means rolling another cigarette. Unlike many smokers, Brian radiates coiled energy, with a nimble six-foot-five-inch concrete physique and intense focus of a Norwegian berserker, charging off to battle each time he reaches the river.

He has a facility for conversation stoppers, habitually emphasizing his listener's name like any good salesman. Talking about his even bigger brother, "the Wedge," whom Brian followed to the river in 1970: "*Jon,* he could snap your neck off in ten seconds."

About his mother, whom he described on the telephone to me, before mine died: "She's one of my best friends, and neither one of us should feel bad about puttin' our moms in the nursing home, because one day you'll thank your kids for doin' it for you."

Even riding a kayak, under his red helmet, he's easily identified by his walrus mustache and dense brown hair protesting ponytail confinement. His face is reddened, maybe from burst blood vessels as much as his time outdoors, yet he repeatedly refuses sun lotion. It's tempting to perceive Brian as a boy who never grew up, hiding behind a booming baritone, a petite Park Service archaeologist wife, Jen, and a slough of business obligations. But as Jen explains, he's often up all night shocking fish in the river, and when he's off the river, he's fixing engines. With the advent of stray gray hairs and his ailing mom, the realities of middle age have begun hitting home. So the prospect of paddling several days across Lake Mead took him by surprise. He couldn't remember the last time that he hadn't been paid to be in a boat.

"That might tickle my yard arms," he said over the phone when I first invited him last fall. "But we might not get along." We needed to break bread somehow. So in early September, while he prepared to take yet another work trip through the Grand Canyon with Jen, I took them out to dinner. For dessert, Brian gave me the keys to his house, truck, boat trailer, and the custom-made New Zealand boat so I could further explore Lake Powell. The implication of this litmus test seemed clear. If I survived without destroying his essential work tools, he'd paddle with me to Hoover Dam.

I'd only spent several hours with him, so his trust and generosity were unnerving. "What if I wreck the boat, Brian?"

He lowered his glasses and squinted at me, trying to take better account. Giving me a bruising clap on the shoulder, he announced, "I have confidence in ya, *laddie.*"

I tried again, knowing that this budding friendship could just as easily go south if something went wrong. "Why don't you let me put down a deposit with your company?"

He rumbled, "Get the fug-outta-here."

I threw him the keys to my Prius as a trade, and later learned Brian found another ride and left my car parked in his driveway.

On the side, while he's not contracting out boatmen and logistics for science trips, or running GCMRC boats as a researcher, he owns the Humphrey Summit Ski and River Supply in Flagstaff. At the USGS field office after my Grand Canyon trip, after Brian handed a young boatman a paycheck as a contracted employee, he said, "So you're *boss-man,* eh?"

"Never call me *that,*" Brian replied, immediately showing the youthful rower his distaste for hierarchal relationships. Brian spun around to deliver the next paycheck with his characteristic bear hug.

He is a gentle judge of character, hiring more than a fair share of misfits, brash Jimmy Deans, and down-on-their-luck boatmen, even trying to give some of them a shove on a new life path away from the river. Seasoned boatmen refer to him as a big brother who blows young swampers away by remembering their names a year later, a once-renowned partier now settled into the bliss of married life and a fulfilling river career.

He's perplexed by the crowd of boatboys unable to put up with hardships: low pay, bad food, miserable weather, rowing under hangovers or high-risk conditions over long periods of time. In earlier decades, suffering had been accepted as a necessary part of apprenticeship. "Unbelievable, isn't it, *Jon*"— he drops his voice a decibel on the *name* of whomever he is speaking to or about—"what pussies these *kids* are. We need to get 'em out there and make 'em swim a few rapids."

Anything related to water spins Brian's turbines. In the winter, when it's frozen, he's an unlikely picture of grace: a muscular hippie and former ski racer floating through powder. In summer, he prefers it wet: on a surfboard at his sister's coastal home in Mexico. He's the only boatman who routinely runs Lava Falls in the aluminum-bottomed sport boat he loaned me for Lake Powell.

The kayak hasn't yet been built to fit his frame, but once shoehorned inside, the boat wags with him like a mermaid's tail. Because he's not content to merely work the Grand Canyon, his ease with moving unwieldy and expensive scientific gear through dangerous rapids has made him the go-to man for Hollywood river shoots. He has worked behind the scenes on many films to cart actors, cameramen, and movie-making tonnage through white water. Brian gets the work because he's skilled and inspiringly calm in dangerous places, and directors know that he instinctually covers people's backs. While everyone else is working, Brian is artfully playing, as long as he's on the water. If people are tense, he makes them laugh.

He is in love with *all* watercraft. It doesn't matter if it's a houseboat, a Boston whaler, or a well-carved board. Brian will trace his fingers along its contours, tinker with the guts, and then mount up and aim for the chaos of gravity agitating lightweight hydrogen atoms chained to heavy oxygen atoms.

Several years ago, he accepted a job with director Sean Penn, scouting out Colorado River locations for the movie *Into the Wild*. Officially, Brian had been hired as the marine coordinator; unofficially, among the Oscar-winning crowd, he became Sean's drinking buddy. After a while, Penn suspected that Brian's charisma would be more fully realized in front of the camera. By the time Brian finished auditioning for the role of a free spirit named Rainey to act with Catherine Keener, the director knew that hiring Brian would save the budget millions of dollars. Keener had been pushing Penn to hire the talented actor Philip Seymour Hoffman for the Rainey role.

If Brian wasn't a character actor, seen through the lens of the camera, anyone could see that he was a *character*. Like Sam Elliott trading in his spurs for a motor home, Brian made Rainey into a homespun original, unfettered by pretension.

The movie portrayed the true epic of Chris McCandless (played by Emile Hirsch), paddling from the lower Grand Canyon to Mexico in 1990,* when the Colorado River still ran to the sea. Although Brian took the actor Emile under his wing (like Rainey with Chris) and showed him how to paddle without a stunt double through the rapids, Emile coached Brian on how to act.

His cameo lasted nearly a half hour, as long as the movie's famous thespian William Hurt appeared on the screen. From the perspective of the marine coordinator, playing the husband of an award-winning actress was as challenging as paddling through Lava's final tail wave with no kayaking experience.

Since *Into the Wild*'s release in 2007, Brian has good-naturedly suffered the gibes from boatmen everywhere. "Hey," a friend asked him up at Lees Ferry, "will you still talk to me now that you're famous?"

Today, a dozen miles below Diamond Creek on the river, a boatman drinking beer in the shade is surprised by Brian paddling past on his surfboard. "Yo, Brian," he yells, "I mean, *Rainey*, what're *you* doing here?"

At the last riffle below Bridge Canyon, a raft stenciled "Hualapai" pulls up as Brian is giving us surfboard lessons. Every seasoned boatman on the river recognizes Dierker, who jumps off the board, strides over to his raft, and digs through a boat locker. Instead of a permit, he hands the Hualapai guide a Humphrey Summit T-shirt.

"Lake Mead's going down," the guide says as he cranks the engine back up and waves goodbye, "Pearce Ferry Rapid is getting bad." Brian rubs his hands with glee. *This,* I can see my companions thinking, *is going to be interesting.*

For a hundred miles, the northern bank remains Grand Canyon National Park, but the southern bank is now Hualapai Indian Reservation. As the tribal council argues that it owns half of the river, the national park won't fight the claim until the Hualapai attempt to show that possession is nine-tenths of their law. Given the march of progress on the reservation, the Hualapai would not object to a river pipeline of water (in short supply on their plateau above), a jetty, or even a dam.

In the 1960 go-go years of cheap cement and the busy-as-beavers Reclamation, Dominy proposed placing another Colorado River dam on their

---

The young rebel McCandless explored the famous river to plunge farther "into the wild"—the title of Jon Krakauer's insightful book upon which the movie was based.

reservation at Bridge Canyon. The Hualapai stood to profit immensely from a dam, Dominy said, just like the Navajo prospered from Glen Canyon Dam, trading off their land to make room for Page, Arizona. No matter that the proposed Hualapai reservoir would doom native fish, and drown Havasu Creek, Lava Falls, and dozens of other rapids, as well as historic ruin sites and scenic canyons. The lake, Dominy said, would be beautiful.

Dominy Lake, Brower jeered. Dominy insisted that it would be called Hualapai Lake.

In *Encounters with the Archdruid,* McPhee recorded Brower's reply:

I'm prepared to say here and now, that we should touch nothing more in the lower forty-eight. Whether it's an island, a river, a mountain wilderness—nothing more. What has been left alone until now should be left alone permanently. It's an extreme statement, but it should be said.

"That, my friend," replied Dominy, "is debatable."

The all-powerful commissioner had been working for three years to place two dams: one at Bridge Canyon where Brian handed over a T-shirt to the Hualapai, and the other in Marble Canyon, several dozen miles below Glen Canyon Dam. Both dams would have harnessed hydropower from a thousand-foot descent between Lake Powell and Lake Mead. Although 140 miles of reservoirs behind the two new dams would not have irrigated or supplied anything beyond the turbines, electricity sales would have helped Reclamation finance a $10-billion plumbing network. Dominy schemed to move water a thousand miles from the Columbia River in Oregon to southern California, several hundred miles from the Colorado River through the Arizona deserts, and a couple dozen miles from Lake Mead into Las Vegas. Because California politicians were eager to ditch their salty, 242-mile Colorado River Aqueduct, they backed the plan. Secretary of the Interior Udall had high hopes that the unused water and power could be used to graft on a new leg of the Colorado River into his native Arizona, so he too stood behind the bulldozing Dominy. But at zero hour, the year before Dominy floated down the Grand Canyon with Brower, a Northwest politician smelled a rat and passed legislation that would prevent Reclamation from stealing Columbia River water for the arid Colorado River Basin.

Dominy let go of the Columbia. Undaunted, he continued pressing other water buffalo politicians to help build the Grand Canyon cash-register dams. On paper, the sale of hydroelectricity would have financed Udall's expensive

Central Arizona Project (CAP), a 336-mile aqueduct diverting river water east through Phoenix, then south to Tucson. But Dominy underestimated Brower. The country's most rabid eco-emissary had already lost Glen Canyon and had no intention of sacrificing the lotus flower of all national parks. Three months before their raft trip, Brower financed $15,000 in full-page ads in the *New York Times* and the *Washington Post*, headlined:

NOW ONLY YOU CAN SAVE GRAND CANYON FROM
BEING FLOODED . . . FOR PROFIT

He continued to take out craftily headlined ads in other national newspapers:

SHOULD WE ALSO FLOOD THE SISTINE CHAPEL
SO TOURISTS CAN GET NEARER THE CEILING?

An anonymous public official, but not Dominy (who wouldn't have hesitated to take credit for the attack), sicced the IRS on Brower's Sierra Club, warning the organization that it could lose its tax-deductible status if it continued to influence dam-building legislation. Brower, of course, broadcast this news as part of his campaign. As the Sierra Club had its tax-exempt status revoked, this government interventionism increased the flood of letters to congressmen, protesting the dams.

In public speeches around the country, the fiery orator Brower told his audiences that he had no objection to Reclamation destroying the Grand Canyon, as long as they built the public another. As Brower traded insults with Dominy while floating Grand Canyon waters that one wanted to save and the other wanted to impound, the commissioner counted his aces in Congress. Surely, Dominy thought, empathy for the environment had little place in a society that would benefit from dams.

Fifteen months after the ads to save the Grand Canyon, Sierra Club membership practically doubled to 67,000. Two years after the most public of all Colorado River fights began, President Johnson signed a bill authorizing CAP, the Las Vegas aqueduct, and a New Mexico dam that would stop the Gila River from flowing to the Colorado River. Amazingly, Brower had kept the dams out of the Grand Canyon. For all of his evangelism, the campaign broke the bank and the Sierra Club fired him.

Brian directs our gazes up to the southern rim: a sandstone-colored paper clip hangs 65 feet out over a nearby side canyon. The $30-million glass-floored structure is the Grand Canyon Skywalk, paralyzing its suspended visitors with a gut-wrenching view of the Colorado River a mile below their feet.

Hidden behind the rim are a couple thousand tourists mingling at a faux cowboy village, overnight cabins, several restaurants, gift shops, a budding visitor center, and an interpretive Indian village. City slickers from as far away as China are also offered Hummer tours, horseback rides, white-water trips, or covered boat rides. The map shows the hidden resort encircling a jet airport and helipads.

Although helicopters are not permitted to descend into Grand Canyon National Park, we're constantly being buzzed below Diamond Creek and outside the park boundaries. This runs contrary to Park Service philosophies because of the noise pollution and recent fatal crashes here. For its next attraction, the $2.8-million-a-year Grand Canyon West plans a rim-to-river gondola.

"We can hardly begrudge 'em for making their own perilous way down the river of American capitalism," Brian says while standing up and taking lazy strokes on his surfboard. "They tried a casino and it went bust, so why shouldn't they profit from their natural heritage by sharing it with tourists?"

He explains that their nomadic ancestors once roamed five million acres of the Grand Canyon, which was reduced to a million-acre reservation in the late 19th century. During the war with white settlers, more Hualapai were killed through disease than gunfire. The 1,400 surviving tribesmen live in the town of Peach Springs, Arizona, 30 miles above the river, battling poverty and a cultural affinity for obesity.

On our second full day below Diamond Creek, the river is still moving, albeit sluggishly from the back pressure of Lake Mead. One rapid after another is buried. At Separation Canyon's flooded debris flow, we pass the junction that led to the death of three men on Powell's journey.*

Later on during that mutinous August day, Powell came to yet another basalt-strewn waterfall, which, like Lava Falls upstream, he named "Lava Cliff Rapid":

---

*Seneca Howland, O. G. Howland, and William Dunn had suffered the Major's authoritarian leadership long enough. Unwilling to run the Separation Rapids, they spend days walking out, carved their names on a rock, then disappeared. Most river experts believe that Mormons, fearing federal spies, murdered Dunn and the Howland brothers by mistake. No trace of the men has surfaced.

Just after dinner we come to another bad place. A little stream comes in from the left, and below there is a fall, and still below another fall. Above the river tumbles down, over and among the rocks, in whirlpools and great waves, and the waters are lashed into mad, white foam.

He directed the men to walk above a cliff on the north side, leashing their boats on long ropes along the river below. Back on board in tranquil waters, the Grand Canyon's walls shrank farther behind with each oar stroke.

The cliff Powell walked around has now vanished beneath a ponderous river stirred into a mocha latte, seething with seven decades of trapped silt, lining the river bottom into Lake Mead. "Ahh, in the name of Christ, *boys*." Brian releases the throttle on the flimsy looking johnboat that he and the biologist have freed from its hiding place in the tamarisk, and shouts over to us on our raft, pushed by a 25-horse Honda. "What have we done to our river?"

We find Surprise Canyon, a major tributary coming down on river right, bustling with researchers seeking out the endangered leopard frog. As usual, the scientists all know Brian.

As the fifth of six children, he exudes an easy magnetism that makes him the center of every party. When he leaves the canyon, he admits to a small crisis of disintegration. Each time he comes back down to the river, he refills his tanks. He's kept it up for four decades: sleeping on the ground, logging immortal hours, and although his risk quotient lies between that of a stuntman and a firefighter, he's only been hurt twice in the canyon and never while boating.

Twenty years ago, while sleeping out of the pouring rain in a cave along the river, he accidentally cut his leg open to the bone on a piece of sharp schist. He spent the night alone, trying to stop the bleeding with his leg elevated, hand firmly pressed over the wound. Because a sick elderly man was being airlifted out from nearby Phantom Ranch, Brian hitched a free ride out on the spare helicopter seat. To close the wound required 24 stitches.

On another trip, while sleeping on the ground, he was bitten by the venomous brown recluse spider. Rather than stop the river work to be evacuated, he ran up a trail to the South Rim holding his softball-sized swollen arm in the air to seek medical treatment. He hiked back in four days later to continue collecting data.

During yet another research trip on Lake Mead, he was bitten by a black widow spider. This time, his rear end grew bigger than a volleyball. So he simply ingested antihistamine and learned to withstand jokes about what a big ass he'd become. Although boatmen know Dierker pushes the envelope with his boats on the river, it doesn't hurt his reputation that his accidents only occur after he puts his head down to sleep.

For two decades, he spent 250 days a year working on the river. His job shifted from rowing clients to working with scientists. "You name it," he says, refraining from the first-person pronoun to emphasize the team effort: "we do fish shocking, surveying, terrestrial vegetation, bird trips, archaeology studies, sediment transfer stuff, herpetology studies, recreational impact studies for the Park Service, et cetera."

Brian has done seining trips, but he has also mastered shocking fish out of the river with an electrically charged ball hanging off the bow of his boat. The procedure is well suited to catching nonnative fish that swim near the surface, so they began a massive culling project to reduce the nonnatives reducing the natives. He spent many months between 2002 and 2006 shocking, analyzing stomach contents, and killing 30,000 fish. Native species were measured, weighed, and gently released back into the river. After the first two years, word about their "death camp" got out among potential volunteers, and Brian had a desperate time finding help.

"For people who had never killed an animal before," he says, "it was pretty grim." When they returned to camp with several hundred writhing fish, they'd euthanize the nonnatives in a chemical bath and dissect them. Although they killed mostly trout, the euthanized carp wouldn't fit in the industrial-strength meat grinder, so they set up a miter saw to pare the fish down.

"The weird part of this work," Brian says, "aside from all of our nightmares about the killing, is that ravens normally follow raft trips and dive into camp for scraps as soon as you head downriver. But the thing about the death camps is that we got to noticing that we never, ever saw ravens."

Their work took place amid the drought, reducing the cold reservoir water, and warming the Colorado River by several degrees. Meanwhile, the chub population increased. But the bureaucrats couldn't agree if the culling or the temperature increase, or both, had worked in the chubs' favor.

Brian believes that Reclamation and Western Area Power, which broker the dam's hydroelectricity, have "walked all over" the Grand Canyon. Yet the scientists' alarming reports have slowly tamed the development-oriented, power-selling Reclamation into polite managers. "Can you imagine the mental angst that those good ole boys must be goin' through?" he asks. "One day controllin' the world, the next day they're being controlled by little chubs."

He starts his deep bass chuckle, blowing air through his mustache, and then we're all laughing with him.

The river turns north and slows after the last canyon and stalls in the backwaters beyond Grand Wash Cliffs. Lake Mead shows its bathtub rings stretching out a mile beyond the river. Pearce Ferry, like Hite Marina on Lake Powell, closed its boat ramp in 2001, as Lake Mead began shrinking. The new river channel is roaring, its water forced into an unnatural elbow while trying to catch a draining reservoir. A repeat of the extraordinary wet winters between 1982 and 1986 would refill the two reservoirs, but some say it will never happen.

As the river declines, tourism bureaus keep up a steady flow of propaganda about how Lake Mead has experienced a cyclic rise and fall of water since the reservoir began filling in 1935. "In the mid-fifties and sixties," they say on the website, "the lake sunk ten feet lower than today." But Reclamation's historic water chart shows that this drought is part of a long and unprecedented decline.

Two Scripps Institution of Oceanography researchers recently claimed that there's a 50 percent chance that the lake will be too low to store water for farms and cities by 2021, and a 10 percent chance it'll be gone in 2013. Although much of the data for their claim came from Reclamation, that agency doesn't believe that global climate models are regionally accurate enough to predict Lake Mead declines. Reclamation called the Scripps report "gloom and doom."

The researchers used a formula that showed annual changes in the storage (S_n) of Lakes Mead and Powell as equal to Lees Ferry flow (Q_n) minus Colorado River consumed (C_n), minus water stored by the reservoir banks and evaporation (L_n). The equation looks like this:

$$S_{n+1} = S_n + Q_n - C_n - L_n$$

Because "n" equals one year, they multiplied it by 50 years with a 20 percent water loss from climate change. The simulation shows the probabilities of when Mead will lose its water.

Many scientists regard the claim as alarmist, if not media mongering, so a diverse group of scientists and researchers from Boulder, Colorado, studied the claim. These scientists believe that the two researchers omitted nearly one maf of inflow, while overestimating the loss from reservoir banks and evaporation.

"The risks to water supply on the Colorado are serious," concludes the Boulder group, "but rather than being in a state of immediate crisis, there is a window of opportunity to craft effective policies to respond to these threats." Adjusting the formula, the scientists found that the 50 percent chance of depletion would occur at least 14 years later, in 2035. The two researchers then retracted their claim.

The numbers-crunching, model-making speculation from diverse experts shows that the Colorado River probably isn't going to be cavitating the dams anymore. From my father's point of view, this would simply be another example of how mathematics can solve the ills of the universe.

Brian and I climb a bluff above Pearce Ferry to perform our own analysis of Lake Mead. From this perspective, the reservoir could be a giant tilted goblet, pouring into the faraway mouths of Las Vegas and Hoover Dam intakes. Because the rim of the glass is wide and the bottom is narrow, the distant elevated salt stains show that more than half of the margarita is missing.

Before we can begin our cocktail hour, we have a rapid to deal with. My friends Adrian Glasenapp, Brian Scranton, and Mark Lellouch are no strangers to white water, but they're all looking askance at the strange and silt-formed wave below.

In the years since Lake Mead was first plugged, no reservoir in the world has accumulated as much silt, even though Glen Canyon Dam and other upstream sediment-catching concrete has slowed the accumulation. When the reservoir started losing water ten years ago, 200 feet of accumulated silt blocked the river and forced it a half mile west to cut a wobbling, bifurcated channel around a ledge of sandstone. East of the bedrock, it's an impassible waterfall. To the west and below our feet, waves beat on the shore, carving out the overhanging bluff we're standing on and repeatedly pulling wholesale acreage into the river with an echoing, "*ChusssssssSSSSSSSh!!!*"

In the middle of the current, a curling ocean-shaped, dark-chocolate wave makes Lava Falls' infamous yet pellucid V wave seem friendly. Brian says he's never seen this most unnatural of all rapids so steep before.

Hit that monster, I'm thinking, *and a yard sale of swimmers and coolers will get thrown into a ballroom-sized corner of misshapen waves, holes, and floating debris.*

Brian claps me on my shoulder, attuned to my thoughts. It's time for him to take the biologist's delicate johnboat through the wave—an unpleasant prospect at best. Yet Brian is one step ahead of everyone else, anticipating a good time, assured of his survival. Because he long ago mastered playing up tension amid hamstrung boaters, he strangely holds out his hand for me to shake goodbye and says: "I love you, *Jon*" then runs to the boat.

Vintage Dierker. We crack up laughing. As the river is reshaped, corralled, and compromised, at least boatmen are making the best of it.

Last year, to address the shrinking reservoir storage, Secretary of the Interior and Colorado Water Master Dirk Kempthorne met with representatives and water managers from the seven member states in Las Vegas, amid the garish fountains of Caesar's Palace in Las Vegas. Kempthorne made historic changes in the Law of the River.*

Prior to 2007, Glen Canyon and Hoover Dams managed Lakes Powell and Mead as two independent reservoirs. Now, according to Kempthorne's Interim Guidelines, the two reservoirs will operate together to meet delivery obligations for the length of the river. If the drought continues, Lake Powell will be drawn down first, keeping Mead full. In wetter conditions, Powell will refill while Mead is drawn down—to the chagrin of California, now receiving the lion's share of Mead water deliveries. In the worst-case scenario, the new guidelines show how consecutively lowering reservoir levels will then mandate a tiered series of lowered dam releases. All seven-member states and Mexico will share these water shortages.

Brian sets the shaken biologist in the bow for trim ballast, tells him to hang on, then coaxes out every one of the 25 horses available as he accelerates down the tongue, banks right along the granddaddy wave's biceps, and hydroplanes over a powerful eddy blocking the reservoir. Although Brian has gunned the boat's bow up at an alarming trim several feet above the water, he seems happily braced with his right hand on the starboard gunwale and his left on the tiller. Soon as the bow drops to prelaunch level, the biologist turns and shouts back his appreciation, muted by the roar of Pearce Ferry on a bender. From its resting place under the stern thwart, Brian produces the bottle of Jameson. The rapids would be a "6" if you're counting from 1 to 10, and for the rest of the crew, it's a quick cheat in Brian's nimble snout raft pushed by an outboard. Adrian and I pack up our cameras and bushwhack around it on foot.

---

*The Law of the River includes the 1922 Colorado River Compact (sharing 16 maf per year to 7 states), the 1928 Boulder Canyon Project Act (authorizing Hoover Dam and the All-American Canal), the 1944 Mexican Water Treaty (1.5 maf per year), the 1964 Arizona v. California decree (2.8 maf to Arizona, .3 maf to Nevada, and 4.4 maf to California), and the 1968 Colorado River Basin Project Act (authorizing the 336-mile CAP canal in Arizona, more dams, and the aqueduct to Las Vegas). These laws were the headliners amid smaller, yet crucial pieces of legislation, such as the prior appropriations doctrine, dating back to the 19th century.

Eighteen miles remain to the South Cove takeout. The wind is pushing clouds of silt and breakers that would tempt most boaters to beach it, but we follow Brian. His right hand is braced around the Jameson, his left on the throttle. He rides the breakers laterally until they foam over the transoms, then dips into their pockets and remounts the next cresting wave. The biggest waves repeatedly add gallons of sloshing ballast. So Brian repeatedly takes the boat ashore to bail it out. Because more than one friend has accidentally broken limbs riding with him in such extremes, he puts the biologist back on the raft and refuses to substitute any more people for ballast. We hunch over in our rain jackets, soaked by the spray, eyelids aching with silt.

"I'd rather have a bottle in front of me," Brian yells above the wind, "than a frontal lobotomy!" Suddenly we're laughing again.

Long-horned range locusts stand on silt banks, kicking past stray sprigs of tamarisk for whatever unsalted greenery can be found chasing the lowering reservoir. The water is warm as cooling cow pies, the sky a desert-washed blue. Even the Redwall limestone, blushing back in the Grand Canyon, is bleached out along the shores of Lake Mead. The whole landscape is a weary-looking monotone, swept by angry wind and encircled by dark, tombstone-shaped buttresses of crumbling conglomerate.

If Lake Powell is Dominy's Jewel of the Colorado, Lake Mead is Where Boatmen Go to Die. For 30 miles, we haven't seen a human soul.

That night, alone on the deserted boat ramp of South Cove, hunkered down out of the wind in a tamarisk hollow, Brian and I polish off the Jameson. Seventy miles distant, Las Vegas brightens a fifth of the sky with the yellow glow of a thousand parties. But with the master of the Grand Canyon telling stories, I'd rather be here in the desert than in any metropolis on Earth.

Before closing our eyes, we agree that it'll take several days to paddle to Hoover Dam. We make a pact to leave early every morning to beat the wind.

At dawn it's apparent that Brian is remarkably fit for still water paddling given all of his river time driving motorboats. During small route-finding quests on the large lake, he puts in a quick vote, easygoing as Bart the Bear off the movie set. Otherwise, he leaves the decisions and pacesetting to me. He's come here many times before, while filming *Into the Wild* and hauling biologists around for research. If he knows the reservoir well, he's being discreet and letting me enjoy a sense of discovery in a place I've never paddled before.

In the reservoir's morning calm, each new sterile horizon looks familiar. I'm sorely tempted to put my head down and paddle out of the drudgery of stilled river as fast as possible. Instead, the hours speed by with stories about family, mutual friends, and our time in the wilds.

Over the long weekend, we consider it good luck that a cold front is blasting the lake. This keeps the stinkpots in drydock, the temperatures in the low seventies and an otherwise flat lake hopping with waves. Like clockwork each afternoon, the cold front slips karate chops of turbulence under the warm air layer of the desert and directly onto the thermal mass of North America's largest man-made lake. The water begins bouncing, and the wind whistles into our cockpits.

We pass grebes diving for sushi. Gabbling coots hunt for lake-bottom roughage. Quail dart through the scrub oak.

At a sandstone reef recently exposed by the receding reservoir, Brian—like a civil-minded boatman—rights a submerged warning buoy, held down by a concrete disc. A large, glistening black widow spider, dazed by sunlight, struts from an underwater air pocket in the signpost pipe. We both jump and crab backward to our kayaks on the far side of the islet.

Because our tongues are sticking to the roof of our mouths, Brian bends toward his stern compartment and discovers that our two-gallon bag of drinking water has leaked dry. Even for one accustomed to river as beverage, here in the dead drain of concentrated pollutants, the empty water bag is grounds for a string of choice expletives. Instead, Brian chuckles: "Wellllll, lookee here!" His sleeping bag and spare clothing are sopping wet. Utterly unflappable, he reaches into the stern compartment of his yellow Prijon kayak, cups his hands, lifts them up, and takes a long swig of dirty water.

"Wanna drink, *Jon?*" His giggling is contagious.

This Friday evening, Temple Bar Marina is nearly empty. Half a mile above the docks, on sand that the marina used to float above, a jackrabbit skitters through browning tamarisk. A rabid-looking coyote stands watching from the shade.

In the bay, distant migrating phalarope lift off and land in eerie formations. The flock is God's own malleable clay: a parallelogram, a rope, confetti blown wide into mimicry of the shimmering windblown water, then flying back together again in tight, isosceles-triangle formation.

On Saturday, a lone houseboat sneaks toward Temple Bar in the midday calm. As the wind picks up, Brian aims for Lake Mead Narrows, a dozen miles away. Within minutes, the fetch created by 30-mile-distant waves traveling down Overton Arm have created a tumbling cross-swell. Every paddle stroke demands a quick brace on the opposite side to stay upright. Brian appears blithely occupied, so I mimic his movements as a model of stability. He's amazingly steady in the confusing reservoir chop, wielding his paddle like a Viking battle-ax. Although it's fun now, the water will go wild halfway across to the Narrows, where the wind is whipping the reservoir white.

I shout to Brian and point to the nearest land, a mile away: "Want to turn with the wind and head to Gypsum Reefs? I don't feel safe about crossing."

"That's probably wise," he replies. Left to his own devices, Brian would have beelined across. If rolled over by a wave, he too would have performed an underwater roll: pulling down on his paddle and snapping his hips.

We surf into a cove, where I breathe a giant sigh of relief. Brian groans as he unfolds his legs out of the kayak, but otherwise, he's at home as an otter backstroking through the storm-tossed Pacific. He flaps out his soggy sleeping bag down directly on the beach next to his kayak. Thirty yards above, I pitch my tent behind a windbreak of tamarisk and zipper it closed to the spiders, scorpions, and snakes.

Sticks and rocks at the waterline are festooned with tiny striped clams. In two years, these zebra mussels,* along with quagga mussels, have multiplied like a computer virus as their spore has migrated throughout the Lower Colorado, encrusting boats, dam meters, drains, and pipes.

"Should we wiggle our legs?" Brian asks, pointing uphill, eager to get away from the lake. A brief desert rain shimmers like ice on the tall grass.

We walk up a half mile onto a layer of recently surfaced travertine that resembles coral. The mineral-rich reservoir has carved out strange fins and gaping caves, so we crawl through and clamber up the disfigured knob. Brian is fearless, planting his Chaco sandals like climbing shoes. The friable volcanic rock breaks away in our hands.

Jets wink overhead on final approach for Las Vegas. Above the distant surf is the Virgin River delta where Powell ended his trip. "It was a strange and delightful sensation," his perennially nervous oarsman Bradley wrote. "For my part, I felt as Dante probably felt as he crowded up from Hades."

A year later, Congress awarded Powell $12,000 to perform a mapping survey of the Colorado River and its tributaries. So he took a shorter river trip

---

*Ukrainian vessels cleaning their bilges introduced quagga and zebra mussels to the Great Lakes in the 1980s, and since then, the mussels have wreaked havoc on many U.S. lakes. Reclamation budgets millions of dollars annually for divers to clean the mussels from the underwater intakes on an increasing number of Colorado River dams. Although carp occasionally eat the mussels, the invasion is so pervasive that engineers are now experimenting with underwater toxins.

and bailed out halfway through the Grand Canyon. For another dozen years, secured by larger government appropriations, he led mapping crews around the West. His study of Native Americans and the arid land beyond the 100th meridian gave him a perspective matched by few. Toward the end of this "Powell Survey," he produced a "Report on the Arid Lands of the West."

His findings of scant water were not well received. Even the elected officials of the most arid Western states refused to believe that their land couldn't support millions of irrigated acres.

Powell drew conclusions from observing every region: community *ejidos* in Mexico, Mormon irrigation techniques in Utah, and mining camps in California. He advocated small farms, based upon accessible and plentiful water, contrary to the false promises of Manifest Destiny pushing homesteaders toward dry soil.

In 1881, when the newly elected President Garfield appointed Major Powell director of the U.S. Geological Society in Washington, D.C., his study of Western landscapes guided him in shaping policy. His USGS would become the precursor to the Reclamation agency. Above and beyond his fascination with geology, Powell dedicated himself to solving the riddle of watering the arid lands. In 1888, Powell undertook a Western irrigation survey to show where dams, reservoirs, and other hydraulic works could be placed.

Based upon his extensive mapping from the previous decade, he told his irrigation survey team: "[T]hat the ends in view are not actual construction by the Government but plans and estimates for the use of the people and Reports should be prepared in the simplest manner possible." In addition to keeping irrigation at small, modular community scales, he imagined dams as tall as 84 feet (Hoover Dam is ten times higher). He foresaw reservoirs storing up to 50,000 acre-feet (Lake Mead has 500 times the capacity). And he didn't plan dams on the Colorado River.

The bold pragmatism that safely steered him down the wild river, combined with a Midwesterner's naiveté about wealth and power, would spell his undoing amid the treacherous politics of Washington. Powell became a fish out of water.

The evening sun throws cloud shadows and a startling new dimension onto the bleak, unnatural-looking lakescape. Brian is still subdued, devoid of his usual shaggy-dog tales. Cast under the soft sunset colors, my companion appears depressed.

He finishes licking closed another cancer stick and lights it up. "*Jon,*" he confesses, sucking in deeply, "the saddest part of my life is coming here to this so-called *lake,*" blowing out a smoke ring, "a dead zone after all my time spent in the canyon."

It's a half-hour taxi ride from Lake Mead to Las Vegas. Cresting a hill with a view of the city, I find the casinos and skyscrapers bathed in burnt-looking smog.

"You're kidding," the cabbie says, "the Colorado River doesn't reach the sea?"

"For nine years the delta has been bone dry," I say.

He's appalled about the idea of a trip that requires tenting out on the river because of all the "wackos gone loose in the wilderness." I reply that I've never had a problem while camping, but during several short visits to Vegas, I've observed what appear to be the same sorts of people on the Strip.

He looks back into the rearview mirror as he pulls up to the hotel. "Well, I don't camp out in Las Vegas."

I find June and the boys in the marbled-floor lobby of the MGM Grand Hotel. I must look like a wacko from the wilderness with an old backpack, unkempt beard, ripped shorts, and a dirty T-shirt, so I open the door for myself and smile to the wary-looking doorman and porter. They don't offer to carry my bags.

I lift the boys up in a double bear hug. Alistair has the undercut chin and long legs of my mother. Nicholas's brown eyes are the same color as his mother's—my striking wife. June's eyes are so big—evocative of Twiggy—that her girlhood friends still call her "Buggy."

A year ago, we discovered that our mutual attraction might be more than random chemistry. Our family trees show that our direct ancestors both emerged from a Pilgrim ship. A half century later, June's great-grandfather (eight times removed) Ichabod Bartlett married my great-grandmother (eight times removed) Elizabeth Waterman.

Although hardly noble lineage the odds of both being a Pilgrim descendant and marrying one are long. And this distant kinship might trump mere hormonal or intellectual attraction.

I recognized June Duell on Mother's Day 1997, in a photograph. Her face radiated warmth, mischievousness, and for lack of a better word, familiarity. I tried to meet her. But she refused to consider dating an "old man" 12 years her senior.

Four months later, when I tracked her down and met her in Wyoming, I found the photographs had not exaggerated. As she first caught sight of me, she thought: *This is my husband*. We found a strange and instant rapport. She altered the reclusive bachelor habits that could have ruled my life; I helped her quit smoking.

Seven months later, on the first day of spring, while cross-country skiing in a backcountry meadow, I got down on one knee and asked her to marry me. Then we had a difficult spell while I finished kayaking alone across the Arctic. As our first son arrived, I began staying closer to home. Now my journeys are elevated by seeing the world through the future of my sons, and through the unlikely reconnection of a family separated by the centuries within our American melting pot.

"Hey, Dad," Nicholas taps me on the shoulder, pulling me out of my reverie while smiling at June, "what did the fish say when it swam into a wall below Lake Mead?"

"I give up."

"Dam," he smiles.

In the MGM, an inexpensive room gives us a small window overlooking air-conditioning ducts on a tarred roof that lights up neon green after the unseen sunset. Because Las Vegas happens to be the only place I can see my family—flying back from a visit with June's sister in California—it doesn't matter where we stay.

In the hallways, we're confronted by life-sized celebrity cutouts. "Who are they?" Nicholas asks.

"Sammy Davis Junior, Frank Sinatra, and Dean Martin," I say, "movie stars."

"Yeah," he asks, "but who are they really?"

Outside the MGM Grand, along the well-lit street, we're pleasantly surprised to find synthetic grass. This is the largest hotel in Las Vegas, so it uses more water than any other building in town, but only modest amounts on a per-room basis, because of low-flow faucets and low-flush toilets.

As we walk down the boulevard, identifying more fake lawns, we're pleased to see this trend toward low-water-consumption xeriscaping. Although there are many garish displays of water and a surfeit of thirsty palm trees, the music-accompanied cannonades of fountain water at the Bellagio come from a natural spring rather than the Colorado River. Still, the Bellagio uses more water per room than any hotel in town, despite its recently installed xeriscaping.

The Waterman lawn-adverse family knows that up to 70 percent of water in America goes to landscaping or lawn watering. In the desert, this water use is further compounded by the heat and high evaporation rates.

Southern Nevada breaks down its most important resource into "consumptive water" (nonrecyclable) versus "nonconsumptive water," recycled in a wastewater plant discharged into Lake Mead—crediting the water authority to redraw the same quantity of Colorado River. The casinos fuel the local economy but buy only a surprisingly small 7 percent of the water supply and use less than half consumptively.

Another practice of water conservation being implemented throughout the drying Southwest is a tier system that increases the unit price of water as more is used. If it costs more, you use less. Las Vegas casinos subscribe to the highest tier but consume less Colorado River than any local users. Residents take more than half of the total water and then use 70 percent of it for consumptive landscaping. Commercial businesses take 14 percent of the water with modest landscaping use, and consumptive golf courses (many of which don't use gray water) buy 8 percent of the total water supply and let it all evaporate on the greens.

"Hey," tow-headed, blue-eyed Alistair yells, scrambling ahead to the next casino lawn, ripping out pieces of grass and throwing it up in the air, "what are they thinking? This is *real* grass!"

Although "lush" Vegas is hardly a model of efficiency, every municipal water operator in the world is watching. While other southwestern cities prepare for water shortages in decades ahead, southern Nevada has already reached the future.

Their frugality all started in 1922, when the Colorado River Compact was being negotiated outside Santa Fe, and sparsely inhabited Nevada had little influence among the six more populous member states. It came away from the negotiations with just 4 percent or 300,000 acre-feet of Colorado River per year. That occurred before Bugsy Siegel came and jump-started a paradise of casinos. The town celebrated its water through lavish fountains and faux volcanoes spewing colored water. Even as the drought hit, Las Vegas gained a half million new residents in subdivisions rife with swimming pools, artificial lakes, and green lawns. The former railroad stop became one of the fastest-growing cities in the nation.

So the Southern Nevada Water Authority (SNWA) initially targeted the most consumptive use of water: lawns. SNWA pays $1.50 for every square foot of lawn its residents or business owners voluntarily tear out to be replaced with xeriscaping. As interest waned last year, they marketed a $2-per-square-foot special. In the ten years since the turf-replacement program started, 100 million square feet of lawns have been converted to colorful gravel, boulders, or desert-friendly plants on more than 5,000 residential and commercial properties. Over seven years, Greater Las Vegas has saved 55,000 acre-feet (18 billion gallons) of water on lawn watering alone.

Still, Las Vegas uses more landscaping water than other southwestern cities because of limited rainfall and its infatuation with lawns. Indoor consumption is also high, which implies that residents are using inefficient appliances and water fixtures. The mindset of residents in Las Vegas is that they live in a plentiful oasis that will stay green from money if not water—even though their river and aquifer are shrinking—and it's their patriotic duty to keep up with the Joneses and celebrate the Great American Lawn. Residents of Tucson and Albuquerque receive more distant water diversions from the Colorado River and long ago reconciled that they live in the desert and had to embrace xeriscaping.

Many climatologists predict that the scant four inches of annual rainfall that evaporates over Las Vegas will diminish. Even the lower basin division of Reclamation calculates that, by 2050, the Colorado could run short of water 58 percent to 73 percent of the time.

To understand the extent of the coming crisis, I spend a morning 30 miles east of town along the puckering shores of Lake Mead. After driving through a fenced region protecting the endangered desert tortoise, I step into a metal cage. We're lifted by a crane above a 30-foot-wide vertical shaft.

A mile off, the receding Boulder Basin arm of the reservoir is a surreal blue against a charcoal-tinted landscape with thinning tamarisk. To the west is the Las Vegas pumping plant and water intakes. It's only a matter of time before the lake sinks under these pipes.

The foreman in the cage radios the crane to send us straight down the hole where another tunnel for a pipe is being drilled. We sway soundlessly 200 feet down through limestone, where three hard-hatted workers dressed in storm suits and lit by halogen beams drill horizontally toward the reservoir. Lake water sprays from the rock above. After five minutes, ears ringing from the horse-sized drill hammering against fossilized seabed, I signal to the foreman that I've had enough and we climb back into the cage.

After drilling another three miles out beneath the center of the reservoir, they'll lay the pipe and punch it through the bottom of the silted-over Colorado River bed. Then Las Vegas will be able to drain every last drop of its shrinking allotments from the lake—until the surface drops to 1,025 feet above sea level and the lower basin states (according to the Interim Guidelines) will renegotiate shortages. At some point, the Hoover Dam turbines will no longer run, and the Western grid will stop emitting electricity to over a million people. Right now the lake is at 1,115 feet above sea level and slowly sinking.

Because the $1-billion pipeline might not be completed before many Las Vegas fountains go dry, the SNWA is trying to pipe in aquifer water from 300 miles away in central Nevada. But this gambit has been stalled until an environmental impact statement is completed because of potential habitat damages and loss of water to Nevada and Utah farmers. The city pursues every option, such as buying water rights from the Colorado tributaries, the Virgin and Muddy Rivers.

The future of water in southern Nevada is the responsibility of SNWA's General Manager Pat Mulroy. She meets me in the hallway of the water authority headquarters on the 14th floor of a LEED (Leadership in Energy and Environmental Design)-certified building, shared with the U.S. Green Building Council offices. I'm carrying an empty MGM Grand pitcher, so she jokes that we should fill it with beer.

"I was thinking we might be able to fill it with water," I reply, vying for a photograph of her pouring a glass. "Do you have any left?"

"As long as we drink it," Mrs. Mulroy says, "then it's nonconsumptive use." She's trim and sports a healthy tan. Since she took this position 19 years ago, she's halved the gallons-per-capita-a-day (GPCD) consumption. In 1989, residents used 350 GPCD—twice New York City's, which receives ten times the rainfall.

Enviros like to compare lush Vegas's present 165 GPCD to Albuquerque's 110 and Tucson's 114. But the 2005 metric, even when calibrated to residences, has too many anomalies—such as climate differences and casinos being counted as single-family residences—to compare apples to oranges.

Twenty years ago, Mrs. Mulroy's first task was to unify the region's seven disparate water districts. Once these local municipalities signed onto the SNWA agenda, she gained the leverage to reduce water consumption. When she decided that conservation could no longer forestall supplementation, she began reaching out to other states and proposing water-exchange programs and endorsing pipelines. Mrs. Mulroy is lauded by casino owners for showing them how to save money and appeal to their water-conscientious clientele. But to those distant ranchers who might be subjected to her long-reaching transbasin diversion plans, she is the water buffalo incarnate.

Mrs. Mulroy, a Democrat, can hit from either side of the batter's box. In one moment, she talks about greenhouse gasses and climate predictions. In the next, she's promoting expensive, energy-intensive solutions such as wastewater plants, pumped diversions, or desalination plants. Whatever it takes to buy southern Nevada more water.

In fall 2007, Pacific Institute and Western Resource Advocates released a report analyzing water use in Las Vegas. Although lauding the city's innovations in landscaping water conservation, the "Hidden Oasis" report pointed out that the water authority uses more electricity than any Nevada consumer. Five percent of it comes from the Hoover Dam, but like the rest of the Southwest, most of the energy comes from coal-fired power plants. Although the water authority has a healthy portfolio of wind and solar power energy sources, until futher developed, green energy would only dim the lights of Las Vegas. According to the "Hidden Oasis" report, "the SNWA's use of one million megawatt-hours of electricity each year releases up to 450,000 metric tons of carbon dioxide into the atmosphere. Potential future greenhouse gas emission targets and rising energy costs suggest that water agencies should develop strategies to minimize energy-intensive diversions and water uses."

The report recommends that Las Vegas increase water conservation in the casinos by 30 percent and in residences by 40 percent by incentivizing low-use water fixtures and raising the cost of water. To be fair, if Mrs. Mulroy managed water in a less arid Colorado River city like Denver, she'd be widely praised, instead of simply respected. As a representative of profligate Sin City, she has to accept the controversy of the territory.

She's 56, dressed formally and both of her children are out of the nest. Compared to the bureaucratic clutter observed in other Western water managers' offices, SNWA mission control is a carefully orchestrated glimpse of the future. Along with antique pieces of furniture, the spacious earth tones of her office contrast violently with the view out the windows: alleys, rooftops, and enough casino cement to balance the Hoover Dam's weight opposite the surrounding foothills. It's an inspiring perch for a water manager who wants to change the Western landscape.

I've come from the river, so Mrs. Mulroy talks about its historic flow: "Somewhere between nine and eleven million acre-feet of flow is where we'll end up." She uses her index finger for emphasis, discussing a river that had originally been estimated to run much higher. She keeps such intense eye contact that there's no mistaking that she means business. "Some years we may see 14 [million acre-feet]," she continues. "To think that those years of high flow will come back is wishful thinking. As water managers, if you get it, great! But if you don't, you've got to have a fallback."

Seen through her crystal ball, the West is not going to be able to produce, divert, and deliver the ever-increasing amounts of water to match its growing population. As a short-term solution, she believes that water use has to flatten through wastewater recycling and water conservation.

"For the longer term," she turns to confront me fully from her chair, her hand slicing air above the water pitcher, "the Colorado River basin has to start looking outside of the box." She's generally referring to the "Big Suck" technique loathed by all ecologists: transbasin diversions. Then she gets specific, talking about how the state of Colorado took water from wet areas west of the Rockies to solve the Great Dust Bowl on the eastern plains. As a natural progression, she mentions how changing climate will increase the precipitation in the Lower Mississippi Basin.

She won't say it first, so I have to ask if this means a Louisiana-to-Colorado pipeline. "Yes," she says, as if it's my idea. "Why not bring water from a flooding river system to a region that has no water?"

(Of course, when I later mention this fantastic diversion to the water managers in Tucson and Denver, they call it, respectively, "magic water" that has "moved through too many sets of kidneys.")

Some of my conversation with Mrs. Mulroy focuses on making the West a better world for our children. By the time I leave, a half hour late in her busy appointment schedule, she takes a long drink from the glass next to the pitcher. I'm wishing that she lived next door so that she could give landscaping counsel to all of our water-happy neighbors.

Back on the streets of Las Vegas, we hold our boys' hands tightly, and Alistair often rides on my shoulders. This might be the wonderful world of Oz for adults, but it's not for children. Cirque du Soleil won't admit little people into its shows, so we settle for viewing the cramped aquarium at the Mandalay Bay Hotel. It's fitting that Las Vegas's biggest aquarium showcases predators, mostly sharks.

As we walk back to our hotel, a tour operator for Grand Canyon West hands me a brochure. I ask if he would recommend the trip to the Hualapai Reservation.

"I took the tour once and learned all about it," he says, "but then I started partying in Las Vegas and I've forgotten everything that I used to know."

June and I laugh out of politeness, but we move the boys on quickly. Because MGM's pool is our boys' version of paradise, we spend an afternoon splashing and playing with Alistair and Nicholas, surrounded by vacationers clutching multicolored drinks in outsized-stem decanters. The "Hidden Oasis" advice on efficient use of water at swimming pools is that city subdivisions need to develop more community rather than private pools. Still, Las

Vegas is the only southwestern city that requires pool covers to minimize evaporative water losses.

Back in the casino cave, devoid of sunshine, the gaming floor layout is designed for entrapment. During our second trip to the jungle-themed restaurant, holding our breath as we walk through clouds of cigarette smoke, we get lost. If you can't find the way out, the synergistic impulse is to join all the other pale-faced men and women working the slots and tables in a collective, hypnotic compulsion.

I need to get out of here, I'm thinking, *and go back to the river.*

On our last of two short nights, lying on the couch to let the boys sleep on the bed, we're suffused by the green glow from the artificially lit roof. We've been together for only one full day for the last month and a half. My predawn ride back to the river will come all too quickly, and I'll be alone much of the coming month. June knows that being troubled about my mom or with other issues won't promote the best survival instincts, so she asks, "How's your head?"

"Never better," I say, knowing that any other answer would make her demand that I come back home. As for her, the boys take up every minute of her day, so she at least has their companionship.

I tell her that I'd be lost without her and our children. The first time we met, on my way back from a long journey, June learned that adventuring makes me whole. Sleeping on the ground and watching birds and the challenges of hard-won miles through the wilderness have always brought me a sense of peace and accomplishment. But when you lose your mother, it's easy to feel inexplicably abandoned and lost, with the clock ticking off the seconds of your own shortening life.

The best chance for "a good four score and seven years," as my mom once told me, is to stay true to one's passions, but never stray far from family. I thank June again for letting me take the journey, then quietly kiss the sleeping boys goodbye before walking out the door.

MAJOR POWELL VERSUS RAMPANT GROWTH

At dawn on October 16, I meet friends at the bottom of the Hoover Dam, its white concrete glowing with the first rays of the sun. Compared to the heat of the surrounding desert, the river consists of cold, bottom-of-the-reservoir water. If we'd come an hour earlier, we would have put our kayaks in 20 feet higher to catch a release of water spinning the turbines so that several million Westerners can turn their lights on, heat up their coffee, and scramble their eggs.

According to Reclamation's taxpayer-financed book, *Reclamation: Managing Water in the West,* the Hoover Dam "proclaimed victory over the rampaging Colorado River and provided the means to divert water for the benefit of southern California irrigation and urban water supplies."

Once the world's largest dam and hydroelectric generator, it is now dwarfed by the monstrosities fragmenting rivers in Egypt, China, and South America (the same dams that Reclamation engineers visit as consultants). From below, the structure is gargantuan. Its concrete could build a two-lane highway from coast to coast.

One hundred and twelve men died to build this dam. An unknown number more died of carbon monoxide poisoning from working in tunnels alongside gas engines and dump trucks. Company officials attributed these deaths to pneumonia, and officially writing off these fatalities as "death by natural causes" kept the books cleaner and the insurance premiums low. Like flogging the peasants to build the Mahmūdīyah Canal to Alexandria in 1820, the bosses enticed starving men during the Great Depression to work by paying them 68 cents an hour, plus meals, with two unpaid days off per year. They had to buy company health insurance, but if they were one of hundreds who dropped from heat exhaustion on 130-degree days or were crippled by "pneumonia," they were cast off with no medical care.

The "Six Companies" that built the dam hired only two dozen black men and no Chinese among a workforce of 5,000. In 1931, as the men protested for better working conditions, company enforcers broke the nonunionized strike with guns and clubs. They fired the malcontents and hired thousands more scabs waiting in line.

Spawned with a blatant disregard to human rights, it proved fitting that Hoover Dam would kill a wild river, shunt flow to the delta, and destroy one of North America's richest wildlife estuaries. It would also doom the pike minnow downstream and help to add four more fishes and several birds to the endangered species list. In the irrigation rush that filled the void downstream, Native American lands and rights were trampled.

Many of the old-time construction workers and their families still call it Boulder Dam, blaming President Hoover for the Great Depression. They were housed in a construction town, Boulder City, that sprang up overnight like Page, Arizona. Boulder City overlooks the dammed-up Black Canyon, with its Boulder Dam Hotel, containing the Boulder Dam Museum. Boulder City, three dozen miles away from its namesake canyon, is one of seven SNWA municipalities connected to 160 miles of Lake Mead water tunnels.

From 70 stories below, one can imagine how the dam allowed the modern West to be won: Towns were built in its floodplain, far-off cities received water and electricity, and agribusiness flourished where the small farmer had failed. According to the dam's memorial plaque to the dead workers, they gave their lives "to make the desert bloom."

Although hundreds of lives may have been saved or nourished through flood control, even the greatest structure in the world cannot totally contain the river. In 1983, the storm floods that rinsed around and root-canaled Glen Canyon Dam's tunnels were bypassed at Hoover Dam and caused the same cavitation.*

Downriver, the flood raced through Davis, Parker, and Imperial Dams. For the first time in a half century, a lower-basin flood wreaked havoc all the way through Mexico to the Sea of Cortez. At least seven people lost their

---

*An experimental Hoover bypass in 1941 showed engineers how water cavitation would damage the tunnels, but they ignored it until the 1983 bypass forced them to patch and carve air slots in the tunnels.

lives. Hundreds of homes were destroyed. Losses reached $80 million, while parts of California and Arizona were declared federal disaster areas.

Seen from river level, the volcanic chasm of Black Canyon begins below a dam landscape warted with electric towers and an interstate highway, complete except for its final jump across the Colorado River. Once finished, the massive bridge will take thousands of cars per day off the dam's art deco–styled crest. Homeland Security will then shut down the single-lane highway to through traffic.

We push off into a current that will run for a dozen miles to the reservoir called Lake Mohave. At each stop, we tie our boats off so they won't float away in the unpredictable ebb and flow of Hoover Dam's turbine releases.

We're following the lead of a self-effacing but accomplished outdoorswoman from Boulder City. Izzy Collett owns Desert Adventure guiding, with the motto *Best Dam Paddlin' in Vegas!* She has generously volunteered to show off Black Canyon to me and my friends, Smokey Knowlton and his wife Judy, paddling a canoe, and Tom Lacy, plugged into a tiny play kayak. We clamber into caves, hot springs, and slot canyons running with water warmed by geothermal springs. The lowered river reveals thousands of invasive quagga and zebra mussels, festooning the walls amid passing brown lumps of yet another aptly named invasive species: rock snot.

At lunch, Izzy plays her flute. For the afternoon, a friend trades me his surfboard for my kayak. With desert bighorn sheep clattering on the cliffs, we share our histories.

For Tom's 50th birthday last year, to celebrate his father's kayaking passion, he snowshoed up to La Poudre Pass headwaters in Colorado, kayaked most of the upper river, and rode speedboats across Lakes Powell and Mead, to finish his journey at Hoover Dam. Tom, a financial investor, celebrated in Las Vegas two months after he began.

Thirty years ago, Smokey wanted to take his two teenagers, Ron and Randy, on a great adventure before they left home and started their own lives. Because the Knowltons were not experienced kayakers, and careful planning would have quelled spontaneity, they were clueless about white water. They each set out from Kremmling, Colorado, rowing souped-up rowboats called Sport Yaks into the tumult of Gore Canyon.

While immersed chest deep in a steaming Black Canyon hot springs, Smokey says, "Our first day nearly proved to be our last." Their only guide to the river was a basic road map, so they had no idea that the placid Middle Park waters dropped into the most hairball of all Colorado River rapids. They managed to sneak and portage and bluff their way through until they saw that they would be thoroughly pummeled, if not killed, in ten-foot waterfalls. They were rescued by a passing railroad car that portaged their boats out of Gore Canyon.

Chastened but not yet beaten, they all voted to continue. As an innovator in his California motorboat business, Smokey fastened the three stubby rowboats into a triangle with one-inch tubing, plopped a 14-inch inner tube on the bow of each boat, and used a canvas decking to hide the mess. Because their adventure took place in the bicentennial year, they flew an American flag from driftwood tied to the bow. For steerage, they added a ten-horsepower Mercury outboard to supplement their rowing positions on either side.

Like the Clampetts backfiring their overloaded Model-T into modern Beverly Hills, these river-billies had transformed their inadequate rowboats into the most ungainly craft to travel the Colorado. Still, the Knowlton family showed as much pluck and courage—or family solidarity—as Powell. Smokey named their boat *River Love.*

Smokey wore a paisley shirt and his signature black riverman's derby flourishing pins. They were proud of their white-nosed, stubby version of a Grand Canyon snout boat. As they continued downriver, onlookers frequently laughed at the outlandish craft. The boys turned the tables on these elitist nonbelievers by painting a smiley face on the bow. Thereafter, they laughed with the onlookers, toasting with their Pabst Blue Ribbons.

In Westwater Rapids, they broke an oarlock and flooded their outboard as *River Love* spun closer and closer to the dangerous hole in Skull Rapids. With little room to spare, Ron pulled the engine back to life, and they scooted out of the rapids in their twisted-up boat, lashed together with a thousand feet of polypropylene. Smokey and sons knew they could no longer substitute luck for technique. Nor would the Park Service grant permits to any yahoo equipped with an inner tube, so they found guides for Cataract and Grand Canyons. Boatmen still pointed at the absurd-looking *River Love,* but Smokey's humility and sincerity in taking his boys the length of the river impressed people.

Below Lake Mead, their biggest challenges were in portaging the big boat over six more dams and reaching the sea through the shallow, shifting mudflats. On October 7, they stood sucked up above their ankles on the river delta and posed for a photograph while bracing their American flag. Since the Knowltons' accomplishment, no one else has run to the delta from Kremmling or its Colorado headwaters.

Smokey has based his life on the river, splitting his time with Judy, renting out their riverside home on Lake Martinez, Arizona, while living an increasingly popular Southwest lifestyle as "mobile home tramps." Several years ago, Ron inherited Smokey's paddleboat business hauling "snowbird" tourists escaping northerly climates for a short dinner ride on the Colorado River. The Knowltons all take an active role in river cleanups, surveys with Reclamation, and historical site upkeep.

Smokey is a fit 70-year-old cancer survivor, versed in holding a canoe paddle or a tiller. He was named for the orchard fires his foreman father set off on the morning of his birth, to keep the orange groves from being destroyed by the southern California frost.

At the Willow Beach boat ramp, we pose for a group portrait and say our goodbyes. After picking up another two gallons of water, I continue paddling through river that stalls into reservoir. An elderly woman buzzes past on a recreational watercraft, a johnboat heels toward capsize with overweight fishermen, and a red-shouldered hawk watches all.

My paddle strokes clomp on with the metronome beat of a walking horse, past the sunset, on through a rising full moon. A "Veterans for John McCain" bumper sticker covers a "Warning" buoy on a submerged rock that would ruin a powerboater's day if the coming election distracted their driving. Dwindling Park Service budgets leave private citizens rescuing injured boaters and cleaning up the littered landscape. Fortunately, the Nevada riverbank is protected by the Black Canyon Wilderness Area, and as a concession to paddlers, motorboats are prohibited on Sundays.

In the water below, a glade of cottonwoods drowned a half century ago by the reservoir is draped in algae, with blurry carp shadows flitting around the trunks. Outstretched rock snot–slick tree branches reach up toward the air from their watery graves. I'm half-spooked by the moonlit arms beckoning from underwater, so I pull ashore and step out onto a dark bank: plunging hip deep in soft plough mud. It takes a half hour to crawl free, dig out my sandal, and rig a driftwood plank so I can pull the kayak ashore without plunging into more quicksand. To clean off the stinking, sticky black mud, I jump back into the reservoir from a cliff, then climb back out on volcanic rock walls sharpened by quagga mussels. While I stand still in a hot canyon breeze to dry off, great blue herons croak at the moon like maddened bullfrogs. On a high bouldered shore, hopefully protected from the dam's rising and childishly frightened by the dark, I quaff merlot and hit dreamland in a sweat.

Sleep is no refuge. I dream of Mom announcing that she's leaving Dad, as in divorce. But even while sound asleep I reconstruct reality by thinking that she's leaving because she's dying. The dream jumps through time and has me trying to console Mom about her mother dying: She wails, pushing me away.

I bolt upright in my sleeping bag and wake up by unzipping the tent door to make certain the trees remain underwater, that the reservoir is not crowding my camp. I'm safe, but the rotting algae on the shoreline stinks like a septic field. With no one to turn to, I flick on the headlamp and confess to my journal.

Is life about saying goodbye again and again? In that dream, I gave my mom a big hug when I told her I was sorry about her mom dying.

Because I can't see or talk to Mom anymore, I know that my subconscious conjures her up because I'm missing her. I dream of her in a way I never did while she was alive.

After Mom died, we flew east with the boys for her service in a Unitarian church, surrounded by the leafy woods of Durham, North Carolina. We lit a chalice, read poetry, and listened to Mom's many friends sharing memories. Unexpectedly, her African American neighbor stood up to say that he didn't really know our mother. She had cheerfully greeted him in the last months before the hospice nurses had come, and although he didn't say it, she had no reason to be so friendly because the police had repeatedly called on *her* to ask of his whereabouts so they could serve him with a warrant for some petty crime. Although this made us nervous for our mother's well-being, she threw the police off his scent because she trusted her neighbor intuitively on the strength of his good character. In the church, he told us about her cheerfulness and her asking about *his* health, never mentioning her terminal illness, as she went off for another long walk around the neighborhood. When she died, he was so stricken by the news that he had to come tell us about the support system that he lost.

He sat back down in the pew, alone, and I caught my brothers' equally surprised looks. Our mom meant so much to such a wide community of friends, but we scarcely knew her. Like many children processing their grief for a dead parent, the regret for our arm's-length love stings more than anything else.

When I leave in the morning, groggy from a lack of sleep, ringtail cat tracks circle the tent but avoid the crayfish remains, belly-up in the mud. I arch my back and paddle double speed against the headwind, trying to ignore the motorboats. As the decaying waters drop into clearer, deeper reservoir water, beaches are littered with balls, plastic bottles, sandals, paper plates, and toilet paper. In place of desert bighorn, wild burros roam the shores, snipping at tamarisk and braying from the brakes beyond. A cigarette boat passes in an ear-splitting roar, a half-minute in front of a prodigious wake. The bikini-clad crew clutches tight to their brontosaurus-mobile, piloted by Fred Flintstone himself.

I spend three days paddling across the 50-mile-long Lake Mohave, shaped like a big-bellied, long-necked cormorant reaching its bill toward Hoover Dam. For the first time in hundreds of miles, the Colorado River runs straight south, carving toward Davis Dam and Laughlin City, Nevada. My second night out, I have to drive a hungry burro out of camp before he nibbles holes through my kayak. Flightless roadrunners play hide and seek along the banks, while carp follow my kayak to shore, begging for handouts.

Each night my sweaty T-shirt and wet shoes dry out in the desert air, hung from the paddle propped against the kayak. Paddling 20 miles day after day in the October heat causes me to pass out as soon as I lay my head down inside the tent.

Unlike well-groomed Lake Powell, the moldy Lake Mohave marinas could be vastly improved with a Hoover tsunami. On my third day, I'm met at Davis Dam by Helen Howard, an energetic grandmother, photographer, and guide. Before the approaching security guard reaches us, she confides, "This World War Two earthen structure would be the easiest of the big dams to blow up." I laugh out loud.

As we cart my kayak up over the crest of the dam, I try to tell Helen that I can manage the load alone. But it turns out she's as spry and strong as a woman half her age, walking across boulders with over a hundred pounds of loaded kayak. As usual, no take-out ramp is provided for paddlers to continue down the river past the dam.

Because I had phoned the dam site yesterday afternoon to let them know that I'd be passing over at midday, the baby-faced security guard introduces himself politely, without challenging me. Steve has a radio in his left hand and a gun on his right hip. In six years, his only emergency arose when Helen's kayaking clients pulled their kayak over the dam in the dark. After the kayaks were searched, a dozen squad cars turned off their flashing lights, the officers holstered guns, and the hapless couple was summarily dismissed.

Steve is escorting us off the dam because pedestrians aren't allowed on top. He can't answer my question about how many cfs the dam is running. "There's two to three turbines running," he says. "Hear 'em?" The whole dam is vibrating.

"All three are each running six thousand cfs," Helen adds.

The dam was built in 1951, to control Hoover Dam releases and generate electricity for southern California. Unlike the bigger dams upstream, the enormous fluctuating releases from Davis—up to 20,000 cfs in a day—wreak havoc on backwaters and riverbanks downstream.

The early Reclamation director Arthur Powell Davis would have been oblivious to the ecological repercussions. Davis first championed hydroelectricity and the mega Boulder Dam while Reclamation bequeathed his name upon this mini dam. Davis got his first federal job when his uncle John Wesley Powell, director of the ambitious Western survey, pulled strings in 1882. In 1914, Davis led Reclamation toward trying to build dams big enough to have given his uncle apoplexy. To stop privateers from monopolizing water and power, Davis showed how the feds would provide both water and power for the disenfranchised Southwest.

As Hoover Dam moved forward, according to Donald Worster's *Rivers of Empire:* "If he did not have his own name up there in the public consciousness, Arthur Powell Davis could at least take comfort in that the Colorado was on its way to becoming what he had wanted it to become, a managed ditch running meekly from its headwaters to its mouth under the strict supervision of the federal engineers."

Downstream of Davis Dam, past a bevy of mallards and mergansers, the refrigerated river carries me beneath Highway 68, connecting Arizona to Nevada. In 1987, a shrewd entrepreneur, Don Laughlin, spent $3.5 million building the bridge, then donated it to Arizona and Nevada. If his Laughlin,* Nevada, casinos weren't already booming, his slot machines needed more oil after the bridge. Whatever gas money gamblers east of the river in Arizona saved from the long route up to the Nevada casinos could now be spent on gambling in Laughlin.

An osprey in a thorny mesquite studies a pair of wood ducks shading beneath a verdant Palo Verde tree. On less protected riverbanks, the huge Davis Dam releases have plowed away trees and beaches. The bathtub rings are higher here than anywhere else upriver. Despite the high tides, trash flutters along the riverbank. Across the river on the Nevada side, like a peregrine claiming Manhattan skyscrapers, a bald eagle perches on the faux paddle wheel of the Riviera Hotel & Casino.

---

*When Laughlin built up the gambling scene in the mid-sixties, a post office official insisted that the town be named after him. So the former dam-building town of South Pointe is now called Laughlin.

I drop off my absentee ballot in a mailbox, then pick up orange juice and green tea at a quick mart. Garishly tattooed drunken men are lined up for their purchases of hot dogs and oversize sodas, displaying their flaccid upper bodies, guffawing loudly. The chain-smoking female cashier is pleasantly amused by their company. They jump back into their pickup truck towing a boat and sporting rifle racks and a bumper sticker that reads:

GUN CONTROL IS USING BOTH HANDS

Back on the river, country music blares from speakers on both the Nevada and Arizona shores. I'm on my guard. I've learned how to travel and camp in safety amid polar bears and grizzlies in remote wilds, but sharing a river with ursine men missing teeth is much more terrifying. Last year, a dozen miles downstream, a young man and woman trying to paddle from Wyoming to Mexico were shot at with automatic rifles as they camped out on an island. Although unhurt, they wisely aborted their trip.

Along the Bullhead City shore, a man shouts directions to a lost-looking tourist on a recreational watercraft. "You should go upstream to the dam," he screams to the German tourist like he's deaf. He yells even louder, "Downstream there's incredibly nice homes to see!"

He's right. The diminished river shows one more sector of the economy that will be jeopardized by drought and overallocation: real estate. Surrounded by lavish lawns and showboat houses, one puny bunker on a quarter-acre lot sells for $949,000. If the river leaves these docks dry, the housing market from here to the border will go bust.

On the Arizona side, a basketball hoop is bolted onto a pole surrounded by two picnic benches. The court and dining area lie on an incoming concrete flood canal, as if the locals have given up on rainwater recharging the river.

I ask a man taking a river bath on the Nevada bank what's on the other side of the tamarisk.

"Desert," he says. "Where you going?"

"Mexico," I reply.

"Bull-tonkey!" he says as the current pulls me out of earshot.

I stop for dinner at the AVI Casino, alongside the "Freedom Bridge," marking the border of Nevada, California, and Arizona. Acres of green grass surrounding the hotel are roped off as a sanctuary. At the sandwich shop, a lonely-looking counter woman asks me where I'm going as she makes a sub sandwich. "You're not from around here, are you?"

"It's a long story," I reply. "I live in Colorado, and I'm interested in the river."

"Oh, you mean that flowing cesspool out there?" she replies.

"Where are you from?" I ask.

"Back East," she whispers. "Drugs and drinking here, it's really bad."

"I thought this was supposed to be an *oasis in the desert*?" I ask, referring to the sign out front.

"No, honey, it's really bad." She looks left and right to make sure her boss is out of sight. "Wanna take me with you? I gotta get outta here."

My sentiments exactly, I think as I eat my dinner alone, outside on the trucked-in sand beach. Cowbirds, grackles, honeybees, and red ants stand close or land on me for a handout. The bread is stale and because I'm not likely to break their habituation to casino scraps, I feed all of them. Like the beggars of Old Delhi, they contribute to the richness of the journey.

I paddle through the dusk, along the shores of Fort Mojave Indian Reservation. As a stranger in a strange land, I will paddle until darkness, so I can pitch my tent unseen in tamarisk thickets and leave undetected in the dawn. Blurry evening is my favorite time on the river. Long-eared owls clack their wings overhead, fish jump skyward for flies, and from my camouflaged position along the shaded bank, I can observe fauna emerging from the heat of day to drink from the river.

A fox trots along the California shore for a spell, then ducks back into the shadows. An osprey dives and splashes, but flies away empty taloned.

My kayak drifts unseen beneath three Anglo women having a tailgate party on the Arizona riverbank, clutching beer cans, engrossed in their conversation: "I hate men!" one complains. "I'm ready to have any ol' stranger, screw my husband, 'cuz I'm gonna play around."

From my hidden vantage point, I wonder if the women know that they're enacting an age-old ritual. Before humans descended from apes, we went to the river for renewal, to cleanse ourselves. After bathing, most mammals will pause along the banks, listen to the purring of current, the coyotes howling in the distance, the return mimicry of a loon, or the injured young woman now throwing up into the river.

If it's right, she'll go back to her husband. And she and her friends *will* come back to the river again—to talk, to play with their children, and to fish. Maybe to listen, or to heal too. Just like me.

Two more days downriver, Helen, Smokey, and Judy meet me at dawn in the Topock Marsh in the Havasu National Wildlife Refuge. It's early, a time of awakening for the river's inhabitants, so we paddle quietly, our senses on high alert. As the sun tiptoes above the horizon, we're lost in our own watchfulness.

For every dying or compromised zone, another part of the river is protected by government parks, recreation areas, and refuges. From Rocky Mountain National Park to the alfalfa-furred headwaters; from BLM acreage to the land of industrial oil and gas. From Canyonlands into Lake Powell and freed once again by the Grand Canyon before dropping into Lake Mead. From the Black Canyon Wilderness Area into Lake Mohave, then into the protected waters of the Havasu National Wildlife Refuge.

Reclamation unwittingly created Topock Marsh in the 1940s, by damming Lake Havasu. Although the Colorado River has experienced a net loss of native habitat, hydroelectric dams have built new marshes by flooding water beyond the deep channels and onto adjoining land. Although the middle of Lakes Mohave and Havasu are deep, the reservoir fringes create shallow-water marshes, ideal for waterfowl.

Within a decade of Havasu flooding, Topock Marsh attracted up to 50,000 migrating waterfowl, displaced from their Pacific Flyway by dams in California that completely flooded bird habitat. As the wind sways our kayaks along with the tall grasses, the marsh is busy with mallards and coots, moorhens, marsh hawks and grebes, buffleheads and loons, and a great egret. But these are only the birds we can *see*. Thousands more ducks and geese gabble and honk from the bulrushes, beyond the concrete dike that Reclamation built around the marsh to sieve silt from the river.

Because the water-consumptive plant and wild bird grasses sucked up river that could have been sold to farmers downstream, Reclamation started dredging their diked marsh in 1948. Two decades and millions of dollars worth of silt dredging later, the waterfowl forage could have been napalmed for a lot less money, along with the migrating waterfowl. In place of a rich marsh ecosystem, Reclamation immaculately engineered another miniature deep-water reservoir unsuitable for birds or diverse aquatic life. Duck hunters and fishermen complained vigorously. By the 1970s, media pressure, along with the Endangered Species Act, emboldened the refuge managers to control Reclamation dredging. Now the shallow-watered marsh is home to a large collection of endangered Yuma clapper rails.*

---

*The buff-colored clapper rail is characterized by its long, slightly down-curved bill and short rounded wings. Rallus longirostris yumanensis is endangered at state and federal levels, wherever it is found nesting or migrating through Arizona, California, and Mexico.

The wind is lifting our blades out of the water, blowing us into Topock Gorge faster than we can paddle. Brown dust whistles into our ears and softens the sunlight. As we raise our heads and airborne silt stings our eyes, the Needles dominate the skyline like the Grand Tetons.

Helen, her feet tightly braced in her sit-atop kayak, points out a site where she has seen a mountain lion. Then at Devil's Elbow, adorned with white crosses, we learn about distracted boat drivers repeatedly missing the turn and killing their passengers by crashing into the high rock wall.

We duck our heads against the wind. Smokey jokes about motorboaters who need to renew their licenses; Judy implores him to paddle harder against the gusts.

Through the cola-colored basalt gorge, reservoir back pressure floods small valleys into more marshes. The current pushing against my hand shows the river is still moving, trying to deny that a mere reservoir will stop nature from being drawn to the sea. As we take a break from the gusts on shore, the wind blows Smokey's canoe, then Helen's kayak, up the beach in banging somersaults; we sprint to the rescue. Strong wind has a way of dampening an outing. But I've come to see unpredictable weather, adversity, and marauding animals as the price of admission to real wilderness.

Unfortunately, protected wild lands are not immune to invasion. The riverbanks are rooted bare by wild pigs, escaped from nearby stockyards. Because the pigs are omnivorous, they eat the eggs of nesting clapper rails and American bitterns, then give chase to any creature that blinks. Two months every year, federal hunters wage war against the feral pigs of Topock Gorge.

So the trial and error of reclamation continues: dam the wild Colorado River for crops that feed us and our domesticated livestock; slow the dredges to save the wild birds; release domesticated livestock—pigs in this case—that kill the wild birds.

Helen leads us through flourishing tamarisk beyond the pig wallows to the Hum-Me-Chomp petroglyph site. Long ago, the Mojave Indians pecked varnish off the volcanic cliff walls to expose lighter rock and inscribe human figures, reeds and "♀" symbols. Their petroglyphs are less detailed than the older ancestral Puebloan art in the Canyonlands, but the Mojave were nomadic hunters and gatherers, struggling to survive in a desert. Their art is as spare as the surrounding landscape. We linger for several minutes, take photographs, and return to the river.

We continue battling the wind, past white sand dunes being salt-shakered into the river south of the spires, to the takeout below Topock Gorge. Smokey ballasts my kayak with their remaining fresh water and food before they drive off in Helen's car. I push off and ride with the wind onto the lake, thinking about how privileged I am to have met so many generous people who have given their time and expertise to paddle with me and share their knowledge of the river.

One of the challenges of solo wilderness travel is the potential for disaster rising in direct ratio to the amount of fun that you're having. Each time I ride down a wave in an exhilarating rush of wind and water, I paddle-brace and angle the kayak along the wave edge for optimal surfing. On the lee of every wave, if I'm not mindfully reassessing, I listen to my instincts and "the pucker factor": Imminent death is often preceded by loosening bowels and a discernible tightening of the sphincter muscle.

My mother often warned that I'd break my neck if I persisted in risk taking. But to my way of thinking, the worst-case scenario is that I'll capsize and get my camera gear wet before I can blow up a paddle float and right my kayak.

Finally, too close to shore, having too much fun, I catch a breaking wave that lifts me into a laughing, high-speed ride—scattering a flock of Canada geese—as a whoop of joy escapes from my lips. The wave spits me sideways, high and dry on a mud bar, until the following wave crashes against me, washes over my spray skirt, up to my armpits, and shoves me back into deeper water in a half-controlled slide. I barely hold onto my paddle, knowing it's quitting time.

Behind the "Private Closed to Boats" sign, I find a muddy shore that will allow one tent, ten feet above the waterline, in case the reservoir rises during the night. The landing is slick and green with mucky duck turds and algae—just like most reservoir beginnings. For the first time in four nights, I still have energy to spare because the white-capped reservoir demands pitching camp before dark. So I get out the stove and cook pasta, washed down with the night's ration of wine.

A few kayak lengths away, a sora, cousin of the clapper rail, emerges from the reeds and joins me for dinner. With the feet and beak of a chicken, she pecks into the mud for bugs. Off in the reeds, hundreds of shy cousins gabble their annoyance at my presence. Havasu could easily be renamed Coot Reservoir—although the bird scarcely existed along the Predambrian Colorado River, its numbers have grown with the stagnant water. Coots are undiscerning bottom-feeders, therefore no hunter would think of shooting them for the table. So as drought shrinks Coot Reservoir, the bird has declared these waters its winter feeding grounds.

At the entrance to the Bridgeway Canal, a marsh hawk rips a piece of flesh from a downed grebe. Before I can photograph the kill site, a cigarette boat roars past, oblivious to the "No Wake" signs and sends the hawk airborne. Def Leppard is gusting from their stereo, while the 40-something owner of the boat is perched on the bow, polishing his black paint job. He turns and curses mercilessly at his 20-something girlfriend for steering too close to shore.

A half mile ahead, I paddle beneath one of five arches under the thousand-foot-wide London Bridge. In 1962, Robert McCulloch purchased the old bridge from the city of London. The structure was dismantled stone by stone, shipped to a quarry, sliced, stone by stone, numbered, and then shipped to Lake Havasu. London sold its bridge for $2.5 million, while shipping charges ran the chain-saw magnate McCulloch another $4 million.

A quaint "English Village" open-air mall was built around the bridge after its 1971 completion. Now hundreds of boutique stores are shuttered down for the winter, except for a fudge shop where I buy tepid coffee.

Along the cast-iron balustrade chaining off the brick sidewalks, I introduce myself to an elderly man with a knee brace, retired and moved from California to one of McCulloch's surrounding subdivisions. Don claims that, after the Grand Canyon, London Bridge became the second most visited Arizona attraction. "No longer true," he says. "The summer tourist season isn't enough to sustain this." He waves his hands at the mall, empty but for several hundred loquacious coots, digging for their own fudge along the canal bottom.

"And the speedboat-building business that fed most of Lake Havasu City," he says, "is going belly up."

Cigarette boats still own the canal, cruising back and forth through the 19th-century bridge in clouds of diesel smoke, accompanied by revving decibel levels that would do a Harley biker proud. I quickly paddle back out to the lake to escape the noise.

Arizona's Lake Havasu State Park shores are rife with neatly painted outhouses alongside more than a hundred motorboat campsites. Compared to the wild California shore, the Arizona side—undergoing tamarisk removal—appears as well groomed and accessible as a golf course, except for refuse overflowing the many trash barrels. Still, at every shore I visit on either side of the lake, cryptogrammic soils are crushed by a labyrinth of destructive trails. Toilet paper and garbage bags are snagged in the tamarisk above the high waterline. Although the land resembles the windblown edges of a landfill, the water looks as clean as a high alpine lake. If the wind holds, I'll make it across Lake Havasu before the weekend crush of race boats take over the reservoir.

I spend the night visited by insomnia, camped east of high sand dunes, ringed by dense and tall thickets of tamarisk. Sleeplessness gives me the opportunity to journal, read, and take in the wonder of an upended day. As an owl hoots its mastery of night, I put down a Le Carré novel. A kangaroo rat bounds around my tent, eyes glowing like diamonds from my headlamp. I walk into the luminescent plain of the reservoir: warmer than the air. In the shadowed sand dunes, I'm surrounded by gleaming stars and naked mountains. Leaves crinkle under the passing footsteps of a small mammal circling camp in the thick brush. I'm delighted to know that I'm not alone, that the quiescent river is still home for wild predators. I click my headlamp off to let my eyes adjust to the black, then pad barefoot and silent, quieter than a cat, feeling as alert as any human on Earth, with my senses wide open to all that I might encounter.

A toad sings balefully. The musk of a smoldering campfire fills the air like sweet skunk. Stars repeatedly slip from their moorings and draw tracers across the sky.

I break trail up through the slipping dunes, stopping frequently to listen, quiet my lungs, and align my pulse with the sleeping reservoir. Below the high point, I'm drawn like a marshmallow to the fire by a distant glow from the west. On top in a gentle wind, I'm blown away: The night sky is stolen by the halogen glow of ten-mile-distant Parker Dam and the Central Arizona Project (CAP), its reservoir straw tilted up a mountainside and sequined with floodlights.

Before my trip began, I visited CAP headquarters in Phoenix and flew over the canal running 336 miles from Lake Havasu to Tucson. Modern reclamation in Arizona has greened the desert. At first, dams on the Salt and Verde Rivers diverted most of their water to flourishing post-Hohokam agriculture rather than returning it to the Colorado River. Elsewhere in the dry interior, 150 miles away as the magpie flies, aquifers were pumped lower and lower as Phoenix grew from a small town into a big city. In many places, six-foot-wide subsidence cracks circle the farm fields like earthquake faults, and show the ground dropping along with the underground water.

Parker Dam had been built to control floods and to send water to southern California on the Colorado River Aqueduct. Arizona's lawmakers felt shortchanged by their 2.8 maf allocation of Colorado River water in 1922, so they refused to sign the Colorado River Compact, and Parker Dam construction began without Arizona's permission. In 1934, Arizona Governor Moeur declared martial law and sent 60 Arizona National Guardsmen to prevent the dam from being built on the Arizona shores of the river. The state had already sued and failed in its attempt to stop Hoover Dam.

When the Department of the Interior sued Arizona to desist rattling its sabers at the Parker Dam site, the Supreme Court sided with Arizona because Congress never authorized the dam. After the California congressional delegation floated new legislation for its Colorado River Aqueduct at the Parker Dam, Governor Moeur shrewdly dropped his objections in exchange for the Wellton-Mohawk irrigation project farther down the Colorado River, on the Gila River—the major tributary that New Mexico would reduce to a creek.

Still, Arizona's water buffalos felt ripped off by California taking 1 maf more than its 4.4 maf entitlement. Not until 1963 did a plethora of lawyers restore Arizona to its original 2.8 maf rights, excluding 1 maf of water already captured on the Gila River, a major Colorado River tributary, which dams eventually sucked dry. Still, Arizona has to obey the fine print by giving more water to Native American Arizonans whenever they ask for it.

In 1968, after four decades of lawsuits, Arizona got its giant straw: The Colorado River Basin Project Act authorized federal money to build the 336-mile CAP. The costs eventually grew to over $2 billion. And the water had to be pumped uphill to reach Tucson. Because the two Grand Canyon dams were nixed and hydropower wouldn't be able to push Arizona's liquid gold deep into the desert, the Navajo Generating Station was built on the Arizona shore of Lake Powell.

In *Rivers of Empire,* Donald Worster pithily captured the build-out:

The Central Arizona Project was authorized exactly one hundred years after Powell led his small party down the unknown Colorado and exactly fifty years after the Boulder Canyon Project was passed. In the span of that century, even more so of that second half-century, the southwestern desert had been replaced over much of its extent by an astonishing urban and agribusiness complex, while the Colorado itself had been transmogrified into an industrial artifact, an almost perfectly realized expression of the new imperial West. What those northern rivers, the Missouri and Columbia, were still struggling toward, the Colorado had become—a part of nature that had died and been reborn as money.

On Friday morning, refreshed by several hours of sleep inside my tiny tent, I climb back up the dunes as the stars blink off into a pale yellow sky. Through binoculars, Parker Dam looks like a square-columned Parthenon above the reservoir. Its floodlights stay on until the first sun reddens the concrete walls.

I trudge down past soda cans strewn randomly in the sand. All morning I paddle by fishermen trolling for bass. Cigarette and deck boats race toward Parker Dam. Directly across the lake, the Colorado River Aqueduct is pumping water uphill with Hoover Dam electricity. Farther in the distance, CAP hums in synchronization with the far-off Navajo Generating Station, puffing clouds of sulfur and steam over Lake Powell. On my side of the reservoir, balancing the California and Arizona water diversions with a note of natural grace, the Bill Williams River National Wildlife Refuge infuses another marshland. Cattails are swaying with raucous red-winged blackbirds. The river, draining from the distant Buckskin Mountains, is neatly managed by yet another dam containing the Alamo Reservoir.

At the boat takeout ramp east of the dam, I drag my kayak onto asphalt, dig out a cart stowed in my stern compartment, and give the kayak wheels. With flat webbing looped over my shoulder, holding the bow of the kayak above the ground, I wheel the see-sawing kayak uphill in the breakdown lane, then back downhill onto the busy Parker Dam road crossing the river. The Arizona banks below are cliffed and fenced off a mile downstream by private homes, so I join the stream of car traffic toward the dam crossing to put in on the California side. Although I have pulled heavier sleds through glaciated mountains and across sea ice, wheeling a kayak in Saturday traffic is equally grueling and dangerous—compressing my shoulder muscles and putting me at risk of becoming roadkill. I alternate lanes to avoid oncoming cars, and rush forward to get the heavy kayak back in the water where it belongs.

Outside the Parthenon-deco dam, next to a white cross marking a highway fatality, a security guard stops me. "You can't cross the dam," she says. She's pointing the antennae of her walkie-talkie radio at me as if it were loaded. "There are no pedestrians allowed."

"I just want to put my kayak in the water and continue down the river," I say. "There's no access here on the Arizona side, and the riverbanks aren't cliffed over there on the California side," I point to the beach, then let her in on my travel plans: "I'm paddling to Mexico's Sea of Cortez, and I've got 1,300 miles behind, only 200 more to go."

Her eyes widen with skepticism. "Stand by," she says, and turns to speak to her colleagues stationed inside the thick-walled, faux Roman structure. After a minute she says, "Roger," and as the radio clicks back with two burps of acknowledging static, she turns back and repeats, "You can't cross," she says, "sorry."

"I phoned the director yesterday, and he said he'd give me his support."

"He's off duty this weekend."

"Can you call him at home?"

"Absolutely not."

So I smile and press the remote shutter release for my camera, mounted upright on its tripod in my kayak cockpit like a winking paddler.

"Why are you taking pictures of me?"

"I'm doing a project for the National Geographic Society, and it's my job to take photographs."

She cocks her head, like she doesn't believe me. I can guess why: I'm filthy, clad in sandals, shining with perspiration, and my red T-shirt is stained white with reservoir minerals that look like sweat stains—hardly the National Geographic photographer Robert Kincaid from *The Bridges of Madison County* come to capture the beauty of dams and win a security guard's heart.

"Please don't photograph me again," she says. As she turns to answer her colleagues on the radio and let them know that we're having a civil conversation, I push my remote and the mechanical paddler behind me winks yet again, but she hears it. "I'm sorry, sir, you'll have to leave immediately!"

"Could I quickly walk the sidewalk across the dam so that I won't interfere with traffic?" I ask with a smile.

"No, you can't," she says.

"You can search my kayak," I offer politely, peeved that the passing cars are not being searched. Besides, the crest of the dam is less than a hundred-yard walk.

"Leave now," she says firmly.

"Well then," I say as agreeably as possible, "you leave me no choice but to lower my kayak down those cliffs over there." I point back to the Arizona side of the river dramatically, knowing that sliding my kayak down the steep riverbank will be only inconvenient to me, but might look death-defying to her.

I'm not dealing with a reasonable person, though. "Please be careful," she says, happy to be rid of me.

"Smile," I say, clicking the camera once more.

Across the river, and over the ridge top, the hidden Gene Reservoir is the beginning of more than 1,600 feet of elevation gain for water running through the

Colorado River Aqueduct. The 242-mile pipeline—with 92 miles of tunnels, 84 miles of buried conduit and siphons, 63 miles of canals, 5 pumping stations, and 2 more reservoirs—is the main source of drinking water for urban southern California. Built in the Great Depression that spawned the Hoover Dam, employing up to 30,000 workers, the Colorado River Aqueduct allowed southern California to burst at the seams. The aqueduct was inspired by the water grab that destroyed Owens Valley in 1905, and built the Los Angeles Aqueduct, while both diversions inspired the 1971 Central Valley California Aqueduct diversion to L.A. The Southern California MWD avoided Reclamation, plumbed it all themselves, and eventually reaped the profits. Despite the two other aqueducts, the Colorado River Aqueduct gives 18 million people from Ventura to San Diego about a fifth of their water. If these cities continue to sprawl—following the combustive growth of Denver, Las Vegas, Alberquerque, and Phoenix—they'll need even more.

Given the Californian deserts made into farms from here to Mexico, however, MWD still bows to agriculture. Palo Verde Irrigation District, the Yuma Project, Imperial Irrigation District, and the Coachella Valley Water District—all watered by the river farther downstream—hold senior priorities, taking up to 3.8 maf. As in every state on the river, agriculture predates the growth of southwestern cities. So agriculture, until now, has taken most of the water.

Along the river, I've seen more recreational and real estate use than farmlands. The town of Parker, Arizona, started as an Indian reservation and a railroad town and, several dams later, has turned into the land of cotton gins and bole pickers, plucking one of the most water-intensive crops on the river.

South of the dam and north of Parker, "NASCAR on water" would best describe the "Parker Strip" of the Colorado River. Riverside bars are doing a brisk early afternoon business. I paddle past one floating open-air establishment, tied up with high-horse deck boats and one neon-orange cigarette boat. The stereo is tuned to classic rock-and-roll on the local radio station, "River Rat" (as motorboaters in the Lower Basin proudly call themselves). The gang at the bar turns to watch me paddle past; I wave. One loud patron hoists his beer toward me in a mock toast. "Ahh, isn't that a nice boat!" he shouts sarcastically, followed by a chorus of tittering barflies.

Despite the display of showy fiberglass paint jobs, propelled by diesel engines connected to jet tubes, a stranger to these parts could be excused for thinking the 1983 flood happened a couple of years ago. Many buildings are still condemned, teetering on river's edge like driftwood, stained with agricultural salts, and shuttered tight.

In its wake, on the California side of the river, RV parks and trailer home developments have sprouted everywhere. From one moldy dock, a 40-something woman clutching a frosty drink shouts down: "Hey beefcake, you look in your thirties, c'mon up for a good time!"

"Sorry," I say, pulling off my hat to show her my balding gray head, "I'm 52 and I want to get below Headgate Rock Dam by evening."

She laughs and waves me away.

The porches, beaches, and docks of trailer homes and bungalows built post-apocalypse are lined with lawn-chaired spectators enjoying the river traffic. Water-skiers, parents pulling couch-sized floats filled with screaming kids, and unmuffled drag-racer boats race up and down the river. I'm paddling river right against the reeds and rocks in hopes of avoiding a collision, while blocking my left ear with a hand as the racers go by. Paddling among the drag racers and surfing their steep wakes is as soothing as lying down on the tarmac of an airport landing zone.

The shore participants are nonplussed—Parker probably has the market cornered on hearing aid sales. If anything, I've become part of the show: a paddler trying to keep up with race boats.

"Wanna beer?" a big man shouts from the California shore.

"Sure, thanks." I catch the PBR, and I save it for later in my cockpit netting.

"Where you going?" he asks.

"Mexico."

"Watch your ass. Drug smugglers will shoot holes through you and your boat."

"If I survive the Parker Strip," I reply.

"You ain't seen nothing yet. They'll close the strip for tomorrow's drag races."

Past the rocking Blue Water Casino and its packed parking lot, the river morphs into lake. In front of the tiny Headgate Rock Dam that diverts farm water, I turn west up a marshy slough to a tunnel through the reeds, where I step out onto an abandoned tire and slog through the mud past a cast-off sofa. Wheels back on, I horse the kayak through soft sand and out onto a curving, hilly California highway for a two-mile walk around the dam. I turn on my headlamp to warn oncoming cars.

The sun has set. There's no breakdown lane. Either side of this Saturday night reveler's highway is lined with Colorado River Indian tribes'* No

---

*The tribes include the Mojave, Chemehuevi, Navajo, and Hopi. Their 250,000-acre reservation, created in 1865, stretches 50 miles south. But not until 30 years after the Hoover Dam was built did the government give them water rights to irrigate half of their acreage.

Trespassing signs. My ears are still ringing. But at least I'm off Parker Strip.

In the morning, after hauling the kayak all that way, my neck muscles are strained, locking my head into a stiff forward position. To look at birds or boats behind me, I draw a sweep stroke and swing the kayak around instead of trying to turn my neck. Although I covered only 26 miles yesterday, it felt like 50 with the final portage. So back in the current below the dam, I adopt a lazy paddle stroke. Amid a browning thicket of cattails, I wave good morning to two duck hunters in a skiff camouflaged for the nearsighted.

They shout back: "God bless you!"

Otherwise, the morning is still, without rifle fire. Countless mallards, cattle egrets, and cormorants shyly gabble in the reeds beyond the hunters.

The dredged river is now steered by concrete walls and rocks. These levees, built with public access roads on their crests, would contain a flood much bigger than the water I'm traveling on now. For the last 200 miles to the border, according to Reclamation, they're "correcting the misalignment of the river" by straightening and dredging to "alleviate the decreased efficiency in water use." In other words, a dammed river requires radical chiropractic adjustment. Seen from an airplane, their intent becomes clear: The former brown and silted river floodplain snakes east and west of the realigned and gray dike–confined river channel, surrounded by perfectly rectangular fields of white cotton, golden wheat, and green alfalfa. To the spherically minded federal engineer or hydrographer, the curves and chaos of Nature must be avoided at all costs. Not a drop of water can be lost.

I pull off the straight-as-an-arrow river to refill my water jugs from a faucet outside the Dock Restaurant in the Big River RV Park. I'm surrounded by elderly couples dressed in their Sunday morning best from attending the Baptist church a block away. Everyone is staring at me like a football player on a croquet lawn, so I smile and nod politely. After placing my order, I find the men's room and scrub the river mud off my face.

The restaurant walls are decorated with photographs of kids on dirt bikes, cars ripping up dirt on "the Parker 400" off-road race, and 500-horse neon-colored boats blurring by the hearing-challenged spectators on the Parker Strip. Several large black-framed photographs show the infamous 1983 event above the Parker Strip: the Parthenon belching Niagara Falls into the raging Colorado River.

I introduce myself to the owner, Jim, who slides a glass of iced tea and the grilled processed cheese product on a Wonder bread sandwich in front of me. Then I pose the question framing my disenchantment since Lake Powell: "Will I be seeing a lot of motorboat traffic downstream?"

"No, sir," he says, "you won't be seeing any boat traffic downstream."

"Why's that?"

"Every year this time of year the river runs so thin that no one dares take a boat through. Shifting sandbars everywhere."

"So what's worth seeing between here and the town of Blythe, California?" I ask.

"Not a lot," he says grimly, "unless you're into natural scenery."

Thirty miles later, I pull out my kayak onto a white, carpeted floodplain of invasive Asiatic clams, lean back, and make notes about the day's scenery:

Small herd of deer in flood channel. Bug hatches. Distant [highway] 95.

2 black-crowned night-heron—skittish, landing in tamarisk + bowing it over. Photoed tame-ish white-faced ibis. Then yellowlegs, _____ plover, _____piper—all together!

Can I still dry things overnight on tamarisk? We'll see . . . washed pants. PFD has taken on a smell that transfers to my shirt, so went shirtless, rather than PFD-less today.

The next morning before sunrise, I crawl reluctantly out of my tent, hidden in thick tamarisk. The temperature is a cool 48 degrees. Kayak and tent are covered in thick dew, so I pull on my wet pants to dry them out with body heat. As I brew up coffee, shivering, I stretch and bend my stiffened spine until it feels as naturally curved as old riverbed.

An hour later, I push off into swift current. The temperature has climbed another seven degrees already, so I can tell it's going to be hot today.

Along the Arizona bank, the reeds explode with the wooden clatter—*hkkkk, hkkkk, hkkkk*—of sandhill cranes, trailing long legs beneath slow wing beats, finishing their rest stop south from the Arctic.

After two hours of paddling, I need to get out of the kayak for a stretch and pee. I paddle over to the silt-covered Reclamation dike. As I stand up, three locals get out of their car atop the dike. Each man has a beer and a fishing rod in his hands. Except for the dog they're holding back, they have smiles on their faces.

"Broke down?" the eldest asks kindly.

"No, just stretching."

"You going upstream or down?" he asks.

"I'd really be having a breakdown if I was going *upstream* in this current."
They remain tight-lipped, so I reply quickly, "No, I'm going to the Sea of Cortez."

"You know you'll hit Mexico about a hunerd miles south?"

"Yeah."

"Seen any fish?"

"Lots of big carp," I say, hoping to get a laugh.

No reply, and they're looking at me like the village idiot. "Sorry," I say, "bad joke."

"We're looking for flathead." The leader pokes back his Caterpillar ball cap, maybe thinking about his fried catfish, then asks, "Have you seen a dike?"

He's not joking, so I smile, play it safe, and abstain from insulting him by telling him that he's obviously standing on it.

"Quartzsite."

"Where's that?"

"Thirty miles east."

Then he lets go of the rottweiler, which runs down to greet me on the river's edge, baring his fangs with a low, menacing growl. "Don't worry," the man says, now scratching his crew cut, "Mustard's friendly."

Mustard backs me into the river, drool bubbling out of sharp-looking incisors. The owner chuckles. In desperation, I hand the dog a Clif Bar, and although the flashing click of his teeth nearly takes my finger off, he stops growling after swallowing my breakfast whole.

"He jus' hungry," his owner says. The eldest asks, "You outta gas?" They're all laughing now.

"No, I've got plenty of gas," I say, "but that's all about my diet." Still no smiles, so I push off and wish them plenty of catfish.

"Good luck," the leader yells, "you'll need it!"

Five miles downstream, I get out and wheel my kayak around the diversion dam that irrigates the Palo Verde Irrigation District. I'm ready to be stopped by yet another official. Fortunately, the small dam, encircled by barbed wire, is unmanned.

Reclamation built the dam a half century ago to replace a rock weir and raise the river lowered by Hoover Dam. Since 2005, MWD has paid the Palo Verde Irrigation District to let a quarter of its 121,000 acres of alfalfa,* sudan

---

*In 2007, California grew 1.1 million acres of alfalfa to feed 1.8 million dairy cows in the state, surpassing cotton as the most popular crop in California. Farmers refer to it as "the queen of all forages" because it is resistant to drought and insects; farmers often lay it in the cotton

grass, cotton, wheat, melons, citrus fruits, and miscellaneous vegetables go fallow, giving thirsty southern California cities up to 118,000 acre-feet of extra water annually. Because the valley's crops are worth as much as $158 million per year, MWD pays the farmers $600 per acre to stop watering their fields. The program will continue until 2040.

Palo Verde acquired its Colorado River rights in 1871. Unlike the well-defined "Colorado law"—or doctrine of prior appropriation: first in time equals first in right—California hybridized the new doctrine with old English Riparian Rights law. Over the next couple of decades, the evolving "California Law" allowed Palo Verde farmers rights to water, even if they did not own land on the Colorado River banks.

As John Wesley Powell performed his Irrigation Survey, the Palo Verde Irrigation District's community water rights stuck close to his ideal for irrigation in the "arid regions." His model community, however, would also include scientific support to conserve water. In a series of 1890 articles he published in *Century* magazine, Powell proposed his community-based form of water use. "I say to the Government: Hands off! Furnish the people with institutions of justice and let them do the work for themselves." He felt the same way toward capitalistic ventures—such as the agribusinesses that would later infiltrate many of the southwestern water districts, plowing under the private farmer.

Although he leaned toward being an agnostic who believed in evolution, unlike the creationist Mormons, he had the open-mindedness to study and admire that Utah society's successful community-irrigated farms. His time exploring the Colorado River, surveying the West and researching water availability made him the nation's most respected authority on irrigation. But as his views diverged from the grain of American capitalism, big business–supported politicians began to cut his funding for the USGS.

Politics in D.C. gave him ulcers, while an exposed nerve in the stump of his amputated arm distracted him. Under the magnifying glass of Nevada Senator William Stewart and other mean-spirited congressmen, he began to wither. These politicians were anxious to revive their state's failing economies through irrigation projects. Because they misunderstood aquifers or were unable to grasp how their desert lands lacked enough water for farming, they didn't want to hear Powell's nay-saying reports. So Senator Stewart began to

---

fields to minimize herbicide use. With milk prices climbing, alfalfa appears to be the enduring crop of the Colorado River.

cut deeper, excising Powell's last chance for reform, through his Irrigation Survey within the USGS.

In mid-October 1893, Powell joined an expert crowd of lawyers, engineers, developers, and water buffalos to speak at the second International Water Irrigation congress in Los Angeles. Attendee Charles Rockwood had begun promoting a farmland in the California desert that would take more Colorado River than anywhere. Elwood Mead, a Wyoming state engineer, believed in absolute control over the irrigators who used water. Frederick Newell, like Mead, would rise through the ranks of the Reclamation Service that would supersede the USGS.

The organizer of the event, journalist William Smythe, had recently published his book *The Conquest of Arid America*. He stoked the attendees' fires with his rhetoric about irrigating every inch of the billion acres throughout the West as the foundation for a new empire. Defying the basic principles of Powell's irrigation plans, the delegates agreed to advocate that the federal government build great dams and reservoirs that would exploit every last drop and green the deserts.

On the second day, the Major lectured about his Colorado River exploration. With the right arm of his tweed coat pinned to his side and a graying beard stained with tobacco, the audience craned to see the buccaneer of the Colorado.

This talk had sustained him for a quarter-century of public speaking events. He can be compared to a modern-day alpinist repetitively hitting the after-dinner circuit to boast of his Everest escapades. Powell provided the evening's entertainment, interspersing moments of high drama with his knowledge of the Grand Canyon. "It is a rock-leaved bible of geology," he would say.

His applause had been respectful yet not thunderous. Powell could be severe, professorial, and among this crowd, his nerves were already on edge. They wanted to green the desert. He knew that his only chance to stop them would be through a speech he had to give the next day on water use.

Then Robert Stanton spoke about how his hoped-for river railroad would neatly dovetail into the expansion of the water empire: acting as the vehicle to transport the crops and coal to fuel the West. From the lectern, Stanton had the temerity to denigrate Powell for recalling the past with his ancient Colorado River expedition, rather than promoting the future growth of America.

Stanton's motivations were transparent. Powell had not given him the attention he wanted during his recent visit to D.C. Stanton still childishly blamed Powell for failing to recommend life jackets—resulting in his teammates' drownings on the Colorado River. Although the maimed Powell wore a life jacket on the Colorado, none of his crew did, and none complained either.

The engineer's plans for what Powell called an "impracticable" railroad had now reached the breaking point amid the year's economic depression, and Stanton was desperate to secure funding. Among his gerrymandering, he promoted a hydroelectric dam in the Grand Canyon that might be assisted by Thomas Edison. If Stanton's railroad were built, he predicted it would help the West grow through water. By tapping into the delegates' fervent campaign to build an irrigation empire, Stanton's speech received wide applause. No one recorded Powell's reaction, but Stanton by now represented a widespread development that infuriated Powell.

The following day, he begged a reprieve from the podium, claiming to be sick. But "Wes's" intimates could have guessed his plan: He couldn't leave L.A. without trying to stop the water congress from destroying the West.

On the fourth and last day of the congress, Powell came into the L.A. Grand Opera House knowing that he would scrap his talk on water use. Normally Powell was a lackluster speaker. Although he had plenty of vigor, he often used the cool, distant voice of the scientific observer. Behind a podium, he became the Civil War officer sitting on his horse in the line of fire, calmly directing his men to stand their ground. But among the ruthless water congress, consumed by a wrong-headed passion to wring the West dry, he charged. Like his Methodist father, he used the pulpit, speaking extemporaneously and facing down his enemy:

> When all the rivers are used, when all the creeks in the ravines, when all the brooks, when all the springs are used, when all the reservoirs along the streams are used, when all the canyon waters are taken up, when all the artesian waters are taken up, when all the wells are sunk or dug that can be dug in all this arid region, there is still not sufficient water to irrigate all this arid region. . . . not one more acre of land should be granted to individuals for irrigating purposes.

At first his audience sat stunned. Few knew that they were witnessing the same courage that made him reenlist with an amputated arm, and that allowed him to plunge into the unknown waters of the Grand Canyon. Powell continued with his repetitive rhetorical flourish, learned from endless diatribes amid the D.C. halls of power, but spoken with an honesty that defied those politicians out for his blood:

Gentlemen, it may be unpleasant for me to give you these facts. I hesitated a good deal but finally concluded to do so. What matters it whether I am popular or unpopular? I tell you, gentlemen, you are piling up a heritage of conflict and litigation over water rights, for there is not sufficient water to supply these lands.

The audience booed. They jumped up with heated questions. The most revered man in irrigation had suddenly become the villain for speaking his mind and imploring caution. Even the state senator C. C. Wright, who wrote the California water law that Powell endorsed, suggested expunging his comments from the record, and Smythe accused Powell of debasing their cherished crusade.

Among many general accounts and Powell biographies, Donald Worster wrote the best summation of this crucial event in *A River Running West: The Life of John Wesley Powell*. According to Worster, "Within a few more hours the congress, with its tail a little twisted, adjourned."

One of the attending USGS employees, Frederick Newell, tried to downplay Powell's remarks. Worster continues: "Newell sent a telegram to the Washington office, reporting on how Powell had riled up the delegates. 'The whole crowd jumped on him for some general statements. The Mexican delegate says he liked that—it was the only bullfight he had yet seen in this country.'"

The Major arrived back in D.C., incapable of surrendering to the politicians who would destroy the West through rampant development. In November, he gave congressional testimony about needed USGS allocations and the importance of his work. Predictably, Senator Stewart and his allies then further slashed funding to the USGS, forcing Powell to eliminate scientific programs and let many employees go. If this bureaucratic form of termination offended the Civil War hero, who had given his arm and later life to serving the country, he never publicly complained. Judging by his sudden decline in health, at 60 years old, the political skulduggery must have wounded John Wesley Powell more than the bullet at Shiloh. He resigned five months later.

I stop to camp on a bank 20 feet above the river in Arizona. Before pitching my tent, I have to kick away dried-out cow pies. Across the river in California, the outskirts of Blythe are populated by new but deserted housing developments, bannered with huge "For Sale" signs. Halfway between Phoenix and L.A., Blythe is suffering an economic downturn and job loss more pronounced than most farming towns. As part of the Palo Verde Irrigation

District, when fields go fallow, locals hit the unemployment lines. Although MWD has forked out an additional $6 million for a development fund to reimburse Blythe for its troubles, half of the businesses are boarded up. In the Colorado River Basin, water fuels the economic engine.

At a decent hour, with a cup of coffee clutched between my thighs, I paddle under the Highway 10 bridge, clattering with early morning commuters and cross-country truckers. Although the current gains a couple knots and has swept away exposed sandbars, the buzzing highway noise doesn't fade for another hour.

I'm determined to put in 40 miles, so I paddle tight to the banks to make the scenery go by quicker and provide an illusion of speed. I distract myself from the monotony of paddling by studying the water. Yellow wasps alight cautiously on the river without breaking the surface tension, float, drink, and hover off. Translucent miniature red dragonflies use the water as a trampoline: bouncing up and down in sheer abandon.

Tanned bundles of hay line the fields crowding the river. Kingfishers rattle above me in undulating flight patterns, stitching the river in search of fingerlings, as they have done since the headwaters. Harriers glide past like spy drones. A family of bufflehead ducks allows me to float with them, wiggling their webbed feet alongside alfalfa acres so musty they make me sneeze—scaring the buffleheads into flight.

At regular intervals, incoming canals and pipes spit foaming irrigation water back to its source. The air smells of insecticide. Curious, I paddle into the eddy of a spewing canal, test the water with my right hand, and paddle back into the current. For an hour, my hand feels lit by Bengay.

At a denuded river beach known by locals as Hippie Hole, a svelte doe-eyed blonde in a bikini stands next to a beat-up white Impala and watches her son toddle in the tainted water. As I'm pulled toward her while trapped inside an eddy, she smiles forthrightly and asks: "Have you been catching any fish in your canoe?"

Although I want to stop and learn what she knows about the river, I'm determined to make it to Smokey's and Judy's riverside house in Walters Camp, California, before dark. I badly need a washing machine, clean sheets, and a shower. The river has contaminated me. I wag my head no, wave, and break out of the eddy.

Silt blackens my fingernails and crusts my eyes. My clothing is stiff. I have infected cuts on my fingers. I feel dipped in the ocean, rolled in manure, and parboiled under the sun. Even on 90-degree afternoons, I can no longer justify jumping into the river to cool off. A week ago, I stopped licking my lips for fear of being poisoned by the briny taste of strange chemicals.

I paddle like a possessed man, too troubled to get out of my kayak. The river is a mess. And for the last week, lonely women, perched on the banks like Sirens, have beckoned me ashore.

Walters Camp is a backwater slough of giant salvinia and duckweed so thick that the kayak scrapes to a halt when I mistakenly paddle into it at dusk. The still water used to be the main Colorado River channel, but has now become a wastewater drain for the vast Palo Verde Irrigation District. The speedy current in the dredged, diked river channel avoids Walters Camp like the plague.

Nearly a hundred homes—more than a few sporting "For Sale" signs— line the southern bank. The recently built two-story houses are mixed in with trailers, tastefully jacketed with siding, screened porches, and add-on bedrooms. Several full-time residents watch over the second homes of fishermen or river rats. The common denominator here is a love for the river. Or what's left of it.

The cheapest homes list for a half-million dollars. Unlike in Parker, homeowners have repaired collapsed banks, rebuilt their houses, and got on with living after the infamous 1983 flood. But, thanks to Reclamation and the Palo Verde Irrigation District, no one can sell their place for half their asking price. The river in their backyards has become a stagnant stinking canal.

The water is ropy with invasive, floating tendrils of giant salvinia. If Walters Camp water continues degrading, the noxious aquatic plant won't last long because it can't tolerate brackish conditions. More pressing are the jungle stands of giant cane (*Arundo donax*). First introduced from East Asia to California in the early 19th century for roofing and flood control, it can grow four feet per week and up to 30 feet high. It consumes three times as much water as tamarisk, and chokes out other plants, including tamarisk. Boaters confuse giant cane with the more benign native subspecies, *Phragmites*. The difference is that *Arundo* has psychotropic chemical properties that kill aquatic life and deter nesting wildlife. Over the last few years, it has grown dozens of feet out into the channel and monopolized the Colorado River from Blythe, California, down into Mexico. Unless Smokey and sons have hit the downriver landing sites with a chain saw, the banks are so overgrown that no one can step out of their boats onto shore. Those boaters who brave the hidden underwater obstacles have adapted by picnicking and partying on mid-river sandbars.

If the Lower Colorado is a water fountain, Walters Camp is the spittoon. The fish are infested with Asian tapeworms. Coots are as dense as a foray of European starlings. And the water is browning like the Ganges.

Lack of freshwater recharge allows silt to accumulate, challenging boat passage year-round. The saline Palo Verde Irrigation District agricultural run-off that feeds this canal is also spiced with nitrogen and phosphorus—making the sole water supply for residents downright dangerous, if not illegal.

As part of the increasing water-related litigation from Mexico to Wyoming, the nonprofit Citizens Legal Enforcement and Restoration (CLEAR) water project filed suit against Reclamation in 2006. The Walters Camp action, however, is one of a few claims about pollution rather than water rights. The lawsuit reads that the river "has been allowed to become unusable, inaccessible, nonnavigable, thereby cutting off the public's and CLEAR's use for active and passive recreation, including fishing, swimming, and enjoyment of ecological and aesthetic values. . . . (and continues to be) unregulated, uncontrolled, and mismanaged without regards to water quality, natural resource protection laws and the public's constitutional and public trust rights related thereto."

The suit names Reclamation, the Palo Verde Irrigation District, the BLM, and the USFWS (from the neighboring Cibola National Wildlife Refuge) as defendants.

Like part of a new chapter appended to Marc Reisner's exposé of Reclamation in *Cadillac Desert*, CLEAR's claim continues: "the purpose of this lawsuit is to have this U.S. District Court adjudicate and correct defects in compliance and jurisdiction with water-related resources—including promised and non-extinguished public rights in navigation, access, use and enjoyment of natural resources. These public rights and resources have unlawfully been abandoned or ignored by the Bureau of Reclamation or buried under the cover of overlapping federal and state jurisdictions."

In 2003, Reclamation commissioned an engineering study. The price tag would run $2.5 million to install pipes that would toilet-plunge Walters Camp with cleaner river water. In response, Reclamation then did what the agency does best: nothing.

While taking two days off from paddling, I nurse my car—shuttled from Bullhead City south by Helen—across bouncing, windy dirt roads around desert washes and saguaro. The California river landscape is a monotony of charred volcanic rock, crisscrossed with jeep roads, neatly etched lizard prints, and wandering fox trails. Standing on my rooftop, I look for the distant river, hidden behind a green Mohawk of giant cane and forced out of its straight-line descent by the curving architecture of privately owned farmlands: the only authority in the lower river basin that Reclamation kowtows to. After gunning it through a last sand trap, I take the paved highway past miles of cotton fields, an eerie blur of waving white finery surrounded by jagged boulders in the black-and-tan desert.

The 2000 census lists Palo as populated by 236 people with a median family income of $14,333 per year, but those generous estimates need revision. The lively end of town is lit by a filling station, a bar, and a small grocery store. Once upon a time, the main Colorado River channel ran through Palo Verde, so I drive two blocks east to investigate. The aqua-brown canal makes Walters Camp look clean by comparison. Trash lines the banks, while DDT, fecal chloroform, and E. coli flavor the water at ten times the state and federal limits. No government agency has succeeded in cleaning it up, and every public river access in Palo Verde is posted with Imperial County Public Health Department signs—a dozen years old—that begin in ominous red letters:

WARNING
WATER CONTAMINATED
CLOSED TO SWIMMING
MAY CAUSE ILLNESS

The river's back channel is lined with modest homes that have beaten back the tamarisk and giant cane to bare sand and occasional palm trees. Several domesticated European strains of wing-clipped geese gabble in the water, but boat docks are empty and all the kids are working in the street rather than playing alongside the river. Because Walters Camp is suffering from the same pollution, CLEAR—hoping to fell one giant with two slingshot loads—has filed suit against Reclamation and the Irrigation District for violating the Clean Water Act.

Amid all this splendor, even laundered clothes, a hot shower, and two days of vacation from a kayak do not appease my growing consternation about the appalling neglect of the river. Palo Verde and Blythe are economically depressed with fallowed fields and shallowed water. Walters Camp is deserted. My first reaction is to quit the river and go home. Surely it will only get worse as I continue to Mexico?

Smokey and Judy rescue me with home-cooked meals, beer, and wine. Then they take me to historic sites along the river and indulge me in one of my favorite pastimes: photographing birds. The eyes of coots become glowing red coals through my telephoto lens. With powerful snaking neck muscles, great blue herons spear their long beaks at fish. Marsh hens with comic ruby-lipsticked chicken beaks paddle coquettishly along the edge of the cane. Stocky bitterns stand with bills to the sky in mimicry of the reeds. Owls hoot beyond the reach and light capacity of my camera, while a family of half-tame, subadult foxes prowl the trailer homes.

Renewed, I paddle another 35 miles downriver, past the smell of wild burro urine behind the impenetrable walls of giant cane and along river campsites in Picacho Peak State Park, below the metamorphosed and burned-looking Chimney Peak. This is the route plied by Pacific Ocean steamships since the mid-19th century, until the railroad and Laguna Dam came to Yuma and killed paddleboat commerce overnight.

From the Knowlton family home on the shores of Lake Martinez, Arizona, Smokey hauls me back and forth in an old motorboat to every nook and cranny of river and lake that I can't reach with my kayak. On the water, we find white pelicans, cormorants, osprey, grebes, ducks, and quail. On the desert banks, we study petroglyphs, coyote, bighorn sheep, and a tortoise.

I take a dinner river cruise on the Knowltons' *Colorado King* sternwheeler, retrofitted with a diesel tractor engine. The big boat hauls dozens of hard-partying blue-haired snowbirds, with Smokey's son Ron at the helm, and a jolly employee at the microphone regaling us with a revisionist Colorado River history.

Captain Ron, a redheaded, blue-eyed river devotee, has taken out a patent for a rapidly deployed underwater net to filter out the weed- and oil-polluted backwaters. Concerned about the river running dry, he's also sketched out a hopelessly futurist plumbing system to catch freshwater out on the delta; the high-concept project makes CAP and the Colorado River Aqueduct look like garden hoses. The Knowltons' long-ago junked boat, *River Love,* aptly describes this family's intentions.

Compared to the shallow Walters Camp and Palo Verde, the deeper waters of Lake Martinez—pushed back by Imperial Dam downstream—are flushed clean by the river. Real estate is flourishing. Fishing fanatics, water-skiers, kayakers, and motorboaters exist with an uneasy community of migrating birds and beat-down giant cane.

Smokey joins me for a long day's paddle toward Mexico. In the eastern sky, we watch large military planes disgorging parachutists over the Yuma Proving Grounds. Fighter jets scorch the sky. A white hot-air balloon, tethered high like a disguised cloud, monitors low-flying border planes with radar.

As the river slows into yet another reservoir behind Imperial Dam, mid-week boaters and fishermen wave as they speed by us in their runabouts. The reservoir needs dredging. Even with Hoover Dam and the 27 maf Lake Mead catching prodigious quantities of silt upstream, the relatively modest Imperial Dam and its 85,000 acre-foot reservoir quickly filled up with silt after construction. Reclamation now periodically dredges a 1,000 acre-foot pool right at the dam.

On a plateau above the troublesome river silt, Reclamation built Senator Wash Reservoir for regulatory storage, to capture water from cancelled downstream orders, and to prevent it from flowing into Mexico. Because of structural defects in the second dam, a dark-of-the-night rider allowed the construction of another delta dewatering facility along the border called Drop 2.

Imperial Dam looks like a long-hulled ship gone aground on the river bottom and emblazoned "DANGER STAY CLEAR" so that we won't get sucked away by intakes leading to the storage reservoir above, or whisked down into the silt-separation lagoons below. Built in 1938 to divert water into the All-American Canal, the ship-shaped dam is a monument to several hundred farmers working nearly a million acres to the west. No city or farmlands elsewhere in the basin receives half the quantity of water sent to Imperial Valley: 2.9 maf per year. One trillion gallons.

East of the dam, we load our kayaks onto the jeep driven by Judy. In what we hoped would be a quick portage, we're given permission to drive through the security gate, then we wend back and forth through the labyrinth of irrigation canals circling the river. After half an hour, on a private road, we find running water in an enlarged ditch behind the formidable wall of giant cane. There's no put-in, so we lower our kayaks by ropes and then slither down the bank, leery of placing more than one foot into the dirty water. The once mighty river is now a creek, unnavigable or at least inaccessible to boats bigger than a kayak.

"This is a poor excuse for a river," says Smokey. He's alone in the rear of a beat-up, fluorescent yellow tandem kayak, clad in a neon green "Yuma River Tours" T-shirt. The river elder paddles like he's on a drip line of Red Bull.

"I wonder if there's enough water to even paddle the last 20 miles to Yuma?" I ask.

At the spillway east of the tiny Laguna Dam, we slosh our way out through a thicket of cane and ankle-deep mud, surrounded by plastic bottles. This 1909 canal diversion and silt-trap dam, built long before the giant dams upstream, kicked the Reclamation Service in the pants. Within weeks of its construction, the reservoir filled up with silt and became dependent upon its half-mile-long earthen spillway to pass the river it could no longer store. After this, Reclamation expanded their ambition to build no less than 100 dams on a river system that used to run thick with silt.

Someday my grandchildren might experience mega dams much like the abandoned spillway that Smokey and I are dragging our kayaks across. The dams will be abandoned, grown over with weeds, cracking from dehydration, and free of security guards.

We circle around the final gate, which casts a stream into an even tinier channel below the dam. Thanks to the stepping-stones formed by more than a metric ton of beer cans, plastic bags, cardboard, socks, pants, and other detritus abandoned by local fishermen, we're able to bushwhack through more cane to the last vestiges of Colorado River rapids: a creek dropping two feet over an abandoned barrel. Smokey wheels my kayak loaded with camera gear another 20 yards downstream, and I borrow his empty bumblebee-colored boat so that I can perform one quick act of kayaking grace on this diminishing waterway.

A half dozen miles downstream, at the Gila River confluence, its 1-maf flow is long gone. An out-of-town fisherman stands knee-deep in midstream.

"Any bites?" I ask.

"Shit," he says, "I think it's barren."

Smokey says that the confluence has become a famous party beach, with rowdy revelers cowing the local law enforcement.

By the time we reach the Yuma railroad bridge at sunset, the creek is running 300 cfs—if it ran an inch lower, Reclamation would be breaking the law. I shake hands with Smokey, and Judy takes a picture. I wonder if there will be a river beyond this point.

Cars rattle across the Pacific Ocean Bridge overhead, lovers stroll the beach hand in hand, a dog catches a Frisbee, and I remind myself that if the riparian system has gone haywire, at least the city of Yuma has done right by its river. It took more than a decade and millions in grant money to disassemble the homeless people's sheds, divert canals, and purchase water rights. They created a wetland, planted native trees, and declared war against the invasive plants. Although no city can save the river alone, we can at least respect it as a living resource.

BIRDS AND FARMS

West of Yuma at the Reclamation desalination plant, I look for a guard at the abandoned security gate. A warehouse of reverse-osmosis pipes and federal office space—more massive than a Super Wal-Mart—is surrounded by more warehouses, a dozen water tanks, and a bunkered mixing vat with three giant blenders on its roof, on standby to mix untold volumes of water. A half mile away, the Colorado River shrinks like a magician's act flowing downstream: drawn away by diversions, evaporation, giant cane, and tamarisk.

The Reclamation plant landscaping is Kentucky bluegrass, surrounded by thousands of acres of alfalfa hay, and fed by a canal of salt, selenium, and fertilizers—mixed with several parts water. The Wellton-Mohawk Bypass Canal was built in 1977, to divert 125,000 acre-feet per year of Colorado River turned agricultural wastewater after rinsing through Arizona's Wellton-Mohawk Irrigation and Drainage farmlands.

In the Predambrian Era, these farms could have been watered by the adjacent Gila River from New Mexico, yet that river is dead. As the salty aquifer below the farms rose after Wellton-Mohawk farmers began to irrigate the land, poisoning the crops' root zone, the district installed pumps to pull out the water and drop the water table. Initially, they dumped this salty water into the Gila, where it flowed into the Colorado and then to Mexico, poisoning Mexican crops and creating an international incident in the late 1960s. Eventually, Mexico and the United States reached an agreement about a salinity limit for deliveries to Mexico. As an interim measure to avoid exceeding this limit, Reclamation built a 48-mile bypass canal to dump the saltwater into the eastern edge of Mexico's forsaken Colorado River Delta and the Gulf of California. From a thousand feet up in a small plane, the waste wash from the Wellton-Mohawk Bypass Canal glows in phosphorescent red and white.

Inadvertently, like many of the marshes created by dams upriver, the wastewater filled up an old Colorado River fault-line slough, the Santa Clara, turning several hundred acres of mudflats into a 50,000-acre marsh. Some Mexican farm *ejidos* were submerged, but families were eventually picnicking and swimming in the new Ciénega (marsh) de Santa Clara. More important, the brackish wetland became a nesting ground and migratory stop for 360 species of migratory and resident birds.* Although most of the Colorado River Delta has been sucked dry by agriculture, Ciénega de Santa Clara offers hope through hundreds of thousands of wing beats.

Birds in the Ciénega tolerate the Wellton-Mohawk agricultural waste because the agricultural water simulates a brackish ocean estuary, teeming with cattails and fish. But from the beginning, the canal had only been a temporary disposal conduit.

Once the Yuma desalination plant was built, it would clean the wastewater and send it back into the Colorado River, fulfilling the agreement with Mexico to deliver 1.5 maf per year of water with low salt content. Then the Wellton-Mohawk Bypass Canal would lose most of its volume and gain an even more toxic stew of concentrated minerals discarded by the plant. That would destroy the Ciénega, for during an eight-month shutdown of the canal for repairs, up to 70 percent of the marsh died off, compromising the birds until the canal began running again.

The desalination plant is Reclamation's Augean Stables. It took more than 15 years to raise the $250 million construction costs and lay thousands of

---

*Mexico has assigned protection categories to many of these vanishing delta birds. The threatened species that are rare or uncommon include: the Laysan albatross, brant, and snowy plover. Rare or uncommon species with special protection include: the least grebe, reddish egret, eight different hawks and falcons, the elegant tern, the least tern, and the short-eared owl. Endangered species include the bald eagle and the California black rail. Sadly, formerly endemic species including the fulvous whistling duck, roseate spoonbill, sandhill crane, gilded flicker, southwestern willow flycatcher, Lucy's warbler, and summer tanager are all extirpated in Mexico and have no protection status. Although others—including the Yuma clapper rail, the elegant and least terns, yellow-billed cuckoo, Western screech-owls and short-eared owls, and summer tanager—breed in the delta, but their populations north of the border are jeopardized. In summary, many of the still-surviving birds can become endangered and then extirpated if the delta wetlands are not protected.

reverse-osmosis pipes. Reclamation then realized that they would need another $23 million a year to run the plant. And somewhere along the way, Reclamation learned that they would have to replumb the faulty, old-technology pipes with more efficient pipes. In 1992, they finished, spending the taxpayer dollar equivalent of a small war, but the next year, they kept the plant closed because of an unexpected flood of freshwater down the Gila River.

Without the desalination plant to clean up bypassed Wellton-Mohawk water, Reclamation had to send all of Mexico's low-salt water down from Lake Mead. Several years ago, rather than utilizing a coal plant's worth of energy to suck wastewater through yesterday's reverse-osmosis technology at the desalination plant, and because Reclamation had to fix Yuma's excessive groundwater, they dug 154 wells around the city. Ninety-seven of those wells were used to pump up the water and mix it in with salty Colorado River to sweeten it up and help meet the treaty obligations to Mexico. So for two decades the extravagant monument to farming—the desalination plant—has taken Reclamation's early retirement plan. And the Ciénega continues to flourish.

I realize that they wouldn't fix the security gate to protect a disabled desalination plant, so I drive into the main parking lot and park my tiny hybrid next to the employees' oversize pickups. A lone guard speaking through an intercom mans the front door. I'm buzzed in to get my badge and then am greeted by the cordial plant operations manager, Len Martin.

His second-floor office, devoid of windows, is lit by a shipyard welding glare of fluorescent light. As a portal into his world, he swivels his computer monitor to show me a PowerPoint schematic of the Yuma wells, monitored by salinity gauges and flow meters. Len's job is to make sure Mexico gets 1.5 maf of water that's no more than 115 ppm saltier than what runs through the Imperial Dam.

"Hell," he says, "they're always bitching that they don't get enough water. In 1998, we gave 'em three million acre-feet extra!" Len is referring to a flood year that forced Reclamation to bypass extra water—more like *dumping* than *giving* it to Mexico. He chews on his pen in consternation. "They're unbelievable."

I ask what causes the surplus of groundwater in Yuma. He hesitates, thinking how this might be explained. He wears a professorial-looking pair of rimless, stainless-steel framed glasses. He's burly, pushing 60, with a two-week-old beard and a sporty mustache.

With two hands, Len pantomimes the vast sweep of Colorado River Basin sinking and narrowing toward Yuma and then fanning out over the Mexican delta. "I don't see what the problem is down there," he says. "They've got 800 wells sucking up groundwater and they won't tell us how much. It's some sort of trade secret." Len adds that no one really understands the vast system of subterranean water here, and the cost to map it would be astronomical. Although I want to ask how much less the mapping would cost compared to the desalination plant, this is obviously a sore subject, so I leave it alone.

Instead, I ask about the plant reopening.*

"Let's run it for a year and see what it does," Len says, echoing the water operators' words.

"As the canal flows shrink and become saltier," I ask, "won't this doom the birds of Ciénega de Santa Clara?" A year earlier, I canoed through the marsh and watched birds flocking through the air as the sun sank over the western mountains. If one accuses Reclamation of playing God with the river, their Ciénega is a success that mortals only create by accident.

"I don't care about a bunch of birds," Len replies. "Twenty percent of the canal water *could* be saltier. The Ciénega needs to come up with a plan to get more water." (A year later, spurred on by enviros, Reclamation agreed to team up with nongovernmental organizations and Mexico to provide an additional 30,000 acre-feet of water to protect the Ciénega.)

Reclamation has always been in charge of reclaiming water rather than preserving species. Len is a former military man and advocate for simplicity who would prefer living aboard his wooden trimaran sailboat. He's not shy about defending the Reclamation mission of moving water as efficiently as a new surge of troops.

"I've heard that there's a lawsuit against Reclamation for the polluted water in Walters Camp and Palo Verde?"

"They've tried to sue us before," Len waves his hand, "and it'll never go anywhere in the courts."

I hadn't expected him to be this candid, so I ask, "Really?"

"Straightening out the river at Walters Camp is nothing but a pain in the ass," he says, watching me write, craning toward my river-stained journal. I tilt it away.

"I didn't know that it could be straightened," I ask. "Don't they just want

---

*In May 2010, California, Arizona, and Nevada water operators will pay $14 million of the estimated $23.2-million cost to crank up the desalination plant at one-third capacity; the feds will cover the rest. In exchange for a temporary financing of Reclamation's expensive plant, the three states will receive a water credit to take the same acre-footage of Colorado River that would have been discarded down the Wellton-Mohawk Bypass Canal into Mexico.

to put some pipes through the dike and restore the Colorado River flow?"

He switches to a more philosophical viewpoint: "We've got another two hundred years at this river business maybe. . . ."

"And then it'll be all gone?" I ask.

"Pretty much."

"Most people are saying it'll happen a lot quicker," I add.

"It's overallocated, it's oversubscribed," Len continues. "Right now, the allocation allows people to take out more than you have. It's a matter of future growth and how people use their allotments."

"Like the green grass out front?"

"Yes," Len says, suddenly on my page, "that's right! Why do we have green grass? We can't put water back in the river from all that we create here."

Before continuing to Mexico, I need to understand exactly how farms use the Colorado River. According to Len Martin, Arizona agriculture took 95 percent of the water in 1975; agricultural water use shrank to 80 percent in the 1990s. As cities continue to grow, farms continue to shrink.

From Yuma, I drive an hour along the All-American Canal on Interstate 8 to Imperial Valley. The busy highway initially cuts through huge sand dunes, buzzing with off-road vehicles and two canals: an old ditch wind-loaded by the sand dunes, paralleling a concrete-lined aqueduct. These canals lie inside a tall brown iron fence, keeping a few immigrants south of the border.

The canal siphons up the Colorado River at Imperial Dam and sends the precious, desilted fuel 80 miles west to the vessel of Imperial Valley. Because porous sand and clay line the old canal, it leaks south like a sieve. So Mexican farmers pump up the leaking All-American Canal water from underground to irrigate their fields (as a supplement to the 1.5 maf that Reclamation delivers to Mexico through the regular channel). When they close the old canal in a few weeks, the informal drain to Mexico will be plugged.

In the 1980s, southern California relinquished almost 1 maf of water to let Arizona take its fair share and to slow Lake Mead's free fall. Desperate for more water, San Diego convinced California to pay most of the cost to cement the leaky All-American Canal so that San Diego could take whatever had been lost to Mexico as a yearly credit out of Lake Havasu.*

---

*The state legislature authorized $200 million to help pay for construction of the canal-lining project and another $55 million in voters propositions.

Mexico will pay dearly. The loss of 68,000 acre-feet (or 25 billion gallons) of leaked water will dry up several thousand acres of farmland and five times as much wetland on the delta.

I drive through an agricultural check station and tell the uniformed official that I'm not importing any produce that might contaminate the farms ahead. Westbound on the highway, I set my clock back an hour for California time, and count five border patrol SUVs in one mile. I am journeying backward in time, tracing the course of Mexico losing most of its Colorado River to the United States. I turn north off Interstate 8 and continue driving downhill toward the Salton Sea.

For millions of years, this below-sea-level plain acted as a natural receptacle for Colorado River floods. The entire region is filled with old river sediment, and from a geologic point of view, like the region surrounding Yuma, this is all delta, the final sand trap of the river.

After ancient northbound floods filled up the Salton Sink (or Sea), it evaporated as shifting silt and sand formed dams and flipped the river back south to the Gulf of California. In drier centuries past, Spaniards named the white, shimmering bowl of southern California "the Colorado Desert." Nineteenth-century California railroad workers and salt miners called it the Valley of the Ancient Sea.

In 1901, East Coast developer Charles Rockwood (who booed John Wesley Powell at the irrigation congress) teamed up with an inventive hydrologist, George Chaffey (who secured corporate bank investors). Rockwood picked Chaffey for his prior successful network of pipes enriching orchards in Riverside, California, and an irrigation project in Australia. Chaffey's avarice amid the socialized farming community down under, along with his shady lieutenants, brought him charging back to California to make real money again. His first move was to rename the Colorado Desert. In the spirit of empire building, he called it the Imperial Valley. Then he set his men on building a canal.

Chaffey put a headgate in the United States and ran his new channel 60 miles west though Mexico. Utilizing a flood path better than any engineer's design, he ran his canal into an ancient river, *el* Alámo (cottonwood) running north to the United States.* In exchange for this trespass, half of the water went into Mexico farm fields, developed by American entrepreneurs. In

---

Chaffey named his newly dug diversion the Imperial Canal. As a well-traveled Canadian born to English parents, Chaffey would have known that the Imperial Canal in China reaped fortunes in shipping by connecting Peking to the Yellow River.

Imperial Valley, Chaffey and Rockwood sold farmers Colorado River water at 50 cents per acre-foot and advertised it as the cheapest water anywhere. Through the homesteading act, the federal government sold the farmland for $1.25 per acre. Rockwood then began beating the publicity drums to bring in more farmers.

The September 1901 *New York Tribune*'s "Reclaiming a Desert" detailed hundreds of settlers rushing into the lower Colorado River farmlands. Later that month, the *Philadelphia Press* ran "Nile Dams Surpassed by Greatest Irrigation System in the World" about Imperial Valley soil, which "carries greater fertilizing properties than does the water of the Nile. . . . made by the great Colorado River, the shavings, as it were, produced by the carving out of the Grand Canyon of the Colorado, the grandest and most awful work of nature on the whole broad face of the old earth."

Issue number 29 of the November 1901 *Imperial Press*, published in Imperial, California, next to the Imperial Lands Company, carried the motto: "Water Is King—Here Is Its Kingdom." The paper, naturally, gave explicit instructions on "HOW TO GET A RANCH."

As Rockwood and Chaffey sniffed their fortunes, the silt-laden Colorado River exasperated them to no end. As soon as they dug silt out of their Imperial Canal, it plugged up again. Without water, farmers began losing their crops.

Chaffey and Rockwood dug new canals. Within months, the dredge couldn't keep up with the gargantuan silt loads drifting in from the main river, which carried three million tons of silt *per week*. In winter 1904, to prevent the Reclamation Service from taking over these "navigable waters" belonging to the United States, Rockwood built an unprotected headgate south of the border and began digging another bigger-than-ever Alamo Canal that ran into the Alamo River, turning north toward Imperial Valley and crossing the border at Calexico, California.

In February 1905, the Colorado River sent an early, unexpected flood crashing through Rockwood's makeshift wooden headgate. Eventually the river widened the Alamo Canal and sucked in the entire river freighting arc-loads of silt. Rockwood's flood roared down the Alamo and New Rivers, inhaling reservoirs and scouring Imperial Valley fields, and carrying off homes and bawling livestock.

The unrelenting wave belittled the short-lived floods of other river basins. Rockwood had waved the red cape north and unleashed the beast. All winter, spring, and summer, the river flooded north. The surge continued for another year.

Chaffey quit. Rockwood sued and alleged that his former business partner had been stealing money from their company. Instead of praising the miraculously fertile farmlands and engineering genius of Rockwood and Chaffey, national newspapers turned their coverage to the raging, foaming flood. For the first time in recorded human history, the Colorado River gained a new set of rapids. Tourists came to gawk at a river gone wild. The nation fell spellbound as their American Nile created a new sea.

Alas, in February 1907, the press hailed America's railway king as the new Moses. E. F. Harriman parted the waters and returned them to the Gulf of California. Harriman paid almost $3 million for his railroad to dump a billion tons of rock to turn the river. Although it had happened here before as a natural process, human meddling created California's largest body of inland water faster than a dam could be built. In two scant years, the Colorado Desert had been humidified into the Salton Sea. It covered 376 square miles.

Rockwood's empire went bust. Harriman bought Imperial Valley for the bargain, below-sea-level price of $200,000. Then he fought with the American entrepreneur farmers south of the border, trying to steal back the Colorado River from Imperial Valley.

As the silt-enriched farmlands came back to life, developers sensed unlimited potential in the fecund abatement of flood. Imperial Valley had been started by corporate bankers and then rescued by a railroad magnate. Despite disaster, the miraculous farmlands suddenly represented the new capitalistic model for harnessing water in the West.

The Reclamation Service—grown from the trunk of Powell's felled Irrigation Survey—sprang into action. Director Frederick Newell couldn't help taking an abrupt turn from his earlier course. Two decades before, while working with Powell, Newell had espoused community-based irrigation. But those utopian ideals were now a notion of the past.

In 1912, Newell began pushing government water diversions and farm networks run by "a business manager whose experience and ability are comparable to those of the general manager of a railroad or any other large industrial institution." Newell was talking about a nascent type of farmlands commerce that wouldn't enter the American lexicon until the 1950s:

> **ag.ri.busi.ness** (*ag'rə biz' nis*), *n.* farming and related food-processing and marketing businesses operated as a large-scale industry.

He was also describing how farmlands needed mega dams to protect and sustain the crops. Newell jumped aboard with the irrigation congress, floating big government dams and corporate agribusiness.

North of the American border town of Calexico, I drive past grazing sheep. Until the recent E. coli scare, a quarter million sheep were pastured on Imperial Valley hay fields. Now farmers contracted with corporate buyers (such as McDonald's) are bending over in compliance. For instance, these farmers can't sell their crops if field tractors have driven over roads where sheep trucks may have dropped dung, which would contaminate the fields. As per the "marketing order" enforced by corporate buyers, Imperial Valley trappers flag the paths used by any mammal—from voles to coyotes—through the fields. Then all crops within 50 feet of a flag are discarded.

Over pale-green lettuce fields, I watch thousands of white-faced ibises temporarily clouding the sky like the birds of Alfred Hitchcock. I drive slowly, while semi trucks—their shocks dampened with the tonnage of produce—honk at me, hanging out the window of my Prius with binoculars. I see species hunched over crops and inspecting their lunch: cattle egrets, snowy egrets, a barn owl, curlews, terns, great blue herons, marsh hawks, a peregrine falcon, mountain plovers, and ring-billed gulls. I could spend weeks in rapture watching the birds of Imperial Valley.

Near the town of Westmorland, I drive past dizzying rows of water-filled ditches, busloads of Hispanic pickers, and sprinklers throwing Colorado River water across fields scowling with brown furrows. Twenty-nine miles west of the All-American Canal, I stop to interview Al Kalin in his carrot fields. Built as wide and unstoppable as a combine, he threshes right into business. "If you eat carrots most anywhere in the United States, from March through May," he says, "you're eating carrots from Imperial Valley. From November to December, it's the same with winter lettuce."

Initially, he's hard to read. Kalin has the passive face of a poker player. He could be a redneck farmer or a progressive grower. His hands are callused, his mind is quick with numbers, and his home county, Imperial County, is run by Democrats.

He invites me to pull a pinky-sized carrot out of the ground, clean the dirt off, and pop it into my mouth: crunchier and sweeter than any comparable vegetable in a supermarket. He grows them under contract for the Grimmway Company—a corporate agribusiness.

To the south, a hired hand shoots harmless shotgun "cracker rounds" toward a flock of snow geese, circling off through the sky like a dissipating white cloud. My delight at these Arctic migrants feasting in the desert evokes the surprise I had as a boy on the Boston Common, seeing live reindeer graze next to a Santa Claus sled.

Al sees my excitement, and as he nods in lieu of a smile, I sense a birdman kinship. Then he mops his brow with a handkerchief.

Imperial Valley swelters at 120 degrees in summer, rains less than three inches per year, and doesn't drop below 50 degrees in winter. The frost-free, sunny landscape is a year-round terrarium—a surreal patch of lushness surrounded by cooked mountains, steaming geothermal plants, and red-hot solar farms. Al's farmhouse, shaded by mesquites, lies ten miles from the San Andreas Fault. "In my lifetime," he says, "four or five seven-Richter-scale earthquakes have shaken this place. You never get tired of unbroken dishes."

Earthquakes and blast-furnace heat are part of the natural cycles here, whereas floods are forgotten along with Rockwood. For farmers, the ancient Colorado River soils still offer legendary fertility—heavily salted by sodium, selenium, magnesium, and iron. For birds, the region is an invaluable stop in the Pacific Flyway. The Salton Sea and surrounding farmlands support 400 species of winged migrants and year-round residents.

Al Kalin earned a bachelor of science in ag management from Cal Poly, with secondary studies in game bird management. He and his brother farm 1,700 acres on the southeast corner of the Salton Sea, at the farthest reaches of the Imperial Irrigation District. As a complement to his full-time labor of farming, he directs Imperial Valley's Landowner Stewardship Program for the Audubon Society. From his point of view, although the birds lost the Colorado River Delta wetlands, they have found refuge in the Imperial Valley and the Salton Sea.

"Everyone wants to talk about the cute, cuddly little burrowing owls," Al says, "yet they have a negligible effect on the crickets that eat our crops. Still, it would be nice to have more burrowing owls," he adds.

"But another species, the barn owl, eats our gophers. Gophers cause field washout that fills the drain ditches with more silt. And six barn owl chicks can eat a thousand gophers."

So he installed owl nest boxes. Then he figured out that stacked hay offered better protection than uninsulated nest boxes. "Eighty-five bales can support four barn owl nests," he says. Although it sounds simple to provide hay amid all of the alfalfa fields, Al had to ask farmers to leave out a permanent stack of bales so that the hay nests wouldn't be picked up and trucked out of the valley.

Al helped get out the news that cattle egrets, white-faced ibises, and curlews eat crickets and cutworms on Imperial Valley's staple crop: hay. "So," Al says, lifting up his "Ducks Unlimited" ball cap to scratch his thinning hair and smile, "we're using birds to our advantage."

In 1917, his father came to farm Imperial Valley, then known as "the Cotton Kingdom." Three years later, the entire 473,000 acres of croplands were in place, and as California's Central Valley took over cotton, Imperial Valley became the "Cantaloupe Capital." Two decades later, Reclamation built the All-American Canal. For farmers, the canal works in tandem with the mega dams upstream: holding floods and straining silt (but not salts). As Imperial Valley became the fifth most productive farmlands in the country, resorts flourished along the briny yet relatively clean waters of the Salton Sea.

Lacking an outlet, the lake evaporated, but kept all of its salts. Agricultural runoff added fertilizers and other chemicals. The New and Alamo Rivers added polluted water from Mexicali and Calexico. By 1970, no one would swim in the water anymore, forcing the resorts to shut down. Fish piled belly up on the beaches. Whereas the Pacific Ocean is 3.3 percent salt, the Salton Sea is now 4.4 percent.

The lake drops a half foot each year, escalating the salinity almost a whole percent each year. Wind sweeps the evaporated minerals off the shore and onto Imperial farm fields, damaging the crops. From a mile away, I catch the rotten-egg smell of the chemical-encrusted Salton Sea, redolent of yet another catastrophe.

That isn't the only way of life draining away. Although Al Kalin has followed his father's footsteps, his three children do not plan to take up farming. Nor will he push them. Even if they were interested, they would face competition from giant agribusinesses, genetically modified crops, increasingly thirsty southwestern cities, and the free market pricing of farm products (arguably controlled by corporate agribusiness). According to Al, each new generation of farmers earns less than their parents did.

"This wasn't the case 30 years ago," he says. "It's hard to afford a new tractor now. Before, we got a new tractor every two years. And the labor to fix one now is the same as what a plumber would charge at your house."

In an organic confluence of old and new, Al's fondness for duck hunting has led to an interest in saving water. The migratory hunting stamp he buys each year with his hunting license contributes to wildlife refuges. He drives a diesel truck and talks precisely about carbon credits. At first glance, his livelihood might be perceived as contradictory. He may be misunderstood by those urban enviros who don't know about their food sources, but by acting as a conscientious farmer, he is a native naturalist and advocate for Colorado River preservation.

He's one of only a few farmers in the valley utilizing drip irrigation, and it's on his dime. Although this reform is a logical step toward a more sustainable future, most farmers avoid drip irrigation. The piping is expensive. It has to be painstakingly laid an inch under the topsoil, and in the conservative world of farming, it's newfangled, little-known gadgetry. But through Kalin's progressive-minded irrigation, and his stewardship of the birds, he has shown traditional farmers the future. Despite the initial cost of the pipes, he seldom needs the tractor to furrow his fields using drip irrigation—so he saves on tractor repair and fuel costs. By delivering his fungicides, fertilizers, and insecticides under the soil through drip irrigation pipes, he no longer needs costly aerial crop spraying. And by getting rid of the high evaporative water loss of irrigating crops with sprinklers, he saves a lot of Colorado River water. Drip irrigation worked for his onions, so he's thinking of expanding the system beyond 70 acres.

If the water-efficient irrigation catches on in the farm fields, as it has in the newly lined All-American Canal, whatever gets saved by the Colorado River will be denied to the Salton Sea and sent to junior water rights holders elsewhere in California. Evaporation will cause the lake to shrink. The chemical concentrations will increase. And the Salton Sea birds prized by farmers will be in a world of hurt. For every potential solution created through well-intentioned conservation, another link in the chain is altered. Consequently, nature lovers have recently begun decrying water efficiency as a sole Colorado River cure.

Yet the problem in Imperial Valley must be answered by more sustainable, if not efficient farming methods. Most notably, the beef* and dairy industries consume more water (and hay) than all the cities in the nation. Alfalfa hay is Al Kalin's star crop. "Lettuce is a gamble because of fickle market demands and the E. coli scare," he says. "Melons are the same way."

Imperial Valley is to hay as Afghanistan is to opium. Six hundred and fifty of Al's 1,700 acres are swaying with the green shoots of alfalfa hay. Most

---

*According to Ecological Integrity: Integrating Environment, Conservation and Health, 12,009 gallons of water are required to make 1 pound of beef—1,000 times more water than it takes to grow 1 pound of wheat.

of Imperial Valley's farm fields grow hay. Although Imperial County has the largest number of cattle feedlots in California, elsewhere the state has enough dairy cows to rival the rubbed-out plains bison. Still, the hay is mostly shipped west and out of the country for dairy cows, whereas huge numbers of feedlot cattle in Imperial Valley take minimal hay so that they can be plumped by corn and other ingredients, and then slaughtered for beef.

"Hay fuels the dairy shed," Al says. "This is the hay that makes the milk, ice cream, et cetera. Without the hay from the Imperial Valley, you might have to go a thousand miles to find enough to fuel the southern California dairy shed. Might as well produce it right here, close to all the lactating cows that depend upon it."

On top of the extra requirements for cattle, the water itself has to be watered. With all the upstream farms and cities running water through innumerable sets of kidneys, Imperial hay farmers are forced to use extra water to rinse the salts away. "You're from Colorado," Al reminds me, "your Grand Junction Mancos shale sends us all the selenium."

The newly diapered, leakproof All-American Canal, originally completed in 1942, cannot clean out the selenium-loaded salts of the river. In 1955, Imperial Valley farmers began building a grid of underground drains to catch the salts and prevent the ground from getting waterlogged—the same issues confronted by Wellton-Mohawk farms in Arizona. By this point, 1,400 miles down the Colorado River, every acre-foot of water carries one ton of dissolved salts. The astounding figure of 32,227 "miles of tile drainage grid lines have been installed underneath Imperial Valley farms," Al says, reciting the mileage faster than I can jot it down. He waits until my pen stops moving and finishes: "That wastewater is captured by another 1,400 miles of ditches."

Depending upon the type of soil and how fast it will percolate water, the drain lines are spaced as close as 75 feet apart and as deep as 7 feet down. When lines become clogged with manganese or iron oxides that block the drains, the minerals can be blown out with a high-pressure hose. Theoretically, these underground lines will allow Colorado River farmers to overcome the salinity issues that killed ancient farming civilizations. Like all drains, however, the toxicity runs downstream to the next user—in this case, to the Salton Sea. To Al's way of thinking, if the 700 ppm salt delivered to his farm from the All-American Canal water were eliminated, he'd use 25 percent less water.

He places his water order each day before noon, and the Imperial Irrigation District, working closely with Reclamation, has to deliver it to him within three days. "It costs me $18 per acre-foot," he says, "but we're not buying the water, we're paying for its delivery." If the Imperial Irrigation District raises the cost—which many enviros suggest as a tool for conserving the Colorado River—or when thirsty city dwellers overrule hungry cows, Al Kalin will be forced to sell the farm.

His potential buyers? L.A., San Diego, Las Vegas, Phoenix. Or the same bankers and corporate barons that Charles Rockwood and Reclamation tried to introduce to the Colorado Desert a century ago. Although Imperial Valley's family-owned farms have mostly escaped the morally bankrupt control of corporate agribusiness, it is also the final drain of Colorado River water: a model of Faustian contradictions.

In late November, beneath the thundering railroad bridge in Yuma, I settle into my Alpacka raft on dry land, Velcro myself in, and then hop the boat forward until I'm in the cool river. From here to the sea for the next 100 miles, the pack raft will be my best friend. As the river dries up, I'll deflate it and carry it in my pack.

For the first day, I'm accompanied by Mark Lellouch, a French- and Spanish-speaking Québécois cum Arizonan. He's also a salaried enviro, making him the most uncommon of Colorado River species.

Mark works for the Tucson-based Sonoran Institute, one of a dozen nongovernmental organizations trying to salvage the delta. The hope is to restore pulse river flows to the delta and secure a dedicated base flow to grow flora and fauna. Before the drought, irregular flood releases in the 1980s and 1990s helped keep the delta green and the wetlands alive, in spite of the huge loss of water Post-DamNation. Now, up to 95 percent of the delta has shriveled without floods. The water that could keep it alive is expensive, clamored after by faraway cities and farms.

Mexico's treaty allotment of 1.5 maf per year is one-ninth the amount of water that used to enrich both the delta and the sea. That one-ninth of river rinses through Mexican farmlands, picking up fertilizers and salts. What isn't lost to evaporation eventually trickles into the sea. Seen in a satellite photo, the Mexican section of the delta appears as a barren plain, contrasting with the fertile fields of Mexicali and Imperial Valley, and puddled by wetlands: the Ciénega, El Doctor, Campo Mosqueda, the Ecocamp area, and El Indio. Contrary to popular belief, Mark tells me, the delta is not yet dead. Although I've already confirmed this during an earlier visit, I plan to see more in the coming weeks.

Despite the best intentions of Colorado River Basin scientists, numbers-crunching water operators, and reclamationists, the best way to come to grips with a river is to sleep on its banks, swim in it (water conditions permitting), and travel its length no faster than the current. If we can't understand that the river is a *living* resource, rather than a mere resource, then the delta and its waters from here to the source are doomed. Or so I'm thinking as Interstate 8 and its drone of traffic fades to the west.

After the long jog west past Yuma, paralleling the All-American Canal, the shrunken river turns Mark and me south toward Mexico. Garbage and tires burning south of the border throw an acrid veil over the country-side. We take three hours to paddle past the RV parks and golf courses to the Morelos Dam. From across the border, we can hear the barking dogs of Mexico, running loose in Algodones—population 3,000, including 350 dentists who cheaply repair American teeth, and scores of cut-rate, prescription-free pharmacies.

The L-shaped Morelos Dam, built by the terms of the 1944 treaty, allows Mexico to send the last significant slice of Colorado River west to the fields of the Mexicali Valley. Unless the river is in flood and the southern gates are opened, the water that travels down the old riverbed is barely enough for a creek.

At a takeout plowed through the giant cane—where Mexico, California, and Arizona join—we meet U.S. Border Patrolman Ben Vik. He's dressed in a forest green uniform and ball cap, with a portable Motorola radio that seldom leaves his left hand and a double-action Beretta 96D "Brigadier" on his right hip.

He escorts us below the dam, and we pick our way through the mud, waffled by many footsteps walking toward America. Ben examines the tracks closely. He picks up a disintegrating sandbag, placed by would-be immigrants to create a dike for four-wheel-drive vehicles attempting a flight to freedom. Once across the riverbed border, their real gauntlet begins: over fences and irrigation canals; past Border Patrol officers in jeeps, planes, and helicopters; then onto the most undesirable jobs in the Southwest. These illegal aliens will work twice as hard as the average American, educate their children on the school systems' largesse, and visit emergency rooms for free. But without our Hispanic labor force, communities across the nation would shut down overnight.

Officer Vik won't paddle or walk with me down the 23-mile, east-west border called the limitrophe:

li-mə-trōf, -tròf\
From Latin *limit-*, . . . boundary + Greek *trophos* feeder,
from *trephein* to nourish.

Ben agrees to drive another dozen miles south on the limitrophe to pick us up at dusk. Mark and I reinflate our rafts and splash across a wet concrete platform under the red louvered gates of Morelos Dam. I climb up on a 20-foot-high rusting red door of steel, reach over the top, and touch the last vestige of a river on the other side, stilled in a brown pool, awaiting delivery to Mexicali farms. This is the only Mexican dam on the Colorado River.

The man sitting in a guardhouse on the Mexican side doesn't care about a gringo clambering on his gates—an unthinkable transgression on any U.S. dam. If I were to wade across the waist-deep water pouring out from under one floodgate and then stroll into Mexico, the fishermen on the other side would welcome me to their country.

Yet Ben has already explained that if I bushwhacked back into the United States several miles downstream without an escort, "*if* the *coyotes* don't slit your throat," I would be surrounded by border patrolmen or Homeland Security officials.

In a soft voice, he adds that one of his colleagues had been run over and killed last year by a drug smuggler who had rammed his car through the fence. He won't give me any details, other than saying that the Border Patrol is the single most dangerous job in U.S. federal law enforcement. This might explain why Ben—normally relegated to desk duty—looks so jumpy here at the border. He wishes us luck, and as we're swept off through a skein of bobbing plastic bottles, he adds that drug smugglers would find our portable little pack rafts useful.

The narrow stream whisks us through the giant cane, as thick as dining room table legs, fibrously strong as bamboo, and fragrant with chemicals very similar to the hallucinogenic ayahuasca. With the jungle towering above us, the algae green water fostering strange microbes, and desperate nomads purported to be haunting the western bank, we could be paddling down an Amazon tributary.

A suitcase swirls in an eddy. Abandoned clothing and shoes dot the overgrown banks. Luckily, I can point out the different birds as a distraction: "Hey," I say, "a bittern!"

"Where?" says Mark, busy fiddling with his camera.

"There, a black-crowned night-heron!"

"Where?" he asks. But it too disappears.

"Another!" The humpbacked glossy green bird slides quickly out of sight and into the shadows. Fish dimple the surface. Unseen animals, or smugglers, rattle through the cane.

Mark lingers, taking photographs. I'm as jumpy as Ben, prompting Mark to hurry up.

It's dusk, prime time, according to Ben, for smugglers to ford the international boundary. I turn on my headlamp, and then turn it off just as quickly, so I can't be seen.

As a heron stops squabbling, we hear hushed Mexican voices and the putter of a small outboard. I hold my breath. The stream is only ten feet wide and there's nowhere to hide. The current pulls us around a bend toward a dented-in skiff, bristling with fishing rods instead of guns, and smoking with an underpowered outboard engine. Three middle-aged men are riding just above the waterline, protected by an inch of freeboard. They smile proudly and hold up a quiver of tilapia, carp, and white fish: tonight's dinner. I breathe a sigh of relief.

Mark tells them I'm headed to the sea, and they nod politely. Every few years the limitrophe along the border fills with water, one man says, and it's the best fishing anywhere. He says that he and his friends have been fishing here for decades—whenever *gringolandia* sees fit to dump some extra water south through the Morelos Dam.

Mark asks if they've ever seen any *narcotraficantes* (drug runners) or *coyotes*. They all shake their heads no.

In the morning, Ben takes me to meet Colin Soto on Cocopah reservation land. Ben unlocks a padlocked gate. We drive in and then get out on the limitrophe riverbank. Ben leaves us alone because there's no love lost between Border Patrol, which Colin disdains for locking up his reservation to chase nonexistent drug runners, and Cocopah, which the Border Patrol has little time for,

In all of his adult years on the reservation, this is the most water that Colin has seen. For a moment he appears animated, boyish. Last week, two days of abnormal rain flooded the Gila River. The United States bypassed the water to Morelos Dam, which bypassed the water into its old riverbed.

Eight thousand Kwapa, or people of the river, lived here before borders existed. After being assimilated into both countries, perhaps 1,500 American Cocopah and Mexican Cucapá remain. As a boy more than 60 years ago, when water still regularly ran south, Colin swam the big river back and forth, without Border Patrol interference. "It was my passage into manhood," he says, "before signing up for Vietnam."

He served two more tours of duty, then became a cop and a teacher in L.A. Several years ago, Colin came home to retire in the Cocopah town of Somerton, Arizona. Here he has found roots and a community otherwise unavailable to a man of his heritage.

We sit down on the riverbank in the shade of a cottonwood, and he talks about what's left of the river. His face is sun bronzed, highlighting perfect white teeth, while his hair is pulled back in a queue beneath his brown ball cap:

25th INFANTRY DIVISION
1966–1970
CHU CHI, VIETNAM

Colin has gone to D.C. to tell congressmen the same things he is telling me. Through the Endangered Species Act, the Kwapa now hope that pulse flows can be returned to the delta and to Kwapa lands to sustain birds like the willow flycatcher and Yuma clapper rail. But he is frustrated. His voice drops to a weary monotone. Even if lawmakers could be forced to care about little birds, he says, they don't care about the river or his people.

"The river is life," he says, sweeping his catcher's mitt of a hand toward the channel. "And when the river is gone, there will be no life." He looks away, choked up, a tear running down his cheek.

He's the last person I would've expected to see crying.

Ben drops me at yesterday's takeout, and although I'm not expecting to interview any drug runners, a Border Patrol helicopter and a Cessna Super Cub buzz me on my way downstream. Despite these annoyances overhead, it's a pleasure to be alone. Over the last few months, listening to the gurgle of water, watching birds, and engaging long-dormant instincts is a pursuit that often defies companionship.

I weave back and forth through a thickening stream, climbing over strainers of cane and cottonwoods. But I'm getting nowhere. After two false starts, I'm lost in a maze. So I turn and paddle back upstream against the current. On the U.S. side of the border, a scant distance below where Ben dropped me off several hours ago, I deflate the raft on a rare sandy opening, fold it into my pack and begin bushwhacking toward daylight. The cane is almost impenetrable, growing out of a knee-deep swamp, but by crawling and pushing my pack in front of me, while trying not to break the psychotropic plants in front of my face, I gopher through: ripping my shorts, scratching my arms, soaking my clothes, losing the reading glasses tied around my neck, and knocking out the right lens of my sunglasses. I wriggle up a loose slope of boulders, wrestling with the strong-armed tamarisk, until I burst out into blinding sunlight.

I catch my breath on a dirt road and shrug on my pack. The river is hushed. Dogs bark to the west. Birds wiggle through the darkened brush.

After a half hour of walking along a dirt road alongside the Wellton-Mohawk Bypass Canal, inside the 15-foot border fence, I wave to an officer with a shiny shaved head, cruising the canal strip in his Border Patrol ride. Because I'm heading south, and because he's already heard the radio chatter about me—the crazy gringo bound for Mexico—he simply waves back and I continue walking.

A few minutes later, I turn to see if I'm being watched. Sure enough, a mile up the canal, Mr. Clean is watching me through his binoculars. So I walk another mile, turn, and look again: He's gone.

I throw my pack raft into the Wellton-Mohawk Bypass Canal and climb down three rusty ladder rungs, mostly out of sight, and plop into my boat—careful not to burn my skin with agricultural wastewater salty enough to kill crops. *Well,* I figure, *if it's good enough for the Ciénega birds, it probably won't kill me.* The current is flowing faster than I can run.

Whooshing toward a dark tunnel that sucks in all the water, I make a quick calculation: A foot of headspace will give me just enough room. So I bend backward into limbo position, point my paddle like a spear along the water surface, and scrape my nose along the moldy ceiling. Then I'm free again. Every half mile, I limbo back and squeeze through another constricted tunnel.

In an hour's time, scarcely paddling, the rush of brine carries me nine miles. Ben drives up alongside me and the canal in his SUV, fresh from his lunch break in a San Luis restaurant. He rolls down his window, and keeping pace with me, checks his speedometer: "Ten miles an hour. How's it going?"

"Better than bushwhacking through the swamp along the old riverbed," I say, knowing that he needs to kick me out of the canal. "Man, it was thick over there."

"See any Mexicans?" he asks.

"No," I smile, "but lots of tracks. I'm making great progress."

"Uh, Jon," he says, ever polite, "we can't let you paddle in there."

"Why?"

"The farmers wouldn't like it if they knew you were in their canal," he says.

What Ben is not saying is that he's afraid Border Patrol will be held liable if I drown.

No farmer worth his water allotment cares about the canal of used-up Colorado River. The millrace carries the salts and chemicals from the Wellton-Mohawk dairy shed and farmers' fields to be dumped—as fast as possible—in the wilds of Mexico. Luckily, Ben is repatriating me from the canal at a broad river swale called Hunter's Hole. Over the last month, Mexican and American volunteers have uprooted, plowed over, and burned out the tamarisk. Ben and I walk toward the scant river through brown sand and newly planted cottonwoods to a riparian habitat restored.

"We like this clearing," Ben says. "No brush makes our job easier, because illegals can't cross here without us spotting them from the fence," he points backward.

"Boy, I can't remember seeing this much water here before," he continues, "almost two inches running into Mexico."

Ben, like most Americans, doesn't know how our neighbors lost their river. It started during the Colorado Compact negotiations, when American officials refused to give Mexico a seat at the table. The chair, Herbert Hoover, was guided by America's 1898 Harmon Doctrine, created so that gringolandia could hoard the Río Grande River. The doctrine declared that all water emanating from the United States belonged to the United States.

Even after Mexico lost the Río Grande to the Attorney General A. G. Harmon's opportunistic doctrine, Mexican diplomats for decades argued that they deserved 3.6 maf—or nearly one-quarter—of the Colorado River water. Yet Hoover chose to abide by the Harmon Doctrine. The 1922 Colorado River Compact allowed the seven-member states to seize 16 maf without specifying Mexico's share.

In 1936, the reformist President Lazaro Cárdenas nervously watched the construction of the All-American Canal. Because it would curb most of the water from flowing down the Colorado River and into the Mexicali farm fields by the Alamo Canal, Cárdenas ordered American entrepreneurs to liquidate their farms in Mexico along with all their Chinese field hands (Mexicans were not allowed to work on these farms). A year later, because the American owners hadn't complied, and Cárdenas faced a popular Mexican riot against the American imperialists, he kicked the Americans out and nationalized the lands. Mexican citizens were awarded 2,000-acre farms as ejidos. Cárdenas sold the remaining acreage as private *colonias*.

The chess game continued. Although Mexico had regained ownership of its farms, the United States still controlled the water. In the wake of Hoover Dam, Reclamation proudly erected Parker, Davis, and Imperial Dams. As the reservoirs filled, the United States still had plenty of water left over for Mexico. But everyone knew that burgeoning American agriculture would eventually shortchange its southern neighbor.

Mexico then built more than a million acres of farm fields around Mexicali. Cárdenas vainly hoped that their expanding agriculture would convince the United States to provide an equivalent amount of Colorado River water. Even though American entrepreneurs no longer owned Mexicali farms, they owned the gin mills and processing plants for Mexican crops. And American bankers financed 95 percent of the farms.

The new Mexican President Manuel Avila Camacho received a letter from a relative exemplifying the crisis:

> The cotton will be lost if our "good neighbors" don't loosen water from the Colorado River. These gentlemen are our "good neighbors" since 1847 and they either make war on us or drag us into it according to their desires. Be concerned for us, Manuel, and save the region.

In 1941, Reclamation released a wall of water into Mexico that destroyed their entire cotton crop. Two years later, Camacho pleaded with the U.S. Department of State to control its water so that another cotton crop wouldn't be destroyed. The water was released in yet another flood that limited the year's harvest.

Near the close of World War II, the United States abandoned the Harmon Doctrine and announced a Good Neighbor policy. Mexico signed the 1944 International Water Treaty presented by the United States. Mexico gave up asking for 3.6 maf of water and reluctantly accepted 1.5 maf.

The half-century-old match infuriated Mexican diplomats. As the Mexicali farming infrastructure nearly crumbled over the next 20 years—recovering only through a manufacturing industry exporting goods to America—up to 10,000 illegal pickers moved to Imperial Valley.

Unintentionally, Mexico opened up another export business. The Alamo River and the New River—the most polluted river in North America—began flushing Mexicali's wastewater north of the border. To prevent agriculture from being tainted, the water skirts the Imperial farm fields and dumps into the Salton Sea. The river contains nearly a hundred toxins and cancer-causing agents such as mercury, PCBs, toxaphene, and benzene; DDT; and two dozen viruses, along with strains of typhoid, cholera, and hepatitis. In the 1980s, floating next to tires and animal carcasses, the thick green soup of Mexican revenge often contained human bodies.

Unlike the Wellton-Mohawk Bypass Canal flushing into the Ciénega, it seemed unlikely that Mexico would ever take back its discarded water. Finally, with recent American government financing, Mexico agreed to treat the wastewater, take it out of those U.S.-bound rivers, and send half of it south to the delta.

Exactly where I'm bound.

THE MEXICAN DELTA

Pete McBride and I spend two days packing in Yuma. During the six months since we parted in the headwaters, Pete has taken trips down Cataract and Grand Canyons, photographing and learning about the river.

I never know if Pete is going to be brooding or flipping up into handstands. But this is why his companionship works. He's a lot like me. One of our differences is that he has a lot of girlfriends. He's a catch: a dressed-down, worldlier candidate for the *Bachelor* show.

Both of our families and friends have warned us about the surge of drug-related violence in Mexican border towns. I promise June and the boys that I'll be careful, but remind them that the U.S. media dramatizes foreign news. Although I'm no stranger to Mexico, McBride will be my secret weapon south of the border: Fluent in Spanish, he has spent years of his life traveling on the cheap throughout Latin America.

On December 2, we wave to the Mexican customs officials at San Luis Río Colorado, and work our way through the border town frenzy to hail a cab. After standing firm on his price—300 pesos ($40)—the cabbie drives us two miles to the north-south border below the limitrophe. Pete and I find floodwater still running under the bridge, and we slap high-fives. The cabbie says that we're only *media loco* (*half* crazy) for going all the way to the sea, and bumps our fists. We laugh like boys.

Below the bridge, we test our lungs by filling up the pack rafts. With no current and ankle-deep water, we paddle past plywood shack homes and

children flipping stones into the water. Although we can still hear the flatu-
lent passage of unmuffled trucks on the highway, we're sucked out of sight
amid a dense tangle of tamarisk into a delta gone desert. We're relieved to
have left border town madness behind and focus on the difficult task of finding the right route to follow.

We portage our rafts around shallow sandbars. Still, every ten yards of
paddling seems like a gift. "Can you believe this, Pete? I never expected we'd
find water running south of the border!"

In lieu of a reply, Pete is frowning about the brown water. Less than two
miles from the bridge, the creek narrows, then pools to a stop against a dam
of tamarisk. The water is festooned with plastic bottles, foam cups, a con-
dom, and tires. I try to hop out, sacrificing only one foot, but along the
heron-V-tracked shore of river's end, both feet are sucked into fetid ooze that
makes me catch my breath and arch my back. It's foaming with phosphates.

"Will we get sick from stepping in it?" Pete asks from behind the lens of
his Nikon.

"Gross" is all I can say. We're only partly concerned about our health.
Mostly we are dismayed, because we know the river as a force of nature near
our homes and throughout its roaring canyons. Upstream, the boiling river
has flipped us out of boats; south of the border, it has congealed to malodor-
ous gravy.

We're reduced to walking the route that steamships rode 120 years ago
on the mighty Colorado. As we bushwhack and trudge through the sand
washed out of the Grand Canyon, our thermometer reads 93 degrees, and
we're sweating out water as fast as we can drink it. The sand is pockmarked
by tracks of bobcats, raccoons, and coyotes. Every hour we break for five minutes and sip our day's two-quart ration of drinking water. But it's not enough.

Each time we slip back under our packs, we groan anew. Pete is carrying
two lenses, two cameras, and a tripod. Each time I grouse about my pack,
my companion asks if I want to lift his heavier one, which we both know
would cripple me. By the time the sun fades over the distant Sierra del Mayor,
dappled a brilliant orange through the bent rays of Mexicali air pollution, we
let our packs crater the riverbank, a dozen feet above one of many desiccated
water courses. Then we pass a bottle of tequila.

In the distance, dogs bark. A bulldozer growls. Truck horns blare. But at
least we're alone, in a wilderness of tamarisk and sand that Mexicans avoid
like the plague. Today it's a ditch-riven desert, but tomorrow, depending on
Reclamation, Morelos Dam, and the gods of rainfall, it could flood once

more. Bereft of stars, the northern horizon above the halogen-illuminated border fence throws shadows for ten miles.

After a pasta dinner, we break out our respective mystery novel and adventure travel book, and turn on headlamps. We're sound asleep within minutes.

As dawn bakes straight into the heat of day, we agree to lift the ration and drink more water to ease the pressure of pack straps cutting into our shoulders. Our fingers, lacking circulation, are swollen and tingling.

We started with three 2.5-gallon nylon bags of water that weigh 60 pounds. I have a satellite phone to arrange our pickup on the border, a three-pound tent to quell my arachnophobia, two lightweight titanium pots, a video camera, and a two-ounce stove. Pete has a bomber sleeping pad system with a toasty sleeping bag, plenty of extra clothes, and an iPod to indulge his passion for music. Pete's pack is a back breaker and although mine is 20 pounds lighter, I'm carrying my minimalist gear, except for the tent, in a lightweight, shoulder-strapped duffel without a functional waist belt. This "dry pack"—superb for strapping onto a white-water raft—wasn't meant for hot backpacking.

The Sonoran Desert's 2.4 inches of annual precipitation makes it the driest place in North America. Drinking even more water, we agree, will lighten our loads and prevent us from getting dehydrated. So we grumble our way south, as the precious gallons dwindle from our packs. By noon, we're dehydrated, pissing yellow instead of clear urine. By early afternoon, our path is blocked by a sudden copse of giant cottonwoods, shading an agricultural drain piped into the former riverbed, covered with green scum and guarded by a reluctant-looking heron above the pond. "Hey, Pete," I suggest, "we can boil and drink this water!"

Pete says nothing. He has that grim look like his pack just got heavier. So I repeat my remark about the water, add that maybe it is a bit fermented, but we're very thirsty.

Then Pete sets me straight, revealing the folly of my ways: "Are you crazy? This water's carrying enough pathogens to make E. coli taste like lemonade!"

So we abandon the riverbed and follow our noses up the drainpipe, past a sagging outhouse, and into an ejido owned by several Mexican farmer families. We're trailed by two snarling, mangy hounds doubling as doorbells. Unlike American dogs, these animals have been repeatedly beaten, so we put up with their noise, and they keep their distance.

Pete asks a man my age—stooped from his labor in the fields—if he can sell us some water. He smiles, and his family jumps into action. Before we know it, he's pouring precious water that he bought at the local market into our bags, while his wife cooks us bean burritos, and his son passes us glasses of Coca-Cola. The soda costs little more than water, and judging by the brown teeth, it's more popular.

Pete tells them that we're trying to reach the sea. So they recommend that we paddle in the irrigation canal alongside their onion fields. In Arizona, paddlers get kicked out of irrigation canals; in Mexico, farmers invite you to jump in. We want to pay the family for feeding us, and although we offer once more, they shake their heads. We know enough about rural Mexico not to abuse their hospitality.

Surrounded by young boys, I blow up my raft, mount it like a kneeling camel, and then ride four feet down the steep slanting walls of the canal. I hit with a splash, flooding several gallons of water onto my lap. The boys clap in glee. Just as my slide is slowed by water, I'm missing my sons with a dull ache that starts in my throat, moves under my sternum, and will stay in my chest all evening.

As the boys chase us, we catch up to their fathers, holding a net and walking either side of the ten-foot-wide agricultural canal. A third man swims behind the net, pulling the net off snags along the canal bottom. After a half mile, Pete photographs them posing with dinner: a big bass, a catfish, and a minnow. As the sun sinks back into its reddened home behind the mountains, one of the fishermen offers to drive us to his house for dinner and a sleeping berth on his dining room floor. We politely decline in favor of a dawn start.

The boys leave us with tangerines. We thank them and their fathers, shaking their hands. *Vaya con dios*, they say, sitting shoulder to shoulder in the cab and bed of a battered miniature pickup.

Pete lies down on hard ground under a scraggly mesquite tree that will keep the dew off his sleeping bag. I pitch my tent in a roadside ditch. We begin indulging our dreams alongside the swish of farm water, beside a fallow field with a felled cow bellowing its death throes to the stars. We're strangers in a land of suffering animals, inhabited by a people so generous they'd give us the last beans off their tables, even though they've been robbed by our forebears.

We move southwest, averaging 15 miles a day, stringing together irrigation canals that vaguely point toward the Gulf of California. Half of the time, we're lost in the dried-out maze of riverbeds cut by farm fields, canals, roads, and railroad tracks. Pete flags down a pickup truck and asks for directions. They contradict the last set of directions.

This man, Jorge, a ditch inspector, is driving a brand-new Ford. He gives us his business card and insists that we call him if we need help. In Spanish he tells us: "I like American adventurers! Mexicans just sit around and eat beans and say '*mañana!*'" We shake our heads, but because he's laughing, we laugh with him.

A low flying crop-duster plane bisects our path, followed by a troop of snowy egrets, buzzing directly over us on another narrowing canal. Burrowing owls cum jack-in-the-boxes pop their heads in and out of nest holes along the canal. I see my first avocet of the entire trip: black and long beaked to match its legs, like an avian clown.

On our third night out, we camp in an alfalfa field along an irrigation canal thickly layered in duckweed, its crumbling cement walls coated in brown slime. I cook freeze-dried chili on the stove with our last two gallons of water. Dinner conversation is a series of grunts, owing to a day of repeated portaging and strong-armed paddling through thick, stilled gunk.

My sleeping pads puncture when I lie down on a hidden strand of barbed wire. As Pete snoozes in comfort atop his two pads, I make my bed in the agricultural product that drinks more water than any Colorado River crop: hay. In the silence surrounding midnight, a local farm dog catches our scent and, in a frenzy of barking, charges across the field to attack. Ten yards from the tent, I give him my best dog whispering voice: "Bad boy, go home." And it works.

In the morning, we debate our whereabouts on the latest 1:250,000-scale map, but it seems that this shifting, dried-out monster of a delta has defied its cartographers. So we consult a GPS downloaded with larger-scale Mexican maps. I carry it in my hand like a Border Patrol officer clutching a radio. Although the two-inch screen shows us as a blinking triangle amid the vast sweep of Colorado River, the GPS omits the roads and irrigation canals that we've been crossing. So we continue steering through frequent polls of passing Mexicans and constant east-west route corrections.

On the strength of the GPS finally matching up with a piece of landscape, we walk away from all roads and farmlands down a deep river channel, filled only with sand and tamarisk. Coyote tracks dent the river bottom, and stillness comes over the cottonwood forests as we plunge deeper into no-man's-land. According to our small-scale map of the delta, we're walking down a Río Colorado channel that should dump us into the still active tributary, Río Hardy.

By now my feet are swollen with white blisters oozing clear fluids and wetting my socks. The last few months of sitting in boats with sandals has splayed my feet into fat, lazy appendages unaccustomed to shoes. So I have taped on moleskin, cut with holes to take pressure off the bulging blisters. With frequent doses of anti-inflammatory ibuprofen to cool each fiery footstep, my feet should carry me to the Río Hardy, where we can sit down and begin paddling again.

Our tongues are sticking to our cotton-dry mouths. Our packs are light, empty of water.

Several miles down the wild, dried-out channel, we find a cement-mortared well, dug into whatever circulatory dribble might exist below the riverbed. After introducing ourselves to the well owner up on the bank, we find Carlos strangely tentative and wary about two strangers walking onto his remote plantation. But we know that he knows that we're harmless gringos. So we attribute his cool air to shyness.

As we stand over the well, he says that it took him ten days of shoveling until he hit water 45 feet down. His body is as sinewy and straight as a stalk of giant cane.

We ask him if it's okay to take a drink. "Okay," he replies. We lower the bucket, then wind it back up. Pete hands the first cup to me, the team guinea pig.

I spit the alkaline liquid out immediately. Even if I could gag it down, my lower intestine would be limed white as the walls of Carlos's well. "*Gracias,*" I say to him, "*no me gusta Río Colorado agua.*"

Pete tells Carlos that we've come so that I can make it all 1,450 miles from the headwaters to the sea. "*¿Media loco?*" Pete asks him about my plan.

"*No es* media *loco,*" Carlos replies, "*Es* muy *loco.*" Pete and I laugh, but Carlos stands sullen and sulking.

Carlos is growing watermelons, he tells us.

"*Watermelons?*" asks Pete, astonished. Carlos nods and then quickly changes the subject to say that we better look out for *narcotraficantes* farther down the river.

Under his grass-roofed *palapala* above the river, we offer to pay him for real drinking water. Carlos may be standoffish, but because he's a Mexican at heart, he refuses our money and uses his market-filled jug to refill our empty bag. After a long discussion over our map, he convinces us to leave the south-trending riverbed and walk the road west toward the Río Hardy. There's no reason not to trust his directions. Our meeting is an instance of the time-honored linkage of strangers amid the wilderness. We shake his hand in appreciation and, as we lift up our despised packs, he once again warns us about *narcotraficantes en el Río Colorado.*

"¿Es verdad?" Pete asks.

Carlos shakes his head and replies that it's true, we'll get our asses shot off if we're not careful. We wave good-bye. As we wind our way through a labyrinth of obscure sand roads toward an equally obscure stony road west, we realize that our well-digging friend has deliberately tucked himself quite deep in the wilds.

Hobbling west, on a road graded in large, sharp stones that jab my raw feet with every red-hot step, I ask Pete if he believes Carlos about the drug runners. Pete replies: "And you think he's really growing *watermelons?*"

Late that afternoon, we sip Clamato juice *cervezas* and chat with 70-something Jesús Mosqueda. His Campo Mosqueda cabins and cantina straddle the suspiciously jade-colored Río Hardy. Unlike most Mexicans, Jesús is prickly, and we're about to find out why.

Campo Mosqueda adjoins his popular RV park, frequented by weekender Mexicans. Today the camping area is abandoned. With the exception of a gringo from Washington State who generously buys us lunch, few American tourists visit Camp Mosqueda. The water smells like a sewer.

Jesús's resort is situated on the western edge of the Colorado River Delta, south of Mexicali. In the Predambrian, the Río Hardy bubbled up from hot springs now commandeered by a Mexican geothermal plant. For the last couple of years, the sluggish Río Hardy has averaged 23 cfs. This stream filters through the Las Arenitas wastewater plant, completed in March 2007, that has removed half of the toxic sewage from the America-bound New River and sent it south to Mexico's delta.

Because no Mexican laws govern "agricultural wastewater" rife with nitrogen and insecticides, Mexican and American conservationists are raising funds to build a treatment wetland, combination wildlife sanctuary and park, to prevent algae blooms in the Río Hardy. Until this wetland is completed and fecal chloroform counts are lowered, flora and fauna will continue to suffer in the oxygen-starved water. "There's been a problem with algae in the river," Jesús says understatedly. But this is only part of his grievances about what upstream users have done to the river.

I mistakenly ask for cheese (*queso*) in my quesadilla: *"Quiero quesadilla con queso, por favor."*

Half good-natured and half annoyed with Americans, Jesús Mosqueda teases me, then corrects my redundant Spanish request. After he gives our food order to the cook, he comes out from behind the bar, sits down, and shares the story that has made him into a local rock star.

Jesús sued Reclamation and won.

During the 1983 dam bypass floods that devastated towns upstream, Campo Mosqueda and its farm fields were inundated by a wall of water and mud. Salt destroyed Jesús's crops and his shrimp farm. Although most Mexican entrepreneurs gave up and abandoned their flooded businesses on the delta, Jesús and his L.A. lawyer dug their heels in for a long, expensive court case. Reclamation arrogantly claimed that Campo Mosqueda had been historically subjected to frequent floods, and that dams, with the exception of the 1983 bypass, saved Jesús from yearly annihilation.

Jesús countered by enlisting the services of an elderly Cucapá, who stood like Mother Mary on the witness stand. She described the Río Hardy of her girlhood and its mesquite forest, how the floods of yesteryear swept to the east, down the Colorado, not the Río Hardy. Jesús rested his case.

After a five-year battle, the court gave Jesús restitution. "I never told anyone how much I got," he says. "I put it in the bank and I've used it here and there to help the *campo*." He subsequently was sued by the Mexican feds, who wanted a piece of his American reward. But he won that bizarre case too.

In his example, Jesús has shown a potential way to the future. Because he is an honorable man who recouped his losses, his destroyed farmland has been restored into a thousand-acre wetland. And his lawsuit has shown how we might use endangered species—or a people who derive their living from the wetlands—to restore the delta. The dapper man with a pencil-thin mustache has set an international legal precedent.

"Good luck," he says as we blow up our rafts in the mud alongside the glowing, barely flowing stream, "you'll need it."

Recently, Jesús was asked a lot of questions about his dirt airstrip by men that he calls "mafia." He doesn't say it, but he implies that they were drug runners. So on his own initiative, without a word from the cowed military, he plowed up the airstrip.

With Highway 5 to San Felipe to the east of us, Pete and I drop into darkness as the sluggish Río Hardy sucks us into confusing overgrown tamarisk braids. At first we follow the current, but as it diminishes, we begin to beat our way through: hopping over small brush dams, and getting poked by snags and swarmed by mullets.

Behind me in the dark, Pete yells, "Ahh, yikes!"

"You okay?"

"A fish just bounced off my chest!"

The night air is wet with dew. Because my boat and sleeping pads are deflated, and a snag has punctured the raft hull, my rear end is submerged in water.

I'm chilled. My feet are throbbing. And all the Clif Bars in the world won't replenish me.

Fortunately, the swamp opens up to a sluggish meandering stream, and we paddle south, west, and then east past banks of giant cane and occasional abandoned camps prowled by barking dogs. We have to keep paddling. The bushwhacking and route finding have slowed us down by several days, and because the satellite phone isn't working, we can't reschedule our pickup date with a Mexican boat driver from an ocean fishing village. Once the river deposits us onto the vast mudflats of the delta, amid drug-running territory, only a motorboat can pull us out.

I call a halt at 9 p.m. I'm shivering, numb. The only campsite is a weed-covered, snake-strewn yard next to a shuttered-up vacation cabin. Otherwise, the giant cane is so thick we wouldn't be able to stand up.

At an algae-covered boat ramp, it takes me three tries to step out of my boat. Now I'm beyond shivering. Today's effort—coupled with dehydration and raw feet—has knocked me off my game. I'm hypothermic. I begin running in place and try to get blood running to my brain and back to my limbs. Pete gets the message and fires up the stove for hot tea.

Finally, I sit down in the thorny weeds, warm enough to shiver again. "Pete," I say, "my feet are infected."

"Bad?"

"I don't know, but I can barely walk."

In the morning, I can't fit my swollen feet into my shoes. For lack of anything better to do, we paddle another few hours toward the last road access at the restored wetland known as Ecocamp. Then we debate our options.

Pete doesn't have to convince me that we need to go home. In the last week, we've made a synergistic team and it would be foolish to split up. Even if we were both healthy, if we went all for the delta, we have limited food and no pickup. Although my feet might hold up for a couple of days of paddling, the Río Hardy runs dry more than a day's walk from the sea. Nor do I have antibiotics in the first aid kit. And my feet are pulsing in a salsa beat.

So we pack up the boats and begin hitchhiking north in late Sunday afternoon traffic on Highway 5. Out of scores of passing cars, we see only two American license plates. Although Americans would never stop for strangers south of the border, who can blame the Mexicans for hitting their accelerator pedals? We're dirty, bearded, and for all they know, we could be those same armed and dangerous Americans they watch on TV.

After an hour, we resort to a trick that carried me around the shores of Lake Powell. Pete holds out a 500-peso ($71) bill. Within five minutes, a pickup truck carrying four beefy machinists screeches to a halt.

"Where you going?" Pete asks.

"Mexicali," they say. "Jump in back."

From the bed of the pickup, we introduce ourselves through the rear window. Pete tries to pass them the 500-peso note; they refuse and pass us two cold beers. We can't refuse.

Pete is shooting photographs for fun. None will go to print. Still, he works methodically, never wasting a shot, framing the image precisely because he doesn't allow his pictures to be cropped. He doesn't like to talk shop when it comes to photography so I leave him alone as he takes in the passing blur of landscape and instinctually interprets colors, shapes, and form.

With this brawny Cézanne creating the images, I'm content to keep my camera packed and describe the scenery in my journal as we coast along the highway:

> Distant smoke plumes from geothermal plant. Closeness of the sere mountains painted black along the Rio Hardy. Stench of cow manure on fields in southern Mexicali—alfalfa w/ rotating graze of cows, green, green, green alfalfa.

That night, I clog up our Mexicali hotel room shower drain with the brown grime and concentrated pesticides and phosphates of a river cum sewer. Once the soup swirls down the drain, the salts are on their way back to the Río Hardy.

I lie atop clean sheets, raise my feet upon a pillow, and close my eyes. I'm going home. Over the last few busy weeks, I realize, I've stopped thinking about my mother. So I wonder: *Where is she now?*

Neither of us has reached the sea. Too many dams and diversions and farm fields. The carbon and atoms of her ashes may have been blown over the divide, down into La Poudre Canyon and east to the plains of Colorado. Or she may have floated down over the Shadow Mountain, Granby, and Windy Gap Dam spillways, past the pasturelands, and into the tumult of Gore Canyon. But who can say how far she's gone?

Now that I have to head home, stung by our retreat from the delta, I begin obsessing yet again about my mother. Even though pulling the plug is a smart move, even though Pete and I have agreed to return after the holidays, I'm wondering, aside from my own unfinished business on the delta, have I fulfilled my obligations as a son? Can I let go of my mother now?

A year ago, my brother Rick agreed to phone me from North Carolina to tell me when her time had come. At the end of January, he reached me on my cell while I was skiing with Nicholas on Snowmass Mountain. Mom's breathing had become progressively more labored. Rick didn't think she'd last the weekend; I told him I'd catch the next flight out, and Rick relayed the news to Mom in person. She couldn't say yes or no, show thumbs up or down. But her eyebrows scrunched together, showing Rick that she was annoyed about having to wait for me before she could die.

I caught a plane the next morning. Although Rick had prepared me, when I reached her bedside that afternoon, I was horrified. The woman who had brought me into the world and formed my earliest, most lasting image of beauty had been reduced to a living mummy. Her shoulders were two large stones above a shrunken torso; her head seemed hugely out of proportion to her shrunken body. I kissed her on the cheek and put my hand on hers outside the blanket, not wanting to chill her by pulling off the blanket. She moved her hands, trying to free them, so I took her hand out and held her clenched-together fingers.

I nearly lost it. I was holding a claw, not my mother's hand.

She began shuddering, heaving, but her eyes were too dry to cry. The hospice nurse's voice reminded me that we weren't alone. "Kay," she asked, "are you in pain?"

"No," I said, "she's just crying."

I couldn't join my mom. We'd always played a game of tight control and willfulness. I am my mother's son, and for her sake, I had to be the unflinching master of my emotions. I couldn't let her know how shocked I was by her appearance, how wretched I felt about her pain. She needed all of her strength for dying rather than putting up with weepy sons.

The fluid in her lungs induced spasms of coughing that had been threatening to drown her every day for more than a month. She was being pushed under to drown, and then inexplicably pulled back—or forcing herself up—so she could have another day of nurses wiping her bottom and wetting her lips.

Another day of listening to classical music on the radio.

Another day of listening to her sons talk at her over the phone.

Another day of unmitigated pain: being consumed from within by the growing cancer cells in her rectum. Until her last speaking moment, she had refused painkillers, and now the hospice nurses didn't dare administer the drip morphine.

All bone and distended abdomen, she had become a victim of malnutrition. Her cancer-ravaged muscles were so sore that the nurse repeatedly propped her up a few degrees with a pillow under her left or right side to relieve her rock-hard buttocks.

She was parched, her kidneys emptied, totally dehydrated. When I pinched the flesh on her arm, the skin remained distended.

Rick came back. He sat on the opposite side of her bed, touching a shoulder knob attached to a birdlike arm.

"It's all right, Mom, we're here, Rick and me. We want you to know that you can let go."

She started crying again. But even this simple act of release was made painful by a face contorted by jutting cheekbones, a mouth dried wide open to battle for air. Her eyes were also wide open and unseeing, her skull sheathed with translucent skin.

I'd stayed with Mom for a long afternoon, but she seemed a stranger. In desperation, I searched for some recognizable sign of my mother: Her hair had come back in black instead of gray, neatly covering the brain surgery scar above her ear.

I told her that it was snowing in Colorado, and that we had more snow than ever before in the normally dry month of January. Although it was cold, our solar home and panels were working well, giving us free hot water from the sun. I told her that I'd been down to the delta, viewing birds in a place called the Ciénega, and I was shocked by the lack of water in the Colorado River, but that I was looking forward to my journey from the headwaters that spring.

I don't know how much she understood.

We asked her to blink if she felt any pain. Nothing, but she may have been beyond blinking.

As the nurse walked away, Mom grimaced, pulling her lips tight against her upper teeth and furrowing her brow. She wanted to tell us something, but she couldn't speak. She fell asleep in exhaustion. Her eyes lay open, veiled gray with cataracts, and except for the rattling from her chest, she looked half gone.

I wanted her to die right away. This wasn't my mother, I thought.

That night, Rick went home and I sat by her bedside. Twice she fell into paroxysms of drowning, and each time I called Rick so we could both be there for her. My brother, an M.D., should've been wrecked. He'd been look-ing in on her daily for months and if the self-described *hole in his heart* was getting bigger, he didn't show it. Twice that night Rick went home as our mom fought back to the surface, unable to let go. Finally, she gave me too no choice but to go to sleep.

In retrospect, she was playing me and Rick. She wanted us to go. She wanted to die alone after we got the good-byes out of the way.

"Good night, Mom," I kissed her on the forehead, "I love you."

I lay in the bed upstairs, thinking I'd spend the morning with her. After all, everyone knew Mom as the Steel Magnolia. But downstairs, she had her own plan. The nurse was napping. Mom knew she could leave without subjecting Rick or me to her final agonies and terror. Shortly after mid-night, she felt herself being pushed back underwater, but this time, she let go and drowned.

The hospice nurse yelled my name. I ran downstairs. I wanted to cry but couldn't. I hadn't been raised that way. Mom's skin was cold, and her eyes focused on something up beyond the ceiling. The room smelled sour even though she had nothing to void and could no longer push and pull air with her collapsed lungs.

She had waited for me to come and say good-bye. It was a gesture I would never forget, but still I felt no relief.

Nor do I feel relief today. When a parent dies, something dies inside of us. So now I think about her with unconditional love, but in the same way, I think about the delta, numb and infected by a river running out of a wastewater plant. She wouldn't have chosen to be remembered this way. Yet Kay Waterman also bore her own unspoken sadness. As an intensely private person, she would have been cross about my airing our family laundry. At least she would have respected my honesty.

After being unable to let her go, I've realized that the death of a mother or a river is too much to bear. It is only fitting, if we want meaning in our lives, for us to carry these losses everywhere we go. To remember.

Pete and I catch a ride home from Yuma with a friend in a small plane. I revert to being a couch potato, happy to play with the boys. Most of my friends raising children talk about how quickly the time goes by as parents. But Nicholas's and Alistair's gift to me is in slowing down the clock and allowing me to see the world, even the Colorado River, with new eyes.

At our family outing to *The Nutcracker* in Aspen, Alistair stands up on his chair so that he won't miss a second; Nicholas, already a fan of this ballet troupe, is equally spellbound. The performance is high art, with enough athletic grace and storytelling nuance to stir the soul of any Grinch, but what moves me the most is watching two boys transported in wonder.

At home, we invent jokes, sing, tickle one another, laugh, and hold races. Every moment assumes an importance that reawakens my own boyhood.

June is aghast about my cherry-colored sausage toes. She tries to take me to the doctor's office, but I respond by taking twice-daily herbal footbaths, resting, and changing the bandages. In a week. the swelling goes down and my feet turn white again. I stop wearing sandals and slip my feet into winter boots.

Two weeks before Christmas, my dad calls. He has been having trouble breathing. His chest is painful. The doctor says that he'll deteriorate quickly without heart bypass surgery.

I volunteer to fly to Boston to stay with him in the hospital. Characteristically, he says no, so I wait a few days and then try again. He claims that he can't bear the pressure of having visitors around his bed. I want to say that I'm no visitor, I'm his son, but I'll have to be satisfied with writing it here and letting go to accept my father's needs.

Dad is inside of me. Just like Mom. Our bodies are mostly water, and surrounding that water I carry the same DNA, genes, facial structure, and bones as my parents. I will pass on their strengths and weaknesses—the genes for disease, the reclusiveness, the athleticism, the math formulas, the impulsiveness, and the love of nature—to my own children.

We believe that nurture is stronger than nature, so June and I raise our children differently than our parents raised us. We ask our parents to substitute books or games or crafts—instead of plastic toys—for Christmas gifts. We spend a lot of time knitting, drawing, or gluing together bits of paper. I take the time with our boys to build frozen-water men, ski and sled down frozen water, throw frozen-water balls, shovel the frozen water off the decks, and take the boys out plowing frozen water off our long driveway.

I still read to the boys at least once a day. As a six-year-old, Nicholas is increasingly interested in what he calls "chapter books": *The Chronicles of Narnia, The Wee Free Men,* or *Alice in Wonderland.* With Alistair's prompting, we return to our old favorites: *Cat in the Hat, Doctor De Soto,* or *Walter the Farting Dog.*

In 1968, the year June was born, she was given the Dr. Seuss book *McElligot's Pool.* Like *The Lorax,* the scuffed 40-year-old edition of *Pool* resonates for us. We read it over and over and over. The illustrated story is about a farmer telling a boy that he will not catch any fish:

The pool is too small.
And, you might as well know it.
When people have junk
Here's the place that they throw it.

Through the power of his dreams, the boy sets out to show the farmer that he's wrong. There are fish in the pool, and although the boy is never shown hauling out any whoppers, he can visualize them below: An Australian fish with a pouch. Or a fish that's a grouch. A sea horse, an eel, a sawfish, circus fish, and fish that go "GLURK" from down under the murk.

This *might* be a river,
    Now mightn't it be,
        Connecting
            McElligot's
                Pool
                    With
                        The
                          Sea!

In our books, our play, and our daily lives, we remain connected to the Colorado River, even if it is no longer connected to the Gulf of California. The water that will flow toward the sea is also part of us. We use it for the plants, showers, baths, shaving, and cooking. We wash our clothes, our hands, dishes, and food with it. Years ago, to protect our groundwater, we stopped using bleach and phosphates. According to our water softener, we use 140 gallons a day, or 51,100 gallons a year—one-seventh of an acre-foot of water. We drink it, while our toilets use more water (one gallon per flush) to push our water-filled wastes back into the ground.

Still, like most Americans, we've had water surrounding us for all of our lives. Some of us are even named after it. And we take it for granted.

Pete and I return to what's left of the river in mid-January. This time we carry a reliable satellite phone, noninflatable foam sleeping pads, three liters of wine, satellite photos marked with longitude and latitude lines to match up to the GPS, eight days of food, antibiotics, and 11 gallons of water.

At the Ecocamp, we share our wine with the caretaker, Alfredo. The Río Hardy water is still green as the eggs from Dr. Seuss, but Alfredo has painstakingly hacked the giant cane off the riverbanks over the last month. In the distance, wild pheasants crow like chickens. Mullet jump out of the water; Pete flinches.

Mosquitoes are out in force. By comparison, Highway 5 is a distant drone. Alfredo, sitting at his campfire next to the one-man trailer that is his home, with dented-in windows taped with cardboard, calls Ecocamp *tranquillo* (calm). "No dogs, or spiders, or snakes."

He and other restoration workers are paid $20 per day by the Ecological Association of Users of Ríos Hardy and Colorado (AEURHYC), Pronatura (the Mexican version of the Sierra Club), and the Sonoran Institute. Their goal is to market the camp as an ecotourism resort for fishermen, boaters, and schoolchildren. Six years ago, these nongovernmental organizations built a 300-foot dike, El Tapon, that simulates a natural dam created by floods in the 1980s. The resulting 800-acre wetland supports a myriad of birds and other wildlife. However, until the wastewater-treatment plant is fixed at the polluted Río Hardy source, Alfredo must truck in water from Mexicali to water the newly planted mesquites of the Ecocamp. The last time the river flooded here, he says, was in 1983.

"I hope to God it does again," he says, not looking for a disaster, but just hoping for more water.

We say good night and go off to our berths under the thorny trees.

Deep asleep in my tent, I have a nightmare about dying in the delta, but I'm not shown how I will meet my end. There is no drug-runner gunplay or fluid filling my lungs, but instead the colorless play of my subconscious coats me with muck and makes my hands useless mittens. Even worse, the most lucid part of the nightmare has me watching my sons grieve after I'm gone. As an inversion of dealing with Mom's death, now I'm worried about them and how they'll cope with their sadness if I screw up by never coming home again.

As we inflate our rafts in the morning, I am scared for my boys. The intensity of this dread, this fear of the future, is something I never felt before having children.

Whether I have foreseen my own death, or that of the river, the implications of the dream are clear: I want to give my sons an intact future. And I don't know how to do it.

I don't breathe a word of the dream to Pete. Similar nightmares have troubled me on bigger adventures, and through caution and luck, I've let these premonitions serve as trail markers. But if you dwell on imminent disaster or morbid dream analysis on an expedition, fear can spread like a contagion to your partners. So following the lead of my reticent dad, I keep it to myself and lash my dry pack onto the bow of the raft to counterbalance my weight in the stern.

From the mud bank, we cinch ourselves inside our rafts and slide down into the shocking green, phosphate-rich water, wave thanks to Alfredo, and work the paddles like metronomes. Our double blades go *"Ka-chunk, Ka-chunk, Ka-chunk,"* taking us down the river in coarse rhythm, powering our boats like musical instruments.

Several miles downstream, we meet a fisherman poling a wooden skiff and pulling up his seine nets. The floor of his leaky boat has a slim pile of flopping bass and several mullet. He's from Mexicali, in his early forties, but like most hardworking Mexicans, he could be mistaken for a much older man. Pete asks if it's okay to take a few pictures. After showing us his catch, apropos of nothing, the fisherman says, *"Los federales se cagaron en el río* (the government has shat in the river)." There used to be a lot more ducks here too, he tells us. He's angry, scowling.

We smile and ask him directions, but he's unhappy. As we leave, he says even more emphatically: *"El agua es encarta cagada* (the water is full of shit)."

Of course, he's right. But I'd like to believe that we can expect more for the Colorado River.

As a writer, when I get stuck, I try to leave my own head and imagine the perspectives of friends or family. Although I can hardly read their minds, the technique sometimes gives me the proper words and, if I dig deep, a better understanding of the complex world that we live in.

My dad would calmly use math to tease out the answers for our own mortality, or for a river running dry. The "catastrophe theory," in particular, could explain a lot. The theory came from the 1960s work of a French mathematician, René Thom.

Catastrophe theory shows how small changes in a variable within a natural system can lead to sudden huge changes. A common example is the change of water after exposure to heat, transformed from the melting solid of ice, to liquid water, to gaseous steam.

The types of catastrophe theory are called butterfly, swallowtail, fold, and cusp. The cusp can be used for natural events when catastrophe can be averted. It looks like this:

$$V = x^4 + ax^2 + bx$$

Water engineers have applied it when V is the variable of flooding streams that hit the main stem of the Colorado River in Utah. On a river out of control, or here on the delta where the river has stopped, the cusp formula offers a chance to balance multiple variables—like restoring pulse water flows—to return to a state that would avoid catastrophe. Doctors have also used the cusp to study and treat cancer.

In the last year, I have experienced these cusp events: swimming through gnarly rapids to shore, Mom getting sick, the boys battling high fevers, or Dad recovering from heart surgery. Four out of five times, the variables—strength, antibodies, and excellent medical care—averted catastrophe.

The fold type of catastrophe ($V = x^3 + ax$) explains our own short lives. There is no avoiding a fold catastrophe because our single control factor is time. When time stops, catastrophe strikes.

Seen through this theory, my mother had lived out most of her years. Even without cancer, her time would have run out.

Nature works under a different set of variables than humankind. Rivers are not meant to die in our lifetimes. The cusp catastrophe allows numeric expansion for a force of nature created more than five million years ago. Our Colorado River came before us, and with human intervention as a crucial variable, it can last long after we're gone.

Mathematics, my father believes, can solve the ills of the world.

We eat cheese and tortillas atop El Tapon. Unlike most dams, this dike shows a noble effort to hold onto the withering delta. Pissed-off fishermen, hoping to restore their catches downstream, have dug a three-foot trench and fish passage through the dirt dike.

We paddle onward, although it's often hard to find the current. When I look up from studying the map, the water clears. It feels different here: Leaves click in the breeze, the air is vibrant, animals swish through the brakes. Somehow a thin slice of delta has survived. I am amazed at the river's capacity to endure.

The serpentine braids lure us down one wrong turn after another, despite our map and satellite technology. This is the river of legend. The river of a century ago that the great conservationist Aldo Leopold wrote about in *A Sand County Almanac*:

Dawn on the delta was whistled in by Gambel quail, which roosted in the mesquites overhanging camp. When the sun peeped over the Sierra Madre, it slanted across a hundred miles of lovely desolation, a vast flat bowl of wilderness rimmed by jagged peaks. On the map the delta was bisected by the river, but in fact the river was nowhere and everywhere, for he could not decide which of a hundred green lagoons offered the most pleasant and least speedy path to the gulf. So he traveled them all, and so did we. He divided and rejoined, he twisted and turned, he meandered in awesome jungles, he all but ran in circles, he dallied with lovely groves, he got lost and was glad of it, and so were we.

To my surprise, the river is as wild as I've ever seen it, temporarily lush with water that must have arisen from underground. I can't count all the rattling kingfishers, the hundreds of circling mallards, the scores of cattle egrets.

Ravens caw. Fish jump. Ospreys dive.

A coyote sings at the approaching dusk. Then a loon cries back in eerie mimicry.

Around us appear green herons, black-crowned night-herons, and cormorants. Salt grass beards the ground.

We camp in the tamarisk, alive with mosquitoes feeding songbirds. Although the mesquite trees are long gone, the giant cane hasn't yet gained a foothold. Like reentering the headwaters, we're transported, if only briefly, back to the Lorax's glorious place, where the grass is still green and the Swomee-Swans ring out in place.

Enveloped in this small bubble of life, I feel hope for the entire river. As for the delta, the dream of Mexican and American conservationists is to allow a single 60,000 acre-foot release each year from the border, supplemented by an equal quantity of water in a "pulse flow," spread out over three months. Compared to the many pricey canals and dams on the river upstream, the costs would be trifling. Measured by our obligations to the next generation and the river as a living resource, after a century's neglect and abuse, we have no choice but to take action.

In the morning, we paddle down past pintail ducks, curlews, ibises, plovers, and loons. As the river narrows, we can feel it gathering momentum, rushing for the sea.

Then, like sudden cancer, it all changes. Half the river disappears into a thirsty delta. Mountains jut as dried-out knobby shoulders above the horizon, while abandoned fishing boats poke their vertebral remains up out of the ground. The delta cracks up into a crusty old mud puddle that stretches as far as we can see. This is the final leach field for the river, but here the kidneys have finally given out. All is caked in salt.

The river cum creek halves again, picks up speed, then shoves us into deep mud and disappears. Just like that it's gone.

We crawl out of the muddy glue, dragging our rafts up onto a dirt track. Instead of a punctured floor, Pete finds that one of our precious water bags has spilled out into his raft. "Good work, Pete," I say, desperately looking for levity, "that'll lighten our loads now that we're through paddling."

We've reached our limitrophe of river: swallowed up by an ancient delta as big as the sky, with no ocean in sight. We scrape the sticky mud off our feet and the rafts, and then we shrug it all back onto our shoulders and walk south. This time the weight is almost too much to bear. Crab and fish skeletons litter the desert, and all afternoon we step gently across the scabbed remains of the Colorado River.

ACKNOWLEDGMENTS

My source-to-sea journey was the highlight of two and a half years of research and travel. Without the logistical and psychological lifeline that so many friends and family extended to me—before, during, and after the trip—I'd still be trying to figure it all out.

Please see *www.jonathanwaterman.com* for related Colorado River media and more information on the following supporters.

Luther Propst initially suggested my Colorado River Project. He and his Sonoran Institute colleagues—Mark Lellouch, Francisco Zamora, Joaquin Murrieta, and Edith Santiago—provided invaluable information and support.

As an Expedition Council grantee at the National Geographic Society (NGS), I am grateful to the ever-ready counsel of Rebecca Martin, Angie Sanders, and John Francis; at NGS Books, my insightful editor Amy Briggs, Barbara Brownell at the helm, and Kevin Mulroy for signing me up; at Conservation Projects at National Geographic Maps, the skilled Frank Biasi oversaw the conception and production of the map inserted in the hardcover first edition of this book.

Margaret Bowman, with the the Walton Family Foundation's Freshwater Initiative, generously funded most of the NGS map. In hopes of influencing policy throughout the basin, we put together a team of expert map advisors, all of whom gave generously of their time: the Nature Conservancy's Taylor Hawes, Environmental Defense Fund's Jennifer Pitt (who also proofread most of this book), Kay Brothers of Southern Nevada Water Authority, Crystal

Thompson of the Colorado River Water Users Association (the latter two organizations also contributed to map production costs), Sam Spiller of the U.S. Fish and Wildlife Service, Norm Henderson of the National Park Service, Reclamation's Bruce Williams, the Colorado River Water Conservation District's Eric Kuhn, Dave Wegner from the House of Representatives Subcommittee on Water and Power, and Western Resource Advocates' Bart Miller.

To New Belgium Brewing, an employee-owned company that depends upon the headwaters and solar power to sustain its brewery, thanks for the beer, financial support, and your "save the river" campaign. Bottoms up to Adrian Glasenapp (a river companion), Kim Jordan, Bryan Simpson, Jenn Orgolini, and Greg Owsley.

For financial contributions, I'm grateful to Brian Scranton of Chaco who joined me on the river and shod me; Caron Obstfeld with Clif Bar, who fed me; and the Kenney Foundation of Denver.

Equipment supporters include Sheri Tingey of Alpacka Rafts, Landis Arnold at Prijon kayaks, Heather McGarry at Teko socks, Joe Vernachio of Spyder/Cloudveil, and Caroline Middleton Duell of Elemental Herbs (particularly for introducing me to her sister, June, in 1997).

I'd like to thank my cohorts in adventure: the redoubtable Pete McBride, Bruce Kime, Michael Freeman, David Schipper, and Michael Brown of Serac Adventure Films (along with his documentary team, Krista Barbour and Tyler Jones).

Many others helped me, through their various talents and selflessness: Bruce Gordon and Jane Pargiter of Ecoflight; Laura Stone, Rudi Engholm, Will Worthington, Dick Stone, Jim Grady—all of Lighthawk; John McBride, Robert Wolford, Bud Tillotson, Dorothy Dines, Lloyd Palmer, Kirsten Peterson, Carol Wood Duell, Bill Wolverton, Chris Reeder, Renée Cameto, Jill Rundle, Matt Halter, Sarah Baden, Colin Daviau, Jenny Stone, Brian Rasmussen, Eric Paddock, Betsy Scruggs, Maureen Meehan, Claudia Bray, Gene Longo, Jim Page, Walt Ruthenburg, Kimberly Keisling, Izzy Collett, Helen Howard, and the Knowlton family: Judy, Randy, Ron, and Julie.

For proofreading, I appreciate the time and expertise of Pacific Institute's Mike Cohen, grower Al Kalin, journalist Alison Pattillo, and attorney Ken Ransford.

Although Marc Reisner's *Cadillac Desert* is the entertaining pièce de résistance of Western water follies, the luminous books by Donald Worster, *Rivers of Empire* and *A River Running West*, also served as invaluable references. In addition, I frequently consulted Wallace Stegner's compelling book on

Powell, *Beyond the Hundredth Meridian;* John Wesley Powell's own story, *The Exploration of the Colorado River and Its Canyons;* Charles Bergman's excellent *Red Delta;* John McPhee's classic *Encounters with the Archdruid;* and the learned *Cataract Canyon,* by Robert Webb, Jayne Belnap, and John Weisheit. My reading list flows on and on as written proof that the Colorado River is America's iconic waterway.

More than anyone else, the river people—my friends and water operators—inhabit these pages. Over two years, I conducted many interviews. To prevent the book from running on into another volume, I couldn't tell everyone's story, even though all interviewees contributed to my education: Matthew Andersen, Jeff Sorenson, Barbara Ralston, Bill Parsons, Matt Fahey, Dave Speas, Andrea Alpine, Stacy Chesney, Chips Barry, Robert Walsh, Jack Simes, Lonnie Gourley, Len Martin, Kara Lamb, Noble Underbrink, Bill Sloan, Tom Lacy, John Williams, Don Metzler, Dave Pitzer, Jenny Ross, Gary Niles, Bill Hedden, Rich Ingebretsen, John Laccinole, Ruth Kirschbaum, Wilfred Whatoname Jr. and Sr., Dave Knutson, Dan Bean, Tim Hurton, Glenn Barnes, Eric Leaper, Ted Wang, J. C. Davis, Pat Mulroy, Bob Navagatto, Chris Avery, Lisa Shipek, Rodney Glassman, Charlie Flynn, Fred Phillips, Carlos Dominguez, Ben Vik, Colin Soto, Jesús Mosqueda, Brad Udall, Peter Culp, Osvel Hinojosa Huerta, and Karl Flessa. My apologies to anyone I may have forgotten.

I am indebted to the generosity of boatmen from Colorado to Mexico, epitomized by Brian Dierker, Steve Young, Carol Fritzinger, and Smokey Knowlton. Through their passion for the riparian corridor, they show the future of Colorado River sustainability.

This book is also about how a river runs through family. In most instances, we're beholden to our mothers, but for this narrative the inspiration I got from my mom, Katherine Waterman, is incalculable. To my dad, Peter Waterman, and my brothers, Diedrich and Jeremy: thanks for allowing me to shine a narrow beam into our lives, at least from my own frame of reference.

Ditto to June, Nicholas, and Alistair Waterman—my gneiss within the deepest canyons. I am in their eternal debt for supporting the desk time and granting my long leaves to the river.

GLOSSARY

Acre-foot: Equal to 325,851 gallons, or one acre of land, one foot deep. An acre-foot can supply two single-family households for a year.

Adjudication: The process of confirming through the existence of a *water right* by court decree for priority among other water rights, according to seniority if there is not enough water to meet the needs of users.

Algae bloom: The rapid growth of aquatic plant life caused by fertilizers, detergents, or other compounds running off from agricultural or urban areas. Algae decreases oxygen for fish and native plant life.

Ancient Puebloan (Anasazi): Basket-making culture that flourished along the desert areas of the Colorado River from A.D. 100 to 1300.

Aquifer: An underground geologic formation containing water.

Arid/semiarid: Describes the relative lack of precipitation. Arid areas receive less than 10 inches of rain per year. Semiarid areas receive between 10 inches and 20 inches per year.

Basin: An area of land that collects water as either snowmelt or rainfall and drains into a common body of water, such as a stream or a river.

Black side up: Boatmen jargon for a flipped raft, as in the color of the raft's bottom.

BLM: The Bureau of Land Management is the Department of the Interior agency that manages 253 million acres of public land in the United States, mostly in the West. Its mission is to sustain the health, diversity and productivity of this acreage for the use and enjoyment of the public.

Boil: Unpredictable upwelling of water found beneath river rapids; also used to connote an upwelling of bass, feeding on insects.

CAP: The Central Arizona Project, a 336-mile aqueduct from Lake Havasu through Phoenix, ending in Tucson.

CBT: The Colorado Big Thompson Project, a transbasin diversion, pulls water from the wet, western side of the Rockies and the Colorado River to the dry, eastern plains.

cfs (cubic feet per second): One cubic foot of water passing by a single point for one second.

Colorado River Basin Salinity Control Act (1974): The frequently amended, congressional legislation that maintains salinity levels for the entire river.

Colorado River Compact: The Upper Basin (Colorado, Wyoming, Utah, and New Mexico), and the Lower Basin (Nevada, Arizona, and California) were each given 7.5 maf of water per year. In surplus water years, the Lower Basin gets an extra 1 maf of water. Mexico's share, 1.5 maf, was allocated during a separate 1944 treaty. Modern tree ring analysis shows that the river runs at about 15 maf per year, rather than the 17.5 maf doled out by the 1922 Compact.

Consumptive use: Water that does not return to its source after being used.

Desalination: Removing dissolved salts from brackish groundwater, seawater, or portions of the river contaminated by crop returns.

Diversion: Removing water from its natural course or location through ditches, canals, reservoirs, pipelines, aqueducts, wells, pumps, or hoses.

Drip irrigation: An efficient conservation practice where small, steady flows of water are released to individual plants through an underground network of irrigation tubes.

Drought: Caused by below-average precipitation over long periods of time.

Eddy: Whirling convergence of currents, often near large boulders, that will hold or tip unwary boaters.

GCMRC: The Grand Canyon Monitoring and Research Center, a branch of the USGS that was established in 1995, to measure the effects of Glen Canyon Dam operations on natural and physical resources along the Colorado River from Glen Canyon Dam to Lake Mead.

Headgate: Located at the top of a diversion or along a ditch or canal to control the amount of incoming water.

Hydraulic: Dangerous river feature that creates a current akin to a front-loading washing machine, which will trap boats and bodies. Swimmers caught in these features can sometimes kick-swim free along the lowest and least powerful point of the cycle at the river bottom.

Invasive (or exotic) species: Recently introduced and foreign flora and fauna—such as tamarisk, giant cane, Russian olives, carp, zebra and quagga mussels, or speedboaters—that often have a detrimental effect upon the river or riparian corridor.

Irrigation or water districts: Public organizations that divert water to the district users for farm irrigation or municipal use.

maf: million acre-feet; see *acre-foot.*

MWD: The Metropolitan Water District of Southern California.

Nonconsumptive: Use of water that does not consume or deplete water through its use. Septic fields or hydroelectric turbines are examples of nonconsumptive water use.

Petroglyphs: Ancient Native American art pecked onto dark, desert rock.

Pictographs: Ancient Native American art drawn with gypsum, dye, or urine.

Post-DamNation: An era that describes river conditions after the dams had been built.

ppm: Parts per million refers to the amount of dissolved salt in water.

Predambrian: Boatmen lingo that refers to conditions of the river in the era before dams had been built.

Prior appropriation: The dominant water law in the American West. The first person or senior *water rights* user to put water to a beneficial use has first rights when there is not enough water to meet the needs of more junior water rights holders or water users.

Recharge: The flow of water into a groundwater basin or aquifer. Recharge occurs naturally or through human intervention that reinjects water into the ground.

Reclamation: The Bureau of Reclamation, within the U.S. Department of the Interior, opened western settlement through massive water projects to irrigate arid lands. Working only in the 17 states west of the Mississippi, Reclamation now manages water rather than building new dams or diversions. Initially John Wesley Powell's USGS tried to establish the forerunner of this agency through the Irrigation Survey. Then in 1902 the Reclamation Act created the Reclamation Service. In 1923 the agency was renamed the Bureau of Reclamation.

Riparian area: Sensitive ecosystems, with unique flora and fauna and dependent upon a wet river environment, that serve as a transitional zone between waterways and uplands.

Salinity: Refers to the amount of salts dissolved in water. High salinity levels are toxic to fish, crops, and native plants. As the Colorado River irrigates desert farm fields, it picks up salts from natural deposits and contaminates the water returned to the river.

Salt: Sodium chloride (common table salt) and other easily soluble elements such as calcium carbonate (limestone or gypsum), magnesium chloride, or potassium chloride.

SNWA: The Southern Nevada Water Authority.

Spillway: The troughs on dams that release water during flood conditions, as an alternative to sending water through the normal bypass tunnels.

Strainer: A tree or obstruction lying across the current that will pin and crush people caught on its upstream side.

Transbasin diversion: Diverting water from one river basin to another is consumptive use because no water from the diversion will return to the basin of origin.

USDA: The U.S. Department of Agriculture develops and executes government policy on farming, agriculture, and food. Also aims to meet the needs of farmers and ranchers, promote agricultural trade and production, work to assure food safety, and protect natural resources—which includes the battle on "noxious weeds."

USFWS: The U.S. Fish and Wildlife Service is the agency that administers national wildlife refuges. The agency is also in charge of protecting endangered species.

USGS: The U.S. Geological Survey. John Wesley Powell and Senator Garfield conceived this Department of the Interior agency to monitor lands and their resources, including water, through science. After the first director, Clarence King, retired early, the newly elected President Garfield appointed Powell to the post.

Water buffalo: Brought into popular usage by Marc Reisner in *Cadillac Desert* to describe developers and reclamationists who hoard water. Otherwise, *Bubalus bubalis* describes an animal of the Old World tropics used to freight large troughs of water.

Water right: A private property right that establishes in what priority water users may use water for a beneficial purpose. A water right allows diversion of a certain amount of water, in a specified order among other water users. The older, or more senior, the water right, the fewer other water users whose needs must be satisfied before users are allowed to divert water. The younger, or more junior, the water right, the greater number of senior water rights that must be satisfied before a junior right can divert water.

Watershed: Land that catches precipitation and drains into the river.

Xeriscape: Describes landscaping—gravel, arid native plants, rainwater catchments, etc.—that conserve water.

INDEX

RUNNING DR